The Routle _____ ᴸ_ _____ reader to
important _____ ____ ___ ____ _____ __ ___ _____ __ ___ _____y period.
Through them an informed, reliable and accessible guide to the ideas that have influenced
political activity and thought in the twentieth century is provided.

Recognizing that the majority of people tend to associate an individual with a particular
idea or movement, the editors have deliberately chosen a biographical approach. Each
entry includes a brief biography, an outline of major ideas and suggestions for further
reading. The difficult and sensitive task of selection has been decided on a 'theorists' and
'practitioners' basis subdivided into three basic categories: those who have actively
engaged in politics; those whose reflections have influenced political movements and activity; and those whose writings have enhanced our understanding of politics.

This second edition extends the list of entries to 174, written by over 100 contributors
who are leading authorities in their fields. The fully revised list includes Third World
political theorists, those who have influenced new movements based on the issues of gender, ethnicity and ecology whose ascendancy will continue into the twenty-first century,
and the most prominent Western thinkers. This will be essential reading for students of
politics and philosophy as well as for those interested in the backgrounds and ideas of the
major political theorists of the twentieth century.

Robert Benewick is Professor of Politics at the University of Sussex. **Philip Green** is Sophia
Smith Professor of Government at Smith College, Northampton, Massachusetts.

The Routledge Dictionary of Twentieth-Century Political Thinkers

Second edition

Edited by Robert Benewick and
Philip Green

London and New York

First published 1992
by Routledge
11 New Fetter Lane, London EC4P 4EE

Second edition 1998

Simultaneously published in the USA and Canada
by Routledge
29 West 35th Street, New York, NY 10001

Typeset in Times by RefineCatch Limited, Bungay, Suffolk

Printed and bound in Great Britain by
TJ International Ltd, Padstow, Cornwall

British Library Cataloguing in Publication Data
A catalogue record for this book is available from the British Library

Library of Congress Cataloging in Publication Data
The Routledge Dictionary of Twentieth-Century Political Thinkers/
edited by Robert Benewick and Philip Green. – [2nd ed.]
Includes bibliographical references and index.
1. Political science – History – 20th century – Dictionaries.
2. Political scientists – Biography – Dictionaries.
I. Benewick, Robert.   II. Green, Philip.
JA83.R725   1997
320'.092'2 – dc21
[B] 97–11585

ISBN 0–415–15881–8 (hbk)
ISBN 0–415–09623–5 (pbk)

Contents

Introduction

This book is a direct response to those who need an informed, reliable and ready guide to the ideas that have influenced political activity and shaped political thinking in the twentieth century. Careful consideration has been given to developing an approach that will be the most useful to readers while at the same time encouraging them to explore the subject further.

It is our firm conviction that most people identify an idea, concept or system of thought with a particular individual. With this in mind we adopted a biographical rather than a thematic approach. Each major entry includes biographical material relevant to understanding the political ideas of the person under consideration, a brief discussion of those ideas and a short and thereby manageable list of their most important writings as well as a selection of commentaries.

The process of inclusion and exclusion is not only difficult but sensitive. Those included fall roughly into three groups: those with ideas who have actively engaged in politics; those whose reflections have influenced political movements and activity; and those whose writings have enhanced our understanding. For the first group of thinkers, whose ideas were clearly secondary to their political activity in significance, we have emphasized biographical data; but for the most part the entries are primarily short essays in the history of ideas.

The inclusion of both theorists and practitioners is not the only way in which this reference work is special. We have focused exclusively on the twentieth century and in doing so have deliberately moved beyond the boundaries and traditions of Western political thought. Not only have we included important non-Western political theorists but also those whose ideas have influenced new movements based on ethnicity, gender and ecological concerns. Finally, in order to achieve what we believe to be a unique and better balanced work of reference, we have recruited a wider field of expert contributors.

The second edition includes new entries on thinkers whose ideas have grown in influence as we approach the millennium. Since it is also an enlarged edition we have been able to respond positively to the recommendations of our colleagues and critics by correcting some important omissions, rewriting and expanding original entries and updating bibliographies.

Phoebe Schreiner was instrumental in the preparation of this edition, but as before, the editors happily accept exclusive responsibility for whatever biases persist.

R. B.
P. G.

Contributors

All uncredited short entries are by the editors.

Adorno	Douglas Kellner, Department of Philosophy, University of Texas at Austin
'Aflaq	Peter Sluglett, formerly Centre for Middle Eastern and Islamic Studies, University of Durham
Althusser	Edward Benton, Department of Sociology, University of Essex
Arendt	Mary Dietz, Department of Political Science, University of Minnesota
Aron	Robert Colquhoun, Department of Advanced Studies in Education, Goldsmiths' College, University of London
Atatürk	M. Naim Turfan, School of Oriental and African Studies, University of London
Bahro	Edward Benton
Barrès	James Q. Graham, Jr, Professor Emeritus, Department of History, Bowling Green State University
de Beauvoir	Kate Soper, Department of History, University of North London
Ben Gurion	Donna Divine, Department of Government, Smith College
Bentley	Leo Weinstein, Department of Government, Smith College
Berlin	Roger Hausheer, Department of Modern Languages, University of Bradford
Bernstein	Henry Tudor, Department of Politics, University of Durham
Bloch	Stephen Eric Bronner, Department of Political Science, Rutgers University
Bobbio	John Keane, Centre for the Study of Democracy, University of Westminster
Bookchin	Martha Ackelsberg, Department of Government, Smith College
Buber	Dan Avnon, Program in Cultures, Ideas and Values, Stanford University
Buchanan	Barbara Krug, Rotterdam School of Business/Erasmus University
Bukharin	Michael Haynes, School of Languages and European Studies, University of Wolverhampton
Cabral	Cedric Robinson, Department of Political Science, University of California at Santa Barbara
Camus	David Sprintzen, Department of Philosophy, C.W. Post College of Long Island University
Castro	Carollee Bangelsdorf, School of Social Science, Hampshire College
Chomsky	Ronald Lunsford, Department of English, University of North Carolina
Clément	Ann Jones, Department of Comparative Literature, Smith College
Cole	Paul Hirst, Department of Politics and Sociology, Birkbeck College, University of London
Croce	Richard Bellamy, Department of Politics, University of Reading

Crosland	Raymond Plant, St Catherine's College, Oxford
Dahl	James S. Fishkin, Department of Government, University of Texas at Austin
Daly	Moira Gatens, Faculty of Philosophy, Australian National University
Delphy	Ann Jones
Derrida	Sue Golding, School of Politics and Policy Studies, University of Greenwich
Dewey	Alfonso J. Damico, Department of Political Science, University of Florida
Djilas	David Dyker, School of European Studies, University of Sussex
Du Bois	David Levering Lewis, Department of History, Rutgers University
Durkheim	Kenneth Thompson, Department of Sociology, the Open University
Fanon	Cedric Robinson
Firestone	Alison Jaggar, Department of Philosophy, University of Cincinnati
Foucault	Athar Hussain, Centre for Asian Economy, Politics and Society, London School of Economics
	Joan Cocks, Department of Politics, Mount Holyoke College
Frank	James Petras, Department of Political Science, State University of New York at Binghamton
Freire	Marcela Gajardo, Facultad Latinoamericana de Ciencias Sociales, Santiago
Freud	Joel Kovel, Bard Center, Bard College
Fromm	Michael Maccoby, Maccoby Group, Washington, D.C.
Galbraith	Philip Green, Department of Government, Smith College
Gandhi	Bhikhu C. Parekh, Department of Politics, University of Hull
Garvey	Louis Wilson, Department of Afro-American Studies, Smith College
Gentile	Richard Bellamy
Gilman	Ann J. Lane, Department of Women's Studies, Colgate University
Goldman	Alice Wexler, Riverside, California
Goodman	Taylor Stoehr, Department of History, University of Massachusetts at Boston
Gorz	Larry Wilde, Department of Economics and Public Administration, Nottingham Trent University
Gramsci	Stuart Hall, Department of Sociology, the Open University
Griffin	Jacqueline Stevens, Department of Political Science, University of Michigan
Guevara	Carollee Bangelsdorf
Gutiérrez	John R. Pottenger, Department of Political Science, University of Alabama at Huntsville
Habermas	Peter Dews, Department of Philosophy, University of Essex
Hall	S. A. Jhally, Department of Communications, University of Massachusetts at Amherst
Harrington	Maurice Isserman, Department of History and American Studies, Hamilton College

Hayek	Raymond Plant
Heidegger	Michael A. Weinstein, Department of Political Science, Purdue University
Hilferding	Tom Bottomore, Late Professor Emeritus, School of Social Sciences, University of Sussex
Hitler	Robert Benewick, School of English and American Studies, University of Sussex
Horkheimer	Stephen Eric Bronner
Illich	John Papworth, London
	Kirkpatrick Sale, New York
Iqbal	F. A. Nizami, Centre for Islamic Studies, University of Oxford
Jabotinsky	Donna Divine
James	Ivar Oxaal, Hull, England
Kautsky	Stephen Eric Bronner
Kelsen	Keekok Lee, Department of Philosophy, University of Manchester
Keynes	Wayne Parsons, Department of Political Studies, Queen Mary and Westfield College, University of London
Khomeini	Sami Zubaida, Department of Politics and Sociology, Birkbeck College, University of London
King	David Levering Lewis
Kita	Germaine Hoston, Department of Political Science, University of California, San Diego
Kohr	Kirkpatrick Sale
Kollontai	Barbara Clements, Department of History, University of Indiana
Kristeva	Ann Jones
Kropotkin	Martha Ackelsberg
	Myrna Breitbart, School of Social Science, Hampshire College
Laski	Michael Newman, School of Languages and European Studies, University of North London
Lenin	Neil Harding, Department of Political Theory and Government, University College of Swansea
Li Dazhao	Chen Shuping, People's University of China
Liang Qichao	Chen Shuping
Lippmann	Richard Crockett, School of English and American Studies, University of East Anglia
Lorde	Lisa Tuttle, Argyll, Scotland
Lu Xun	Chen Shuping
Lukács	Istvan Meszaros, Professor Emeritus, School of European Studies, University of Sussex
Rosa Luxemburg	Stephen Eric Bronner
Lyotard	Sue Golding
MacIntyre	Philip Green
MacKinnon	Jacqueline Stevens
Macpherson	Frank Cunningham, Department of Philosophy, University of Toronto
Malatesta	Nunzio Pernicone, Department of History and Politics, Drexel University

xiii

Malcolm X   Louis Wilson
Mannheim   David Kettler, Bard Center, Bard College
Mao   Chen Shuping
Marcuse   Douglas Kellner
Mariátegui   Harry E. Vanden, Department of Political Science, University of
                   South Florida
Markovic   Larry Wilde
Maurras   James Q. Graham, Jr
Merleau-Ponty   Diana Coole, Department of Political Studies, Queen Mary and
                   Westfield College, University of London
Michels   Joel D. Wolfe, Department of Political Science, University of
                   Cincinnati
Millett   Lisa Tuttle
Mills   Richard Gillam, Department of American Studies, Stanford
                   University
Mitchell   Jane Flax, Department of Political Science, Howard University
Morgenthau   Charles L. Robertson, Department of Government, Smith College
Mosca   Richard Bellamy
Mussolini   Robert Benewick
Narayan   Bhikhu C. Parekh
Niebuhr   John W. Cooper, James Madison Institute, Tallahassee, Florida
Nozick   Robert Benewick and Philip Green
Nyerere   Harry Goulbourne, Cheltenham and Gloucester College of
                   Higher Education
Oakeshott   W. H. Greenleaf, Professor Emeritus, Department of Political
                   Theory and Government, University College of Swansea
Ortega   Andrew Dobson, Department of Politics, University of Keele
Orwell   Bernard Crick, Professor Emeritus, Department of Politics and
                   Sociology, Birkbeck College, University of London
Ōtsuka   Germaine Hoston
Pareto   Richard Bellamy
Pashukanis   Robert Fine, Department of Sociology, University of Warwick
Pateman   Elizabeth Meehan, Department of Political Science, Queen's
                   University of Belfast
Plekhanov   Chris Arthur, Brighton, England
Popper   James Farr, Department of Political Science, University of
                   Minnesota
Poulantzas   John Solomos, Department of Sociology, University of
                   Southampton
Rand   Jacqueline Stevens
Rawls   Amy Gutmann, Department of Politics, Princeton University,
                   Roberto Alejandro, Department of Political Science, University
                   of Massachusetts
Reich   Joel Kovel
Rorty   Norman Geras, Department of Government, University of
                   Manchester
Rowbotham   Valerie Bryson, Politics Division, University of Huddersfield
Roy   Bhikhu C. Parekh

Russell	Alan Ryan, New College, Oxford
Sandel	Philip Green
Sartre	Istvan Meszaros
Schmitt	Joseph Bendersky, Department of History, Virginia Commonwealth University
Schreiner	Joyce Berkman, Department of History, University of Massachusetts at Amherst
Schumacher	Kirkpatrick Sale
Schumpeter	Nicholas Xenos, Department of Political Science, University of Massachusetts at Amherst
Shari'ati	Sami Zubaida
Shaw	Stephen Ingle, Department of Political Studies, University of Stirling
Skinner	Lyman Tower Sargent, Department of Political Science, University of Missouri at St Louis
Sorel	Larry Portis, The American University in Paris
Stalin	Alan Foster, School of Politics and Policy Studies, University of Greenwich
Strauss	Arlene Saxonhouse, Department of Political Science, University of Michigan
Sun Yat-sen	Chen Shuping
Tawney	Raymond Plant
Taylor	Alice Hearst, Department of Political Science, Smith College
Trotsky	Norman Geras
Uno	Germaine Hoston
Veblen	Rick Tilman, Department of Public Administration, University of Nevada at Las Vegas
Voegelin	Mary Dietz
Walzer	Philip Green
Washington	Louis Wilson
The Webbs	Norman MacKenzie, Professor Emeritus, Institute of Continuing and Professional Education, University of Sussex
Weber	Robert Holton, Research School of Social Sciences, Australian National University
Weil	Mary Dietz
Williams	Stuart Hall
Wittig	Ann Jones
Woolf	Lee Edwards, Department of English, University of Massachusetts at Amherst
Yoshino	Germaine Hoston
Zetkin	Lisa Tuttle

Twentieth-Century Political Thinkers

Max Adler   1873–1937

Austro-Marxist philosopher and supporter of
the post-First World War workers' council
movement in Austria, best known theoretically for his attempt to establish Marxism as a
scientific sociology in the modern positivist
sense.

See also

Hilferding.

Works include

Kausalität und Teleologie im Streite um die Wissenschaft,
 Vienna, Wiener Volksbuchhandlung, 1904.
Der Soziologische Sinn der Lehre von Karl Marx, Vienna,
 Wiener Volksbuchhandlung, 1914.
*Die Staatsauffassung des Marxismus. Ein Betrag zur Unter-
 scheidung von soziologischer und juristischer Methode*,
 Vienna, Wiener Volksbuchhandlung, 1922.
Soziologie des Marxismus two volumes, Vienna, Wiener
 Volksbuchhandlung, 1930.

Other works

Tom Bottomore and Patrick Goode (eds.), *Austro-
Marxism*, Oxford, Clarendon Press, 1978.

Theodor W. Adorno
1903–1969

Theodor W. Adorno was born in Frankfurt,
Germany, into an upper-class bourgeois fam-
ily. The son of a German Jewish father and an
Italian Catholic mother, Adorno studied
philosophy, psychology and musicology at the
University of Frankfurt, where he received his
Ph.D. in 1924. He also engaged in profes-
sional music training, studying piano and
composition with the modernist composer
Alban Berg. During the 1920s and early 1930s

Adorno edited a musical journal, *Anbruch*,
and continued his studies of philosophy. He
completed his *Habilitationschrift* on Kierkegaard in 1931 and began teaching at the University of Frankfurt. He there became associated with the Marxist-oriented Institute for
Social Research with which he worked for the
rest of his life.

Upon Hitler's rise to power, Adorno first
emigrated to England and then joined the
Institute for Social Research in exile at
Columbia University in New York. During
the 1930s he became closely connected with
the institute's attempt to develop a critical
theory of society. This involved him in one of
the first attempts to develop a Marxian critique of mass culture, which Adorno and the
institute discerned was becoming ever more
significant as an instrument of ideological
manipulation and social control in democratic
capitalist, fascist and communist societies.
Adorno first developed this critique in studies
of popular music. In a 1932 study, 'On
popular music', he argued that music was
commodified like everything else in capitalist
society and should be analysed as a commodity produced primarily for its exchange value
and its success on the market. This marketing
of music led to the reduction of culture to
preconceived formulas and codes, thus producing what Adorno and his colleagues saw as
a degradation of culture.

Adorno also studied the effects of popular
music and utilized Lukács's category of 'reification' to describe what he perceived as the
degrading effects on consciousness of music
reduced simply to rhythms and lyrics which
could be easily memorized and hummed. During the 1930s Adorno carried out further studies of music, working with the 'father of mass
communications research', Paul Lazarsfeld, at

the Princeton Radio Project and later at Columbia University on one of the first sustained research projects on the effects of popular music. Later, Adorno was also to work on one of the first attempts to develop a critical analysis of television, producing an article on 'How to look at television' in 1954.

Adorno also participated in the intradisciplinary research projects at the institute and worked on their researches into fascism and antisemitism. When the institute broke up in the early 1940s – with its director, Max Horkheimer, going to California for health reasons and other members like Herbert Marcuse, Franz Neumann, Leo Lowenthal and Otto Kirchheimer going to Washington to join the US government in the fight against fascism – Adorno went to California. There he worked closely with Max Horkheimer on the book that became *Dialectic of Enlightenment*. Horkheimer and Adorno moved away from the Marxian emphasis on the primacy of political economy to stress the importance of the project of the domination of nature, from the Greeks and Christians to the present. Consequently, they placed technology and what they called 'instrumental reason' at the centre of their new sociocultural theory, displacing the primacy of class struggle as well as the Marxian theory of crisis.

Drawing on the institute's previous research into mass culture, Horkheimer and Adorno developed a theory of the culture industry that produced the first systematic Marxian critique of mass culture and communication. Horkheimer and Adorno argued that although mass culture purported to be mere entertainment it was a vehicle of ideology that served as a powerful instrument of social control; from this perspective, mass culture was eminently political, and the critique of a society's dominant ideologies should focus serious attention on mass culture. On Horkheimer and Adorno's conception, mass culture produced a system of products that idealized the existing society and suggested that happiness could be found through conformity to its institutions and way of life. The culture industries thus provided contemporary capitalism, and fascism and state communism, with powerful instruments of domination that secured the power of hegemonic institutions over individuals and contributed to the decline of the individual through their growing control of thought and behaviour.

Horkheimer and Adorno also presented a variety of theses on antisemitism and a set of aphorisms which expressed their growing pessimism and sense that totalitarian social powers were coming to control the entire world. Adorno pursued the aphoristic strategy in a collection of short entries written during this period and published in 1951 under the title *Minima Moralia*. In the introduction to this book Adorno situated the text within the project of developing a critical theory of contemporary society, though the main focus was on culture, everyday life and 'the teaching of the good life'. His aphorisms evoke the growing power of society over the individual and the desire for individual emancipation and happiness, as when he writes, 'Perhaps the true society will grow tired of development and, out of freedom, leave possibilities unused, instead of storming under a confused compulsion to the conquest of strange stars. . . . *Rien faire comme une bête*, lying on water and looking peacefully at the sky, "being, nothing else, without any further definition and fulfilment", might take the place of process, act, satisfaction, and so truly keep the promise of dialectical logic that it would culminate in its origin. None of the abstract concepts comes closer to fulfilled utopia than that of eternal peace' (pp. 156–7).

In *Minima Moralia*, and other essays of the period, Adorno continued the institute's studies of the stabilization of capitalism and the integration of the working class as a conservative force in the capitalist system. In such a situation, deeply influenced by his sojourn in New York and California, Adorno only saw the possibility of individual revolt. He also feared, however, the resurgence of authoritarianism in the United States and collaborated on a ground-breaking collective study of *The Authoritarian Personality* with a group of Berkeley researchers. The project embodied the institute's desire to merge theoretical construction with empirical research and produced a portrait of a disturbing authoritarian potential in the United States. Adorno was responsible for elaborating the theoretical implications and helped design the research apparatus.

In the early 1950s he returned with Horkheimer to Germany to re-establish the institute in Frankfurt. He continued his studies in sociology and culture, though he turned to philosophy during the last years of his life. During the 1950s he participated in the institute's sociological studies of education, students, workers and the potential for democracy. Adorno wrote many sociological essays at this time and participated in the debates published in *The Positivist Dispute in German Sociology*. Adorno defended the institute's conception of dialectical social theory against positivism and the 'critical rationalism' espoused by Karl Popper and other neo-positivists.

Increasingly critical of communism and sceptical of Marxism, Adorno engaged primarily in cultural criticism and studies of philosophy and aesthetics during his last decade. Deeply shocked by Auschwitz and the Holocaust, Adorno's criticism became ever more negative and oppositional. In the postwar period he became increasingly known as a champion of modernist *avant-garde* art, which he saw as the most powerful weapon of liberation. Although he followed Lukács and other Marxist theorists in his sociological and ideological approach to culture, he broke with standard Marxian normative aesthetics, which championed realist art *à la* Lukács or political modernism *à la* Brecht. Adorno, by contrast, championed *avant-garde* modernism, which he believed carried out the most extreme negation of existing society and culture. Thus in 'Commitment' he polemicized against Brecht, Sartre and 'committed' literature, and championed Kafka, Beckett and other exponents of what he saw as extreme negation of existing society.

While Adorno's last major published work during his lifetime, *Negative Dialectics*, was deeply philosophical, his essays were often directed towards the political issues of the day, and he continued the politicization of cultural criticism that he had helped inaugurate in the 1930s. Although many of his students were active in the German student movement in the 1960s, Adorno was highly critical of the movement and even called in the police during a student occupation of the institute during an anti-war protest. His estrangement from the student movement and the sharp criticism that he received from student activists hurt him deeply and he died suddenly of a heart attack in 1969 with his *magnum opus*, *Aesthetic Theory*, still unpublished, though it soon appeared posthumously.

While Adorno's contributions to philosophy, sociology and cultural criticism are immense, his major political contributions reside in his politicizing of these disciplines, showing that all have a deeply political dimension. Thus his studies of Wagner's music dramas and of Husserl's and Heidegger's philosophy emphasize their political import, as do his studies of mass culture. Increasingly sceptical of standard varieties of political action, and pessimistic concerning the possibilities of emancipatory political change, Adorno championed individual rebellion and resistance and will be remembered as an uncompromising critic of existing societies and politics and a champion of individual emancipation.

See also

Heidegger, Horkheimer, Lukács, Marcuse, Popper, Sartre.

Works

The Authoritarian Personality (with others), New York, Norton, 1950.

'How to look at television', *Quarterly of Film, Radio, and Television* VIII (spring 1954).
Prisms, London, Neville Spearman, 1967.
Dialectic of Enlightenment (with Max Horkheimer), New York, Herder, 1972.
Negative Dialectics, London, Routledge, 1973.
Minima Moralia, London, Verso, 1974.
'Commitment', in *Aesthetics and Politics*, London, Verso, 1977.
'The social situation of music', *Telos* 35 (spring 1978).
Aesthetic Theory, London, Routledge, 1984.
Kierkegaard: Construction of the Aesthetic, Minneapolis, Minn., University of Minnesota Press, 1989.

Other works

Susan Buck-Morss, *The Origins of Negative Dialectics*, New York, Free Press, 1977.
Martin Jay, *Adorno*, Cambridge, Mass., Harvard University Press, 1984.
Douglas Kellner, *Critical Theory, Marxism, and Modernity*, Cambridge, Polity Press, and Baltimore, Md, Johns Hopkins University Press, 1988.
Frederic Jameson, *Late Marxism*, London and New York, Verso, 1990.

Michel 'Aflaq   1910–1989

Michel 'Aflaq, one of the founders of Ba'thism, a form of pan-Arab nationalism, and its best-known ideologue, was a Greek Orthodox Christian, born and educated in Damascus. Between 1929 and 1933 he studied philosophy at the Sorbonne, where he was influenced by the writings of Bergson; in addition, he made no secret of his admiration for National Socialist Germany, which he saw as a model for his ideas of a synthesis between nationalism and socialism. While in Paris he met his fellow countryman Salah al-Din al-Bitar, and the two stayed in close contact on their return to Syria, founding what was to become the Ba'th Party in the early 1940s. (The precise chronology of the foundation of the party is disputed: the Syrian Ba'th traces its origins to the teachings and writings of Zaki al-Arsuzi (1900–69), while the Iraqi Ba'th claims descent from 'Aflaq and Bitar.) 'Aflaq was secretary-general of the Ba'th Party for most of his later life, first between 1954 and 1965, then again from February 1968 until his death; in addition, he was Syrian Minister of Education for a few months in 1949, and worked as a secondary schoolteacher in the 1930s and 1940s.

During the heady years of the early 1950s, when Arab nationalism was much in vogue, the Ba'th Party gained a considerable following in Syria, and branches were founded in other Arab countries, notably Iraq. The party was conceived of as the instrument through which the Arab world would eventually be united, and its publications and declarations referred to the various Arab states in which its branches were located as 'regions of the Arab nation'. Unfortunately for the Ba'th, however, enthusiasm for unity (combined, it must be said, with a profound suspicion of communism) led the leadership to confuse appearances with reality. In 1958 'Aflaq and Bitar encouraged the Syrian branch, which was then in a relatively powerful position, to dissolve itself as the price of Syria's entry into a union with Egypt, since Nasser was not prepared to tolerate political parties. The experiment collapsed within three years; in 1963 a group of Ba'thist officers seized power in Syria, and in 1966 an intra-Ba'th *coup* effectively ousted 'Aflaq and Bitar. The main consequence was an open breach between the Syrian and Iraqi wings of the Ba'th (the latter supporting 'Aflaq), amounting in practice to the creation of two Ba'th parties, a situation which has continued ever since. 'Aflaq went to Baghdad in 1968, and remained there as titular head of the party for most of the rest of his life.

The main message of Ba'thism as it appears in 'Aflaq's writings is the assertion of the underlying unity of the 'Arab nation' from the Atlantic to the Gulf. The Arabs are one people who have been divided by imperialism and Zionism; their rebirth (*ba'th*) can come only when they unite against the enemies which surround them. Antagonism to the idea of the Arab nation must be fiercely, even violently, resisted; 'the antagonistic idea does not exist by itself', he wrote in 1959, 'it is embodied in persons who must perish, so that it too must perish.'

'Aflaq, a Christian, asserted that Islam was the 'prime moment' of Arabism, in which Christians and Muslims could participate together; 'the Arab Christians', he wrote in 1943, 'will recognize that Islam is [a part of] their national culture ... they will cherish Islam ... as the most precious moment of their Arabism'. Ba'thist 'socialism' is vague in the extreme ('socialism is a necessity which emanates from the depth of Arab nationalism itself'); it is anti-communist – 'we represent the Arab spirit against materialist communism', 'Aflaq wrote in 1943 – and does not recognize class struggle.

'Aflaq was always described by those who knew him as an ascetic, shy and intense figure, living a simple and unpretentious life, with little interest in worldly affairs. He looked to political activists or to regimes to implement his fervent desire for Arab unity; to Nasser in 1958, to the Iraqis Qasim and 'Arif in the same year, when he tried to persuade them to bring post-revolutionary Iraq into the United Arab Republic, to the brutal gang leader 'Ali Salih al-Sa'di, whom he supported as leader of a splinter group of the Iraqi Ba'th in 1963, and finally to Saddam Husain, perhaps the most unsavoury of them all, who used the slogans of Ba'thism as the 'ideology' of his regime.

Works

Most of 'Aflaq's writings were originally essays or newspaper articles; the items below are collections of these, together with a few translations.

Fikratuna (Our Idea), Beirut, 1948.
Fi Sabil al-Ba'th al-'Arabi (In the Cause of the Arab Ba'th), Beirut, 1953, 1959, 1963 (editions vary considerably).
'Commémoration du prophète arabe (1943)', trans. J. Viennot, *Orient*, 9, XXXV (1965), pp. 147–58.
'Nationalism and revolution', in S. G. Haim (ed.), *Arab Nationalism: an Anthology*, Berkeley, University of California Press, second edition, 1976, pp. 242–9.
Choice of Texts from the Ba'th Party Founder's Thought, Florence, 1977.

Other works

P. Seale, *The Struggle for Syria: a Study of Post-war Arab Politics, 1945–1958*, London, Tauris, second edition, 1986.
M. Farouk-Sluglett, and P. Sluglett, *Iraq since 1958: from Revolution to Dictatorship*, London, Kegan Paul, 1987.
P. Seale, *Asad of Syria: the Struggle for the Middle East*, London, Tauris, 1989.
S. al-Khalil, *The Republic of Fear: Saddam's Iraq*, London, Hutchinson Century, 1990.

Louis Althusser   1918–1990

It is no exaggeration to say that the ideas of Althusser and his associates set the agenda for Western Marxist intellectuals, and indeed for many radical non-Marxists, from the mid-1960s into the late 1970s. Arguably, too, much of the 'postmodernist' and 'poststructuralist' literature of the subsequent decade is the legacy of Althusser's unremitting deconstruction and renewal of Marxist philosophy. Althusser has been credited with raising Marxist philosophy to a new level of sophistication and with effectively 'de-Stalinizing' it by bringing it into creative engagement with non-Marxist philosophies and other traditions of modern thought: most significantly psychoanalysis, structuralism and linguistics. But he has also been vigorously denounced by his detractors for the sterility of his 'theoreticism', for his evacuation of human agency from the Marxist understanding of history, and for the crypto-Stalinism of his politics. There are recent signs of a new and positive re-evaluation, but the partisanship surrounding Althusser's work has been so intense that a balanced assessment is difficult to achieve.

Althusser was born in Algeria. Most of the Second World War was spent in a prisoner-of-war camp, and after it he went on to complete his studies at the Ecole Normale Supérieure, where the historian and philosopher of science Gaston Bachelard was his supervisor. He went on to become a distinguished philosophy teacher at the Ecole, and was a member of the French Communist Party from 1948.

The publication in 1965 of *For Marx*, a collection of his essays of the early 1960s, and of a collaborative work, *Reading Capital*, had a rapid international impact. In these works Althusser challenged the humanist moralizing which had been the dominant critical response of anti-Stalinist Marxist philosophers. Althusser's project was a critique of Stalinism from the left, which would involve both a renewal of Marxist philosophy and an associated defence of historical materialism as a scientific discourse: only in this way could the left move beyond moral condemnation to an analysis of the causes and conditions of Stalinism and of the strategic possibilities of revolution in the West. Althusser's procedure was to utilize ideas drawn from a distinctive French tradition of history of science, together with structuralist principles of 'reading', to offer a radically new interpretation of the formation and content of the writings of Marx.

The writings were subjected to a historical periodization, the most important element of which was the identification of an 'epistemological break', separating the humanist and Hegelian problematics of the early works from the emergent problematic of a scientific 'historical materialism' which took shape from 1845 onwards. In basing themselves on the early texts of Marx, and insisting on continuity between them and the later works, the humanist Marxists had failed to recognize all that was significant and innovative in Marx's intellectual achievement – the conquest of the whole 'continent' of history for science. The mere trading of quotations could not decide the issue, since what was at stake was the 'problematic' – the underlying nexus of concepts which determined both the questions posed and the silences of the empirical text. This problematic could be exposed only by a disciplined practice of 'symptomatic' reading, whose great exemplary exponent had been Marx himself in his critique of political economy.

What is yielded by this symptomatic reading, practised on the later works of Marx (primarily *Capital*), together with some texts by Lenin and Mao? First, a series of respects in which the new problematic of historical materialism makes a decisive break with the philosophical ideologies of its prehistory, and, second, a network of substantive theoretical concepts for historical periodization and social scientific analysis. The philosophical ideologies against which historical materialism is pitted are, primarily, essentialism, historicism, humanism and empiricism. Against essentialism in social theory, historical materialism, in Althusser's version of it, advocates a concept of society as a 'de-centred totality', a complex combination of practices, each with its own specific conditions, relations, dynamics and effects on the totality. No practice is to be regarded as a mere 'epiphenomenon' or manifestation of any other, and, in political practice in particular, the reduction of class struggle to the economic struggle between capital and labour is to be resisted. Social and political struggles located at different sites within the social formation mutually condition and 'over-determine' one another. The rejection of essentialism is logically connected in this way with anti-historicism. Since there is no single 'essential' contradiction leading of necessity to a higher-level revolutionary synthesis and supersession, it follows that fundamental transformations in the forms of social life are to be thought of as contingent outcomes of a 'fusion' or 'condensation' of multiple contradictions and struggles. There is no place here for history as a linear sequence of stages leading inexorably to some pre-defined end-state, a doctrine so often masquerading as the Marxian view.

Althusser's 'anti-humanist' reading of Marx has been, perhaps, the most controversial of all his innovations. At the most banal level, Althusser's critics have taken it to be a moral doctrine – a kind of systematic misanthropy – whilst others, more plausibly, have recognized in Althusser's theoretical anti-humanism a down-playing of the role of self-conscious agency (individual or collective) in the making of history. In fact a number of quite distinct theses are confused together in

Althusser's anti-humanism. One of these follows directly from the rejection of historicism. In so far as that ideology postulated communism as both the outcome of historical development and the fulfilment of human potential – full human self-realizations – a form of humanism is implicit in it. A rejection of historical teleology would carry with it a rejection of that form of philosophical humanism. But Althusser also attempted a synthesis of structuralist and Marxian principles of social explanation in rejecting the 'humanist' understanding of social relations as the products of social action in favour of a view of the consciousness, identity and activity of human agents ('subjects') as effects of their positions in the structure of social relations. It was this doctrine which most offended Althusser's radical critics, in seeming to rule out a causal role for autonomous human agency in revolutionary change, but, paradoxically, it is this element in Althusser's thought which has survived the fragmentation and dissolution of his own intellectual project and remains at the core of post-structuralism. Finally, Althusser advocated what might be called 'epistemological anti-humanism', the thesis that the social formation is never 'transparent' to social actors, who always and necessarily live their relationship to the social conditions of their existence in the domain of ideology. This, again, offended humanist Marxists, for whom the future communist society would be rationally intelligible to its citizens, by contrast with the mystification and false consciousness endemic to capitalism.

Althusser's anti-empiricism in epistemology was also closely connected with this form of anti-humanism. If social reality is not 'transparent' to its agents, then observation cannot be the proper foundation for objective knowledge of it. Knowledge is an achievement, won through a social practice of critical engagement with given (ideological) conceptual forms. 'Science' is not given in experience, but is rather the product of intellectual labour, a distinct, irreducible 'theoretical practice'. Despite his insistence upon a radical

distinction between ideology and science, and upon the objectivity of the latter, Althusser never resolved the dilemmas implicit in his attempt to combine a relativist-inclined historical understanding of the production of knowledge with an orthodox defence of the 'scientificity' of historical materialism.

Althusser tended to leave the more concrete elaboration and application of the specific historical concepts of structural Marxism to his associates and pupils. Attempts to establish distinctively Marxist conceptions of the state, ideology and 'civil society', and of the mode of their 'relatively autonomous' combination with economic structures under the determination 'in the last instance' of the latter; to develop and update Marxian class theory in a form adequate to challenge non-Marxist sociological scholarship; and many other projects, flowed directly from these new openings forged by Althusser in the early and mid-1960s.

But partly under the weight of its own internal tensions and contradictions, partly in the face of the severe political challenges of the uprisings of Paris, in May 1968, and their aftermath, the Althusserian project began to disintegrate. This can now be recognized (as Althusser himself has asked) as a symptom of the current crisis of Marxism itself, and, indeed, of the whole socialist tradition.

In a spate of self-critical activity, Althusser himself led the way in the demolition of his own intellectual achievements, denouncing, especially, the 'theoreticism' of his early work, and advocating a new conception of philosophy as a 'revolutionary weapon'.

Althusser suffered from a serious depressive illness, which appears to have become more intense after 1968. In 1980 he was admitted to St Anne's Psychiatric Hospital in Paris, having confessed to the killing of his wife, Hélène. The retrospective verdict on his work will almost certainly be that he was one of the major Marxist intellectuals of the twentieth century. If he is also the last, that may well turn out to have been his own paradoxical contribution to our history.

7

See also

Lenin, Mao.

Works

For Marx, London, Allen Lane, 1969.
Reading Capital, London, New Left Books, 1970.
Lenin and Philosophy and other Essays, London, New Left Books, 1971.
Philosophy and the Spontaneous Philosophy of the Scientists and other Essays, London, Verso, 1990.

Other works

Norman Geras, 'Althusser's Marxism: an account and assessment', *New Left Review*, January–February 1972, pp. 57–86.
Alex Callinicos, *Althusser's Marxism*, London, Pluto Press, 1976.
T. O'Hagen, 'Althusser: how to be a Marxist in philosophy', in *Marx and Marxisms*, Cambridge, 1982, pp. 243–64.
Edward Benton, *The Rise and Fall of Structural Marxism*, Basingstoke, Macmillan, 1984.
George Elliot, *Althusser: the Detour Theory*, London, Verso, 1987.

Hannah Arendt   1906–1975

Arendt spent her childhood in Königsberg, the famous eighteenth-century centre of the German Jewish Enlightenment. Her university years, from 1924 to 1929, began at Marburg under the tutelage of Martin Heidegger and the theologian Rudolf Bultmann. Heidegger's *Existenz* philosophy, especially his radical enquiry into ontology and his emphasis upon 'existentials', decisively influenced Arendt's theorizing and provided a guiding framework for her later work. After a year at Marburg, Arendt moved briefly to Freiburg, where she studied with the phenomenologist Edmund Husserl, and then on to Heidelberg, where Karl Jaspers was just beginning his three-volume *Philosophy*. Jaspers's appreciation of Socratic exploration and his philosophical emphasis on freedom, community, plurality and dialogue played as significant a role in Arendt's thinking as Heidegger's anti-philosophy. In 1928 she completed her dissertation, 'Der Liebesbegriff

bei Augustin' (The Concept of Love in St Augustine).

In the waning years of the Weimar Republic, Arendt began a postdoctoral project on German romanticism and grew increasingly attentive to the problem of antisemitism and the social psychology of Jewish assimilation. The question of what it means to be an outsider, a '*parvenu* or pariah', she explored in detail in *Rahel Varnhagen*, and in her later Zionist writings. Her increasing involvement with the German Zionist Organization, along with growing antisemitism and repression, led to her arrest and brief detention in 1933. Shortly after Hitler's rise to power and the burning of the Reichstag she left Germany for France. In 1941, as Vichy materialized, and following internment in separate French prison camps, Arendt and her husband, Heinrich Blücher, escaped to the United States.

From the early 1950s until her death in 1975 Arendt taught at numerous distinguished universities in the United States. Along with other German *émigré* scholars, including Hans Morgenthau, Franz Neumann, Leo Strauss, Eric Voegelin and the Frankfurt school of critical theorists, Theodor Adorno, Max Horkheimer and Herbert Marcuse, she was instrumental in reshaping the discourse of political theory in American academia. Arendt's own writings on this matter defy easy categorization and stand outside the familiar classifications of left or right. One of the hallmarks of her political theorizing is her rejection of almost all modern schools of thought as appropriate starting points for political enquiry. She preferred to turn to German philosophy and the Western tradition of political theory – especially Aristotle, St Augustine, Machiavelli, Hobbes, Rousseau, de Tocqueville and Marx – to guide her thinking, as she once put it, 'in the gap between past and future'.

At least four expressly political themes dominate Arendt's work. All reflect her lifelong concern to explore the meaning and conditions of human action or the *vita activa*:

the unprecedentedness of totalitarianism in the modern age and the need to comprehend its evils; the theoretical and practical task of rescuing politics from 'the social', and in the face of contemporary crises; the importance of revitalizing our understanding of freedom as a communicative practice involving speech, action and plurality; and the guidance offered by the legacy of American republicanism for the founding of a free political order.

The Origins of Totalitarianism established her reputation as a major political and social thinker. The title, however, is misleading. Arendt's concern was not to undertake a genetic study of twentieth-century totalitarian systems but rather to probe the historical meaning of what she once referred to as 'the elements of shame' in modernity – antisemitism, imperialism and racism. The English title, *The Burden of our Time*, better conveys Arendt's ultimate intention: to find out the main elements of Nazism and Stalinism, trace them back, and probe the social realities that crystallized in 'total domination'. The central argument of this ambitious enterprise is that no totalitarian system can succeed without the bureaucratization of terror, especially in the form of concentration camps. An array of other themes and issues crowd the book, however, underscoring the scale of Arendt's enterprise: the social psychology of mobs and elites; a critique of nationalism and the 'statelessness' it foments; the problem of pan-movements and continental imperialism, race and bureaucracy, ideology and terror. Despite its pell-mell character, *The Origins* bears a quality that distinguishes all Arendt's subsequent political texts: it attempts to generate our thinking about what it means 'to be' in the world, rather than explaining human behaviour or social systems in causal, scientific fashion.

The Origins established Arendt's reputation; *The Human Condition* secured it. The influence of Heidegger is seen in the book's concentration upon 'existentials' that describe being in the *vita activa*: labour, work and action. But the purpose of *The Human Condi-*

tion is unique to Arendt: she seeks to restore the primacy of politics as action in the world and thereby secure its *raison d'être*, freedom. In telling the story of how action has been subsumed by labour and work in the modern world, Arendt fully displayed her affinity for thinking in terms of overlapping conceptual distinctions. It is only through action, the most thoroughly reduced human activity, and its corresponding condition, plurality, that human beings reveal their individual distinctiveness publicly, through shared speech and deed, and thereby realize freedom. In true Heideggerean fashion, Arendt implicates the tradition of Western philosophy – from Plato to Marx – in the disastrous transformation of the *vita activa*. But the real core of *The Human Condition* lies in its powerful, albeit pessimistic, exposure of the alienation of the contemporary world, and the book's celebration of freedom – as the glory of self-revelation through shared speech and deed in the public sphere.

The prevailing ideas in *The Human Condition*, of politics as an end in itself and of freedom as constituted by citizens participating together in the public realm, resurfaced in *On Revolution*, where Arendt used them to take the measure of the American and French revolutions. In what proved to be a highly controversial argument, she claimed that the French revolution succumbed to 'the social question' and thereby subverted itself by failing to found and sustain a public space for action. By making 'abundance' rather than freedom their aim, and the alienation of poverty rather than the founding of arenas of action their end, the French failed to secure institutions for freedom and, along with them, a true revolution. By contrast, Arendt's account of the American revolution, with its homage to the founders' *constitutio libertatis* and republican forms of government, proclaimed the American experience an unambiguous, if not decisive, success. In the final chapter Arendt warned that contemporary Americans are in danger of losing the 'treasure' their revolutionary tradition betokened. This was a theme that reappeared in *Crises of the Republic* (1972). In *On Revolution*, as in her earlier writings, Arendt wove a cautionary tale about the meaning of politics and the fate of freedom in the modern world. But once again she was assessed primarily as a social scientist and historian, and by those standards her work was found wanting.

Reaction to *Eichmann in Jerusalem*, which overshadowed the publication of *On Revolution*, was even more critical. The subtitle, *a Report on the Banality of Evil*, captures Arendt's most famous judgement: Eichmann, and other functionaries of totalitarianism like him, are best understood neither as monsters nor as cogs in bureaucratic machines, but rather as 'terribly and terrifyingly normal'. Eichmann, Arendt argued, had no motives for doing what he did; he exhibited both a stultifying thoughtlessness and a lack of imagination. He was banal, an ordinary perpetrator of evil. To those unfamiliar with Arendt's other writings her judgement of Eichmann seemed, at best, to be a case of extreme understatement, at worst the whitewash of an accomplice to genocide. Yet her portrait can also be read as a merciless exposure of the sort of normalcy that enables a human being to obfuscate totally the nature of right and wrong. Arendt held Eichmann accountable to the principle of freedom and the human requirements she set for the public realm: the capacity to think representatively, exercise reflective judgement, revere and practise speech as a form of freedom, and respect the opinions and the beingness (plurality) of one's fellow citizens as equals and peers. On all these counts, thoroughly in keeping with Arendt's respect for human freedom and her awareness of the fragility of the web of human relations, Eichmann was damned. In a postscript to the controversy aroused by her book, 'Truth and politics' (*Between Past and Future*), she attempted to clarify the nature of factual truth and the kind of political thinking to which she had held Eichmann responsible.

In assessing Arendt's work as a whole it is useful to call upon Jaspers's observation that one can be philosophically systematic without producing a system, a totalizing order of thought. Arendt's work, including her last, unfinished and most purely philosophical text, *The Life of the Mind*, is systematic without a system. A rich set of concepts, ideas and principles, particularly her appreciation of the uniqueness of politics as a realm of distinctive action, is carried throughout her writings. Yet her consistent practice of political theorizing as 'pearl diving' rather than system-building renders her work less a philosophical *opus* than a perpetual invitation to 'think what we are doing' as citizens in the modern world.

See also

Adorno, Heidegger, Horkheimer, Marcuse, Strauss.

Works

The Origins of Totalitarianism, New York, Meridian, 1951.
Rahel Varnhagen: the Life of a Jewish Woman, New York, Harcourt Brace, 1957.
The Human Condition, Chicago, University of Chicago Press, 1958.
On Revolution, New York, Viking Press, 1963.
Eichmann in Jerusalem: a Report on the Banality of Evil, New York, Viking Press, 1963.
Between Past and Future, New York, Viking Press, 1968.
The Life of the Mind, New York, Harvest, 1978.

Other works

Margaret Canovan, *The Political Thought of Hannah Arendt*, New York, Harecourt Brace, 1974.
M. Hill (ed.), *Hannah Arendt: the Recovery of the Public World*, New York, St Martin's Press, 1979.
Elisabeth Young-Bruehl, *Hannah Arendt: for Love of the World*, New Haven, Conn., Yale University Press, 1982.
George Kateb, *Hannah Arendt: Politics, Conscience, Evil*, Totowa, N.J., Rowman & Allanheld, 1984.
L. P. Hinchman and S. K. Hinchman, eds, *Hannah Arendt: Critical Essays*, Albany, N.Y., State University of New York Press, 1994.

Thurman Wesley Arnold 1891–1969

New Deal 'trust buster' and member of the school of legal realism.

See also

Galbraith.

Works include

The Symbols of Government, New Haven, Conn., Yale University Press, 1935.
The Folklore of Capitalism, New Haven, Conn., Yale University Press, 1937.

Raymond Aron   1905–1983

Born in Paris, Aron studied philosophy at the Ecole Normale Supérieure, where he was a close friend of Sartre. From 1930 to 1933 he was a French *Lektor* in Germany, where he witnessed the rise of National Socialism and encountered neo-Kantian philosophy, phenomenology, Marxism and German social science. On his return to France he published *German Sociology* (1957), in which his admiration for Max Weber – a major influence – is apparent, followed by his doctoral thesis, *Introduction to the Philosophy of History*, primarily an epistemological work which explores the relationship between philosophical and social thought and political action.

With the fall of France, Aron – patriot, Jew and unwavering liberal democrat – left for England in June 1940 and became editor of the successful Free French review *La France Libre*. On returning to France he turned to journalism and was for thirty years the influential political columnist of *Le Figaro* (1947–77), after which he joined *L'Express*. His anti-totalitarian convictions led him to adopt a forthright anti-Soviet position during the Cold War; breaking with Sartre, he joined the Gaullist Rassemblement du Peuple Français and published a celebrated study of Marxist and French fellow-travelling ideology, *The Opium of the Intellectuals*.

From 1955 to 1968 Aron was Professor of Sociology at the Sorbonne. The main academic writings of this prolific period include *Peace and War*, a major treatise on international relations in the twentieth century; *Democracy and Totalitarianism*, a comparative sociology of monopolistic and pluralistic political systems; *An Essay on Freedom* (1970), a neglected analysis of the problem of liberty in modern society; and *Main Currents in Sociological Thought*, the text of his justly famous Sorbonne lectures on Montesquieu, Comte, Marx, de Tocqueville, Durkheim, Pareto and Weber. At the same time the political journalism continued unabated; Aron was an early advocate of Algerian independence and a severe critic of the student revolt of May 1968 (*The Elusive Revolution*, 1969).

Aron was appointed professor at the Collège de France in 1970, and this last phase of his life includes a dispassionate analysis of US post-war foreign policy, *Imperial Republic* (1975); *History and the Dialectic of Violence* (1975), a critique of Sartre's political philosophy; and a late masterpiece, *Clausewitz: Philosopher of War* (1983), a study of the Prussian military theorist and his impact on twentieth-century strategic thinking.

Although respected in the Anglo-American world, in French intellectual circles Aron's political liberalism and anti-communism had long made him a somewhat isolated figure, often compared unfavourably with Sartre. This gradually changed, however, in the last decade of his life, especially with the impact made by the publication in France of Solzenhitsyn's *The Gulag Archipelago*. Aron now wrote one of his finest polemics, *In Defence of Decadent Europe* (1979), a plea for liberal Western society in the face of the persistent seduction of Marxist ideology and the threat of Soviet imperialism. A series of television interviews made him known to a wider public – the text, *The Committed Observer* (1983), constitutes one of the best introductions to his life and thought, as well as giving the flavour of the man; and the publication of his *Mémoires* (1983), a few weeks before his death, at last enabled him to be appreciated as a lifelong champion of liberty and truth, arguably the greatest political sociologist since Max Weber.

11

See also

Durkheim, Pareto, Sartre, Weber.

Works

The Opium of the Intellectuals, London, Secker & Warburg, 1957.
Introduction to the Philosophy of History: an Essay on the Limits of Historical Objectivity, London, Weidenfeld & Nicolson, 1961.
Peace and War: a Theory of International Relations, New York, Doubleday, 1966.
Democracy and Totalitarianism, London, Weidenfeld & Nicolson, 1968.
Main Currents in Sociological Thought, London, Penguin, 1968.

Other works

Roy Pierce, *Contemporary French Political Thought*, London, Oxford University Press, 1966.
Ghita Ionescu, 'Raymond Aron: a modern classicist', in Anthony de Crespigny and Kenneth Minogue (eds.), *Contemporary Political Philosophers*, London, Methuen, 1976.
Judith A. Hall, *Diagnoses of our Time: Six Views on our Social Condition*, London, Heinemann, 1981.
Robert Colquhoun, *Raymond Aron: the Philosopher in History, 1905–1955*, London, Sage, 1986.
Robert Colquhoun, *Raymond Aron: the Sociologist in Society, 1955–1983*, London, Sage, 1986.

Mustafa Kemal Atatürk
1881–1938

In tracing the political thought of Atatürk, the soldier and statesman, three events of his career are prominent: he was the first national leader to check by force of arms the apparently irresistible expansion of the Great Powers into the Middle East; he founded upon the ruins of the Ottoman Empire a new nation state, the republic of Turkey; he transformed Anatolian Turkish society from its fundamentally religious frame into an essentially secular structure.

The transformation constituted a national revolution quite distinct from other revolutions of this century, principally owing to the personality of its leader. Atatürk, as a member of the Ottoman elite, albeit a dissentient one, had no deliberate hand in the destruction of the established state; indeed, he fought for

years (1909–18) to defend it. Such a background was instrumental in shaping the form and character of the Turkish revolution and was crucial to the formation of a political thought that was pragmatic, though possessing a clear coherence, and related to the course of political events.

It was the threat to the existence of the Turks of Turkey and their violent reaction to it in the War of Independence (1919–22) against the allies and their proxies which made Atatürk the leader of the resistance and set the revolution in motion. Atatürk's was a vision of social order fashioned out of long reflection on the disorder he lived through. He knew what was; he deduced what ought to be. So he reconstructed the state as a republic for which he aimed to create, especially through education, an appropriate citizenry. Though his political thought constitutes a theory of universal validity, Atatürk was aware that he must live with the consequences of its specific application. He introduced no wholly novel ideas; his originality lay rather in the reinterpretation of familiar concepts to form a viable method of tackling an actual situation. However, in order chiefly to retain its flexibility and acceptability, he never systematically set down his thinking.

Atatürk sought to establish an inherently capitalist nation state based upon the principle of popular sovereignty, whose moral substance would be a conscious synthesis of native and universal elements. His vision of social order assumed a modern state inclining towards social democracy in which ideas that had taken root in Reformation Europe would be grafted on to the liberated Turkey through the complementary concepts of contemporaneity and nationalism.

Contemporaneity derived from the rationalist essence of civilization, contemporary civilization being, in Atatürk's usage, equivalent to but not identical with civilization in Western Europe. And Atatürk was determined to cultivate the principle of rational enquiry as the ultimate arbiter in society, in order to gain individual self-awareness and thence national integration. Central to his concept of contemporaneity, that of a world civilization in which every nation might participate, was recognition of the multiplicity of its origins, not least among them medieval Islamic civilization. Civilization was thus linked with the idea of progress as technological development compounded with moral improvement. In fact Atatürk held the current state of the Islamic world to be lamentable, and his idealist philosophy ascribed this to a question of attitude; over the centuries Muslims' gradual retreat from rationalism to blind acquiescence in theology had rendered them defenceless and submissive. His view of the intellectual history of Islam strengthened his conviction that the weight of rigid orthodoxy must be lifted from Turkish society, not merely for the sake of the people but for that of Islam itself, which he felt needed cleansing of its irrational and inflexible accretions. Atatürk envisaged, therefore, a secular society wherein the existence of Islam would be dependent upon the voluntary adherence of the individual Muslim. He conceived contemporaneity in a Turkish setting which would bolster intrinsic values towards this mental emancipation of the Turks – a conceptual revolution he believed vital to prepare them for the secularizing institutional reforms he planned. Aware as he was that secularism itself was liable to undermine the traditional bonds of Muslim society, Atatürk strove to nurture that national loyalty already evoked among participants in the War of Independence into an intense nationalism, whether combined with faith in Islam or, preferably, serving as a substitute for it. In this sense, nationalism would be the rediscovery and reassertion by the Turks of their Turkishness. For this, Atatürk postulated a nationhood founded upon the prerequisites of common polity, vocabulary, territory, ancestry, history and morality – the sum of which exactly fitted the Turks; yet the exclusivity of the definition moved him to concede that ultimately anyone was a Turk who considered himself such. Moreover, he generalized nationhood to include every group with a distinctive linguistic and historical background and a continuous awareness of it, provided they could establish and maintain their independence.

Atatürk stressed that for nations, as for individuals, life was a struggle and those who succumbed must blame themselves. His anti-imperialism in this respect was unique. He looked forward to the colonial peoples freeing themselves from their oppressors, by armed force if necessary. The increase in political awareness that they gained thereby would ensure jealous guard of their new-found political liberty. They ought then to direct themselves towards contemporaneity and the creation of genuine modern nations, responsible for and answerable not only to the citizenry or a section thereof but also to the citizens of the nation as individuals. This kind of nation-building would be their responsibility alone, and only thus, as fully independent nation states, could they hope to survive in the contemporary world.

In sum, a kind of Pythagorean 'harmony of the spheres' underlies Atatürk's thought. A self-proclaimed nation, conscious and assured, is a coherent whole relative to its constituent individuals; yet the nation is also part of a larger entity, a civilization. Thus nationalism and contemporaneity become complementary to one another in the idea of unity in diversity. Contemporaneity, fostering the integrative tendency of contemporary world civilization, involves a break with the past while nationalism with its self-assertive tendency serves as a counterbalance, providing a continuity with the past beneath even the most drastic social reforms. This conjunction of the concepts of contemporaneity and nationalism, the holistic view of the political universe, forms the core of Atatürk's thought with regard to his Janus-like Turks, and relates directly to his belief in the efficacy of psychological change, the power of ideas. For it was Atatürk's *dirigiste* conviction that, without first changing the individual, true development of society was impossible.

Works

Works by Atatürk, comprising speeches, statements, declarations, treatises, diaries, letters, handwritten and dictated notes and unsigned articles, together with secondary materials in many languages, are to be found in:

M. Gökman, *Atatürk ve Devrimleri Tarihi Bibliyografyası/ Bibliography of the History of Atatürk and his Reforms*, Ankara, Kültür Bakanlığı, 1981–3, three volumes.

The English version of Atatürk's major six-day speech (without its original documents) is:

M. K. Atatürk, *A Speech Delivered by Ghazi Mustapha Kemal, President of the Turkish Republic, October 1927*, Leipzig, Koehler, 1929.

Other works

G. Tongas, *Atatürk and the True Nature of Modern Turkey*, trans. F. F. Rynd, London, Luzac, 1939.
N. Berkes, *The Development of Secularism in Turkey*, Montreal, McGill University Press, 1964.
A. Kazancıgil and E. Özbudun (eds.), *Atatürk: Founder of a Modern State*, London, Hurst, 1981.

Rudolf Bahro   1935–

Though best known for his contribution to the West German 'Green' movement in the 1980s, Bahro's first and perhaps most substantial statement as a political theorist was his critical analysis of 'actually existing socialism', written in East Germany during the 1970s. Bahro was born in 1935 in Silesia. He became a committed Marxist and party member in the German Democratic Republic, carrying out a series of trade union, cultural and organizational jobs. Though always independent and reform-minded, his decisive break with the political elite of Eastern Europe came with the Warsaw Pact invasion of Czechoslovakia in 1968. Unlike many East European dissidents, Bahro analysed the formation and structure of what he preferred to call 'proto-socialist' states from a resolutely Marxist standpoint. But, again, Bahro rejected the common tendency among left-wing critics of these societies to see their development as some kind of deviation from or 'betrayal' of classical Marxist principles. They should, rather, be seen as a quite distinct type of historical form, with their own spe-

cific structures, dynamics and antagonisms. They are not a post-capitalist stage, *en route* to communism, but, rather, represent an alternative, non-capitalist route to industrialism.

But the technological dependence of the non-capitalist economies on the economically more developed capitalist world subordinates them to the world market, and industrial technologies themselves carry with them a commitment to 'factory despotism', centralized bureaucratic administration and an expansionist dynamic. Alienation is as pervasive a feature of the East as it is of the West. The 'alternative' proposed by Bahro is a project of universal human emancipation through cultural revolution, in which 'compensatory needs' for power, possessions and consumption are displaced in favour of an 'emancipatory interest' in many-sided individual self-realization.

Bahro's book was first published in the West in 1977, and he was imprisoned as a Western spy by the East German authorities, only to be released in 1979 after an international campaign. On his arrival in West Germany, Bahro aligned himself with the newly emerging Green movement, becoming a leading activist and intellectual of its 'fundamentalist' faction. During the 1980s significant shifts in his outlook occurred, especially his adoption of a global perspective in which the key premise was a belief in nature-imposed absolute limits to industrial growth. Given his already established view of the interlocking of both capitalist and non-capitalist forms of industrialism in a single expansionist system, it followed that human survival itself was threatened by the continuation of this capitalist industrial monolith. Those who have an interest in human survival must become socialists, but, equally, all who favour social justice must conceive it in terms of ecological sustainability.

The impossibility of generalizing Western levels of material consumption to the Third World requires the industrialized world to think of the 'good life' in ways which make far fewer demands on a finite world. This goes against the short-term material interests of industrial workers in both Western and Eastern Bloc countries, so that class antagonisms in the industrial societies, as well as the East–West conflict itself, must be seen as secondary to the primary contradiction of North and South. Strategically, this means that the Greens must avoid the temptation to ally themselves with the traditional organizations of the working class. Instead, they must work for a fundamental change of consciousness and culture, towards a deindustrialized society of self-sufficient local communes, oriented to meeting basic needs. Bahro's position is avowedly utopian, and the growing tendency of the Greens to pragmatic political compromise led to his resignation from the party in 1985.

Works

The Alternative in Eastern Europe, London, Verso, 1978.
Socialism and Survival, London, Heretic, 1982.
From Red to Green, London, Verso, 1984.
Building the Green Movement, London, New Society, 1986.

Other works

Raymond Williams, 'Actually existing socialism', *New Left Review*, 120 (March–April 1980), pp. 3–19.
Ulf Wolter, *Rudolf Bahro: Critical Responses*, New York, Sharpe, 1980.
Boris Frankel, *The Post-industrial Utopians*, Cambridge, Polity Press, 1987.

Paul Baran   1910–1964

American Marxist political economist and co-author of the best-known critique of American capitalism.

See also

Frank.

Works include

The Political Economy of Growth, New York, Monthly Review Press, 1957.

Monopoly Capital (with Paul Sweezy), New York, Monthly Review Press, 1966.

Maurice Barrès   1862–1923

Novelist, journalist and politician, Maurice Barrès was one of the major figures in the reorientation of French nationalism in the period 1890–1914. Often credited with being the first to give nationalism a new and more exclusionary meaning, his novels and newspaper articles moulded a generation of young French intellectuals to accept an instinctual and cultural nationalism that emphasized the concept of a national community based on the mythic solidarity of 'the earth and the dead'.

Barrès came from a well-to-do bourgeois family of Lorraine notables and was educated at the *lycée* of Nancy before going to Paris to continue his legal studies. But he had little interest in the law and, once settled in Paris, launched himself in the literary world in 1884 by writing and publishing his own short-lived review. The success of his three novels of the *Culte de moi* series, with their themes of intellectual self-discovery and cultural rebellion, made Barrès the idol of the Latin Quarter and one of the most important intellectual influences on the new generation of educated French just emerging from the *lycées*.

Barrès began as a political activist with the Boulangist movement in 1889. Winning as a 'radical revisionst' candidate on an anti-semitic, anti-parliamentary platform in Nancy, Barrès's Boulangism united several of his literary themes: hostility to the rigid structures of bourgeois culture and education, and contempt for the parliamentary system and its leaders, whom he saw as responsible for France's decline as a culture and as a world power. The victory of Boulangism, by chasing the 'barbarians' from power, would, in Barrès's view, purge the political system and revivify French culture at the same time.

Barrès's 1889 campaign also stressed a vague socialism and a populist antisemitism in an attempt to build a politically expedient bridge to the workers of Nancy. The attempts to reach the working class through socialism would eventually fade from Barrès's political rhetoric. With the Dreyfus affair, in which Barrès played a leading role as an anti-Dreyfusard supporter of the army, the antisemitism was to become more strident.

Although Barrès's electoral defeat in 1893 corresponded with the general decline of Boulangism, nationalist politics had become part of his search for identity. It was the Dreyfus affair that completed his transition to a mystical and authoritarian nationalism and linked his anti-parliamentarianism and antisemitism with an environmental and biological determinism that was expressed most clearly in his 'political' novels of 'national energy' – *Les Déracinés* (1897), *L'Appel au soldat, Leures figures* – and in *Scènes et doctrines du nationalisme.*

Although he was deeply involved with most of the major nationalist organizations, such as the Ligue de la Patrie Française and Charles Maurras's Action Française, and ultimately served as president of the Ligue des Patriotes after Paul Déroulède's death, Barrès's influence on the generation that came of age just before the First World War ultimately owed more to his writing than to his organizational skills. His novels, essays and unceasing journalistic activity were his principal contribution to the reorientation of French nationalism and to making antisemitism and anti-parliamentarianism respectable among pre-First World War intellectual circles.

See also

Maurras.

Works

L'Appel au soldat, Paris, Fasquelle, 1900.
Leures figures, Paris, Juven, 1902.
Scènes et doctrines du nationalisme, Paris, Juven, 1902.
La République ou le Roi: correspondance inédite (with Charles Maurras), Paris, Plon, 1970.

Other works

Michael Curtis, *Three against the Third Republic: Sorel, Barrès, and Maurras,* Princeton, N.J., Princeton University Press, 1959.
Robert Soucy, *Fascism in France: the Case of Maurice Barrès,* Berkeley, Cal., University of California Press, 1972.
Charles Stuart Doty, *From Cultural Rebellion to Counterrevolution: the Politics of Maurice Barrès,* Athens, Ohio, Ohio University Press, 1976.

Otto Bauer   1881–1938

Austro-Marxist, editor of the theoretical journal of the Austrian Social Democratic Party (of which Adler was also a leading member, and like Adler, Bauer was on the left wing of the party), best known for his analyses of the Austrian and Russian revolutions and his opposition to Bolshevik-style revolution, exponent of what he called the 'slow revolution' and an early supporter of the thesis that post-war capitalism had entered a phase of rationalization.

See also

Hilferding.

Works include

Nationalitätenfrage und die Sozialdemokratie, Vienna, Wiener Volksbuchhandlung, 1907.
Kapitalismus und Sozialismus nach dem Weltkrieg I, Vienna, Wiener Volksbuchhandlung, 1931.

Other works

Tom Bottomore and Patrick Goode (eds.), *Austro-Marxism,* Oxford, Clarendon Press, 1978.

Simone de Beauvoir 1908–1986

De Beauvoir was the most important influence on modern feminism and a major figure of post-war French existentialism. During her philosophical studies at the Sorbonne (1926–9) she came in contact with Maurice

Merleau-Ponty and Jean-Paul Sartre, with whom she was later to join in founding *Les Temps Modernes* (1945), the major organ of the non-communist left in France. With Sartre she formed the most enduring and crucial relationship of her life.

Sharing in Sartre's 'conversion' to political engagement as a result of the war experience, she published in 1945 *The Blood of Others*, a novel centred on the moral dilemmas posed by support for a resistance movement whose acts of sabotage had been systematically met with German reprisals against innocent civilians. The preoccupation of her early novels with the formulation of an ethical position which is both responsible towards the condition of others and uncompromising of the freedom of the individual is continued in her philosophical essay *The Ethics of Ambiguity* (1947). Relying as it does on the supposition of an inherent human capacity for freedom, and on respect for its preservation, *The Ethics ofAmbiguity* is more a statement of an existentialist credo than an argument for the unconverted. It is marked, none the less, by the same alertness to the tensions created for Sartre's existentialism by the existence of material and social constraints on the individual's freedom, which informs the argument of *The Second Sex* (1949). Vexed as it is by the difficulties of arguing that women are both free, transcendent, human subjects and cast into the condition of 'otherness' in virtue of patriarchal culture, *The Second Sex* remains today the most important philosophical treatment of femininity.

As a political manifesto *The Second Sex* has come under criticism within the contemporary feminist movement for its 'masculinist' conception of feminine emancipation. In her demand that women should transcend their 'otherness' by engaging in traditional masculine pursuits and fighting for parity of status in a world whose norms and habits have been fixed by male predominance, de Beauvoir, it is said, is insensitive to the economic, social and emotional factors which make this project either unrealizable or undesirable for many women, is too disdainful of the maternal dimension of women's lives and fails to appreciate the value and socially regenerative potential of distinctively feminine attributes and perspectives. The feminism of *The Second Sex* is certainly open to all these charges, though they are moved from 'eco' or 'maternal' or 'difference' feminist positions which can themselves be accused of conserving aspects of feminine 'otherness'. Moreover, de Beauvoir's model of liberation, for all its abstraction from the material context of most women's lives, did spur the mobilizing demands (for abortion, birth control, civil rights) of an initial feminist politics in the post-1968 period out of which emerged a more distinctive socialist–feminist formation. De Beauvoir herself, in fact, regarded socialism as a condition of female emancipation and indeed for much of her life thought it sufficient to the overthrow of patriarchy. Hence her description of herself as becoming a 'feminist' only through her active involvement in the Mouvement de la Libération des Femmes in 1971 when she committed herself to fighting on 'specifically feminist issues independently of the class struggle'.

Prior to the MLF engagement her political arguments and activities had cohered more closely with those of Sartre. They were marked, broadly, by her advocacy in the post-war decade of an existentialist 'third way' through the politics of the Cold War; by her opposition in the 1950s to French government policy in Algeria (the cause of much public opprobrium and some danger to Sartre and herself), and the occasion of her documenting the torture of a young Algerian woman in *Djamila Boupacha*, of 1962; by her hostility to US intervention in Vietnam and participation in the Bertrand Russell tribunal on war crimes; and by a flirtation with Maoism in the early 1970s. She was relatively uninvolved in the events of May 1968, by which she professed herself not deeply shaken. Alone, or with Sartre, and in her later career very much as a 'celebrity figure', she travelled extensively, and her diaries offer political reflections of a largely journalistic character on these visits together with a record of Sartre's own political interests and activities. Her experience of America is documented in *America Day by Day* (1948), and of China in *The Long March* (1957).

As she was never a political analyst by disposition and was always irked by the more humdrum organizational aspects of movement politics, her political contribution is largely that of an intellectual commentator fired by a deep moral sense but at times blinkered by the perspective of her own personal, and rather exceptional, circumstances. Her Sartre-influenced amalgam of existentialist and socialist commitments is by no means as incoherent and damned by voluntarism as her more sectarian Marxist detractors would have us believe. But it is true that her responses display a certain impercipience and impatience towards those dimensions of social and political life which get in the way of adherence to pure moral principle and complicate the rationalist's solutions.

See also

Merleau-Ponty, Sartre.

Works

The Blood of Others, London, Secker & Warburg, 1948.
The Ethics of Ambiguity, New York, Philosophical Library, 1948.
America Day by Day, London, Duckworth, 1957.
The Long March, London, Weidenfeld & Nicolson, 1958.
Djamila Boupacha, London, Deutsch, 1962.
Memoirs of a Dutiful Daughter, Harmondsworth, Penguin, 1965.
The Second Sex, Harmondsworth, Penguin, 1972.

Other works

Anne Whitmarsh, Simone de Beauvoir and the Limits of Commitment, Cambridge, Cambridge University Press, 1982.
Alice Schwarzer, Simone de Beauvoir Today: Conversations, 1972–82, London, Chatto & Windus, 1984.
Mary Evans, Simone de Beauvoir: a Feminist Mandarin, London, Tavistock, 1985.
Judith Okeley, Simone de Beauvoir, London, Virago, 1986.

David Ben Gurion 1886–1973

Among Zionism's founders David Ben Gurion, born in Plonsk, Poland, was unique. As Israel's first Prime Minister and Minister of Defence he saw the dream of a Jewish state come to fulfilment. His formal education was limited, but he was an avid reader and a prolific writer. His speeches, essays, books and diaries were intended not only to strengthen his political position but also to remake Jewish consciousness. Political office gave him the opportunity to define Zionism's immediate goals, but writing Zionist history relentlessly, day by day, provided the possibility of producing an eternal historical perspective.

Ben Gurion was a labour Zionist. In his view, exile had distorted Jewish society, primarily by preventing Jews from engaging in productive labour. Jewish life in the diaspora was obsolete and destined to expire with its practitioners. Only a state sustained by a population of productive Jewish citizens held out any hope of Jewish survival. Only a Zionist socialist ethos could instil a level of altruism sufficient to build a Jewish economy and polity in Palestine. A capitalist economy would not induce an adequate degree of cooperation or dedication. Jews had to be reintroduced to agricultural and industrial labour.

Ben Gurion advocated the 'conquest of labour' not simply to exclude Arab workers from the Jewish economy but also to condition Jews to the virtues of work and to alienate them from the idea of exploiting others. He rejected strict Marxian categories and denoted artisans, farmers, small shopkeepers and clerks as workers. Sensitive to the underdeveloped economy of Palestine, Ben Gurion argued that physical labour provided a mandate for the working class to establish economic and political dominance without a class struggle. Only the working class could orchestrate the weak, passive, disparate Jewish people into an independent and powerful nation state. A strong working class was both the prerequisite of sovereignty and a condition of its worthiness. This kind of Jewish state would create an exemplary society which would serve as a model of equity and justice to the world.

The establishment of Israel in May 1948 was a turning point for Jewish history and Zionist ideology, according to Ben Gurion. No authentic Zionist could live outside the state's borders. Ben Gurion extolled the virtues of statehood. The machinery of state would absorb operations once carried out by voluntary organizations. As a natural consequence of discrimination, Israel's highly divergent population adhered to values inimical to the ethos of a modern state. Israelis had to learn not to subvert the authoritative exercise of state power. A new national ideology which prepared Jews for self-government had to be formulated. Loyalty to state institutions must displace commitment to political party and union. Israelis must be made to respect authority.

Works

Israel: a Personal History, New York, Funk & Wagnall, 1971.

Other works

Arthur Hertzberg (ed.), *The Zionist Idea*, New York, Meridian, 1959.
Amos Elon, *The Israelis: Founders and Sons*, New York, Holt, Reinhart & Winston, 1971.
Michael Bar-Zohar, *Ben-Gurion*, London, Adama, 1978.
Shlomo Avineri, *The Making of Modern Zionism*, New York, Basic, 1981.
Shabtai Teveth, *Ben-Gurion: the Burning Ground, 1886–1948*, Boston, Mass., Houghton Mifflin, 1987.

Arthur Fisher Bentley
1870–1957

Academic, journalist, political activist, but for many years a private scholar and sometime co-worker with John Dewey on the foundations of logic and communications theory, Bentley is known in American political science primarily as the pioneer figure in the study of group behaviour, of 'pressure groups' and 'interest group activity'. Bentley was convinced that the activity of human beings in groups was the fundamental datum – indeed, the only accessible datum – available to describe and understand the social behaviour of people. He opened a two-fold campaign in *The Process of Government*, written during his early years as a journalist. Explicitly and repeatedly he insisted that his book was an attempt to fashion a tool for analysis of human behaviour in strictly empirical, descriptive terms. With the activity of humans in groups as the raw material, strict description of manifest or palpable activity would yield a scientific understanding of human behaviour. In fact, as Bentley liked to put it, the complete description would be the complete science. In this aspect of his work Bentley sought to reject all reliance on ideas, ideals, concepts and what he derisively called 'mind stuff'. What groups were, what they did, what they sought, were to be found in observation and description, with no anticipatory conceptual framework or limiting paradigm to bias the observation and so distort the description. Such application was to be made at all levels. The most palpable, manifest group activities, taken together 'in system', as Bentley put it, were, when adequately described – 'stated' – the real process of government in its various expressions as legislative, executive and judicial processes. And, mysteriously, groups whose activities were not 'external', manifest or palpable, but only 'potential', were also to be sought and stated. Thus would a full statement, in system, be achieved. His concern was to outline methods, not to get final results. Something approximating a research protocol whose value could be demonstrated only in its use by others, many others, was what Bentley offered. 'Bentleyan' came to mean descriptive of activity, free of 'mind stuff' but with purposes, discussion groups and goals contained in the activity and stated in the description. The Augean stables of classical and post-Machiavellian political theory were to be cleansed of their noetic dross and concern with 'human nature'. Thereafter, group activity in all its overlapping and intersecting phases would allow an anoetic description, free of 'mind stuff' – the complete and true science of humans.

Of the difficulties this enterprise entailed, the greatest was to understand the key term 'group' in all its rich variety. Bentley offered 'activity' as one explanatory synonym, and 'interest' as another. Group, group activity, interest or interest group, all used interchangeably, were as close to description as Bentley would permit himself to come. He rejected the suggestion that a definition or definitions might help, insisting that the workers in his vineyard were to follow activity wherever it led, 'heedless of definitions'. And, in truth, those who have taken up his call to fashion a tool have concentrated on description of group activities, often inattentive to analytical acuity. In these respects Bentley contributed greatly to the behaviouralism of the latter half of the twentieth century.

There is in addition a second effort articulated in *The Process of Government*, one that is less coherently stated and also, characteristically, shared, but with little critical attention, by his more enthusiastic followers. In his account of the development of group interpretation Bentley says that the starting point for practical purposes 'is, of course, Karl Marx'. But Marx's class theory is rejected as too rigid and abstract, with too great an emphasis on the 'economic basis of groupings'. Bentley's own interest in economics, in 'the economic life', is repeatedly affirmed. However, it was not Marx but rather Ludwig Gumplowicz who, before Bentley, had come closest to articulating the nature of the group process. And, in doing so, Gumplowicz had convinced Bentley that, in Gumplowicz's words, 'the only possible solution of the social question lies in a harmonious co-operation of the social groups as far as that is possible'. So, in addition to seeking a method, Bentley was also involved in trying to get results – reformist results in a world he characterized as corrupt, exploitive, full of conflict. But Bentley's

tough, hard-headed scepticism about group protestations of good intentions, ideals and noble goals was conditioned by a remarkable meliorist expectation. He was apparently persuaded that in 'our government' there are 'rules of the game' which limit group striving for dominance, power and the subordination of the mass of people so characteristic of 'the economic life'. In touching tribute to American progressivism, Bentley expected that 'the lion when he has satisfied his physical need will lie down quite lamblike, however much louder his roars were than his appetite justified'. The 'social question' would be answered benignly within the constitutional rules of the game.

None of Bentley's later works focuses centrally on politics, government or economics. Only one – *Relativity in Man and Society*, an admittedly lesser achievement – paid some attention to political and social processes. A dedicated scholar, his writings were directed towards communications theory, foundation theory in mathematics, pragmatism and repeated, varied and successively abandoned attempts to develop a scientific terminology for use in his (and some of John Dewey's) areas of interest.

See also

Dewey.

Works

The Process of Government, Cambridge, Mass., Belknap Press, 1908.
Relativity in Man and Society, New York, Putnam, 1926.
Knowing and the Known (with John Dewey), Boston, Mass., Beacon Press, 1949.

Other works

Herbert Storing (ed.), *Essays on the Scientific Study of Politics*, New York, Holt, Rinehart & Winston, 1962.
Sidney Ratner and Jules Altman, *John Dewey and Arthur F. Bentley: a Philosophical Correspondence, 1932–1951*, New Brunswick, N.J., Rutgers University Press, 1964.
Paul Kress, *Social Science and the Idea of Process: the Ambiguous Legacy of Arthur F. Bentley*, Urbana, Ill., University of Illinois Press, 1970.

James F. Ward, *Language, Form, and Inquiry: Arthur F. Bentley's Philosophy of Social Science*, Amherst, Mass., University of Massachusetts Press, 1984.

Adolf Augustus Berle
1895–1971

American lawyer, economist and diplomat. Member of Franklin D. Roosevelt's 'Brain Trust'.

See also

Galbraith.

Works include

The Modern Corporation and Private Property (with Gardiner C. Means), New York, Harcourt Brace, 1968.

Isaiah Berlin   1909–

Born in Riga in 1909, and brought up in St Petersburg, Isaiah Berlin came to Britain in 1921 and is widely recognized as one of the leading philosophical defenders of liberalism in the twentieth century, and one of the foremost historians of ideas writing in English. Unlike most of his British and American contemporaries in the field of political thought, whose approach has tended to be ahistorical, formalistic and narrowly focused, the range of Berlin's philosophical, historical and cultural interests has been dauntingly wide: the sheer colour and diversity of his writing is one of its most distinctive marks. Nevertheless, salient peaks can be singled out to reveal a coherent mountain chain.

A founding member in the 1930s of the tendency that came to be called 'Oxford Philosophy', whose principal members were himself, A. J. Ayer, John Austin and Stuart Hampshire, he has maintained throughout his career an unswerving adherence to empiricism and a scrupulous regard for conceptual clarity. He was already sceptical as an undergraduate of his teachers' treatment of political philosophy as consisting in a timeless dialogue with 'dead contemporaries' such as Plato, Aristotle, Hobbes, Locke, Kant and Mill. His own research into Karl Marx and his precursors, especially the *philosophes* of the French enlightenment, which produced his minor masterpiece, *Karl Marx: His Life and Environment* (1939) profoundly altered his outlook. For Berlin discovered two things. First, that Marx and Marxism were, albeit transformed by the historicizing influence of Hegel, the most recent expression of the enlightenment belief in a single objective structure of discoverable laws governing history and the development of human society. Second, that against this view, which is itself embedded in the central two-thousand-year-old monist–rationalist tradition of Western thought, according to which there is one world, one method and one (in principle discoverable) body of logically coherent knowledge on all matters, fixed for all people and all time, a great rebellion arose from which sprang the major movements that characterize the modern era.

Already in the writings of Machiavelli, Berlin detects a fatal crack in monolithic monism (*Against the Current: Essays in the History of Ideas* (1979)). For him, Machiavelli was the first to reveal the need for an absolute choice between two equally valid but mutually exclusive moralities: the meek, individual Christian ethic of selfless charity, and the collective ethos of ancient Republican Rome with its self-assertive *virtú*.

It is, however, in the works of the seminal figures *Vico and Herder* (1976) that Berlin identifies the first radical, systematic break with millennial Western monism dating back to Plato. And it is out of their ideas, developed and modified, that Berlin has built up his own extremely complex and sophisticated brand of liberal pluralism. Vico produced a series of novel ideas which have had a revolutionary impact on subsequent thought. He was the first to claim that people do not have an unvarying human essence. They understand history, which they make, in a way which they cannot understand; nature, which they do not make; that the 'inner' knowledge we possess as agents is more thoroughly intelligible to us than the detached 'outer' knowledge obtained by observation. He invented the idea of a culture, all of whose products bear the stamp of its pervasive pattern, and envisaged a plurality of such cultures. Vico believed that all human activities and institutions are not just functional but above all forms of self-expression; that permanent standards in ethics and aesthetics do not exist and that all things human should therefore be judged by the canons of their own time and place; and that the two traditional types of knowledge, the deductive and the empirical, must be enriched by a third – what later German thinkers termed *Verstehen* – i.e. reconstructive imaginative empathy. Here is the origin of the cardinal distinction between the sciences and the humanities. It both undermines belief in universalist principles and blows an irreparable breach in the monist belief that knowledge must be in principle one and undivided. Herder, in turn, is seen by Berlin to have uncovered some of the principal categories which have come to dominate and transform the modern world. These include populism, or the belief that people can realize themselves fully only as members of an identifiable culture with roots in language, tradition, history; expressionism, or the notion that people have a vital need to express themselves and that all their works are 'voices speaking' which communicate a total vision of life; and pluralism, or the recognition of an almost endless variety of cultures and systems of values, all equally ultimate, and incommensurable with one another, so that the belief in a universally valid path to human fulfilment becomes conceptually incoherent.

Henceforth all was changed. For although neither Vico nor Herder is correctly described as an irrationalist or a subjectivist, the ideas of these Counter-Enlightenment thinkers mutated into ever more radical and influential forms in the hands of later movements and thinkers. In particular, German Romanticism (on which Berlin delivered the Mellon lectures in 1965, and has published essays in *The Crooked Timber of Humanity* (1990) and *The Sense of Reality* (1996)) tended to dissolve the notion of objectivity altogether in favour of the ceaseless striving of creative will. This led on to increasingly extreme, and finally violent and inhuman movements, both in the arts and in political life. Historicism, nationalism, fascism, voluntarism, relativism, subjectivism, existentialism and the many strains of modern irrationalism – but also, paradoxically, pluralism – may be traced back to this profound shift in our basic categories.

This brings us to the question of where Berlin, as an empiricist and a believer in rational methods, stands in this great mutation of ideas, of which he is the foremost living historian and the most rationalistic heir. The answer to this question contains the key to Berlin's contribution to twentieth-century political thought. For if Vico and Herder are right, it is the case both that entire systems of equally valid objective values may conflict with each other and also that value may conflict with value within the selfsame system and the selfsame individual, with no possibility in principle of appeal to mediating rational standards. Agonizing choices, which neither reason nor empirical knowledge can settle, are thus a normal, ineliminable feature of the human lot. Moreover, provided the values people live by fall within the common human horizon and do not conflict with the fundamental sense of what it is to be a human being, then there is room for them in the great and growing realm of human values, past, present and future.

A major revolutionary consequence of this is the impossibility of utopia in principle: no conceivable world *logically* could unite all the objective goods and ultimate values pursued by human beings. The whole notion of a single true path to perfection, for the individual as for the species, is destroyed. This weakens the foundations of the great majority of political and ethical doctrines in the mainstream of Western thought, from Plato to the French Enlightenment, Marxism, 'scientific' liberalism and beyond.

In view of the heterogeneity of values, we must according to Berlin be especially on our guard against abuse of what he has called 'positive liberty', i.e. liberty as self-mastery and self-realization (in 'Two Concepts of Liberty', in *Four Essays on Liberty* (1969) an essay which has determined the framework for serious discussion of liberty since its appearance in 1958). For while this is indeed a genuine end, the danger is that in the hands of monists and voluntarists it tends to take on sinister shapes. First, he claims, they assume that the pattern of goals pursued by human beings is, if not identical for all, then at least capable of being brought into a rational harmony. Second, they slide from empirical finite selves to some transpersonal collectivized notion of 'self', of which the former are mere elements – the nation or the state, as with National Socialism and Fascism, or even, as with Marxism–Leninism, the whole of humanity as a species-being on the march towards a single final goal. Then the individual's 'true' liberty comes to consist in the unresisting exercise of the role assigned by the relevant social and political experts in the great frictionless collective enterprise. By contrast, Berlin extols the virtues of 'negative liberty' which, in order that human beings should be free to make their own unique choices among conflicting values and outlooks, and so spontaneously build their lives in their own ways, seeks to secure the maximum area of non-interference in the lives of individuals and groups consonant with basic social order and justice.

Finally and relatedly, since 1945 Berlin has been an unsleeping custodian in exile of the great liberal inheritance of the nineteenth-century Russian intelligentsia (*Russian Thinkers* (1978)), rescuing from the Soviet distortion the writings of such figures as Alexander Herzen, who, with his pluralism and his subtle fusion, in his life and in his work, of conflicting Enlightenment and Romantic values, most nearly anticipates Berlin's own position.

See also

Popper.

Works

Four Essays on Liberty, London and New York, OUP, 1969.
Vico and Herder, London, Hogarth Press, 1976.
Russian Thinkers, London, Hogarth Press, 1978.
Against the Current: Essays in the History of Ideas, London, Hogarth Press, 1979.
The Crooked Timber of Humanity, London, John Murray, 1990.
Karl Marx: His Life and Environment, fourth edition revised, London, Fontana, 1995.
The Sense of Reality, London, Chatto & Windus, 1996.

Other works

John Gray, *Isaiah Berlin*, London, HarperCollins, 1995.
Roger Hausheer, 'Introduction', in Isaiah Berlin, *The Proper Study of Mankind*, London, Chatto & Windus, 1997.
George Crowder, 'Pluralism and Liberalism', *Political Studies* 42 (1994), pp. 293–305 (reply by Berlin and Bernard Williams, pp. 306–97).
Claude J. Galipeau, *Isaiah Berlin's Liberalisms*, Oxford, Clarendon Press, 1994.

Eduard Bernstein   1850–1932

The son of a Jewish locomotive driver, Bernstein was born in Berlin. In 1870 he took employment as a banker's clerk, and in 1872 he began his political career by joining the Social Democratic Workers' Party, the 'Eisenachers'. Three years later he attended the Gotha congress at which the Eisenachers united with the Lassallean wing of the German socialist movement to form what was to become the SPD (German Social Democratic Party). However, in 1878 the Reichstag passed legislation effectively making the SPD illegal, and Bernstein went into exile in Switzerland, where, initially, he took employment as secretary to Karl Höchberg, a wealthy supporter of social democracy. A year later he helped found *The Social Democrat*, which became the official party organ. It was published in Zurich and distributed clandestinely throughout Germany, and in 1881 Bernstein became editor-in-chief. In this capacity he collaborated closely with Engels and soon established a reputation for being a Marxist of impeccable orthodoxy and an intransigent opponent of Bismarck's policy in Germany. However, in 1887 he was expelled from Switzerland and moved to London, where he continued publishing *The Social Democrat* and consolidated his relationship with Engels.

The Reichstag elections of 1890 saw the SPD emerge as the largest single party in Germany. Shortly afterwards Bismarck fell from power, and the anti-socialist legislation was allowed to lapse. The following year the Erfurt congress accepted a new party programme, drafted mainly by Bernstein and Karl Kautsky and unmistakably Marxist in orientation. Since the party press could now operate legally within Germany, *Der Sozialdemokrat* ceased publication. Bernstein, however, remained in London and devoted the next few years to journalism and historical research. When, in 1895, Engels died, it was found that he had named Bernstein and August Bebel as his literary executors.

By this time Bernstein had begun to nourish doubts about revolutionary Marxism as a basis for party policy. The terminal crisis of capitalism, predicted by Marx and Engels, had not occurred and, so far as Bernstein could see, was not going to occur. The development of a sophisticated credit system, the emergence of cartels, and improved means of communication, had enabled capitalism to eliminate, or at least control, the periodic crises that had been so marked a feature of economic development in the earlier part of the century. Besides, Bernstein argued, there was no evidence that the means of production were being concentrated in fewer and fewer hands, or that cut-throat competition was eliminating large sections of the bourgeoisie, or that the proletariat was being progressively reduced to abject poverty. Indeed, capitalism was in robust health and seemed likely to

remain that way for the foreseeable future. It was, therefore, idle for socialists to pin their hopes on an imminent collapse of bourgeois society. On the other hand, the advance of democracy in most industrialized countries had enabled working-class parties to enter the political arena, and there was a real prospect that significant reforms could be achieved by parliamentary means. Indeed, Bernstein argued, the victory of socialism might well be accomplished by the steady implementation of socialist principles by democratic and constitutional means.

From these observations Bernstein drew two general conclusions. First, it was clear that Marx's doctrines would have to be re-evaluated critically and, where necessary, 'revised'. Second, the SPD should abandon its revolutionary aspirations and acknowledge that it was now a democratic socialist party of reform.

Starting in 1896, Bernstein developed these views, partly in a series of articles published in *Die Neue Zeit* under the title 'Problems of socialism' and partly in an extended polemical exchange with the English socialist Ernest Belfort Bax. The consequent uproar within the party culminated in the rejection of Bernstein's 'revisionism' at the Stuttgart congress of 1898. Early in 1899 Bernstein published his *Evolutionary Socialism: a Criticism and Affirmation.* It contained a critique of certain fundamental Marxist doctrines (notably the materialist conception of history and the theory of surplus value), a detailed vindication of democratic reform as the best means of achieving a socialist society and a suggestion that a theoretical foundation for socialism might be found in the philosophical idealism of the neo-Kantians. It was to become recognized as the classic defence of democratic, non-revolutionary socialism.

The left-wing opposition to Bernstein, represented mainly by Parvus and Rosa Luxemburg, was now joined by the party leadership. In particular, Kautsky came out against Bernstein with a series of articles published in *Vorwärts* and *Die Neue Zeit*. Bernstein stoutly maintained his position, but, at the Hanover congress that autumn, his 'revisionism' was debated at great length and, again, was rejected.

In 1901 the warrant issued for Bernstein's arrest was at last withdrawn and he returned to Germany. In 1902 he was elected Reichstag deputy for Breslau, a seat he held until 1906 and again from 1912 to 1918. During these years Bernstein added nothing significant to the position he had developed in the 1890s. However, he continued to advocate his views and, in the party and in the trade union movement, his influence grew. He could not, however, translate that influence into political success. In 1903 he argued that the SPD should co-operate with the liberals in the Reichstag to achieve practical reforms and, in particular, that the party should accept a position in the Reichstag praesidium. At the Dresden congress later that year his position was once again debated and once again decisively rejected.

In 1914 Bernstein, like most German social democrats, saw Germany's entry into the war as an act of self-defence and accordingly voted in favour of war credits. However, he subsequently changed his mind, and for most of the war he opposed war credits and took a strong position on the right of self-determination. In 1916 the SPD split. Bernstein joined the break-away group, the SAG, and in 1917 he joined the newly established radical USPD. When the war ended, however, he rejoined the majority SPD.

After the poor showing of the SPD in the elections of 1920 Bernstein became a member of the commission appointed to redraft the party programme. The resulting Görlitz programme of 1921 abandoned much of the Marxist analysis embodied in the Erfurt programme of 1891 and was widely regarded as owing much to Bernstein's influence. However, this belated triumph of 'revisionism' was short-lived. Reunification with the USPD made compromise necessary, and the Heidelberg programme of 1925 restored some of the basic principles of Erfurt. Otherwise, Bernstein devoted his declining years largely to arguing that the Weimar Republic should recognize imperial Germany's responsibility for the Great War and repudiate the imperial government, thus establishing a new and peaceful relationship with the victorious powers and pointing the way forward for Germany as an integral part of Western European civilization. Once again the 'father of revisionism' was a voice crying in the wilderness. In 1928 he retired from active politics.

See also

Kautsky, Luxemburg.

Works

Die Voraussetzungen des Sozialismus und die Aufgaben der Sozialdemokratie, Stuttgart, Dietz, 1899, trans. Edith C. Harvey as *Evolutionary Socialism: a Criticism and Affirmation*, New York, Schocken, 1965.
Zur Geschichte und Theorie des Sozialismus, Berlin, 1904.
Der Sozialismus einst und jetz, Berlin, 1921.
Das Görlitzer Programm der Sozialdemokratischen Partei Deutschlands, Berlin, 1922.

Other works

Pierre Angel, *Eduard Bernstein et l'évolution du socialisme allemand*, Paris, Didier, 1961.
Peter Gay, *The Dilemma of Democratic Socialism*, New York, Columbia University Press, 1962.
Thomas Meyer, *Bernsteins konstruktiver Sozialismus*, Berlin, Bonn and Bad Godesberg, Verlag J.H.W. Dietl Nach F Gmbh, 1977.

Ernst Bloch   1885–1977

Ernst Bloch was the principal modern theorist of utopia. Born in Ludwigshafen, he grew to intellectual maturity in the midst of a burgeoning movement of 'romantic anti-capitalism' infused with cultural modernism, a certain apocalyptic vision, vaguely socialist aspirations and a new philosophical spirit that stressed the moment of subjective experience. Even as a youth Bloch had come to know important thinkers like Wilhelm Windelband and Eduard von Hartmann. Captivated by the *avant-garde*, whose centre was Munich, Bloch moved to that city, where he studied philosophy, physics and music. After finishing his doctoraté in 1909, with a dissertation on the epistemology of the popular neo-Kantian philosopher Heinrich Rickert, he went to work with Georg Simmel, the famous sociologist and exponent of 'life philosophy', in Berlin. Only then did he move to Heidelberg, where he established a close friendship with the already prominent aesthetician, and future Marxist philosopher, Georg Lukács, who introduced him to the glittering intellectual circle around Max Weber.

The First World War created the conditions for Bloch's unique eschatological reading of Marx, which he then fused with elements of neo-Kantianism, 'life philosophy' and an 'authentic expressionist impulse' to produce his first great work, *The Spirit of Utopia* (1918). This book set the stage for Bloch's later attempts to ground the concept of utopia in the unfinished character of reality as such and to forward a dynamic vision of nature as a set of unrealized potentialities which could become purposive if humanity decided to make them so. Ultimately Bloch would fashion an ontology in which Being would be seen not as a static or finished entity but rather as inherently retaining an unexplored horizon that constantly projects a utopian novum. Thus, whether consciously or unconsciously, human existence is understood as necessarily manifesting 'anticipatory' qualities that point to a utopia which does 'not yet' exist, but which nevertheless stands open to realization.

His encyclopedic masterpiece, *The Principle of Hope* (1959), would analyse such anticipatory utopian projections in the realms of religion, art and philosophy, as well as the daydreams and manifold occurrences of everyday life. Even Marx appears as just one member – albeit the most talented – of a utopian tradition which stretches back over the peasant revolts of Thomas Munzer to medieval mystics, neo-platonism and the thinkers of antiquity. From such a perspective, people are seen as anthropologically motivated by a complex of instinctual drives which bring about a hope of the best world and a sense of

frustration of *Angst* at not attaining it. Rigid 'stage' theories of history thus surrender to a perspective in which the past is not merely dead time but rather the repository of unresolved contradictions which can reassert themselves for good or ill. Indeed, if this outlook informs Bloch's outstanding cultural analysis of Nazism in *Inheritance of our Time* (1935), it also opposes any form of fatalism with a 'militant optimism' that ultimately underpins all efforts in theory and practice to transform the present.

This emphasis on human will separated Bloch from the deterministic Marxism of the social democratic movement and inclined him towards the voluntarism of Lenin and Stalin. But, if his philosophy need not lead to any particular form of socialist politics, Bloch's own attachment to the Soviet Union – to the point where he could support the Moscow trials of 1938 – was not simply *ad hoc.* Indeed, following his anti-fascist exile in the United States, it was logical for him to assume a Chair in philosophy and later to become Rector of the University of Leipzig in East Germany.

For Bloch was primarily concerned with analysing the concept of utopia and calling for further experimental thinking. His works are totally lacking in any specifics regarding how the utopian order might be brought about, what institutions are necessary to ensure its liberating character or even what sociocultural relations should inform it. Even while he was emerging as a steadfast critic of party dogmatism regarding the arts, especially following his famous debate with Lukács over the political implications of expressionism in the 1930s, Stalinist socialism therefore at least provided an objective referent for his speculations.

East Germany was initially happy to welcome a philosopher of Bloch's stature. Rewards and honours were heaped upon him. But following the 1956 Twentieth Party Congress in the USSR, at which Stalin's crimes were revealed, the atmosphere grew ever more stifling. Ultimately the increasing political pressure resulted in Bloch choosing to remain in West Germany while on a visit in 1961 and assume a Chair in philosophy at the University of Tübingen.

Yet Bloch never relinquished his radicalism. His ongoing theoretical attempts to extend the notion of liberation into non-economic arenas like culture and the human personality found fertile soil in the student revolt of the 1960s. In fact, even later, his call for a new interrelation with nature and a non-instrumental theory to deal with it – in works like *The Problem of Materialism* (1972) and *Experimentum Mundi* (1974) – would resonate with many of the most sophisticated philosophers interested in ecology and the Green movement. Indeed, whatever the political and technical criticisms, Ernst Bloch produced an all-encompassing and experimental philosophical standpoint which speaks to humanity's best hopes for the future even while holding on to the most progressive unrealized possibilities of the past.

See also

Lenin, Lukács, Stalin.

Works

Man on his own, New York, Herder, 1970.
A Philosophy of the Future, New York, Herder, 1970.
On Karl Marx, New York, Herder, 1971.
Atheism in Christianity, New York, Herder, 1972.
Natural Law and Human Dignity, Cambridge, Mass., MIT Press, 1986.
The Principle of Hope, three volumes, (eds.) Jack Zipes and Frank Mecklenbury, Oxford, Blackwell, 1986.
The Utopian Function of Art and Literature: Selected Essays, Cambridge, Mass., MIT Press, 1988.

Other works

Frederic Jameson, 'Versions of a Marxist hermeneutic' III, 'Ernst Bloch and the future', in *Marxism and Form*, Princeton, N.J., Princeton University Press, 1971.
Dick Howard and Karl E. Klare (eds.), *The Unknown Dimension*, New York, Basic Books, 1972.
Jürgen Habermas, 'Ernst Bloch: a Marxist Schelling', in *Philosophical–Political Profiles*, Cambridge, Mass., MIT Press, 1983.
Stephen Eric Bronner and Douglas Kellner (eds.), *Passion and Rebellion: the Expressionist Heritage*, New York, Columbia University Press, 1989.

Stephen Eric Bronner, 'Expressionism and Marxism: towards an aesthetic of emancipation', in Bronner and Kellner (eds.), *Passion and Rebellion: the Expressionist Heritage*, 1988.

Norberto Bobbio   1909–

Italy's most distinguished and influential post-war political thinker is not well known in the English-speaking world. This neglect is strange, considering the international relevance of his thinking and his life's long list of achievements. Born in Piedmont, he grew up in what he described as a 'bourgeois patriotic milieu'. His early training was in political philosophy and jurisprudence at the University of Turin. He was arrested and imprisoned twice by the Mussolini regime for sympathizing with the anti-fascist cause. He is a constitutional lawyer by training and an outstanding political philosopher, whose thinking is based on a rich and unusual synthesis of liberal and socialist themes. Since 1984 Bobbio has been a life senator in the Italian parliament and a leading moral conscience of its politics. He is author of nearly thirty books and a courageously independent *franc-tireur* in the columns of *La Stampa* and other influential Italian newspapers and journals. He confesses to anglophilia and enjoys a wide reputation throughout Latin America.

Bobbio is primarily renowned as a brilliant analyst of democracy. In such works as *The Future of Democracy* and *Which Socialism?* he insists that democracy is not an elastic term, and criticizes its twentieth-century vulgarization. Democracy is not a word which can be made to mean whatever the media or politicians choose it to mean. Democracy is a method of arriving non-violently at collective decisions by securing the fullest possible participation of interested parties. 'At a minimum,' says Bobbio, 'democratic procedures include equal and universal adult suffrage; majority rule and guarantees of minority rights, which ensure that collective decisions are approved by a substantial number of those expected to abide by them; the rule of law; and constitutional guarantees of freedom of assembly and expression and other liberties, which help guarantee that those expected to decide or to elect those who decide can choose from among real alternatives.' Democracy, Bobbio explains, is the best method ever invented of checking the unending arrogance and foolishness of those who govern. Democracy enables the ruled to question, rotate or sack their rulers. Democracy thereby helps ensure that the distribution of power is determined by open political contests framed by visible rules. 'Democracy makes the exercise of power visible – against the tendency of all power holders to become invisible, like God.'

For many years Bobbio roasted the Italian left, especially the Communist Party, for undervaluing democracy in this sense. Although Bobbio considers himself a leftist, that does not mean that he speaks the old language of capitalism or socialism. 'The nineteenth-century definition of socialism as the transition from private property to publicly owned property is dead.' Only lovers of democracy can now be counted as leftists, argues Bobbio. To be on the left is to favour more democracy by democratic means. This argument leads Bobbio to question powerfully the (Leninist) belief that liberal, parliamentary democracy is a bourgeois institution. He insists that the historical emergence in Europe and elsewhere of liberal democratic institutions, such as free elections, competitive party systems and written constitutions, represented a great leap forward in the fight for more democracy. For Bobbio a non-liberal democracy is thus a contradiction in terms and in fact. He has always criticized socialists who failed to see that political democracy cannot be reduced to class questions and demands for economic equality. 'If socialism means a society in which ownership of the means of production has been transferred from private hands into the lap of "society" – in the twentieth century that has normally meant the state itself – then the abuses of state power are, and have been, more likely than in a capitalist society.' The

demand for socialism in this conventional sense is undemocratic; whereas the demand for democracy is much more subversive because it calls into question all despotic forms of power.

Bobbio nevertheless rejects as unworkable the Rousseauian dream of small self-governing republics. Too much democracy can kill off democracy. The wholesale politicization of life, the attempt to create a society of full-time political animals, is actually antithetical to democracy. Free time and private life would become a thing of the past. The quality of decision-making would decline. The life of the full-time citizen would be a nightmare of interminable meetings, fraught compromises and endless late-night telephone calls. Bobbio also insists that direct, participatory democracy, which in certain cases would require the public assembly of millions of citizens, is technically impossible in large-scale complex societies. Besides, Bobbio points out, direct democracy thrives upon consensus. It therefore works best when there are a limited number of policy choices – nuclear power or no nuclear power, peace or war, or the legalization or criminalization of abortion. Otherwise the trust, patience and mutual support required within self-governing circles are normally overloaded with many conflicting viewpoints, the clash among which can be resolved only through mechanisms of representative democracy which 'filter out' and simplify the kaleidoscope of conflicting opinions.

Bobbio does not conclude from all this that Western parliamentary democracy as we know it is the alpha and omega of political life. He is convinced that Western democracies contain decadent tendencies, such as the continuing absence of any democratic controls over the use of force in international politics, and the growth of 'invisible government' – governmental or paragovernmental institutions which operate on the shadowy margins of parliament and which, in the eighteenth century, would have been denounced as tyrannical because they are unelected, secretive and publicly unaccountable. Bobbio also emphasizes that parliamentary democracies are hemmed in by accumulations of social power within civil society. The vast majority of citizens have no say in major decisions concerning economic investment, production and growth. Churches, trade unions and many other institutions of civil society remain insufficiently democratic. Bobbio therefore argues for the refinement and extension of democracy – for a post-liberal democracy which enables citizens to vote in many more areas than at present. Political democracy should be supplemented with 'social democracy'. Democracy should be extended from the political sphere (where individuals are regarded as citizens) to the civil sphere, where individuals are regarded variously as men and women, entrepreneurs and workers, teachers and students, producers and consumers. Battles over where citizens can vote should be given as much priority as the struggles in the nineteenth and early twentieth centuries over who could vote.

Works

Which Socialism? Marxism, Socialism and Democracy, Cambridge, Polity Press, 1986.
The Future of Democracy, Cambridge, Polity Press, 1987
Democracy and Dictatorship: the Nature and Limits of State Power, Cambridge, Polity Press, 1989.

Other works

R. Bellamy, *Modern Italian Social Theory*, Cambridge, Polity Press, 1987.
P. Anderson, 'The affinities of Norberto Bobbio', *New Left Review* 170 (July–August 1988), pp. 3–36.
J. Keane, 'Democracy and the decline of the left', in *Democracy and Dictatorship*, Cambridge, Polity Press, 1989.

Leonardo Boff   1938–

Born in Portugal. Roman Catholic priest and liberation theologist who combines Marxism and Christianity to fight poverty and social injustice in Latin America. Enjoined to silence by the Church for his revolutionary activities.

Works

Salvation and Liberation, Maryknoll, N.Y., Orbis, 1984.
Liberation Theology, San Francisco, Harper & Row, 1986.
Introducing Liberation Theology, Maryknoll, N.Y., Orbis, 1987.

Murray Bookchin   1921–

Murray Bookchin, theorist of and spokesperson for social ecology, began his political life in the Marxist socialist labour movement. His disillusionment and frustration with its centralized hierarchical structures led him towards the anti-authoritarian approaches of Peter Kropotkin, Paul Goodman and other social anarchists. Increasingly he has coupled critiques of hierarchical political and economic structures (whether capitalist or socialist) with the articulation of a social ecological vision of participatory, egalitarian 'eco-communities' in which humans see themselves, and act, not as dominators of nature but as participants in it.

Bookchin's warnings about hierarchy in human communities and consequent threats to the environment antedated the ecological and environmental movements of the 1970s and 1980s. Especially in *Our Synthetic Environment* and in articles written during the 1960s and 1970s, and collected in *Post-scarcity Anarchism* and *Toward an Ecological Society*, Bookchin insisted on the connections between the domination of humans by one another and the domination of nature by humans. He asserts that hierarchy (both of humans over one another, and of humans over nature) is a social invention, introduced into what were essentially egalitarian, mutually interdependent communities. Bookchin finds the roots of such hierarchy neither in a presumed human 'drive' to dominate nature, nor as a socio-technological response to scarcity, but in the gradual development of gerontocracies into patristic, patriarchal, statist social systems. His social ecological perspective leads him to argue, further, that no technology is neutral: all 'technics' must be examined in their social context, and evaluated according to their potential contribution to a liberatory social life, respectful of the natural environment.

Bookchin does not simply challenge the hierarchical social, economic and political structures characteristic of contemporary industrial societies, however. His writings – often quite polemical in tone – take to task many 'alternative social movements', including Marxist socialist trade union movements, the 'new left' and environmentalists, arguing that, without a thoroughgoing critique of hierarchy and authoritarianism in all arenas, radical social change will never be truly liberating. Bookchin looks to the Greek city states, medieval communes, anarchist affinity groups, neolithic 'organic' societies and a variety of nineteenth-century utopias to provide examples – however partial and limited – of decentralized, egalitarian, human-scale communities with more fully participatory notions of citizenship, and models for a politics of direct action (1973, 1977, 1982, 1990). The industrial revolution had succeeded all too well in dehumanizing workers, transforming them first into 'mass beings', then into 'hierarchical beings'. We should not, then, look to the traditional 'proletariat' but to feminists, artists, students, young people and members of other hitherto excluded groups for the imagination to guide and inspire the liberatory movements of the twentieth and twenty-first centuries.

While the polemical style of Bookchin's argument often seems in tension with its content, his social ecology represents more a process than a structure, an insistence that any utopistic vision or liberatory movement must begin with its own practices. A social ecological perspective values community while respecting human individuality, striving towards realizing unity in diversity and diversity in unity; it prefers direct action in decentralized groups to mass action directed and co-ordinated by a centralized authority; it advocates the development of technologies that enhance human choice and freedom while respecting the natural context in which humans are rooted; and envisages a fully participatory, self-managing citizenry where people realize their full capacities through exploring their imaginations in co-operation with others.

See also

Goodman, Kropotkin.

Works

Our Synthetic Environment, New York, Knopf, 1962.
Post-scarcity Anarchism, Berkeley, Cal., Ramparts Press, 1971.
The Limits of the City, New York, Harper & Row, 1973.
The Spanish Anarchists: the Heroic Years, New York, Free Life, 1977.
Toward an Ecological Society, Montreal, Black Rose, 1980.
The Ecology of Freedom, Palo Alto, Cal., Cheshire, 1982.
The Modern Crisis, Philadelphia, Pa, New Society, 1986.
The Rise of Urbanization and the Decline of Citizenship, San Francisco, Sierra Club, 1987.
Remaking Society: Pathways to a Green Future, Boston, Mass., South End, 1990.
The Philosophy of Social Ecology: Essays on Dialectical Naturalism, second edition, revised, Montreal and New York, Black Rose, 1995.

Other works

John Clark (ed.), *Renewing the Earth: the Promise of Social Ecology*, London, Green Print, 1990.

Martin Buber   1878–1965

Born in Vienna of a Jewish family, Buber spent his youth with his grandparents in Galicia. Influenced by the writings of Kant and Nietzsche, he studied philosophy at the University of Vienna and in Leipzig. He moved to Berlin to study under Georg Simmel and Wilhelm Dilthy. His doctoral dissertation, 'Towards the History of the Problem of Individuation' (1904), was a study of the mystical thought of Nicholas of Cusa and Jacob Boehme. In 1905 Buber began his lifelong study of Hasidism, especially of its communities and its prominent figures. During that period Buber also edited a collection of mystical confessions from various cultures.

Buber's major political and social works were written after the First World War. Influenced by Gustav Landauer, Franz Rosenzweig and Ferdinand Ebner, Buber denounced asocial philosophies, including mysticism. This shift in emphasis included a new understanding of the nature of social reality. He now claimed that 'I' and 'You', the poles of a dialogical relation, have neither meaning nor independent existence apart from the relation into which they enter. In addition, Buber argued that the forms of social life generated by the separate poles of a relationship have an objective, independent existence. Hence, in contrast to his earlier position, in his mature works Buber sought the greater reality of existence not in a person's inner life but rather in the context of the interpersonal. He suggested that the ideal social environment is created by a person-oriented (I–You) attitude to relationships. This quality of the interpersonal Buber called the 'between' *(das Zwischen)*. Buber believed that standing in constant tension with the I–You is an ego-oriented (I–It) attitude to relationships, which he considered the source of alienating social environments such as those prevalent in modern societies. He first established this conception of the interpersonal in his *magnum opus*, *I and Thou* (1923), and developed it in numerous essays written between 1923 and 1965. Some of his more important essays are collected in *Pointing the Way, Between Man and Man* and *The Knowledge of Man*.

Buber identified his political thought as utopian socialism. His major work in political theory, *Paths in Utopia*, was a meditation on modern socialism's misguided preoccupation with the problem of political power, a preoccupation that deflects attention from what (Buber maintained) ought to be socialism's primary concern – the question of social renewal. For Buber the goal of socialism ought to be to render obsolete the modern state, its institutions and its primary modes of relationship, power and domination. This transformation is to be attained in three mutually reinforcing ways: first, by creating a 'true' community as the basis of a new form of society; true community is, however, a mere step on the way to the second goal, the creation of a 'community of communities', a commonwealth of communities bound together by a common trust, a shared relation to the 'eternal' You (God, or any other word designating the primal reality); finally, Buber believed that the goal of the new (global) social system must be the creation of social conditions conducive to the inclusion, and the revelation, of the spirit.

Buber thus envisaged a global system in which the community (and not the nation state) is the basic political and social unit. Buberian communities come into being as a result of the efforts of 'living, active, centres'. These are persons who have found the way to establish I–You relationships with other persons and with the 'eternal You'. This idea was influenced by Buber's belief that great cultures and civilizations originate in the lives and deeds of 'dialogical' persons such as Jesus and the Buddha.

Throughout his life Buber was an active Zionist, identified with its cultural/spiritual (as opposed to its dominant, 'political') wing. His commitment to Zionism provided him with many opportunities to apply his philosophical principles to concrete political situations. Buber supported the form of communal life being developed in the kibbutz, and wrote numerous articles about these co-operative experiments. In a different context, while supporting the right of Jews to return to the land of Israel (Palestine), Buber opposed the creation of a separate Jewish state in Palestine. Instead he proposed a non-state, binational federation as a possible solution of the Jewish–Arab conflict in Palestine. This aspect of Buber's political thought is expounded in essays included in *Israel and the World* and in *A Land of Two Peoples.*

Works

I and Thou, New York, Scribner, 1970.
Paths in Utopia, Boston, Mass., Beacon Press, 1958.

Israel and the World: Essays in a Time of Crisis, New York, Schocken, 1963.
Pointing the Way, New York, Harper Torchbooks, 1963.
The Knowledge of Man: a Philosophy of the Interhuman, New York, Harper & Row, 1965.
Between Man and Man, New York, Collier, 1965.

Other works

Bernard Susser, *Existence and Utopia: the Social and Political Thought of Martin Buber*, London, Associated University Presses, 1976.
Paul R. Mendes-Flohr (ed.), *A Land of Two Peoples: Martin Buber on Jews and Arabs*, New York, Oxford University Press, 1983.
Paul R. Mendes-Flohr (ed.), *From Mysticism to Dialogue: Martin Buber's Transformation of German Social Thought*, Detroit, Wayne State University Press, 1989.
L. Silberstein, *Martin Buber's Social and Religious Thought: Alienation and the Quest for Meaning*, New York, New York University Press, 1989.

James Buchanan   1919–

Born in 1919 on a farm in Tennessee, a Southerner by origin and conviction, James C. Buchanan was sceptical about the East Coast political and academic establishment to the point that he deliberately remained at Southern state universities (Virginia and Virginia Polytechnic Institute 1956–1983). By so doing he demonstrated that a state university background is not an obstacle to first-class research, finally receiving the Nobel Prize for Economics in 1986.

His best-known work, though, is in political economy rather than technical economics. Inspired by the work of the nineteenth-century Swedish economist Kurt Wicksell, and even earlier Italian 'economists' such as Antonio de Viti de Marco, Buchanan resurrected the old European tradition in which economics starts not with the discovery of the market by Adam Smith but two hundred years earlier with the subject of public finance and the question 'What is "good" government?' This question offered him a focus and framework which he relentlessly pursued.

The resurrection of public finance, or 'public choice theory' as it came to be called,

depended (and still depends) on a rigorous debate with neoclassical welfare economics. Its critique of the latter includes an insistence on comparative (positive) analysis, and posits that the only way to judge good government is by its efficiency, which in turn can be judged only by those individuals who are affected by government's actions. As Wicksell had argued before him, Buchanan claims that full efficiency is reached only if there is a unanimous vote (or support) for specific government actions; a majority vote is probably the closest we can get in practicality.

Buchanan's approach to this argument is grounded in *methodological individualism*. Aggregates do not act; the driving force of economic development is therefore not GNP, investment, capital or labour but the individuals who daily decide anew whether to work more or less, whether to save more or less, whether to think of new products or ways to market them. They do so either independently or together. In the latter case the overall outcome is less dependent on the number of people involved, even less on different preferences, than on the institutions within which the collective decision-making takes place. Thus the question is, if aggregates do not act, do institutions such as the state act? In response to this question Buchanan argued that there was a major inconsistency in traditional economic theory. While microeconomics is firmly based on the actions of individuals, more or less hinting that 'the state' in a market economy is nothing but the aggregate of all individual actions, the prevailing theories in public finance and welfare economics are based on a collectivist-organicist view of the state. The state is represented as a supranational entity acting for the common good (an enlightened and benevolent dictator in effect) or is hidden behind a 'social welfare function' that is defined as the collective equivalent of individual utility functions.

Yet, if people react to institutional constraints the way they react to market constraints, i.e. rationally, then different constitutions (of the state) must lead to different outcomes. This reasoning opened the avenue for what has come to be known as *constitutional economics*, Buchanan's great innovation. He showed that the constitution, the electoral system, federalism and the principal–agent relationship defined by the involvement of a state bureaucracy in decision-making play a decisive role in a nation's social and economic development; for these factors create *differential opportunities* for individuals to pursue their self-interest. In *The Calculus of Consent*, Buchanan and Gordon Tullock then applied the analytical tools of neoclassical microeconomics in order to demonstrate these different effects in concrete practice. Beyond this demonstration, Buchanan went on to claim that all institutions, even constitutions, are themselves the outcome of collective choice. People therefore have an incentive to search for forms of government that allow them to transform their individual demands for government action into a corresponding policy supplied at the lowest feasible cost.

Buchanan also has argued that 'market failures' happen on a much smaller scale than has hitherto been assumed, and thus should not be allowed to become the *raison d'être* for large state bureaucracies. In particular a broad range of public goods, which according to standard economic arguments require state provision, can (and often will) be provided more efficiently either by local constituencies or by private organizations ('clubs'). His conclusion is then straightforward: establish local self-government (a federal structure), and allow individuals to establish private organizations for the provision of public goods. On inquiring into the conditions that allow efficient forms of constitutions, as for example the federalist form, Buchanan then concludes that distributional aspects of social organization should be left outside the realm of constitutional choice. Instead, he argues, only behind a *veil of ignorance* – that is, only so long as individuals do not know the distributional consequences of a future constitution – will people settle for the most efficient institutional frame. Interestingly, then, the

same line of reasoning leads Buchanan exactly in the opposite direction from John Rawls, who presumes risk-aversion as a general psychology, and thus contrarily argues that the 'veil of ignorance' will lead constitution-makers to establish a Second Principle of Justice, the Difference Principle, that is precisely redistributional.

Moreover, even after a constitution is established its efficiency can be eroded by *rent-seeking*. When political markets are used by different groups for creating artificial scarcities that are maintained by government regulation (such as keeping markets closed to foreign producers via tariffs, or excluding outsiders by means of state-controlled 'technical' standards, price controls or bureaucratically managed channels of distribution), rent-seekers benefit to the detriment of the overall economy and the taxpayer.

Consequently, the political market can turn into one in which there is an ever decreasing number of institutions which create opportunity for all, but in which instead the demand for and supply of rents meet. The result will be an ever-growing state, a *Leviathan*, which is more concerned with redistribution and regulation than with providing an environment that allows individuals (and succeeding generations) to prosper. Once more, constitutional provisions that limit political rewards for rent-seeking are required. Overall, then, Buchanan's is one of the leading theoretical arguments for a minimal state that maximizes both free-market opportunities and risks, and minimizes regulation and redistribution.

See also

Rawls.

Works

'Positive economics, welfare economics, and political economy', *Journal of Law and Economics*, 2 (1959), pp. 124–38.
Fiscal Theory and Political Economy, Chapel Hill, University of North Carolina Press, 1960.

The Calculus of Consent (with Gordon Tullock), Ann Arbor, University of Michigan Press, 1962.
'An economic theory of clubs', *Economica* (February 1965), pp. 1–14.
Theory of Public Choice (ed. with R. Tollison), Ann Arbor, University of Michigan Press, 1972.
The Limits of Liberty: Between Anarchy and Leviathan, Chicago: University of Chicago Press, 1975.
Freedom in Constitutional Contract, College Station, Texas A&M University Press, 1978.
Liberty, Market and the State, New York, New York University Press, 1985.

Other works

Norman Barry, 'Unanimity, agreement, and liberalism – a critique of James Buchanan's social philosophy', *Political Theory*, 1 (1984), pp. 579–96.

Nikolai Ivanovich Bukharin 1888–1938

Nikolai Ivanovich Bukharin was born in Moscow. He joined the Bolshevik Party as a student in 1906 but his studies were interrupted by arrests and exile. While in Europe he developed his lifelong critical interest in bourgeois social science and this led to his interesting, but occasionally misdirected, critique of marginalist economics, *The Economic Theory of the Leisure Class* (1914).

War in 1914 led him to analyse the nature of modern capitalism. In *The World Economy and Imperialism* (1915) he argued that capitalism could be understood only as a world economy where the internationalizing elements of capital clashed with a tendency for capital to consolidate in 'national units' competing economically and militarily. State intervention in the production of surplus value had culminated in the state capitalist war economies.

During the Russian revolution Bukharin played a leading part in Moscow. Subsequently he had a major theoretical and propagandist role. His Civil War theorizing resulted in *The Economics of the Transition Period* (1920). Although often seen as an uncritical admirer of war communism, Bukharin was aware of the military character of the regime. In 1921 he published *Historical*

Materialism: a System of Sociology, a continuation of his critique of social science and an attempt to examine the conditions of 'social equilibrium'. His philosophical assumptions here produced sharp critiques but the idea of equilibrium was important for Bukharin's subsequent development.

Despite his being Lenin's close associate they often clashed politically, most notably over the Treaty of Brest-Litovsk in 1918. Except on the question of the need to destroy the capitalist state it was Lenin who was the theoretical and political victor. This was one of the factors behind Lenin's doubt, despite his recognition of Bukharin's theoretical eminence, whether Bukharin fully understood dialectics.

After Lenin's death in 1924 Bukharin became one of the most vigorous defenders of the New Economic Policy, and from 1924 to 1929 he was a full member of the Politburo and played a leading role in the Communist International. His views were summarized in *The Road to Socialism and the Worker Peasant Alliance* (1925), in which he argued that the Soviet state was a workers' state, based socially on a worker–peasant alliance, which could grow into socialism through cooperation and a judicious balance of plan and market. These ideas led him to attack the left's arguments about the need for both a faster pace of growth and permanent revolution in favour of the idea of socialism in one country.

Bukharin worked closely with Stalin against the left but in 1928 fundamental differences developed between them. Fearing renewed military threats, the Stalin group began to push for faster industrialization and a harder line against the peasantry as a logical development of the idea of socialism in one country. Bukharin opposed this and in 1929 was condemned as part of the 'right opposition'. In reality he was defeated politically because he lacked Stalin's power base in the bureaucracy and theoretically because his support of socialism in one country meant that he shared many of the underlying assumptions of the Stalin group.

During the 1930s he played a reduced political role, appearing to make veiled criticisms of the official line and to stand for a more humane vision of socialism. However, his condemnation and execution in 1938 after Stalin's third and greatest purge trial is to be explained by the dynamics of Stalinism rather than Bukharin's active opposition. His ideas, however, outlived Stalinist condemnation and distortion not only in the West but also in the Soviet Union, where Bukharin's rehabilitation in 1988 was a major step forward in *glasnost*.

The debate on Bukharin's legacy involves a number of issues. His discussion of capitalism as a world economy clashes with those who start with the national form and his argument that the state is capital challenges the view that the state stands outside the process of production of surplus value. In respect of the USSR there is argument over whether there was a viable 'Bukharinist' alternative to Stalin. Finally there has also been debate over the reinterpretation of Bukharin's work and politics within a liberal framework rather than exploring his strengths and weaknesses as a Marxist.

See also

Lenin, Stalin.

Works

Historical Materialism, Ann Arbor, Mich., University of Michigan Press, 1970.
Imperialism and the World Economy, London, Merlin, 1972.
Selected Writings on the State and the Transition to Socialism, Nottingham, Spokesman, 1982.

Other works

Sidney Heitman, *Nikolai I. Bukharin: a Bibliography*, Stanford, Cal., Hoover Institution, 1969.
Steven F. Cohen, *Bukharin and the Bolshevik Revolution: a Political Biography, 1888–1938*, Oxford, Oxford University Press, 1980.
Michael Haynes, *Nikolai Bukharin and the Transition from Socialism to Capitalism*, London, Croom Helm, 1985.

James Burnham   1907–1987

Best known for his theory that capitalism in crisis would give rise to a new managerial class which would rule both capitalists and workers, Burnham went on to become a leading advocate of American Cold War conservatism.

Works include

The Managerial Revolution: What is Happening in the World, New York, Day, 1941.
The Machiavellians: Defenders of Freedom, New York, Day, 1943.
The Struggle for the World, New York, Day, 1947.
The Coming Defeat of Communism, New York, Day, 1949.
Containment or Liberation? An Inquiry into the Aims of United States Foreign Policy, New York, Day, 1952.
Congress and the American Tradition, Chicago, Regnery, 1959.
Suicide of the West: an Essay on the Meaning and Destiny of Liberalism, New Rochelle, N.Y., Arlington House, 1964, 1975.

Other works

Samuel T. Francis, *Power and History: the Political Thought of James Burnham*, Lanham, Md, and London, University Press of America, 1984.
C. Wright Mills and Hans H. Gerth, 'A Marx for managers', in C. Wright Mills, *Power, Politics and People*, New York, Oxford University Press, 1963, pp. 55–71.

Amilcar Cabral   1924–1973

In the early 1960s Amilcar Cabral emerged from the national liberation struggle of the peoples of Guinea-Bissau and Cape Verde as one of the foremost Third World revolutionary theorists and activists of the century. His work on revolutionary organization and ideology, on imperialist exploitation and on African peasantry and national liberation placed him at the forefront of black intellectuals like Frantz Fanon, Julius Nyerere, Kwame Nkrumah and Patrice Lumumba.

Amilcar Cabral was born at Bafata in what was then the Portuguese colony of Guine. He died in Conakry, Guinea, assassinated by agents of the Portuguese government. His parents were natives of Santiago in the Cape

Verde archipelago, descendants themselves of the mulattoes and *assimilados* produced by Portuguese colonialism as a social instrument for exploiting its African territories. During the years of Cabral's childhood the Portuguese empire was in the midst of what its now fascist architects (the Novo Estado of Antonio Salazar) took to be the 'final' phase of its colonization of its African territories. Insufficient in material and human resources to administer and develop its vast colonies, Portugal conceded monopolies to French and British capitalists and adopted the French policy of 'indirect rule'.

Cabral was selected to be trained as a native administrator by the Portuguese state, receiving a scholarship to the Lisbon Higher Institute of Agronomy in 1945. While studying in Lisbon he was exposed to the anti-fascist student movement, the Portuguese Marxist underground and radical African nationalism. Among his fellow African students at the Casa dos Estudantes do Império were Augostinho Neto (medicine) and Mario de Andrade (literary criticism), who were to serve as leaders of the Movimento Popular de Libertacão de Angola (Cabral was a co-founder). Later they were joined by Lucio Lara, Deolinda Rodrigues de Almeida (who was to die in a Congolese prison after the overthrow of Lumumba), and Eduardo Mondlane and Marcellino dos Santos, leaders of FRELIMO (the Mozambique Liberation Front). 'The colonial situation,' Cabral would write in 1966, '. . . offers the petty bourgeoisie the historical opportunity of leading the struggle against foreign domination. . . .'

Cabral, an outstanding student of agronomy, completed his professional training in 1952, and returned to Guine under contract to the Provincial Department of Agriculture and Forestry Services of Portuguese Guine. There he planned and executed the first agricultural census of the colony, detailing the transformation of Guine into a monocrop economy and the techniques and ethnic organization of land use ('Agricultural census in Guine', in *Unity and Struggle*). But

Cabral's primary interests were political. Already persuaded that European Marxism was an inadequate guide for national liberation in Africa, Cabral employed his colonial post and technical training to determine 'the social ground of the struggle'. He concluded that the peasants most receptive to the idea of national liberation were those whose traditions lacked 'defined organization' and who 'maintained intact their tradition of resistance to colonial penetration' ('A brief analysis of the social structure in Guinea', in *Revolution in Guinea*).

Nevertheless, Cabral concentrated his political work among his own class, the petty bourgeoisie (civil servants, technical professionals, contract employees, small farmers) and 'wage-earners' (non-contract workers, domestic servants, factory, shop, transport, port and farm workers). In September 1956, during one of his authorized visits to Guine, along with his brother Luiz and several others, Cabral secretly organized the African Party of Independence (PAI). In December, upon his return to Angola, Cabral assisted in the founding of the MPLA.

Even before its formal organization, the activists of the PAI had concentrated on organizing a militant trade union, the clandestine União Nacional des Trabalhadores da Guine. And after a series of successful strikes, culminating in the seamen's strike of July 1959, the colonial administration responded by ordering its soldiers to fire upon workers striking at the Pidjiguiti quay near Bissau. Now persuaded that the trade unionist tactic was mistaken, the PAI (designated the PAIGC with the addition of Guine-Bissau and Cape Verdes to its name) determined on a campaign of armed struggle based on the mobilization and organization of the peasantry. For the next three years the PAIGC recruited, trained, organized and prepared its cadres for the liberation struggle.

By 1965 the PAIGC could claim to have liberated 40 per cent of the countryside and had initiated the establishment of people's stores and a campaign to increase rice production in the secured areas. By 1966, with 50 per cent of the interior in the hands of the revolutionists, and with sixty or more of the Portuguese fortified camps under attack, the Portuguese shifted to reliance on air power; later, when the PAIGC regular army absorbed the guerrilla forces, they resorted to bio-chemical warfare. In November 1970 a desperate Portuguese military invaded neighbouring Guinea (the PAIGC secretariat had been based in Conakry since 1959), simultaneously dispatching a secret mission to assassinate Cabral and Guinea's president, Sékou Touré. The plot failed and the captured agents confessed. In 1971, with 30,000 Portuguese troops in the country, the PAIGC launched attacks on Bissau and Bafata. In April 1972 a United Nations special mission travelled to Guine-Bissau and declared that the Portuguese were no longer in control of most of the country. On 14 November 1972 the UN General Assembly voted to recognize the PAIGC as the sole legitimate representative of the peoples of Guine-Bissau. Cabral was assassinated in 1973. Notwithstanding, after nearly fifteen years of war, Guine-Bissau became independent in September 1974.

Cabral's theoretical work was cut short by his untimely death at the age of forty-eight. During his life, however, the liberation struggle propelled his development as a revolutionary theorist. Initially a recruit to Western Marxism, by 1961 Cabral was persuaded that the liberation struggles of colonial peoples superseded class struggle and the antagonism between capitalist and socialist countries as the prime motive force of modern history. Cabral opposed the Marxian formula which posited class struggle as the basis of history, arguing that Europe's experience should not be mistaken for a universal history. Similarly, following the massacre at Pidjiguiti, Cabral and his comrades recognized that the peasantry and not the petty bourgeoisie and the proletariat constituted the social base, i.e. the physical force for revolution. But, unlike Fanon, Cabral did not believe the peasantry were a revolutionary force, nor, as Che

Guevara maintained, that guerrilla movements or *foco* required certain topographical features. Instead he maintained that the peasantry could be transformed into a revolutionary army through political action, armed struggle and national reconstruction. A comparable creativity and sophistication marked Cabral's contributions to the study of history and culture.

Cabral asserted that colonialism not only appropriated national productive forces but sought to usurp a people's history. The culture of the dominated, however, is not easily defeated. Culture, the 'memory' of historical development, contains the 'seed of opposition', and, short of annihilation of the native population, the imperialist powers in Asia, Africa and the New World were compelled to attempt the suppression of native cultures. The imperialist instrument created for this task is a deracinated, culturally alienated and Westernized elite, the petty bourgeoisie. Nevertheless the interests of the imperialist ruling classes and the petty bourgeoisie are not identical. Inevitably the elements within the native class rebel and eventually identify the masses as their political base and the native culture as the source of their ideology. But neither the rebellious petty bourgeoisie nor the native culture is a finished whole. The revolutionary petty bourgeoisie (with its tendency to evolve into a bourgeoisie) must be capable of committing class suicide to avoid betraying the revolution; and the culture of national liberation must continue to expand and develop, integrating the 'positive accretion from the oppressor and other cultures'. Through this process a dominated people reclaim their historical development.

See also

Che Guevara, Fanon, Nyerere.

Works

Revolution in Guinea, New York, Monthly Review Press, 1969.
Our People are our Mountains, London, Committee for Freedom in Mozambique, Angola and Guine, 1972.

Return to the Source, New York, African Information Service, 1973.
Unity and Struggle, London, Heinemann, 1980.

Other works

Basil Davidson, *The Liberation of Guine*, Harmondsworth, Penguin, 1969.
Basil Davidson, *In the Eye of the Storm: Angola's People*, New York, Doubleday, 1972.
Basil Davidson, *No Fist is Big Enough to Hide the Sky*, London, Zed Press, 1981.
Patrick Chabral, *Amilcar Cabral: Revolutionary Leadership and People's War*, New York, Cambridge University Press, 1983.
Rosemary Galli and Jocelyn Jones, *Guinea-Bissau: Politics, Economics, and Society*, Boulder, Colo., Lynn Rienner, 1987.

Albert Camus   1913–1960

A French Algerian, born on the outskirts of Algiers, and raised in one of its poorer neighbourhoods, Albert Camus came to consciousness on the margins of Western civilization. His sensibility was shaped both by his ambivalent attitude towards its culture – awed by its historical accomplishments while repelled by its moral hypocrisy and systematic oppression – and by his deep identification with the joys and sufferings of its working people.

The contraction of tuberculosis at age seventeen brought a sharp metaphysical turn to his reflections, till then focused primarily on the poverty of his home life and the celebration of youth and the body. This emerging sensitivity finds expression in his earliest published works, *The Rightside and the Wrongside* (1937) and *Nuptials* (1938). In these works the search for happiness generates the call to live 'as if', culminating in the celebration of life by a lucid consciousness confronting death.

These literary reflections of his early twenties complemented a period of feverish public involvement in the cultural and political life of what he viewed as the Mediterranean Renaissance. A member of the French Communist Party from 1935 to 1937, he organized a 'Workers' Theatre' in which his vision of egalitarian communal democracy was expressed by the lack of hierarchy, titles or individual bows at the end of performances. In addition to heading the 'intellectuals' cell', and being primarily responsible for adapting, producing and directing numerous classical productions, he dramatized the 1934 struggle of Spanish miners against fascism in his first play, a collaborative 'essay in collective creation' entitled *Revolt in Asturias*. He was ultimately expelled from the party when he refused to go along with its new Popular Front strategy of sacrificing the native population's struggle for human rights to the fight against fascism. From this period dates a growing cynicism about Communist Party policy that only increased throughout his life.

For the next three years he was a crusading journalist for the left-leaning *Alger Republicain* and *Soir Republicain*, attacking the Governor General of Algeria and defending the rights of both French and Muslim working people. This led to the closing down of these papers and his 'pressured' exile in 1940 as the Second World War approached.

During the war he completed the literary–metaphysical work begun in Algeria, producing *The Stranger* (1941), *The Myth of Sisyphus* (1942) and 'Caligula', along with 'The misunderstanding' (1944). These works, which constitute the 'first series' of his work, are devoted to the theme of 'the absurd' with which he has become so closely identified. (A second series on 'Revolt' was completed later, with only suggestions appearing of future series on 'Judgement', 'Love' and 'We are'.) By the absurd, whose 'discovery' he attributes to Nietzsche – probably the major influence on his intellectual development – Camus means only the condition of human beings who desire life to have a transcendent purpose but find themselves in a universe that seems ultimately indifferent to that concern. For him this metaphysical solitude, which characterizes the human condition in the twentieth century, is 'not a conclusion, but only a point of departure'. The challenge is to know whether humans 'can live and create without the aid of eternal values, which, temporarily perhaps, are absent or distorted in contemporary

Europe'. And what are the moral guidelines for such effort?

These questions, made more poignant by Camus's wartime experiences as editor of the Resistance newspaper *Combat*, find initial expression in his *Letters to a German Friend* (1944). The works of his 'series' on 'Revolt', *The Plague* (1947), 'The state of siege' (1948), *Les Justes* (1949) and *The Rebel* (1951), develop a moral and political framework for conduct in a world without 'moral absolutes'. Rebellion attests to the human need for dignity, and the willingness to face death rather than suffer unending injustice. With the 'I rebel, therefore we are' the rebellious outrage at injustice gives birth to the demand for the establishment of a human community in which the integrity of the person will be respected. But rebellion usually requires a radical, if not revolutionary, transformation of institutional injustice which all too often has ended in disaster, in spite of itself. Camus's exposition and critique of the implicit and self-destructive messianism pervading modern revolutionary theory, along with his exploration of the preconditions of dialogic civilization, constitute his major theoretical contributions to Western political thought.

It is as wrong to suggest, however, that Camus counterposed rebellion and revolution as it is to call him a pacifist. Values are grounded in the natural community of human beings in face of death. Intentional killing, except in self-defence, undermines the basis of values. But pacifism would render human beings ultimately incapable of defending their rights. Moral limits must be drawn from within the moral framework articulated by the rebel's outrage. Ends must be balanced with means, since, as actions unfold in time, one tends to become the other. Justice must be balanced with liberty, and the human community must democratically take control over its destiny, without any claim to moral ultimacy.

Finding the emerging Cold War atmosphere inhospitable to moral values and libertarian socialist politics, Camus reduced his public role, left *Combat* in 1947, and focused on his theoretical and artistic efforts. His refusal to sacrifice moral values for Cold War commitment led to his break with Sartre, in 1952, after the latter's publication, *Les Temps Modernes*, had criticized *The Rebel* for presenting a 'Red Cross morality'. The agony of his increasing isolation from Parisian intellectual life in the 1950s – whose hypocrisy increasingly depressed him – finds biting expression in that 1955 'portrait of the aggregate of the vices of our whole generation in their fullest expression' which is Jean-Baptiste Clamence, the hero of *The Fall*.

Cut off from his native Algeria, first by the Second World War and then by the Algerian civil war, torn by the conflicting claims of justice for the indigenous population, identification with French culture, and loyalty to his friends and family – while increasingly alienated from Parisian intellectual circles, especially those of his natural constituency, the left – Camus found himself in a personal and political no-man's-land, anguished by the thought that his creativity was drying up. In addition to numerous private interventions on behalf of both French and Muslim detainees, his major public intervention in the Algerian civil war was an unsuccessful 'Appeal for a civilian truce' in 1956. In 1958 he published his third collection of political essays, *Actuelles III*, an 'Algerian chronicle', in which he presented his more than two decade-long struggle for the rights of the native population along with his defence of a French Algeria.

In 1957 Camus was awarded the Nobel Prize for Literature, for a literary production which 'illuminates the problems of the human conscience in our times' while suffering from his own spiritual crisis and publicly derided as dried up and 'finished'. Yet, in addition to *The Fall*, he had continued to write essays, some included in *Summer* (1953), and the short stories published as *Exile and the Kingdom* in 1957, as well as adapting and producing plays, most successfully Faulkner's *Requiem for a Nun* and Dostoevsky's *The Possessed*, while directing summer theatre in Algiers. He was working diligently towards the goal of having his own theatre – a project upon which he placed much hope for personal revitalization, and which stood on the verge of completion, owing to the assistance of his friend, and De Gaulle's Minister of Culture, André Malraux, at the time of his death in an automobile accident.

See also

Sartre.

Works

L'Etranger, trans. Kate Griffith, Washington, D.C., University Press of America, 1982.
The Myth of Sisyphus and other Essays, trans. Justin O'Brien, New York, Knopf, 1955.
The Rebel, trans. Anthony Bower, New York, Knopf, 1954.
Resistance, Rebellion, and Death, trans. Justin O'Brien, New York, Knopf, 1960.
Notebooks, trans. Justin O'Brien, New York, Knopf, 1965.

Other works

Philip Thody, Albert Camus, London, Hamish Hamilton, 1961.
Germaine Brée, Camus, New York, Harcourt Brace & World, 1964.
Emmett Parker, Albert Camus: the Artist in the Arena, Madison, Wis., University of Wisconsin Press, 1965.
Germaine Brée, Camus and Sartre, New York, Dell, 1972.
Donald Lazere, The Unique Creation of Albert Camus, New Haven, Conn., Yale University Press, 1973.

Fernando Cardoso   1931–

Born in Brazil. An influential member of the dependence school who formulated the notion of dependent development. After a distinguished career in the academy and university administration, he entered politics. Elected to the Brazilian Senate, he became Leader of the Brazilian Social Democratic Party in the Senate, held several ministerial posts including Minister of Finance, and was elected President of Brazil in 1995.

See also

Frank.

Works include

'Dependency and development in Latin America', New Left Review 74 (July–August 1972).

Fidel Castro   1929–

Fidel Castro has consistently been portrayed by a spectrum of commentators, from the right to the left, as the negative side of Mikhail Gorbachev. If Gorbachev is pragmatic, then Castro is intransigent, a 'fossil Marxist'. If Gorbachev is future-oriented, then Fidel is backward-looking. If Gorbachev is credited with heralding the end of the Cold War, then Castro is seen as continuing to evoke it. It seems a strange fate for a man deemed in the past either a sycophant of the Soviet Union or an eternal revolutionary heretic.

Fidel Castro was born into a well-off land-owning family in the easternmost province of Cuba. Early in his career, as a student leader and as a young lawyer, he demonstrated certain of the characteristics which would continue to define him throughout his career: a belief in himself, a sharp single-mindedness of purpose, a powerful nationalist instinct, and a high level of activism. 'History,' Castro once said, 'is a by-product of action.' When Fulgencio Batista seized dictatorial power in 1952 it was Castro who opposed him, first singlehanded in a Supreme Court brief which charged that his dictatorship was illegal, and then as head of a troop of some 130 young people who, on 26 July 1953, attacked the Moncada police barracks in Oriente Province in the belief that the attack would spark an uprising throughout the island. It did not; Castro was imprisoned for several years and, when released, went into exile in Mexico to train for guerrilla warfare, as part of the tactics of a revolutionary movement which had come to be called the 26 July Movement. He returned to Cuba with his motley array of fighters in December 1956; by January 1959 the 26 July Movement was in power. Castro launched the country into a dizzying programme of radical urban, agrarian and educational reforms which in one year managed a 15 per cent redistribution of income and set Castro on what was to become a permanent collision course with the United States. Cuba and Castro became a virtual obsession of six US presidents, who variously sponsored invasions, efforts to assassinate Castro (or even to use dipilatory to rid him of his beard), the creation of a 'secret army' of exiles who were to play a crucial role in both the Watergate and the Iran–Contra scandals and in the arming and training of the contras in Nicaragua, and a more than thirty-year, strictly enforced, embargo against the island.

Castro himself has led and dominated the Cuban revolution since its inception, charting a course through extraordinarily difficult terrain, both domestic and international. On the world stage he has emerged as a leader whose importance and stature are far out of proportion to the size of the country he represents: he has been a crucial actor in some of the most important crises of the post-Second World War world. Within Cuba he has been, from the outset, *the* institution: the only constant in a revolution which has experienced radically dramatic changes. By and large, he has determined those changes: his omnipresence, combined with what may be characterized as a strong streak of paternalism, have, at key moments, blurred the lines between his own personality and the revolution itself. Thus in April 1961, at the moment of the US-sponsored (and defeated) invasion at the Bay of Pigs, Castro's announcement that the Cuban revolution was a socialist revolution was greeted by a public which declared, 'If Fidel is socialist, so are we.' It was Castro who believed in, and set in motion in 1966, the radical Cuban experiment in creating socialism and communism simultaneously – that is, as he said, using consciousness to create material wealth, rather than the other way around. It was he who, in 1970, declared the experiment a failure and began the process of 'institutionalization' which dominated Cuba until the mid-1980s and involved the adoption and adaptation of traditional Soviet structures. It was he who, in 1986, in the face of economic crisis, formally launched the Cuban 'rectification campaign', whose parameters have continued to widen along lines he has by and large determined. And it is Castro who has shaped Cuba's reaction to *perestroika* and *glasnost* in the Soviet Union and the collapse of command socialism in Eastern Europe. Castro sees himself as a spokesman for the entire Third World in noting the absence of any discussion of the Third World in Gorbachev's 'common European home', and the fact that the end of the Cold War between the superpowers does not mean the end of war-ravaged societies in Asia, Africa and Latin America. When he evokes the new Cuban battle cry, 'Socialism or death', the strong currents of Cuban nationalism, which he has embodied during the entirety of his life, collapse into socialism defending the nation, which becomes simultaneously the defence of the revolution and socialism itself. The figure of Castro has loomed so large in the Cuban revolution that it is difficult to imagine that revolution without him: this issue becomes increasingly central as the years pass.

Works

Rolando Bonachea and Nelson Valdes (eds.), *Revolutionary Struggle: the Selected Works of Fidel Castro*, Cambridge, Mass., MIT Press, 1972.
Speeches, New York, Pathfinder Press, I, 1983, II, 1985.

Other works

Tad Szulc, *Fidel: a Critical Portrait*, New York, Morrow, 1986.
Frei Betto and Fidel Castro, *Fidel and Religion*, New York, Simon & Schuster, 1987.
Lee Lockwood, *Castro's Cuba, Cuba's Fidel*, Boulder, Colo., Westview Press, 1990.

Noam Chomsky   1928–

Avram Noam Chomsky was born in Philadelphia. His father, who left Russia in 1913 to avoid being drafted into the Czarist army, was a scholar of medieval Hebrew grammar at the University of Pennsylvania, where Chomsky was educated. Midway through his undergraduate degree, Chomsky came under the influence of Zellig Harris, a noted linguist at the University. Chomsky was drawn to Harris, not because of his work as a linguist but because of his radical politics. However, Chomsky soon took a linguistics course with Harris and eventually wrote an M.A. thesis, in which he applied Harris's structural principles of language to an analysis of Hebrew grammar.

While a Junior Fellow in the Society of Fellows at Harvard (1951–5), Chomsky completed work on his Ph.D., which he took at the University of Pennsylvania in 1955. In that same year he began teaching linguistics at the Massachusetts Institute of Technology, where he has served continuously since that time, now holding the title of Institute Professor. Chomsky is universally given credit for the development of transformational grammar, which has revolutionized the field of modern linguistics. This rationalist linguistics, with its bedrock assumption that every human being is born with the capacity for natural speech, presupposed a universal, cross-cultural linguistic capacity that became the basis of his egalitarian politics as well.

While effecting this revolution in linguistics, Chomsky has committed himself to a radical political agenda closely aligned with the tenets of *anarchism*. He has written numerous books outlining his political beliefs; he has used his invitations to speak in university settings about linguistics as an opportunity to offer lectures on politics; and he has travelled countless miles to civic and church meetings to deliver his radical message. Chomsky is dedicated to getting his message across to the public because of a basic belief, shared by most anarchists, in the individual's ability to know the difference between good and evil and to choose good over evil. This faith in the individual is in contrast to his distrust of all human institutions. According to Chomsky, the only kind of government he would con-

done would be a libertarian government that does not take for itself arbitrary authority and that respects the individual freedoms and creativity of its citizens. By 'arbitrary' Chomsky means authority that does not have its roots in 'Truth'. Thus, a government that gains authority by means of its power or its popularity, or any means other than the 'rightness' of the causes it espouses, is exercising 'arbitrary' power. In saying that a government should respect the 'individual freedoms' of its citizens, Chomsky seems to be calling for a grass-roots government in which citizens band together in something like town-hall meetings and set the agenda for governing from the bottom up.

It is clear that no human governments meet this criterion. Thus, Chomsky is at pains to expose the limitations of democracy in the United States. According to Chomsky, the American government is a 'ratified' democracy, in which the two controlling political parties set the agenda for the populace. The people are asked to ratify the choices that have already been made for them.

According to Chomsky, the agenda of the ruling political parties is set by big business; it is an agenda that is predicated on keeping a huge percentage of the world's resources under the control of a few huge American corporations. When apologists argue that the United States is non-imperialist, Chomsky agrees that it has no designs on annexing other countries. What the United States does is worse: it steals resources from those countries that come under its economic sway. In explaining the international policies of the United States, Chomsky asserts that historians should add a Fifth Freedom to the Four Freedoms enunciated by President Franklin D. Roosevelt during the Second World War. To the freedom of speech, freedom of worship, freedom from want and freedom from fear he would add the freedom to rob and exploit. He argues that America's policies are designed to ensure that it continues to control a wildly disproportionate (relative to its population) percentage of the world's wealth.

From the time he began his political writings at the early age of eleven, Chomsky's main goal has been to reveal the economic basis for interventions into the affairs of other countries. It is telling that his first political writing was an editorial dealing with the fall of Barcelona, since many anarchists point to the Spanish Civil War as a watershed moment in history that provides a glimpse of what could happen if governments were dissolved and individuals were put in charge of their own work. Consistent with his anarchist philosophy, Chomsky sees capitalism (with its focus on profit) as an evil system of government that is designed to rob individuals of the fruits of their labour. Over the course of his life Chomsky has written over twenty books detailing the ways in which American capitalist interests have wreaked havoc in all parts of the world.

Chomsky's political commentary first gained notice during the Vietnam War when he spoke eloquently in opposition to the US involvement in Vietnam (*American Power and the New Mandarins*, 1969). However, his critique does not begin with Vietnam. In that book Chomsky presented a 'revision' of the history of the Second World War, that blamed the United States for backing Japan into an economic corner that made war inevitable.

Some ten years later Chomsky (and Edward Herman) published a two-volume work, *The Political Economy of Human Rights* (1979), detailing the evils of US foreign policy throughout the world. In the 1980s, Chomsky gave particular attention to US actions in Central America, publishing three books: *Turning the Tide* (1985); *The Culture of Terrorism* (1988); and *Language and Problems of Knowledge: the Managua Lectures* (1988). One of Chomsky's most recent books, *Year 501: the Conquest Continues* (1993), offers a panoramic view of what he sees as five hundred years of US terror and oppression, beginning with the treatment of the Native Americans and continuing through the Gulf War.

Chomsky does not limit his criticism to the United States. He makes it clear that all governments are corrupt and corrupting. He focuses his attention on the United States not because it is worse than other governments but because it is the country of his citizenship. This logic may help explain why the other country that comes in for a frontal attack from Chomsky is his ancestral homeland, Israel. In *The Fateful Triangle* (1983) and *Pirates and Emperors* (1986), Chomsky details the ways in which Israel continually acts as a pawn to protect US economic interests in the Middle East and then bullies all of its surrounding countries, under the protection of the world's big bully, the United States.

Throughout his writings, Chomsky concerns himself not only with the evil that governments do but also with the means by which this evil is achieved. If individuals are capable of recognizing and choosing good, how is it that a country such as the United States can be such a consistent force for evil? Chomsky places most of the blame on a system of thought control that the government uses to manipulate the populace. Major culprits, according to Chomsky, are intellectuals and the media. In *Towards a New Cold War* (1982), Chomsky delivers a scathing review of intellectuals in general and Henry Kissinger in particular. In two other books Chomsky lambastes the media for its role in duping ordinary citizens: *Manufacturing Consent* (with Edward Herman, 1988) and *Necessary Illusions* (1989). In these two books Chomsky offers an explanation of how a so-called democratic government like that of the United States deals with dissidents like himself. In some cases the dissidents are silenced. For example, journalists who are offering a 'real' critique of the United States will be silenced because in the end they will have to say that the very newspaper they are writing for is under the control of a corporate world that is involved in terror and killing. They are not likely to stay in the employ of that newspaper after making such a charge.

According to Chomsky there is an even more effective (because it seems so open and democratic) way to deal with dissent. Since the two 'ruling' parties and the major media in the United States are under the control of big business, certain assumptions frame all discussions in the media. For example, in the Vietnam War hawks and doves disagreed as to whether the American policy was 'working', but both camps shared the assumption that the United States intended to be a force for good in Vietnam. This underlying agreement made it impossible for Americans to hear Chomsky when he said that the goal of the United States in Vietnam was to control that country's assets for its (the United States') own use, and that in order to achieve that goal the country had invaded South Vietnam.

Since he holds a position in a respected academic institution and is very competent in his work, Chomsky is protected from those who would silence him literally. There is no need to do so, however, since what he is saying is undercut by the official media; those in positions of power are happy to allow him the 'freedom' to say what he wants.

Still, despite the apparent success of those who would marginalize him and his message, Chomsky continues to promote his cause. He shares the basic belief of the anarchists that, if enough people hear the truth about their government, they will rise up in peaceful revolution. Thus, he continues his many speaking engagements and his prolific writing. His most recent book, *Powers and Prospects* (1996), offers readers his thoughts on, among other things, language, society, governments and human nature.

Works

American Power and the New Mandarins, New York, Pantheon, 1969.
The Political Economy of Human Rights (with Edward S. Herman), Nottingham, Spokesman, 1979.
Towards a New Cold War, New York, Pantheon, 1982.
The Fateful Triangle, Boston, Mass., South End Press, 1983.

Turning the Tide, Boston, Mass., South End Press, 1985.
Pirates and Emperors, Brattleboro, Vt, Amana Books, 1986.
The Culture of Terrorism, Boston, Mass., South End Press, 1988.
Language and Problems of Knowledge: the Managua Lectures, Cambridge, Mass., MIT Press, 1988.
Manufacturing Consent (with Edward S. Herman), New York, Pantheon, 1988.
Necessary Illusions, Boston, Mass., South End Press, 1989.
Year 501: The Conquest Continues, Boston, Mass., South End Press, 1993.
Powers and Prospects: Reflections on Human Nature and the Social Order, Boston, Mass., South End Press, 1996.

Other works

Michael C. Haley and Ronald F. Lunsford, 'Chomsky's linguistic and political thought', in Michael C. Haley and Ronald F. Lunsford, *Noam Chomsky*, New York, Twayne, 1994.
James Peck (ed.), *The Chomsky Reader*, New York, Pantheon, 1987.
Raphael Salkie, *The Chomsky Update: Linguistics and Politics*, Boston, Mass., Unwin Hyman, 1990.

Catherine Backès Clément 1939–

Catherine Backès Clément is a cultural critic, feminist and novelist. Trained in anthropology and philosophy, she was active in the French Communist Party in the 1960s and joined the women's movement in the early 1970s. Exposed by her university training to psychoanalysis, she examined it from a materialist point of view, focusing on the thought of Freud and Lacan in relation to specific social practices in *Pour une critique marxiste de la théorie psychanalytique*; *Miroirs du sujet*, a study of advertising and art forms as media through which Althusserian interpellation works upon the unconscious of the consumer; *The Lives and Legends of Jacques Lacan*; and *The Weary Sons of Freud*. Her commitment to practical mainstream politics is evident in her feminist texts; she questions the usefulness of hermetic, separatist discourses in 'Enclave/Esclave' and analyses a range of cultural forms that constrain women rather than free them in *The Newly Born Woman* and *Opera or The*

Undoing of Women. In the early 1980s she began to write novels exploring cultural diversity, *Le Maure de Venise*, an imaginative reconstruction of the African past of Shakespeare's and Verdi's Othello, and *Bleu panique*, a historical family chronicle of Jewish emigration from Russia and the events of May 1968. She became Director of Cultural Exchanges in the French Ministry of Culture under the then Prime Minister, François Mitterrand. Clément's reputation as an original and positive thinker is based on her combination of theoretical perspectives from many disciplines to imagine and effect, on a public level, what she forthrightly calls 'happiness'.

See also

Kristeva, Delphy, Wittig.

Works

Pour une Critique Marxiste de la Theorie Psychanalytique, Paris, Editions Sociales, 1973.
'Enclave/Esclave', *L'Arc* 61 (1975).
Miroirs du Sujet, Paris, 10/18 (1975).
Lives and Legends of Jacques Lacan, translated by Arthur Goldhammer, New York, Columbia University Press, 1983.
The Weary Sons of Freud, translated by Nicole Ball, London and New York, Verso, 1987.
Opera or The Undoing of Women, translated by Betsy Wing, Minneapolis, University of Minnesota Press, 1988.
The Newly Born Woman (with Hélène Cixous), translated by Betsy Wing, Minneapolis, University of Minnesota Press, 1986.

G. D. H. Cole   1889–1959

George Douglas Howard Cole was a lifelong socialist, whose role as a political theorist was to further the cause of labour. He began his intellectual career before 1914 as a radical Fabian, challenging the statism and collectivism of the Webbs. His early views were much influenced by the wave of strikes and labour agitation then current in Britain, and he attempted to draw positive lessons from it whilst avoiding the excesses of syndicalism. In *The World of Labour* he argued for industrial democracy, advocating that organized labour should work towards taking effective control of industry. Cole supported the principle that industrial power should take precedence over political power, and, therefore, that direct action in society was more effective than seeking to win elections and change society through legislation.

Cole became the leading thinker of Guild Socialism – a movement which enjoyed a short period of relative political success between 1917 and the early 1920s. In *Self-government in Industry* and *Guild Socialism Re-stated* he advocated that industry should be socialized, not nationalized, that production should be organized by 'national guilds' and not officials appointed by the state. The guilds were to exist in each industrial sector; they were to represent all plants and were to co-ordinate production. Each industry was to be a self-governing body, and co-operation between guilds was to be achieved through joint co-ordinative bodies. In *The Social Theory* Cole advanced the theoretical basis of Guild Socialism. He had been greatly influenced by the ideas of J. N. Figgis and the English political pluralists. Like them he argued that society was based on the principle of association, that it was only by associating with others that people could enjoy freedom, and that society should be organized as a plurality of self-governing voluntary associations. As a political pluralist Cole argued that each functionally specific domain of social life should be self-governing. The national 'political' authority was itself a specific functional organization and it should have charge only of certain common needs such as defence. There need not be an omnicompetent 'sovereign' state which claimed the right to regulate and administer every area of life.

By the mid-1920s Guild Socialism had collapsed and the new Labour Party had institutionalized itself as the mainstream. Cole was forced to rethink his thesis of the precedence of industrial power over the political and to redefine his position as a Labour intellectual. Through the 1930s and 1940s he produced an endless stream of books, pamphlets and reports on a variety of topics from planning to social history. He worked tirelessly for the labour movement, but little of his work from this period is of lasting intellectual value, even if it was of considerable contemporary relevance. After the experience of the 1945 Labour government he returned to some of his earliest concerns, arguing that nationalization needed to be complemented by industrial democracy. After his death Cole's reputation as a social theorist underwent a considerable eclipse. With the professionalization of the social sciences, he was too much the all-purpose intellectual and labour propagandist. Recently, however, there has been a renewal of interest in his earlier pluralist and Guild Socialist ideas as the attractiveness and political success of state socialism and collectivism have waned.

Works

The World of Labour, London, Bell, 1913.
Self-government in Industry, London, Bell, 1917; revised edition London, Hutchinson, 1972.
Guild Socialism Re-stated, London, Parsons, 1920; reprinted 1980 New Brunswick, N.J., Transaction Books.
The Social Theory, London, Methuen, 1920; selections reprinted in P. Hirst (ed.), The Pluralist Theory of the State, London, Routledge, 1989.

Other works

M. Cole, The Life of G. D. H. Cole, London, Macmillan, 1971.
L. P. Carpenter, G. D. H. Cole: an Intellectual Biography, Cambridge, Cambridge University Press, 1973.
A. W. Wright, G. D. H. Cole and Socialist Democracy, Oxford, Clarendon Press, 1979.

Benedetto Croce   1866–1952

Born in southern Italy, Croce dominated Italian culture until 1952. His copious writings on aesthetics, history, ethics and politics constitute a comprehensive humanist philosophy, which Croce hoped would provide a secular substitute for the consolations of religion. Originally immersed in studies of an antiquarian nature, Croce began to develop his own philosophy in the 1890s as a result of an examination of Marxist ideas encouraged by Antonio Labriola. Croce praised Marx for separating political considerations from ethical ones. Politics was concerned with the achievement and distribution of power rather than the morality of its use. As a result, politicians should attend only to the practicality of their acts. He later elaborated this thesis in the third volume of his Philosophy of the Spirit, the Philosophy of Practice (1909).

Croce distinguished the theoretical from the practical dimension of life. Whereas the first was oriented towards the spiritual spheres of the Beautiful and the True, the second aimed at the Useful and the Good. These spheres were so related that although the second and fourth implied the first and third respectively, the reverse was not the case. Thus a good act was ipso facto useful but not vice versa. A debate with his friend Giovanni Gentile in 1905–6 had led Croce to treat this thesis as part of a general historicist conception of philosophy. Taking up the Hegelian motto that 'What is rational is real, and what is real is rational', he maintained that human action could be evaluated only according to its utility at a given moment and place. The morality of our acts, like the truth of our thoughts, would be revealed only with the passage of time and the contribution they made to the unfolding of spirit in history.

This doctrine came perilously close to identifying right with might, for it appeared to make success the only measure of a policy's or a regime's acceptability. The danger became all too obvious during the First World War, which Croce interpreted as a struggle to find the strongest and most capable state to give the imprint to the new century. Similar reasons made him an initial supporter of fascism, which he regarded as a valid instrument of class war and the only effective response to socialism. However, he utterly opposed the fascist regime and its totalitarian doctrine, formulated by his former colleague Gentile, which committed the philosophical sin of uniting theory and practice, morals and politics in the theory of the ethical state.

As a result, Croce radically rethought his position after 1924. He now argued that all practical action was 'ethico-political' in nature, for human history was advanced only by the struggle to realize certain moral ideals. This process was open-ended. Any attempt to bring it to a close by declaring the end of history in either the fascist state or communist society was necessarily oppressive and wrong. Croce claimed that his new thesis encapsulated the philosophical core of liberalism, which he equated with acceptance of the dialectical nature of history. He refused to identify liberalism with the traditional liberal practices of the free market and a right-based democracy, since he believed socialist or even authoritarian measures might be more appropriate in certain circumstances. He regarded liberalism as a 'metapolitical' doctrine coinciding with the historicist conception of reality.

Whilst his philosophy offered both solace and a common language to the various antifascist forces, he failed to maintain his Olympian supra-party role after the war. Instead, Italian politics became dominated by the two rival religions he most detested: Catholicism and communism. By the time of his death it had already become clear that his ideas would be remembered chiefly for their influence on the Italian Marxist Antonio Gramsci – a fate Croce bitterly resented.

See also

Gentile, Gramsci.

Works

Filosofia della practica: economia ed etica, Bari, Laterza, 1963.
Philosophy, Poetry, History: an Anthology of Essays, London, Oxford University Press, 1966.
Etica e politica, Bari, Laterza, 1967.

Materialismo storico ed economie marxista, Bari, Laterza, 1968.
La storia come pensiero come azione, Bari, Laterza, 1978.

Other works

Richard P. Bellamy, *Modern Italian Social Theory: Ideology and Politics from Pareto to the Present*, Cambridge, Polity Press, 1987.
David D. Roberts, *Benedetto Croce and the Uses of Historicism*, Berkeley, Cal., University of California Press, 1987.

Charles Anthony Raven Crosland 1918–1977

Anthony Crosland was educated at Trinity College, Oxford, where he returned as a fellow in economics after war service. He was elected MP for Gloucestershire and then Grimsby; he served in the Labour governments of 1964–70 and 1974–77 as Secretary of State for Education, President of the Board of Trade and Secretary of State for the Environment. He died in office as Foreign Secretary in 1977. Crosland was a leading socialist intellectual in the middle years of the twentieth century whose revisionist, social democratic theories had a major influence on the Labour Party.

Crosland saw himself as a revisionist in the mould of Eduard Bernstein. Like Bernstein he rejected the Marxist analysis of modern societies, and defined socialism in terms of ethical goals rather than as based on class and the common ownership of the means of production. He argued that the British economy was no longer capitalist in the classical sense of being dominated by the interests of those who owned the means of production. Ownership had been dispersed, and decision-making power resided more with managers since the trade unions, the extension of democracy and the growth of the welfare state had moved power away from the owners of capital. Socialism had to jettison its Marxist strand to come to terms with what he took to be an irreversible change in power relations. In his view socialism had to be defined in terms of greater social equality and greater social justice. Public ownership was regarded by Crosland as but one of a number of possible means to the achievement of greater equality, the desirability of which had to be judged by its contribution to this goal rather than being seen as a necessary condition of socialism.

In *Socialism Now* Crosland argued for a conception of equality, which, following Rawls, he called 'democratic equality'. He regarded equal opportunity as an important though not sufficient conception of equality for the socialist. Like Rawls, he recognized that some inequality may be necessary for economic efficiency because otherwise the worst-off might actually suffer under equality of outcome. However, he believed that differential rewards should be paid on the basis of a rent of ability rather than desert; in other words, based on incentives, which are necessary to mobilize scarce talent, which is in the interest of all, rather than assuming that inequality represents greater merit on the part of those better placed.

Crosland believed that in a democratic society in which egalitarians had to get elected to office greater social and economic equality had to depend on levelling up rather than down. This meant that economic growth was an essential condition of a more equal society. The fiscal dividends of economic growth would enable governments to use public expenditure to improve the relative position of the worst-off while maintaining the absolute position of the better-off. In addition, growth in incomes had an equalizing effect, at least in terms of equality of opportunity, increasing access to consumer goods such as cars and household appliances which reduced the drudgery of working life. This concern with growth meant that, as shadow environment secretary and as Secretary of State from 1974 to 1976, he had limited sympathy with the incipient development of ecologically concerned socialism.

Crosland placed a good deal of emphasis on the role of comprehensive education as a means to greater social equality in which children of all abilities and from a wide range of backgrounds would have similar educational experiences in the same school. As Secretary of State for Education from 1965 to 1967 he was able to accelerate the move to universal comprehensive education and in DES circular 10/65 he invited all education authorities in England and Wales to submit plans for the reform of secondary education on comprehensive lines.

See also

Bernstein, Rawls.

Works

Britain's Economic Problem, London, Cape, 1953.
The Future of Socialism, London, Cape, 1956.
The Conservative Enemy, London, Cape, 1962.
Socialism Now and other Essays, London, Cape, 1974.

Other works

D. Lipsey and D. Leonard, *The Socialist Agenda: Crosland's Legacy*, London, Cape, 1981.

Robert Dahl   1915–

Robert Alan Dahl is a political scientist who has had extraordinary influence on American writing on democracy. Now Sterling Professor of Political Science Emeritus at Yale University, he served on the Yale faculty from 1946 to 1986 after receiving his Ph.D. there in 1940. He was president of the American Political Science Association in 1966–7 and has received numerous awards, most notably the Woodrow Wilson Foundation Award in 1962 for *Who Governs?*, and the James Madison Award and the Benjamin Evans Lippincott Award of the American Political Science Association. The latter is for 'a work of exceptional quality by a living political theorist that is still considered significant after a time span of at least 15 years since the original publication'. It was awarded in 1989 for *A Preface to Democratic Theory.*

Dahl has spent most of his professional

career writing about the theory and practice of democracy. His work has focused on four main topics: (1) competing models of democracy, (2) normative theories supporting or evaluating one or another of those models, (3) applications of those models to the evaluation of actual regimes and institutions, (4) empirical conditions for the partial or full realization of those models of democracy.

Politics, Economics and Welfare (written with Charles E. Lindblom and first published in 1953) developed the notion of 'polyarchy' as one of the four central processes available for social control in politico-economic systems. Polyarchy was characterized as a process in which non-leaders exert a high degree of control over leaders. A *Preface to Democratic Theory* contrasted 'Madisonian' and 'populistic' models of democracy with an 'American hybrid' characterized by 'minorities rule' – a system in which intense minorities tend to get their way and in which there are many impediments to majority rule.

Who Governs? focused on New Haven, Connecticut, as a test case of the degree to which the American hybrid, at least on the local level, is undemocratic in being dominated by a ruling elite. Dahl countered this charge with the finding that there were competing elites (economic, social and political notables) who were influential in different ways in different issue areas. The system, while not fully living up to democratic aspirations, dispersed power far more than radical critics contended. This book aroused a storm of controversy for its focus on actual decisions rather than on non-decisions or on the shaping of preferences. (See McCoy and Playford and also Lukes for criticisms along these lines; for a vigorous defence of the approach taken in *Who Governs?* see Polsby.)

In *Polyarchy* and *Dilemmas of Pluralist Democracy* Dahl developed further the notion of polyarchy as a partial realization of democratic aspirations. Polyarchies were characterized by seven conditions: (1) control over governmental policies by elected officials, (2) frequent elections of those officials without

coercion, (3) the right to vote for those officials being nearly universal, (4) the right to run for elective office being nearly universal, (5) right of free expression on matters generally relevant to those elections, (6) a right to seek out alternative sources of information, (7) the right to form relatively independent associations or organizations, including political parties and interest groups.

This model of polyarchy falls short of Dahl's ideal model of 'procedural democracy'. The latter includes equality in voting, 'effective participation' (adequate and equal opportunities for expressing preferences), 'enlightened understanding' (adequate and equal opportunities for arriving at one's preferences on any matter to be decided), 'final control of the agenda' and inclusion (membership with its attendant rights being widely shared). Polyarchies are not fully democratic in the sense of procedural democracy because of the limited opportunities for effective participation and for enlightened understanding. Most important, the very 'organizational pluralism' which permits the articulation of interests in the large-scale nation state also distorts the democratic process by permitting existing social and economic inequalities to create effective political inequalities. In 'On removing certain impediments to democracy' Dahl focused on the transformation in the United States brought about by the rise of the giant corporation. In *A Preface to Economic Democracy* he developed criteria for how the sphere of democracy might be extended to corporations and other institutions outside the realm of conventional politics.

Polyarchy proposed an ambitious empirical theory of the socio-economic conditions which favour or impede a transition from a non-democratic regime to one which is at least minimally democratic in the sense defined by polyarchy. Dahl pursued this cross-national work with edited volumes such as *Regimes and Oppositions* (1973) and *Political Oppositions in Western Democracies* (1966) and with *Size and Democracy* (1973, written with Edward R. Tufte) which explored cross-nationally the opportunities and trade-offs offered by differently sized jurisdictions for effective participation and collective preference satisfaction.

In many ways the culmination of Dahl's work can be found in *Democracy and its Critics*. This is a magisterial work in which the normative argument for 'procedural democracy' is fully developed, the limitations of polyarchy are fully explored and the empirical conditions for polyarchy receive a final assessment. In addition Dahl speculates that, just as there was a 'first transformation' in the invention of city-state democracy, and a 'second transformation' in its adaptation to the nation state, we may be on the verge of a 'third transformation' in which the scale and quality of democratic deliberation may both be extended. Democracy may be extended to other institutions within the nation state (corporations, unions) and it may be extended beyond the nation state to international institutions and governing bodies. Furthermore, new technologies and techniques may improve the quality of deliberation within the nation state. Dahl makes a variety of practical proposals along the latter lines.

In *A Preface to Democratic Theory* Dahl defines tyranny in terms of the 'intensity' of opposition to a policy supported by a majority. In *Democracy and its Critics* he develops a notion of tyranny as deprivation of 'primary political rights', i.e. those necessary for the political process. Yet a critic might argue that there are other actions by a majority which might be tyrannical. Depriving a racial minority of equal employment opportunities might, for example, have no effect on primary political rights but it would seem to many to be tyranny of the majority. To the extent that *Democracy and its Critics* deals with issues of this sort, it deals with them in the form of 'dialogues' which leave basic issues unresolved. While the point Dahl makes at the beginning of *A Preface to Democratic Theory* is still true after his own work – that there is no single satisfactory theory of democracy – it is nevertheless the case that his own work is widely regarded as the essential preface to all future serious work on the subject.

Works

Politics, Economics, and Welfare: Planning and Politico-economic Systems Resolved into Basic Social Processes (with Charles E. Lindblom), New York, Harper & Row, 1953.

A Preface to Democratic Theory, Chicago, University of Chicago Press, 1956.

Who Governs? Democracy and Power in an American City, New Haven, Conn., Yale University Press, 1961.

Polyarchy: Participation and Opposition, New Haven, Conn., Yale University Press, 1971.

Dilemmas of Pluralist Democracy: Autonomy versus Control, New Haven, Conn., Yale University Press, 1982.

A Preface to Economic Democracy, Berkeley, Cal., University of California Press, 1985.

Democracy and its Critics, New Haven, Conn., Yale University Press, 1989.

Other works

Charles McCoy and John Playford, *Apolitical Politics: a Critique of Behavioralism*, New York, Crowell, 1967.

Steven Lukes, *Power: a Radical View*, London, Macmillan, 1974.

Nelson Polsby, *Community Power and Political Theory: a further Look at Evidence and Influence*, New Haven, Conn., Yale University Press, 1980.

Ian Shapiro and Grant Reeher, *Power, Inequality, and Democratic Politics: Essays in Honor of Robert A. Dahl*, Boulder, Colo., Westview Press, 1988.

Mary Daly   1920–

American radical feminist philosopher and professor of theology. Her first book, *The Church and the Second Sex*, antedates second-wave feminism. In it Daly argued that the attitudes of the Catholic Church towards women have been and still are misogynistic. At this point in her thinking Daly saw the problems of Catholicism as remediable, provided the Church recognized women's equality. Her second book, *Beyond God, the Father*, marks her definitive break with Catholicism. Daly later maintained that the book signalled her transition from radical Catholic to postchristian feminist. In this book she rejects all Judaeo-Christian religions, maintaining that they are built upon men's fear, envy and hatred of women. From this point on Daly becomes increasingly critical of terms such as 'equality', claiming that culture requires a more radical transformation than a feminism of equality could achieve. The influence of French existentialism (de Beauvoir, Sartre, Camus) and Nietzsche, discernible in Daly's first book, is more pronounced in her middle period. In the latter chapters of *Beyond God, the Father* Daly puts forward a Nietzschean argument for the 'transvaluation of values', that is, for the creation of new values and new forms of moral and ethical life that go beyond the traditional, patriarchally defined opposition between good and evil.

The transvaluation of values involves not only moving beyond traditional philosophical oppositions but also an inventive and transgressive use of language in order to pose possibilities for new forms of life. *Gyn/Ecology*, perhaps the best known of Daly's works, takes up this linguistic challenge. The very title plays on the ambiguity of language by drawing attention to the latent meaning of gynaecology. Whilst the vast majority of medical gynaecologists are men who are institutionally qualified to treat the conditions and diseases peculiar to female biology, gyn/ecologists, in Daly's text, are radical feminists who are concerned with women and the ecological future of the planet. Daly draws on the etymology of various terms, e.g. 'glamour', 'spinster', 'crone', in order to challenge existing meanings, and invents other terms, e.g. 'gynergy', 'gynography', 'fembot', to convey new meanings for women's experience. This draws attention to the political nature of semantics and writing. Daly contrasts the terms 'God' and 'Being', which are nouns in traditional thought, with 'Goddess', 'Be-ing' and 'Be-coming', which she claims to use as verbs, that is, as active and dynamic terms.

In addition to this inventive and transgressive use of language, *Gyn/Ecology* offers an analysis of a variety of cross-cultural practices (Indian *suttee*, Chinese foot binding, African genital mutilation, European witch burnings, American gynaecology and Nazi medicine) which she takes to be indicative of the gynocidal intent of patriarchy. Daly argues that gynocide is at the root of all genocide and that the first step towards the reconstruction of culture is to expose these woman-hating practices. The importance she attaches to identifying and naming these atrocities derives from her belief in the power of language to construct social and political reality. Changing the way in which our social and political lives are represented in language will necessarily involve a change in social and political reality. Daly contends that patriarchal culture is necrophilic, and she exhorts women to counter the destructiveness of contemporary life through the development and expression of their creative biophilic (life-loving) energy. The latter part of *Gyn/Ecology* is a 'celebration' of this biophilic gynergy.

Her most recent book, *Pure Lust*, continues this project of deconstructing patriarchal language and 'sadosociety' whilst offering a reconstructive radical feminist philosophy. Such a philosophy seeks to bridge the gulf between traditional oppositions such as culture and nature, reason and emotion and mind and body by showing how culture is dependent upon nature, reason on emotion and the mind on the body. Daly argues that the patriarchal exploitation and abuse of women and nature are intertwined and must be addressed as such if the planet is to have any future at all. She admits that her philosophy is extreme but reasons that we are confronted with imminent global destruction and only extreme solutions can hope to be effective.

Daly's work is most often criticized on the grounds that it presents a biologistic and essentialist view of men and women, according to which men are innately aggressive and necrophilic and women are innately life-giving and life-loving. Several critics claimed that *Gyn/Ecology* in particular takes an ahistorical approach towards women's social and political situation, and that it fails to respect the specific features of particular cultures. Some have claimed that Daly treats the situation of all women in a monolithic manner, and fails to take account of historical, cultural, racial and class differences between women. Critics have argued, further, that in so far as Daly presents men as essentially irredeemable and places the focus for the future on women and their capacities only, her philosophy is of questionable practical value to the day-to-day realities of social and political life. Still, along with Susan Griffin, she has been and continues to be influential in the American radical feminist movement.

See also

de Beauvoir, Camus, Griffin, Sartre.

Works

The Church and the Second Sex, Boston, Mass., Beacon Press, 1968.
Beyond God, the Father: Towards a philosophy of Women's Liberation, Boston, Mass., Beacon Press, 1973.
Gyn/Ecology: the Metaethics of Radical Feminism, Boston, Mass., Beacon Press, 1978.
Pure Lust: Elemental Feminist Philosophy, Boston, Mass., Beacon Press, 1984.

Other works

E. Manion, Mary Daly: Philosophy, Theology and Radical Feminism, Cambridge, Polity Press, 1990.

Christine Delphy   1941–

Christine Delphy is a feminist sociologist and was a co-founder of Questions Féministes. Delphy was a member of the Mouvement de Libération des Femmes from its beginnings in France and active in the editorial group that began producing the journal Questions Féministes in 1977. Her work begins with a critique of Marxist views of the family, 'Women in statification studies' and 'The main enemy', collected in Close to Home. Arguing that Marx and Engels naturalized the sexual division of labour and obliterated the particular disempowerment of women by equating their status with their husbands' class position, she proposed that women themselves constitute a

class, defined by the unpaid work they do in the family rather than in the market. She also criticized the persistence of traditional gender ideology in what the Questions Féministes collective called non-femininity, that is, the celebration of women's difference from men by French feminists such as Luce Irigaray and the group called Psych et Po (Psychoanalysis and Politics). Her focus on agricultural families as well as urban economies and her rigorously materialist perspective have contributed to feminist debates about housework, the concept of patriarchy and the definition of sexual identity.

Works

'A materialist feminism is possible', Feminist Review 4 (1980).
Close to Home: a Materialist Analysis of Women's Oppression, essays from 1970–81, collected and translated by Diana Leonard, London, Women's Research and Resources Centre/Hutchinson, and Amherst, Mass., University of Massachusetts Press, 1984.
'French Feminist Forum: Questions Féministes/Nouvelles Questions Féministes, 1977–85', Women's Review of Books III, 6 (March 1986).
'Women's liberation: the tenth year', in French Connections: Voices from the Women's Movement in France, ed. and trans. Claire Duchen, Amherst, Mass., University of Massachusetts Press, 1987.

Other works

Michèle Barrett and Mary McIntosh, 'Christine Delphy: towards a materialist feminism?', Feminist Review 1 (1979).
Diana Leonard, 'Introduction', in Close to Home.
Claire Duchen, Feminism in France from May '68 to Mitterand, London, Routledge, 1986.

Jacques Derrida   1930–

Approaching the voluminous literary and philosophical work of Jacques Derrida is not unlike approaching the Sphinx. To grasp the ungraspable, to embroil oneself, willingly or otherwise, in a sometimes crude, sometimes vulgar, sometimes fanciful, sometimes fleeting, sometimes incomprehensible, sometimes contradictory 'love affair with impossibility', as Derrida has so named his thirty-year-plus passionate journey, one needs curiosity, vigilance, patience and flexible ego boundaries. It would not hurt to have, as well, a familiarity with Kant, Hegel, Marx, Kierkegaard, Nietzsche, Husserl, Freud, Heidegger, Levinas, Lacan, de Man, Lyotard, Lacoue-Labarthe, Nancy, Laclau, not to mention Kafka, Joyce, Mallarmé, Saussure. But the 'answer' to this ([post]-modern-day) sphinx riddle holds out the promise of a gift box with two different hinges: the first, as 'deconstruction', the second as the messianic 'promise' of a 'democracy to come'.

At the risk of oversimplification, deconstruction gives precedence to writing over the phoneme of speech. Many names have been attributed, by Derrida, to this move: *différance*, *écriture*, *trace*, *supplément*, *hymen*, *pharmakon*, *marge*, *entame*, *parergon*, etc.; though the umbrella-esque name *deconstruction* is one that he, himself, firmly disdains except 'for the sake of rapid convenience'. Indeed its mention seems more a case of it imposing itself on his work, rather than the other way round. Despite constant disclaimers, we find him as recently as 1980 having to reiterate, once again, a lost ground, musing that 'deconstruction, in the manner in which it is utilized and put to work, is always a highly unstable and almost an empty motif'. This may come as a surprise to the uninitiated and, perhaps also, to scholars, that despite his attempt to avow the contrary, he continues to be hounded by its insurgency.

There are many plausible explanations. But not surprisingly, Derrida himself offers the best: deconstruction is neither a method nor a deliberate 'decision'. It is the 'undecidable' bearing-expression/baring-nakednesss, proper name/naming of an enigma, which 'like all other words', he calmly explains, 'acquires its value only from its inscription in a chain of possible substitutions, in what is too blithely called a "context"': 'Deconstruction is not a method and cannot be transformed into one. ... Deconstruction takes place, it is an event that does not await deliberation, consciousness, or organization of a subject, or even of modernity.'

This enigmatic 'undecidable' is but a strange 'animal'. Something like a peculiar contamination, it is at once exiled to the margins of meaning and yet, simultaneously, constitutes, in its impure 'neither-this-nor-that-ness' an identity-context (i.e., a meaning). As such, it 'names' an impossibility, as if (and to ensure that) the not-nameable aporia or abysm or gap 'exists'. But this is not all that was at stake in Derrida's wrestle with the 'impossible'.

Derrida, with his penchant for 'raising the stakes', does not 'leave it at that', for this contaminated neither/nor-ness occupies a kind of plural or multiple impurity, and, therewith, a 'difference', whose 'root' is, itself, radically violent. That is to say, this unnameable name occupies both a 'difference' (meaning here: 'not-the-same', 'that-which-does-not-fit-in', 'that-which-is-exiled-to-the-margins') and a kind of deferral (the movement of the 'that-which-cannot-be-named', 'the interval of a spacing and temporalising'). This double mark or double movement of difference – a 'double science' he calls grammatology – is re-marked by Derrida as *différance*, replacing the e of *difference* with the a of *deferral*. It is not an innocent [re-]placement. Indiscernible in speech, this deferral/contamination can come to light, be spotted, exposed, only in writing. In this sense, writing is 'more originary' than speech. Its 'origin' is 'it-self'; a kind of 'non-origin-beyond-the-origin', a deep hiatus of continual deferral, which can be nothing other than 'undecidable', and indeed, radically, violently so.

How is it that this non-origin 'origin', this *différance*, at once both violent and undecidable, re-marked upon that tiny little slippage from the e to the a, can be so overwhelmingly effective that it tears down (or claims to tear down) the whole of Western metaphysics? Because once this difference is no longer posed as a mere reflection or mirroring of the oral/said word, this e → a *différance* belies, instead, a 'trace', a tiny micro *grammè*, an 'arche-phenomenon of memory', which, in its doubled non-sayable/deferring mark, remains always-already 'there', before or beyond the logic of the movement of deferral; and blows apart the usual onto-theological metaphysical move, by which Being is understood as a 'something' disentangled from the savagery of exile (of the 'that which cannot be contained' [*différance*]). But Being, indeed life itself, is uncontainable, messy. We are faced with a kind of blasphemous 'infidelity' whereby onto-theology is made to 'submit' to the violence of the text, rather than the other way around. Moreover, as *différance* is also deconstruction, there is no falling back into the empty teleo-logics of an absolute stasis, meaning or truth. Indeed – though this is a contentious point to many critics of deconstruction – there is no falling back to a metaphysics at all. Small-w writing thus begins where The Book ends. As Derrida writes in *Of Grammatology*, 'The subordination of the trace to the full presence summed up in the logos, the humbling of writing beneath a speech dreaming its plenitude, such are the gestures required by an onto-theology determining the archaeological and eschatological meaning of being as presence . . . as life without *différance*. . . . [But if writing is shown to be what it is, then] this trace is the opening of the first exteriority in general, the enigmatic relationship of the living to its other and of an inside to an outside: spacing. The outside, "spatial" and "objective" exteriority . . . would not appear without the *grammè*, without *différance* as temporalization, without the nonpresence of the other inscribed within the sense of the present, without the relationship to death as the concrete structure of the living present.'

Apart from the crushing of 'all dualisms, all theories of the immortality of the soul or of the spirit, as well as all monisms, spiritual or materialist, dialectical or vulgar' – which heretofore emitted/admitted to a future presence as the *logos* of a *telos* striving to clear away imbalance, violence, difference – this infidelity, this 'trace', instead re-presents, in its wake, a future presence without harmony. Indeed, the future is presented 'as a sort of monstrosity', a kind of threat, 'that can only be anticipated in the form of an absolute danger'.

If this be the case, does this then mean that his 'love affair with impossibility', with its paradoxical aporias, is really nothing other than an intractable double nightmare, evacuating hope, ethics, not to mention *jouissance* (pleasure), neatly off the map? In order to tease out an (all too brief) answer, we must turn from the aporetic logic of deconstruction to the promise of democracy. As we will see, it is also a complex corner-hinge.

Violence, chaos and instability are 'fundamental, founding, and irreducible'. This is precisely where the political moment makes its stand. The political, as a hegemonic move, attempts to secure stability, rules, law, force, consent. This 'political' move, and the ethics it implies or expresses, requires a decision. That 'decision', says Derrida, means saying 'yes' to certain discourses, for example, to the discourse on emancipation, in order to secure a future democracy 'to come' (*à venir*). Now this 'yes saying', which is conditioned, also, by the double gesture (in this case, the repetition that marks the event as an event, and the non-incorporated Other to which the 'yes' is addressed), [re-]cognizes the 'yes' as 'the promise'. The promise, as it turns out, is messianic. 'It is not a question of a messianism that one could easily translate into Judaeo-Christian or Islamic terms but rather of a messianic structure that belongs to all language. There is no language without the performative dimension of the promise. . . . Even when I lie . . . there is a "believe me" in play. And this "I promise you that I am speaking the truth" is a messianic apriori, a promise which, even if it was not kept, even if one knows that it cannot be kept, takes place and *qua* promise is messianic.'

Not surprisingly, a double message is at work in the messianicity of 'the promise': (1) a disavowal of any kind of utopian thinking ('There is the future [*il y a de l'avenir*]. There is something to come [*il y a à venir*]. That can happen . . . and I promise in opening the future or in leaving the future open. This is not utopian'); because (2) there is always-already at work an 'inheritance', a ghostly, spectral effect (*Spectres of Marx*), a 'mourn-ingful memory' with which, in and against which, one must engage. This is a promise that takes account of both temporal and spatial disruptions, repetitions, jagged edges, pieces that 'do not fit in'. In ways far more layered than glimpsed at here, the promise heralds the gift of a radical alternative to modernity itself, challenging, as the most recent commentary so well articulates, the usual Hegelian, liberal and communitarian political philosophies around rights, community and violence.

But whether or not it can 'deliver' on that promise, messianic or otherwise, remains to be seen. In a double move, one might say: this is but a moot point while, at the same time, precisely the point.

See also

Freud, Heidegger, Lyotard.

Works

De la grammatologie, Paris, Minuit, 1967, trans. Gayatri Spivak, *Of Grammatology*, Baltimore, Md, Johns Hopkins University Press, 1976.

L'Ecriture et la différance, Paris, du Seuil, 1967, trans. Alan Bass, *Writing and Difference*, London, Routledge & Kegan Paul, 1978.

La Voix et le phénomène: introduction au problème du signe dans la phénomènologie de Husserl, Paris, Presses Universitaires de France, 1967, trans. David B. Allison, *Speech and Phenomena*. Evanston, Ill., Northwestern University Press, 1973.

La Dessémination, Paris, du Seuil, 1972, trans. Alan Bass, *Margins of Philosophy*, Chicago, Ill., University of Chicago Press, 1981.

Spectres de Marx, Paris, Galilée, 1993, trans. Peggy Kamuf, *Spectres of Marx: the State of the Debt, the ·Work of Mourning and the New International*, London: Routledge, 1994.

Geoff Bennington, *Derridabase*; and Jacques Derrida, *Circumfession*, Chicago, Ill. University of Chicago Press, 1993.

Other works

David Wood and Robert Bernasconi (eds.), *Derrida and Différance*, Evanston, Ill., Northwestern University Press, 1988.

Peggy Kamuf (ed.), *The Derrida Reader: Between the Blinds*, New York, London and Tokyo, Harvester/Wheatsheaf, 1991.

Rodolphe Gasché, *Inventions of Difference: on Jacques Derrida*, Cambridge, Mass., and London, Harvard University Press, 1994.

Chantal Mouffe (ed.), *Deconstruction and Pragmatism: Simon Critchley, Jacques Derrida, Ernesto Laclau and Richard Rorty*, London and New York: Routledge, 1996.

Richard Beardsworth, *Derrida & the Political*, London, Routledge, 1996.

John Dewey   1859–1952

Born in Burlington, Vermont, John Dewey published his first article in 1882. In 1952, the year of his death, he was still writing and publishing. This seventy-year writing career produced an enormous body of work. Among his best-known works in formal philosophy are *Reconstruction in Philosophy*, *Human Nature and Conduct*, *The Quest for Certainty* and *Logic*. Dewey's philosophy of education and his programme for reforming the schools are best represented by *Democracy and Education*, perhaps his most widely read book. *The Public and its Problems* and *Freedom and Culture* are the two works of most value for understanding his pragmatist theory of democracy. Dewey was philosopher, educator and reformer. Indeed, he combined these roles so effectively that for much of the first half of the twentieth century he was viewed as America's most important public philosopher.

Along with Charles Peirce and William James, Dewey founded an entire school of philosophy known as pragmatism. At the most general level, pragmatism is a phil-osophy of the practices and actions that we rely upon to make sense of our ideas. Every idea, pragmatism argues, indicates some action to be taken, and that action's con-sequences are the test of the idea's meaning and validity. What most disturbed Dewey about other philosophies is that they lacked this connection with practice or experience. They were unpractical in this very specific sense. Instrumentalism, Dewey's theory of knowledge, is the first principle of pragmatism. Since an idea is intended as an instrument to help solve some problem, the instrument needs to be put to work. To defend this claim, Dewey urged us to look not at thought itself but at what people are doing when they engage in thinking. People often act out of habit, which is sensible enough. But when things go wrong or some difficulty arises in their interactions with their natural or social environment they begin to cast around for some way to deal with the situation. And this casting about is what it means to have an idea. From this activist understanding of ideas it was only a short step to Dewey's concern with such arts of social engineering as education and politics.

Experimentalism is Dewey's description of the pragmatic method of enquiry that complements instrumentalism. Experimentalism can be described as a form of trial-and-error rationalism in which the worth of an idea depends upon the care taken to verify it. Where other philosophies encourage people to value their beliefs precisely according to the degree to which they can be said to be absolutely true, pragmatism insists that the truth of an idea – more accurately, its validity – is relative to the needs of different situations. The usefulness and hence the value of ideas will change with changing circumstances. Experimentalism is also the method and goal that define Dewey's philosophy of education. In 1894 he joined the University of Chicago, where he established the University Elementary School, more commonly known as the Laboratory or Dewey School. Such laboratory schools are still a part of many colleges of education.

As a political theorist Dewey's most lasting contribution is his account of democracy as a way of life. This view runs counter to most prevailing discussions of democracy as group conflict, party competition and the struggle for power. The key to an appreciation of Dewey's alternative theory of democracy is to notice how he connects it with other prominent pragmatist themes. The essence of democracy is located in how people form judgements, communicate with one another, and come together to solve problems. The democratic method can be compared to the scientific method in which the public(s) is conceived as a community of enquirers trying to solve some problem. What matters about formal guarantees of free speech, elections and other democratic institutions is that they make a trial-and-error rationalism possible in politics. A successful democratic politics does not depend on the judgement of each citizen considered separately. It depends rather on the judgement that arises out of the interactions among citizens. Majority rule, for example, is not, as other democratic theories often describe it, simply a method of making a decision. The process whereby the majority is formed, a process marked by free communication and free association, is equally important. When citizens communicate, talk, share their ideas and try them out so as to test their consequences, Dewey believed, you can have a democratic public in fact as well as in name. The familiar features of pragmatism – enquiry, communication, experimental action – here define the essence of democracy as a type of social practice in which individuals work together to form judgements that are political precisely because they arise out of public activities and are about public life.

Dewey understood that the creation of the public was always a local affair in that communication and the arts of political judgement were best practised in small groups. Membership of voluntary associations and local communities can help educate individuals to become democratic citizens. But increasing industrialization, urbanization, geographical mobility, the growth of the state, all pose serious challenges for Dewey's theory of democracy as a way of life.

After Dewey's death in 1952 pragmatist philosophy suffered a period of relative neglect. More recently his philosophy has enjoyed something of a renaissance. Richard Rorty has given Dewey's pragmatism a new academic and public visibility by using it to criticize philosophy's continuing efforts to discover criteria that will certify certain ideas as absolutely true. The work of the German philosopher and political theorist Jürgen Habermas has similarly renewed interest in Dewey's theory of democracy. Habermas's efforts to work out a conception of democracy as a form of ideal communication bears a close resemblance to Dewey's account of the relations between community and communication. Others have borrowed Dewey's idea of democratic community to criticize the excessive individualism of American politics.

See also

Habermas.

Works

Democracy and Education, 1916, reprinted New York, Macmillan, 1966.
Reconstruction in Philosophy, 1920, reprinted Boston, Mass., Beacon Press, 1957.
Human Nature and Conduct, 1922, reprinted New York, Random House, 1930.
The Public and its Problems, Chicago, Swallow Press, 1927.
The Quest for Certainty, 1929, reprinted New York, Putnam, 1960.
Logic: the Theory of Inquiry, New York, Holt, 1938.
Freedom and Culture, 1939, reprinted New York, Putnam, 1963.

A project to publish the collected works of John Dewey is near completion. All are edited by Jo Ann Boydston and published by Southern Illinois University Press, Carbondale, Ill.: *John Dewey, The Early Works, 1882–1898*, five volumes, 1969–72, *The Middle Works, 1899–1924*, fifteen volumes, 1976–83, and *The Later Works, 1925–1953*, up to volume 8, 1981–.

Other works

Edward C. Moore, *American Pragmatism: Peirce, James, and Dewey*, New York, Columbia University Press, 1961.
A. H. Somjee, *The Political Theory of John Dewey*, New York, Teachers' College Press, 1968.
Richard J. Bernstein, *Praxis and Action*, Philadelphia, Pa, University of Pennsylvania Press, 1971.
Alfonso J. Damico, *Individuality and Community: the Social and Political Thought of John Dewey*, Gainesville, Fl., University Presses of Florida, 1978.

Richard Rorty, *Consequences of Pragmatism*, Minneapolis, Minn., University of Minnesota Press, 1982.
Alan Ryan, *John Dewey and the High Tide of American Liberalism*, New York, W. W. Norton, 1995.

Milovan Djilas   1911–1995

Born in Montenegro, southern Yugoslavia, Milovan Djilas was active in the Yugoslav Communist Party before the Second World War. He emerged as a leading figure in the communist-led Partisan resistance movement during the period of German and Italian occupation, 1941–4. In the period immediately after the war he held a succession of key government jobs. Along with Edvard Kardelj and Boris Kidric, he was one of the architects of the Yugoslav system of decentralized socialism, based on workers' councils. Deeply shocked by Stalin's excommunication of the Yugoslav Communist Party and its leader, President Tito, in 1948, Djilas had by early 1950 come to the conclusion that centralized state socialism was inherently bureaucratic, arbitrary and privilege-ridden. In July the same year a law on workers' self-management was passed by the Yugoslav parliament. But the establishment of a kind of market socialism in Yugoslavia was not enough to satisfy Djilas's growing radicalism. Yugoslavia remained a one-party state, and Djilas became increasingly vociferous in his criticism of the activities of the party bureaucracy, which still controlled the country with the help of the secret police. By 1954 Tito, who saw self-management as a way for communists to keep their power, not as a way of relinquishing it, had had enough. Djilas was stripped of his offices and expelled from the central committee of the Communist Party. In 1956 he was sentenced to three years in prison. When his celebrated *The New Class* was published in the West in 1957 his sentence was extended another seven years. Conditionally released in 1961 but swiftly rearrested, he was finally released in 1966, and subsequently lived quietly in Belgrade. After 1972 he was allowed to publish again.

Milovan Djilas's works from the 1950s and 1960s stand today as early classics of the critique of communism. He was not the first writer to pinpoint bureaucracy as a key problem, but he was the first to generalize the argument to all communist systems. The development of market socialism in Yugoslavia since 1950, and its eventual degeneration, has graphically demonstrated Djilas's central point: as long as any given communist party remains a Leninist 'ruling party' its cadres will continue to behave as if they owned the entire capital stock of the country, even if a market-based economic system is in operation. The collapse of communism in the Soviet Union and Eastern Europe and the events of 1989 in China provide further evidence of the acuteness of Djilas's diagnosis.

While primarily a political thinker, Milan Djilas was also a *littérateur* of considerable note. His autobiographical *Land without Justice* presents a vivid and poignant picture of life in a still tribalist Montenegro before the Second World War. He also made a significant contribution to the historiography of the Stalin period through his *Conversations with Stalin*, an account based on his own direct dealings with the Soviet dictator. In his life and writings Djilas epitomizes the rise and fall of Soviet/East European communism in the latter half of the twentieth century.

See also

Stalin.

Works

The New Class, New York, Praeger, 1957.
Land without Justice, New York, Harcourt Brace, 1958.
Conversations with Stalin, New York, Harcourt Brace, 1962.
The Unperfect Society, New York, Harcourt Brace, 1969.

Other works

Stephen Clissold, *Djilas: the Progress of a Revolutionary*, New York, Universe, 1983.

W. E. B. Du Bois   1868–1963

In his 1903 classic, *The Souls of Black Folk*, William Edward Burghardt Du Bois prophesied that the problem of the twentieth century would be the colour line. He was born in Great Barrington, Massachusetts, the year of President Andrew Johnson's impeachment and died in Accra, Ghana, ninety-five years later, on the eve of the march on Washington. His mother was a domestic whose family had lived in the Berkshire hills since the early eighteenth century, while his father, whom he never knew, was an itinerant mulatto barber of French extraction. Scholarships from four New England Congregational churches enabled Du Bois to graduate from Fisk University in Nashville, Tennessee, in 1888. Scholarship assistance permitted him to earn another B.A. in philosophy from Harvard College in 1890.

The first Harvard Ph.D. of his race, his dissertation, 'The Suppression of the African Slave Trade' (1896), became the first monograph of the influential Harvard Historical Series. His next book, *The Philadelphia Negro* (1899), significantly advanced the new field of urban sociology. Ten more monographs in history, politics and cultural anthropology followed, in addition to five novels and three autobiographies. Premier architect of civil rights in the United States, founder of the Niagara Movement in 1905 and a co-founder of the National Association for the Advancement of Colored People (NAACP) in 1910, he was also a principal architect of pan-Africanism.

Du Bois's career divides into four periods: (1) scientific investigation of African-American culture and institutions and of American race relations (the pioneering Atlanta University Studies) while teaching in Atlanta (1898–1909); (2) defence of 'Talented Tenth' values and militant civil rights propaganda while editing the NAACP's *Crisis* magazine (1910–34); (3) economic separatism and Talented Tenth Marxism, again at Atlanta University and at the NAACP (1934–48);

(4) prophetic Marxism and pan-Africanism, as roving renegade and Ghanaian citizen (1948–63).

Du Bois was inclined to draw no distinction between his own fate and that of fellow African-Americans. In *Darkwater* (1920) and *The Gift of Black Folk* (1924) he wrote of African-American qualities of sensibility, humanity and dignity, which he implied were inherent – almost racial. He was among the first American intellectuals to assert that hyphenated Americans were not cultural contradictions but the embodiment of an enriching diversity. He was a principal source of the Black Aesthetic and Black Pride. He also led the way, along with anthropologists Franz Boas and Melville Herskovits, in recovering the major lost civilizations of sub-Saharan Africa, in books such as *The Negro* and *Black Folk Then and Now* (1939). Although he shed its extreme racial chauvinism, the 1897 paper before the American Negro Academy, 'The Conservation of Races', resonated in his thinking until the end. Equally seminal was the elitist 1903 'Talented Tenth' essay, finally renounced in 1947 for a socialist-inspired 'Guiding Hundredth'.

Du Bois's life can best be grasped by examining five pivotal points: (1) the Du Bois–Booker T. Washington controversy, (2) the Du Bois–Marcus Garvey battle, (3) the two departures from the NAACP, (4) the *Encyclopedia of the Negro* project and, finally, (5) the hard turn to the left. In the final analysis, Du Bois's militant ideology versus that of Washington's accommodationism became tremendously important, but it was first the egoes and politics of what Du Bois memorably dubbed, in *The Souls of Black Folk*, Booker T. Washington's 'Tuskegee Machine' that sealed the division within the African-American leadership community. That Washington and Du Bois were also talking past each other to different constituencies – the former to a southern, agrarian, peasant and minimally educated population, the latter to a northern, urban, middle-class and college-educated one – was fundamental to their conflict.

The conflict with Marcus Garvey and his Universal Negro improvement Association was, ultimately, one of power. Most of his ideas could have been made compatible with Du Bois's. At stake was the vital question of the national origins and nature of the social class that would embody black leadership in America: whether it would be parvenu West Indians enrolled behind charismatic Garvey, or the home-grown bourgeoisie loyal to aloof Du Bois, the NAACP and the National Urban League.

In 1934 *Crisis* readers were astonished by two Du Bois editorials, 'Segregation' and 'Separation and self-respect', advocating separate (if co-operatist) racial development in the United States, seemingly along the lines of Booker T. Washington earlier. Du Bois claims that, by 1930, he 'had become convinced that the basic policies and ideals of the [NAACP] must be modified and changed'. It was also painfully clear that the Depression-era plunge of his magazine's circulation meant inevitable loss of editorial control. There were compelling economic as well as ideological and organizational reasons why Du Bois may have decided to depart from the NAACP and simultaneously jolt the thinking of black America.

In any case, the Atlanta University president, John Hope, urged him to chair the graduate sociology programme at the newly restructured, General Education Board-financed institution. The Rockefeller-backed GEB immediately let Hope know of its misgivings, suggesting Du Bois's appointment be limited to a trial year. Something quite dramatic and unexpected needed doing in order to effect Du Bois's transition from the fiery *Crisis* to the stately halls of a Rockefeller benefaction, which the editorials accomplished.

The period from 1935 to 1948 was marked by political experimentation, but also by significant relapses into conventional optimism. On the one hand, there is the magisterial *Black Reconstruction in America*, and there are the fundamental essays 'The Negro and social reconstruction' (1936) and 'Basic American Negro creed' in *Dusk of Dawn* (1940), spelling out his socialist cooperatives plan; yet, as late as 1948–9, there are orthodox civil rights pieces foretelling social democracy in America if the race relations progress of the last thirty years continued 'for another generation'.

After involuntary retirement from Atlanta University in 1944 Du Bois returned to the NAACP. His anti-imperialist book *Color and Democracy* appeared that January. He served as a consulting delegate at the founding of the United Nations in San Francisco in 1945, criticizing the charter's silence about colonialism. Collaborating with Paul Robeson and others on the Council on African Affairs, he presided at the Pan-African Congress meeting in Manchester, England, that year. His 1947 United Nations petition, 'An appeal to the world: a statement on the denial of human rights to minorities in the case of citizens of Negro descent in the United States of America', was a bold initiative for the NAACP. Already shaken by charges of communist infiltration and by new board member Eleanor Roosevelt's 'embarrassment' over Du Bois's UN petition, the NAACP board fired Du Bois in 1948 when he openly endorsed Henry Wallace's presidential candidacy.

Du Bois's avowedly Marxist period began with the March 1949 Cultural and Scientific Conference for World Peace in New York. In 1950, at eighty-two, he ran for the US Senate from New York, on the American Labor Party ticket. On 13 July in the *New York Times* Secretary of State Dean Acheson attacked Du Bois's Peace Information Center as a Soviet front. On 9 February 1951 he and the officers of the PIC were indicted under the Foreign Agents Registration Act of 1936. The Justice Department, however, abandoned its case in mid-trial but the experience was traumatic.

Du Bois's book *In Battle for Peace* (1952) concluded that, for the sake of under-developed peoples everywhere all tactics that constrained American capitalism were fair.

He ignored the Soviet Union's 1956 rampages in Eastern Europe. His passport restored, Du Bois spent 1959 in red-carpet travel through Eastern Europe, the Soviet Union and China, adding to his 1959 Lenin Peace Prize honorary doctorates. In a private Kremlin talk with Nikita Krushchev he persuaded the Soviet Premier to create the Institute of African Studies in the Academy of Sciences.

In 1961 Du Bois petitioned the Communist Party for membership. He believed it was now too late to rejoice at the advent of Martin Luther King, Jr. Presiding over the *Encyclopaedia Africana* in Ghana, Du Bois believed his long life would be redeemed by the triumph of Third World socialism.

See also

Garvey, Washington.

Works

The Souls of Black Folk: Essays and Sketches, Chicago, McClurg, 1903.

The Negro, New York, Holt, 1915.

Black Reconstruction in America: an Essay toward a History of the Part which Black Folk played in the Attempt to Reconstruct Democracy in America, New York, Russell, 1935.

Color and Democracy: Colonies and Peace, New York, Harcourt Brace, 1945.

Other works

John H. Clark, E. Jackson, E. Kaiser and J. H. Odell (eds.), *Black Titan: W. E. B. Dubois*, Boston, Mass., Beacon Press, 1970.

Herbert Aptheker (ed.), *Annotated Bibliography of the Published Writings of W. E. B. Du Bois*, Amherst, Mass., University of Massachusetts Press, 1973.

Joseph P. De Marco, *The Social Thought of W. E. B. Du Bois*, Lanham, Md, University Press of America, 1983.

Gerald Horne, *Black and Red: W. E. B. Du Bois and the Afro-American Response to the Cold War, 1944–63*, Albany, N.Y., State University of New York Press, 1986.

Manning Marable, *W. E. B. Du Bois: Black Radical Democrat*, Boston, Mass., Twayne, 1986.

Arnold Rampersad, *The Art and Imagination of W. E. B. Dubois*, Cambridge, Mass., Harvard University Press, 1990.

David Levering Lewis, *W. E. B. Du Bois: Biography of a Race, 1868–1919*, New York, Henry Holt, 1993.

Emile Durkheim   1858–1917

The foremost French sociologist was born in Epinal, near the German border, a town occupied by German troops during the Franco-Prussian War when he was twelve. He was also Jewish, and France's humiliating defeat led to an outbreak of scapegoating antisemitism as well as more positive reformist responses. His response to these experiences was to put his faith in social science as the best means of combating irrational prejudices, reactionary privileges and customs, and as the best way of inculcating national and rational unity. The liberal republicans who eventually rose to power in the Third Republic after the Prussian war, many of whom had been educated like Durkheim at the elite Ecole Normale Supérieure, encouraged him in his mission.

Durkheim's subsequent university appointments at Bordeaux and then as the first professor of sociology at the Sorbonne were made on the understanding that he would teach courses in education as well as sociology. His course in Paris on the history and theory of education in France was compulsory for all students undertaking the *agrégation* in arts and sciences, and some right-wing critics of his influence in the education system spoke of it as 'State Durkheimianism' because of its ideological affinity with the ideas of the liberal republican regime. It was said that, throughout France, teachers trained in Durkheim's sociology were to be found propagating sociology as an alternative to the preaching of the Catholic priest

In practical terms, Durkheim's influence on politics was mainly indirect, being mediated through the impact of his influence within the educational system. However, in the 1890s, when there was another outbreak of antisemitism surrounding the unjust conviction of the Jewish Captain Dreyfus as a German spy, Durkheim made one of his rare public interventions in the political sphere, defending the position of the intellectual supporters of Dreyfus against the charge that their espousal of individualism and individual rights was anti-social and led to anarchy. Durkheim's defence was an original account of 'individualism' as the emergent 'religion' of a modern society with an advanced division of labour, wherein the human person becomes a sacred object. This 'cult' of moral individualism was opposed to egoistic or utilitarian individualism because it was not a glorification of the self: it was not a matter of each for him or herself, but of each for every other. Eighteenth-century doctrines of individualism had a negative character, concentrating on freeing individuals from political shackles which impeded their development. Such political freedoms needed to be seen as means and not ends in themselves. Political liberties had to be used positively to work towards economic and social justice, removing the harsh aspects of society and making it possible for all individuals to develop their capacities to the full and receive their just reward – 'to each according to his labour'.

Although Durkheim seldom again intervened in the political sphere, his sociology had important political implications. These implications have been likened to the British tradition of non-Marxist, socialist critique of capitalism, as exemplified by R. H. Tawney. Like Tawney, Durkheim was looking for a way of transcending class divisions through social reform, the establishment of a kind of guild socialism based on ethical community with a vision of social justice and power exercised responsibly because it would be grounded in equality of respect for other individuals.

Durkheim had a positive view of the role of the state and a substantive theory of democracy. These ideas emerge in his first book, *De la division du travail social*, and in two posthumously published books listed below. The main conclusion reached in *The Division of Labour* is that there can be no going back to the mechanical solidarity of simpler societies, in which the individual was subordinated to a collective conscience, based on uniformity. The complex division of labour in modern society provides some of the conditions for an organic solidarity based on interdependence and co-operation. But this too requires a moral component and cannot be left to the workings of an amoral market. Existing capitalist societies had taken on pathological characteristics, marked by competition and conflict to satisfy unrestrained appetites. Freedom of contract in the existing situation of inequality simply meant that the strong exploited the weak. In *Professional Ethics and Civic Morals* Durkheim stressed that the situation would be changed only if the state took a more active role in securing the conditions under which individuals could develop their potential, involving equality of opportunity and a drastic reduction in the inequalities perpetuated through the inheritance of wealth. A crucial reform would be the development of intermediate institutions between the individual and the state, so as to consolidate the opinions of individuals and communicate them to the state, and to channel the state's leadership down to the grass roots; such institutions would also act as a buffer between the individual and the state, and balance the power of the state. Occupational associations should be given the main intermediary role in the electoral system and the regionally based electoral constituencies abandoned, as he argued that regional differences in culture and interests were being increasingly eroded by industrialization. These occupational associations, analogous to the ancient guilds or corporations, would combine economic and moral functions. It was this latter suggestion that was seized on by theorists of corporatism and solidarist syndicalism; it even led a few later commentators to link his ideas with fascism. In fact the intention of Durkheim's political sociology was to situate corporativism within the general theory of democracy and of socialism.

The core of Durkheim's political theory is to be found at the point where his discussions of the state, democracy and socialism intersect. The modern democratic state would flourish to the extent that it cultivated pluralism and individual self-realization. These values were to be embedded in the political structures so that they themselves became the object of attachment and commitment, a sacred manifestation of the collective consciousness. In contrast to Max Weber, who tended to picture political leaders as vying for the support of an irrational mass, Durkheim insisted that substantively democratic systems could transform the population into an ever more rational and critical public.

Durkheim's view of democratic socialism was that it required the connection of all economic functions to the 'directing and conscious centres of society'. It was an inevitable development in social evolution because the anarchy of markets and unrestrained appetites led to pathological conflict unless subjected to rational co-ordination and regulation. But the state should confine its intervention to the most general, co-ordinating level; more detailed regulation had to be pluralistic and decentralized into the hands of the people actually involved in production.

Durkheim rejected revolutionary socialism on the grounds that revolutionary changes tended to lead to bureaucratic oppression. Similarly, whilst paying tribute to Marx's work, Durkheim objected that its claim to scientific status was premature. Sociology would proceed more cautiously. Furthermore, Marxist socialism's analysis and programme onesidedly emphasized economic factors at the expense of the moral element in society. Durkheim's sociology focused much of its attention on this moral element, particularly in his last major work, *The Elementary Forms of the Religious Life*. His discussion of the binary structures of culture, especially the sacred–profane dichotomy, influenced the subsequent development of structuralism (e.g. the work of Claude Lévi-Strauss), and has recently been drawn on by sociologists attempting to develop a symbolic approach to politics.

The main weakness of Durkheim's political sociology is that it underplays issues of power and the state, and in this respect it contrasts with the contribution of Weber. Nevertheless, Durkheim's cultural approach to politics is useful in areas such as the analysis of the symbolic codes through which national communities define themselves in terms of inclusion and exclusion. It has also proved useful in analyses of the integrating role of a 'civil religion' in secular society, manifested in rituals such as the inauguration of a president and in interpreting the symbolic significance of reactions to critical events like the Watergate crisis in America.

See also

Tawney, Weber.

Works

De la division du travail social: étude sur l'organisation des societes supérieures, Paris, Alcan, 1893; trans. George Simpson as *The Division of Labour in Society*, New York, Macmillan, 1933.

Les Formes élémentaires de la vie religieuse, Paris, Alcan, 1912; trans. Joseph Ward Swain as *The Elementary Forms of the Religious Life*, London, Allen & Unwin, 1915.

L'Allemagne au-dessus de tout, Paris, Colin, 1915.

Le Socialisme, Paris, Presses Universitaires de France, 1928; trans. Charlotte Sattler as *Socialism and Saint-Simon* (subsequently reprinted as *Socialism*), Yellow Springs, Antioch Press.

Leçons de sociologie, Paris, Presses Universitaires de France, 1950, trans. Cornelia Brookfield as *Professional Ethics and Civic Morals*, London, Routledge, 1957.

Other works

Steven Lukes, *Emile Durkheim: his Life and Work,* London, Allen Lane, 1973.

Jean-Claude Filloux, *Durkheim et le socialisme*, Geneva and Paris, Droz, 1977.

Jeffrey Prager, 'Moral integration and political inclusion: a comparison of Durkheim's and Weber's theories of democracy', *Social Forces* 59, 4 (1981), pp. 918–50.

Kenneth Thompson, *Emile Durkheim*, London and New York, Tavistock/Routledge, 1982.

Anthony Giddens (ed.), *Durkheim on Politics and the State*, Cambridge, Polity Press, 1985.

Frantz Fanon   1925–1961

The emergence of Frantz Fanon as a radical black intellectual in the first decade after the Second World War was both spectacular and of international importance. As a critic of colonialism, and as an uncompromising proponent and theorist of revolution, his name was to become synonymous with militant anti-imperialism and anti-racism. In this manner he followed in the wake of a radical tradition of Caribbean and African francophone activist intellectuals which included (among others) Lamine Senghor, Aimé Césaire, Leopold Senghor, Jean Price-Mars, René Maran and Paulette Nardal.

Fanon was born in Martinique, then a colony of France; his father was a customs inspector, his mother a shopkeeper. In 1943, with the island occupied by the Vichy fleet and Petainist refugees, Fanon left Martinique to join the Free French movement. During the next two years he fought in the West Indies, North Africa (Morocco and Algeria) and Europe, was wounded twice and received the Croix de Guerre for his 'brilliant conduct'. In 1947 he returned to France to study medicine and psychiatry at the University of Lyons. In 1952, upon the completion of his thesis and his marriage to Josie Duble, he took up residence at the Hôpital de Saint-Albain, and published his first collection of essays, *Black Skin, White Masks*. At the end of the following year he was appointed *chef de service* to the government psychiatric hospital at Blida-Joinville, Algeria.

Fanon's return to Algeria coincided with the beginnings of the Algerian revolution's armed struggle. As a colonial subject of the French, Fanon was schooled to observe the tragedy and historic dimensions of Western imperialism. And at Blida Fanon experienced the brutality of colonialism as well as its scientistic mystification. Almost immediately, through contacts on the hospital staff, he became involved politically and professionally with the underground Front de Libération Nationale. By the end of 1956 Fanon had resigned from the hospital; he was expelled from Algeria in January 1957. At Blida he had determined that 'the Arab, permanently an alien in his own country, lives in a state of absolute depersonalization', and concluded,

'A society that drives its members to desperate solutions is a non-viable society, a society to be replaced.' Fanon relocated to Tunisia, taking up his clinical work at the Centre Neuropsychiatrique de Jour de Tunis while assuming a more active role in the FLN's refugee centres and its diplomatic work. And it was through the synthesis of these activities with his work on the FLN's propaganda organs (*el Moudjahid, Resistance Algérienne*) that Fanon was to produce the essays in *A Dying Colonialism* and *Toward the African Revolution* and the case studies reported in *The Wretched of the Earth*.

In *Black Skin, White Masks* Fanon had wrestled only partially successfully with the issues of alienation, racism, science and irrationality. He conceded, 'for a man whose only weapon is reason there is nothing more neurotic than contact with unreason'. And his encounters with ordinary and extraordinary Frenchmen and women were a source of profound disillusionment and betrayal. 'A man was expected to behave like a man. I was expected to behave like a black man – or, at least, like a nigger.' His historical and social 'otherness' was so acute as to instil in him an intellectual compulsion to seek not merely a negation of Western thought but a wholly alternative problematic. In Algeria, in the vortex of a revolution which summoned forth his own paradox, he became an African revolutionary and a Third World theorist.

From his vantage point as a Third World revolutionist, Fanon resolutely unmasked the ideological supports of racism, colonialism and imperialism, and, with equal force of intellect, he also threw into question the socialist project articulated by Marx and Engels. Fanon's social consciousness was first formed at the colonial margins of the West. This placed him in a position to absorb the oppositional world views of the colonial and the colonized. He looked upon the rise of bourgeois society from the outside, and from his perspective the industrial, technological and scientific revolutions commandeered by the bourgeoisies of Europe had not achieved the conditions for human emancipation which Marx had foreseen.

In *The Wretched of the Earth* Fanon maintained that the Manichaean racial order of colonial society transcended capitalist relations. Profit was certainly a reason for the imperialist impulse but the reasoning which characterized the world of the *colon* was profoundly irrational. The native and the settler were not opposing classes. The opposition was between civilizations: 'when the native hears a speech about Western culture he pulls out his knife – or at least he makes sure it is within reach'. In the colonies the proletariat was privileged, pampered and 'bourgeois'. And in the metropole colonialism had invalidated the relevance of class theory. 'It used to be said,' Fanon wrote in *Toward the African Revolution*, 'there is a community of interests between the colonized people and the working class of the colonized country. The history of the wars of liberation waged by the colonized peoples is the history of the non-verification of this thesis.' For Fanon it was not the 'organization of production' but the persistence and 'organization of oppression' which formed the primary social basis for revolutionary activity.

Fanon's revolutionary theory implicated the violence and racialism of colonialism, not its economics, in the dialectic of resistance. In *The Wretched of the Earth* he identified the social base of revolution as the 'country people', the lumpenproletariat and the renegade petty-bourgeois intellectuals. Drawing upon his experience in the Algerian revolution, and on his studies of the revolutionary movements in Madagascar, Indochina and Central Africa, Fanon concluded that it was among the peasantry that one discovered 'the only spontaneously revolutionary force in the country'. Unlike those who were drawn into the urban centres and into close proximity to settler society, the peasantry, as the social base of the first resistance to imperialism, remained self-disciplined during colonialism, nurturing opposition in the folklore and myths of resistance. However, the social and cultural activity of the peasantry was not purely or simply revolutionary. Like the irrationality found among the native population in the towns – sometimes fratricidal, sometimes 'phantasmic' and ecstatic – irrational movements of religious fanaticism or tribal wars appeared in the countryside. He was no less critical of the colonized national bourgeoisie, believing the bulk of this class culturally, psychologically and ideologically pathological. It was the interaction of peasants, lumpenproletariat and intellectuals which crystallized revolutionary consciousness through the experience of revolutionary struggle.

Fanon argued that the war of national liberation occurred in successive stages. He distinguished the 'nationalist phase' of the revolutionary movement – the moment when the national bourgeoisie and the militant trade unions demanded greater privileges – from the 'spontaneous phase' – when the inevitably repressive colonial response precipitated a flight to the countryside by the surviving nationalists and their discovery of the 'coherent' peasantry. It was at this decisive moment that the movement required its most politically sophisticated elements to come to the fore in order to transform resistance into revolutionary war. The radical intelligentsia would provide a leadership which could direct the resistance past the seductions of colonialist counter-revolution, forestall the degeneration of the guerrilla forces into undisciplined nationalists, and obstruct the enlistment of a 'neurotic' lumpenproletariat on the side of the oppressor.

Drawing upon his clinical experience as well as his exposure to French imperialism, Fanon systematized the treatment of revolutionary violence. He pursued its significations philosophically ('It is solely by risking life that freedom is obtained'), psychologically ('violence is a cleansing force'), historically ('the war of liberation introduces into each man's consciousness the ideas of a common cause, of a national destiny and of a collective history') and organizationally ('The practice of violence binds them together as a whole, since each individual forms a violent link in the great chain'). Nevertheless, as Césaire would recognize, Fanon was horrified by violence: 'His violence, paradoxically, was that of the non-violent.'

At the time of his death Fanon was working with his wife Josie on the final drafts of *The Wretched of the Earth*. He has been criticized for dismissing the proletariat, being preoccupied with violence, and romanticizing the peasantry and the party of national liberation. His vision was not complete, yet, given the severe historical and personal conditions under which he worked and the foreshortened life which followed, Fanon's legacy constitutes an important beginning.

Works

Black Skin, White Masks, 1952, reprinted New York, Grove Press, 1964.
A Dying Colonialism, 1959, reprinted New York, Grove Press, 1967.
Toward the African Revolution, 1964, reprinted New York, Grove Press, 1968.
The Wretched of the Earth, 1961, reprinted New York, Grove Press, 1966.

Other works

Renate Zahar, *L'Oeuvre de Frantz Fanon*, Paris, Maspéro, 1970.
David Caute, *Fanon*, London, Fontana, 1970.
Pierre Bouvier, *Fanon*, Paris, Editions Universitaires, 1971.
Peter Geismar, *Fanon: the Revolutionary as Prophet*, New York, Dial, 1971.
Irene Gendzier, *Frantz Fanon: a Critical Study*, New York, Vintage, 1973.
Emmanuel Hansen, *Frantz Fanon: Social and Political Thought*, Nairobi, Oxford University Press, 1978.
Adèle Jinadu, *Fanon: in Search of the African Revolution*, Enugu, Nigeria, Fourth Dimension, 1980.
Marie Perinbam, *Holy Violence: the Revolutionary Thought of Frantz Fanon*, Washington, D.C., Three Continents, 1982.

Shulamith Firestone   1945–

Shulamith Firestone is best known as the author of *The Dialectic of Sex*. This pioneering book was one of the first two full-length theoretical expressions of the feminism that re-emerged in the late 1960s – the other being *Sexual Politics* by Kate Millett, published in the same month, September 1970. Prior to the publication of *The Dialectic of Sex* Firestone was extremely active in such early feminist groups as New York Radical Women and Redstockings, writing articles on abortion, love and 'When women rap about sex' for the influential *Notes from the First Year* (1968) and *Notes from the Second Year* (1970), publications which she co-edited. She is also listed as co-editor on leave for *Notes from the Third Year* (1971).

Initially part of the 1960s new left, Firestone's departure from that movement became inevitable after the August 1967 National Conference on New Politics, held in Chicago. Although a women's caucus had met for days, the convention refused to discuss its resolution or to recognize women wishing to speak from the floor. Firestone was one among five women who eventually rushed the podium, only to be patted on the head and told, 'Cool down, little girl. We have more important things to talk about than women's problems.'

In the late 1960s it was common for the feminist movement to regard itself either as an extension of the civil rights movement or as part of a wider struggle for socialism – a self-conception which encouraged frequent references to women as 'niggers' or as an exploited class. The major theoretical innovation of *The Dialectic of Sex*, an innovation that became a distinguishing feature of US radical feminism, was to deny that women's subordination could be understood as a symptom or aspect of some deeper or more comprehensive system of domination. Instead, Firestone argued that the subordination of women was fundamental to other forms of oppression. By 'fundamental' she meant that women were, historically, the first oppressed group; that women's subordination could not be eliminated by such changes as the elimination of prejudice or even the abolition of class society, both of which Firestone

saw as merely symptomatic or 'superstructural'; and that women's subordination provided a conceptual model for understanding all other types of oppression. In her own work she reversed the usual conceptual priorities by explaining such phenomena as racism and class society in terms of the subordination of women.

Firestone claimed that the basis of women's subordination was ultimately biological, arguing that human reproductive biology had dictated a universal form of social organization that she called the 'biological family'. This basic reproductive unit, consisting of father, mother and offspring, was said to result from what Firestone saw as two universal features of the human biological constitution: that women are physically weaker than men as a result of their reproductive physiology, and that infants are physically helpless relative to adults. The survival of women and children thus required that infants depend on lactating women and that women, in turn, depend on men. In Firestone's view, it was this supposedly biologically grounded dependence of women and children on men that was the ultimate cause of what she saw as the universal fact of male dominance.

Happily, according to Firestone, the material conditions for ending this hitherto inevitable dependence had finally been achieved in the twentieth century with the advent of reliable contraception, infant formula and, above all, the possibility of extrauterine gestation or what were popularly called 'test-tube babies'. She argued that these technological developments provided the means of 'freeing . . . women from the tyranny of their reproductive biology' and diffusing 'the childbearing and childrearing role to the society as a whole, men as well as women' .

Although Firestone's work is often dismissed because of its apparent biologism, it contains a number of themes that run counter to biological determinism. Firestone describes at length how male dominance, though supposedly grounded in biology, is elaborated and reinforced through cultural practices; her analyses of the ways in which male dominance is expressed and strengthened through the ideology of love and romance, for instance, are witty and insightful. Similarly, Firestone's appropriation of Freudian theory 'de-biologizes' Freud by arguing that the development of distinctively 'feminine' and 'masculine' personalities in girls and boys respectively is not a direct and inevitable response to observed physiological differences between the sexes but rather a reaction to differences in the perceived social power of women and men. Thus penis envy is not envy of the male organ but rather envy of male privilege. And in an extremely radical challenge to a form of biological determinism now accepted almost universally in Western society Firestone denies the biological inevitability of childhood, arguing that it is actually a social invention.

Firestone's views were never popular among grass-roots feminists. This was probably due to a combination of factors, including her perception of women's biology as inferior to men's, her negative view of childbirth and lactation, and her confidence in the liberatory possibilities of high technology, a confidence which, in the 1970s, began to seem increasingly misplaced as technology was implicated in a series of medical and ecological disasters. Subsequent feminist theorists were also critical of her work, rejecting what they saw as her biological determinism and especially what came to be called her 'essentialism', that is, her sweeping transcultural and transhistorical generalizations about relationships between men, women and children. Her ingenious reinterpretation of Marxist terminology could also be seen as an inappropriate form of filial piety.

Despite its undeniable flaws, Firestone's work has great historical significance. The opening words of her book, 'Sex class is so deep as to be invisible', encapsulate the original and continuing project of feminist theory, to make women's subordination visible as a political problem. Though few feminists today would endorse Firestone's proposals for resolving this problem, her work broke the ground for a new tradition of autonomous feminist theorizing. She may have been the first feminist in this century to explore theoretically the full significance of women's distinctive role in procreation. Instead of evading or dismissing the issue, she was certainly among the first to set in a feminine context the now increasingly urgent questions raised by the possibility of technically assisted procreation.

Unfortunately Firestone's early articles are impossible to find unless one has access to the rare original issues of *Notes*. None of her articles is among those reprinted in the 1973 collection *Radical Feminism*, edited by Anne Koedt, Ellen Levine and Anite Rapone, even though many, if not most, of the pieces in the volume appeared originally in *Notes*.

Feminist theories of the 1970s referred frequently to Firestone's work, but usually to define themselves in opposition to it. Today her work is neglected and her book is out of print.

See also

Millett.

Works

The Dialectic of Sex, New York, Morrow, 1970.

Michel Foucault   1926–1984

Michel Foucault received his university education first in philosophy and then in psychology. He established his intellectual reputation with his monumental thesis for *doctorat d'état*, published in 1961 as *Folie et déraison: histoire de la folie* and translated into English in an abridged form as *Madness and Civilization*. His fame grew with the publication of *Naissance de la clinique* (*The Birth of the Clinic*) and *Les Mots et les choses* (*The Order of Things*). In 1970 he was elected to the professorship of systems of thought at the prestigious Collège de France. In the 1970s Foucault became a political figure, agitating for prison reform and human rights inside and outside France. In the later part of his life he embarked on a massive history of sexuality.

Foucault's writings consist of around ten full-length books, a number of translations and hundreds of articles, interviews and introductions to books. Although conventionally Foucault might be described as a historian of systems of thought, he distanced his enquiries from the history of ideas, describing those enquiries instead as archaeologies or genealogies. Apart from *The Archaeology of Knowledge* Foucault wrote little on methodology, yet his writings, with their innovative procedures and constant conceptual experiments, have proved a great source of methodological invigoration for social theory.

In the main Foucault's works may be grouped under three headings: (1) analyses of branches of knowledge and discourses; (2) geneaologies of institutions of internment – asylums, hospitals and prisons; (3) investigations of power relations and sexuality. Under the first heading fall above all *The Order of Things* and *The Archaeology of Knowledge.* The French title of the former is ironical, as the work is not about a general relation between 'words and things' but about fundamental configurations of fields of knowledge at various historical periods, which Foucault terms *epistèmes.* Foucault establishes filiations among seemingly different disciplines by demonstrating that the seventeenth-century studies of language (general grammar), living beings (natural history) and wealth and money were all governed by the 'classical episteme'. He also establishes breaks in seemingly continuous disciplines by arguing that nineteenth-century linguistics, biology and economics must be understood not in terms of seventeenth-century grammar, natural history and the physiocrats' and mercantalists' studies of wealth and money but rather in

terms of one another. Together they constitute the modern 'human sciences'.

The Archaeology of Knowledge is a retrospective reflection upon earlier texts and an attempt to produce a conceptual framework for analysing discourses. Here Foucault specifies the difference between his own approach to discourse and the conventional history of ideas and the history of science. He also discards the term *epistème* as smacking too much of 1960s structuralism and instead uses the phrase 'discursive formation'.

Under the heading of genealogies of institutions of internment one can group *Madness and Civilization, The Birth of the Clinic* and *Discipline and Punish.* The asylum, the clinic and the prison with which these texts are respectively concerned are all semi-enclosed domains housing special categories of individuals and governed by projects of cure, correction or reform. In their modern form they emerged at the turn of the nineteenth century with a simultaneity that was not accidental but a function of their intertwined genealogies. All three developed out of the dissolution of older polymorphous regimes of succour, cure and punishment which had prevailed in Europe from the end of the sixteenth century until the latter part of the eighteenth. Not only do asylums, clinics and hospitals share the same ancestry but also, and more important for Foucault, their internal regimes are founded on similar techniques, which he comes to call disciplinary techniques in *Discipline and Punish.* Disciplinary institutions are central nodes in the network of modern power relations. They are also institutional supports of varieties of knowledge: the asylum, of psychiatry and psychology; the teaching hospital or clinic, of modern anatomo-clinical medicine; the prison, of criminology and other socio-psychological discourses. Finally, these institutions are the site of practices which divide individuals into the normal and the abnormal: the mad and the sane, the sick and the healthy, the criminal and the law-abiding.

Relations of power, which can be seen in retrospect as the subject of *Madness and Civilization* and *The Birth of the Clinic*, become the explicit focus of Foucault's later writings, beginning with *Discipline and Punish*. The *History of Sexuality*, published in French in 1976, was to be the introductory volume in a six-volume history of power and sexuality. Three substantial volumes have appeared after Foucault's death; all three seem more exploratory than well finished. But, in combination with *Discipline and Punish* and his later interviews and earlier case studies, these texts exhibit Foucault's political as well as intellectual magnetism for the critical contemporary reader.

This magnetism has a distinctly post-Marxist pull to it. Like other major French theorists in the last third of the twentieth century, Foucault discards the idea of history as moving dialectically through domination to an emancipated end, the accordance of explanatory primacy to the mode of production, the revelation of a truth or reality underneath the appearance of social life, and the faith in a revolutionary class subject. Foucault does not, however, discard the political point of view. He emphasizes the key significance of power, and he allies himself with those in resistance to it. He bequeaths to political theory concepts and studies of normalizing power, truth as a function of power, the local operations and molecular effects of power, as well as the multiple, fractured and localized oppositions to power – concepts and studies that, while tied by different connective strands to the thought of Nietzsche, Weber and Gramsci, are fundamentally iconoclastic and (although Foucault would shudder at the term) original. He also provides stimulation for some of the most rebellious recent tendencies of thought and practice. Almost silent himself on questions of gender and colonialism, although less silent on questions of sexuality, Foucault none the less offers central theoretical support for their analysis in his assertion of the multiple sites and axes of power and resistance; his principle of the

fusion of knowledge and power; his view of power as productive as well as prohibitive; his notion of the discursive imposition of identity on the body; and his repudiation of the ideas of nature, essence and authentic subjectivity. Feminism, gay and lesbian studies, and post-colonial criticism, all have made use of these supports in their own challenges to the cultural production of masculine–feminine, the delineation of normal and perverse eroticisms and the imperial engagements of Western discourses on occident and orient, white and black, colonizer and colonized.

At once a sceptic of collective revolution and a theoretician of fragmented resistance, Foucault is, in the aftermath of Marxism, the exemplary disenchanted radical of our time.

See also

Gramsci, Weber.

Works

Madness and Civilization: a History of Insanity in the Age of Reason, London, Tavistock, 1967.
The Order of Things: an Archaeology of the Human Sciences, London, Tavistock, 1970.
The Archaeology of Knowledge, London, Tavistock, 1972.
The Birth of the Clinic: an Archaeology of Medical Perception, London, Tavistock, 1973.
Discipline and Punish, London, Allen Lane, 1977.
History of Sexuality I, *An Introduction*, London, Allen Lane, 1978.

Other works

A. Sheridan, *Michel Foucault: the Will to Truth*, London, Tavistock, 1980.
C. Gordon (ed.), *Michel Foucault: Power/Knowledge*, Brighton, Harvester, 1980, a collection of Foucault's interviews, with an afterword.
M. Cousins and A. Hussain, *Michel Foucault*, London, Macmillan, 1984.

André Gunder Frank   1929–

Dependency theory has its origins in the works of Karl Pølanyi, who basically centred his analysis of economic development on the centrality of world capitalist market place and relations in shaping national power. Subsequently, in the late 1940s, Raul Prebisch, an Argentine economist at the United Nations Economic Commission on Latin America, elaborated a critique of neoclassical international economic theory. Based on the notion of comparative advantage, conventional economic theory assumed that it was mutually advantageous for northern countries to 'specialize' in manufactured goods, and southern countries in raw materials and food stuffs. Prebisch, basing his analysis on the notion of unequal exchange between centre and periphery, argued that the prices of raw materials tended to be inelastic or under downward pressure, while the prices of finished goods tended to be elastic and to move upward, resulting in a chronic transfer of economic wealth from south to north. A decade later Paul Baran, a Marxist scholar working at Stanford University, in *The Political Economy of Growth* extended Prebisch's analysis of uneven exchange to include the internal mechanism by which states and capital in dominant countries appropriate economic resources (economic surplus) from the periphery, leading to the development of the north and the under-development of the south. Baran focused on multiple international linkages between foreign investors and bankers and local exporters, landowners and political elite and argued that, given their control over markets, labour and resources, little or no capitalist development was possible and that only a socialist transformation would allow for the retention and productive investment of the economic surplus for development.

In the late 1960s Frank borrowed the international elements of Baran's complex political and economic framework, stripped it of its internal class components and popularized what became known as 'dependency theory'. Frank's argument was essentially that development and underdevelopment were not natural stages that all states go through but historical outcomes of unequal inter-state relations, the results of a long-term, large-scale process of surplus extraction and transfer from the satellites or periphery to the metropolis or centre. The outcome of this process was the 'development of under-development', of self-sustaining growth in the north and dependent underdevelopment in the south. According to Frank, the surplus extraction process was repeated internally and led to the uneven development between urban areas and the countryside. Dependence writers thereafter focused on the unity of the international economic system.

Frank's work focused on Latin America, and his polemical writings were intent on demonstrating that Latin America's periods of growth and stagnation were predominantly shaped by its external relations. He argued that economic growth coincided with periods when external ties were minimal (during world wars, depressions) and that the return of Latin America to the world market led to stagnation and crisis. Unlike Prebisch, Frank sought not to reform the terms of international trade but rather to opt out of the world market and base development on autonomous growth. While Frank's writings received a great deal of attention, for their radical prescriptions as much as for their substantive elaboration of dependency theory, other writers, mostly Latin Americans and Caribbeanists, were active in formulating and refining dependency analysis to account for what appeared anomalous occurrences – the growth of dependent capitalist countries. Fernando Cardoso, for example, formulated the notion of dependent development, thus rupturing the link between dependence and underdevelopment. He argued that the emergence of a technocratic state and local capitalists in subordinate alliance with foreign capital could provide the basis of rapid growth based on long-term, large-scale investment and external financing, particularly in a country like Brazil with a large internal market. Other writers further criticized the Frank dependence perspective by arguing that, while all Third World countries were or are dependent, dependence alone did not explain why some developed and others did not, particularly in Asia. Neo-dependence writers attempted to formulate a model which combined an analysis of external relations with internal class forces to determine the divergent outcomes of dependence. The focus in these writings was on the way in which internal forces disposed of externally earned wealth.

In retrospect, the major contribution of dependency theory was its critique of parochial ethnocentric perspectives in modernization theory, which focused on isolated nation states in an ahistorical fashion and which attributed underdevelopment to internal backwardness, i.e. the 'traditionalism' of the south, and overlooked the asymmetrical nature of global power relations. Likewise, dependency theory called into question the optimistic assumption of post-Second World War policy-makers who believed in the linear process of development, that the north was the mirror of the south. Dependency theory brought history back into the analysis, describing the institutional constraints on long-term development, identifying colonial and post-colonial forms of income and resource appropriation and their negative impact on the productive systems of the south. Dependence forced development writers to examine the unequal relations of power between states and not merely to make an inventory of quantitative differences in socio-economic indices. Finally, and more controversially, dependency theory forced Third World policy-makers to focus on developing internal resources and to consider the long-term costs of externally funded development agendas – advice that was, unfortunately, largely disregarded, as is evident in the 1980s, particularly among Latin America's heavily indebted countries. What dependency theory lacked was a clear theory of non-dependent growth, thus giving it the appearance of a political critique rather than a programme for practical policy. Moreover the divergent experiences among dependent countries – the spectacular growth of Korea,

as well as the regressive pattern in Mexico and Brazil – suggested that problems of underdevelopment and development required a more comprehensive framework which examined how inflows of capital were utilized as well as how much capital flowed outward. In this sense, dependency theory appears most useful not as a comprehensive theory but as a heuristic tool, providing insights into specific problem areas and generating hypotheses, rather than providing the totalistic explanations it originally claimed.

See also

Baran, Cardoso, Pølanyi, Prebisch.

Works

Capitalism and Underdevelopment in Latin America, New York, Monthly Review Press, 1967.
Latin America: Underdevelopment and Revolution, New York, Monthly Review Press, 1969.

Other works

Dudley Seers (ed.), *Dependency Theory: a Critical Reassessment*, London, Pinter, 1981.
Sing C. Chew and Robert A. Denemark (eds.), *The Underdevelopment of Development: Essays in Honor of André Gunder Frank*, Thousand Oaks, California, Sage, 1996.

Paulo Freire   1921–1997

Paulo Freire is one of the best known and most influential of Latin American educational thinkers and practitioners, as well as one of the most creative and controversial. Born in Recife, capital of the state of Pernambuco, in the north-east of Brazil, Freire was the creator of a methodological approach which combined the teaching of adult literacy with a critical appraisal of social, economic and political structures; which combined learning processes with the mobilization and organization of the poorer groups in society, in order to overcome situations of dependence, poverty and underdevelopment.

Freire's method is known as the conscientization method of adult education. His pedagogical theory is known worldwide as the pedagogy of the oppressed, or, more recently, as pedagogy for liberation. Both his theoretical and methodological proposals inspired significant literacy campaigns in Latin America, later adopted by various grass-roots movements on a global scale and by the revolutionary government in Nicaragua. At the same time the interpretation of both the theory and the practice of consciousness-raising and political organization among deprived groups has varied greatly in different social, economic and cultural contexts.

Freire's theory is built upon the critical analysis of existing relationships among the educated and uneducated, educators and students. By means of analogy he compared these relationships to those existing in society among the oppressors and the oppressed. He adopted neo-Marxist theories of ideological reproduction theories (such as that of Louis Althusser) from developed capitalist countries to criticize educational systems as one of the ideological apparatuses of the state. In addition, he proposed alternative means by which deprived groups and social minorities may become active participants in socially relevant learning processes, learn to think critically, and participate as a literate and informed citizenry in public affairs. More recently Freire's theory and practice moved beyond straightforward reproductivism towards a wider conception of education and the educational systems of modern societies, in which any educational space, within or outside the school system, is seen as potentially valuable for the promotion of critical consciousness and active participation.

Freire's method was first used in literacy campaigns in several Latin American countries in search of economic growth, social equity and the democratization of sociopolitical systems. Brazil, Chile, Peru and Nicaragua under the Sandinistas (and to a lesser degree Colombia and Ecuador) are among those countries which incorporated Freire's method into governmental educational policy as part of a wider movement towards social, political and economic change. In most of those countries, however, Freire's approach to adult education has never been fully implemented as an alternative educational paradigm.

Ultimately the developmentalist models of the 1960s led to the imposition of authoritarian styles of development and government in much of Latin America, and Freire himself lived in exile for almost twenty years. In many Latin American countries the method was transformed into a mere literacy technique and his more fundamental ideas about participation and empowerment were treated as subversive.

At the same time, and perhaps necessarily, given this context, Freire's ideas and methods have taken on an ideological aura. Several studies of his ideas and method in practice suggested that, whether on account of conceptual or methodological weaknesses or owing to political obstacles, genuine conscientization often hardly took place; or, if it did, it did so more among a limited number of popular leaders than in deprived groups as a whole. Ongoing experience raises a series of questions as to what concrete results might be achieved through the application of his ideas and methods in different political and cultural milieux. There are only a few studies which present clearly and attempt to clarify the objectives, methodology and possibilities of the so-called conscientization movement as a whole. Freire himself from time to time discussed the practice of the movement in different contexts, as well as his own theoretical evolution, which was also influenced by recent educational developments in the Latin American countries.

Freire returned to Brazil, from exile, in the early 1980s. In 1991 he was Secretary of Education for the city of São Paulo, where he lived and lectured. His later concerns had to do with the educational performance of children from lower-income groups, as well as with that of children and adults who cannot participate in an increasingly technically demanding society. Neither, he argued, can perform their duties or articulate their rights as part of an informed citizenry.

As technological progress accelerates, conscientization in theory and in practice continues to be an unfinished agenda. The ideological aura surrounding Freire's work has yet to be demystified, and conscientization (real or alleged) is pursued by groups and agencies with widely differing social and economic objectives. The pedagogy of the oppressed is still more a research agenda than a coherent movement. Its theoreticians and practitioners, though, are united by dedication to the education of underprivileged people in developing (and developed) societies, and to the transformation of social relationships in the classroom as a necessary prelude to the introduction of social, economic and political changes in the larger society.

See also

Althusser.

Works

Education for Critical Consciousness, New York, Seabury Press, 1973.
Pedagogy in Process: the Letters to Guinea-Bissau, trans. Carman St John Hunter, New York, Continuum, 1983.
The Politics of Education: Culture, Power, and Liberation, trans. Donaldo Macedo, Hadley, Mass., Bergin & Garvey, 1985.
Pedagogy of the Oppressed, trans. Myra Bergman Ramos, New York, Continuum, 1986.

Sigmund Freud   1856–1939

Though Sigmund Freud eschewed politics, his influence on twentieth-century political thought has been profound. Freud was not merely the discoverer of a technique for healing mental ills but the originator of a major paradigm shift in the self-perception of society. Psychoanalysis represented the emergence of an epoch of psychological reflection, one of whose effects was to provide a radically different framework for the conceptualization of human consciousness and interaction. Although psychoanalysis has become largely funnelled into the profession of psychotherapy, Freud vociferously opposed this contraction of his vision. He regarded psychoanalysis as a complete synthesis of biology, psychology and sociology. From this perspective innumerable political phenomena came into view and found their explanation. Beyond any particular theme enunciated by Freud, however, are two general notions – one authentic and the other dubious – which have profoundly influenced political thought.

Freud's most important contribution was his systematization of the notion of the repressed unconscious, irrespective of any contents which may be found in that unconscious. This offered a revolutionizing perspective on politics because it added a dimension of hidden meaning to any phenomenon. More, it tied that meaning to other spheres of life, such as childhood, the family and sexuality, which had been at best residual categories in traditional political discourse. Thus one could gain deeper insight into questions such as authority, charisma and nationalism, in which non-rational forces come into play. On a larger scale still, Freud enabled political theory to transcend the limitations of rationalism itself. Not since Plato had such systematic cognizance been taken of the role played by irrational forces in human affairs. For a twentieth century which has witnessed the emergence of the irrational in politics with horrifying force the dimension introduced by Freud has proved of extraordinary usefulness.

The more dubious general notion to have been drawn from Freud – and one which he played no small role in perpetuating himself – may be regarded as an ideological distortion of his principal contribution. For all the brilliance of his insight into the human condition, Freud remained remarkably obtuse concerning the nature of ideology, including, most pointedly, the ideologies inherent in psychoanalysis itself, which he persistently regarded as a neutral, value-free and objective science. Thus armed, he saw fit to ride roughshod over

73

the conceptual ground of history and politics. The results may be summed up under the rubrics of 'biologism' and 'psychologism'. Freud's biologism was reinforced by his medical training and the mechanical–biological synthesis of late nineteenth-century thought. It lay in giving primacy to genetically transmitted patterns of human behaviour. (He even believed in Lamarckianism – the inheritance of acquired characteristics.) And his psychologism was the according of primacy to fantasy over actuality. Freud felt that the model of psychoanalytic therapy – wherein action in the world is stilled in order to become conscious of what had been unconscious – was a distinctly superior mode of endeavour to any attempt to transform reality through political action. This combined shift of emphasis away from more material determinants such as class or the structures of state power plays a conservative ideological role because it focuses upon what cannot be changed or on what is purely individual as against social. Freud thus becomes the great avatar of the fundamentally conservative doctrine that 'the political is the personal'.

There are two main features of Freud's thought wherein his political insights as well as ideology are embedded. The first is his assertion, made in *Group Psychology and the Analysis of the Ego*, that group and social psychology are fundamentally individual psychology writ large. Thus the notions of love, ambivalence, enthralment, etc., which he did so much to illuminate, came to be seen as the molecular constituents of society. The second notion is the one most famously associated with Freud's personal ideology. This was an extreme emphasis on the importance of biological and instinctual factors in human existence, and, of special importance, an interpretation of human instinct (or what would be better called 'instinctual drive') as deeply anti-civilizational.

Freud's conservatism has often been compared to that of Hobbes in its depiction of the natural state of human beings as a war of all against all, requiring authoritarian intervention. The comparison is apt but there are also substantial differences. Where Hobbes emphasized egoistic assertiveness as the mutually repelling factor in natural society, Freud insists that active hostility, embedded in instinctual aggression, is the key repellent force (while egoism is only the narcissistic expression of the instinctual drive). Freud also pays greater attention to ambivalence in human society. This is consonant with his fundamental – indeed, virtually metaphysical – need to see the world in terms of duality. Thus Freud's instinct theory devolves into the 'immortal struggle' between the forces of Eros, which bind society together, and Thanatos, the instinct of death, which generates destructiveness. As elaborated in *Civilization and its Discontents*, his major political work, society is subject to the bivalent instinctual dynamic of love and hate, the result of which is the accumulation of guilt over time. It is this guilt, embedded in the 'cultural superego', which produces the 'discontent' people experience in advanced society – but is also the instrument of civilization itself. Moreover, Freud sees the salvation of the human species emerging in the slow but inexorable growth of science and technical rationality rather than authoritarianism. This view was most fully elaborated in his critique of religion, *Future of an Illusion*.

On a more concrete level, Freud's instinctual dualism and tragic–stoic view of human being was contained in his most famous formulation, that of the Oedipus complex, i.e. incestuous love for one parent, jealous hatred of the other. Freud holds the Oedipus complex as universal, because it reflects innate instinctual ambivalence as played out in the framework of childhood in a bigendered social reality. Indeed, he was so concerned to establish its essentiality that in *Totem and Taboo*, one of his most frankly speculative – and wildly inaccurate – works, Freud claimed to have established a phylogenetic (as well as Lamarckian) basis for the Oedipus complex in a prehistorical totemic slaying and cannibalistic incorporation of a 'Primal Father' by his tribe of sons.

However ideological these formulations may have been (Freud wrote *Totem and Taboo*, for example, following the defection of Jung and Adler from his 'tribe' of psychoanalysts), there can be little doubt that the Oedipus complex epitomizes a dialectic of authority, submission and rebelliousness inherent to class society. The question remains – which only concrete study can establish – as to the essential, innate character of the complex, as against whether it reflects the internalization of a historical arrangement. It goes without saying that the former alternative, which is Freud's, represents the conservative point of view, while the latter would be the view of progressives.

To summarize, in the near run Freud sees humanity as so beset by infantile thinking and instinctual passion as to be incapable of genuine civilization. Only in a remote and by no means guaranteed future will the triumph of technical-instrumental reason produce some kind of reconciliation within humanity and between humanity and nature.

Freud's personal politics were considerably less colourful than his theories. As a young man he desired power, idealizing the Spanish *conquistadores* and Hannibal, the Semitic conqueror of Rome. These urges were soon channelled into his professional medical work, where they undoubtedly drove him onward across the dark seas of his inner exploration. Meanwhile Freud lived an impeccably bourgeois life in all outer aspects. He disliked Bolshevism, showed no interest in Marx (whom he greatly misunderstood), was a lukewarm Zionist (though highly conscious of his Judaism) and engaged chiefly in the politics of the psychoanalytic movement he founded. This he strove arduously to keep free of left-wing influence. Expelled after the Nazi take-over of Austria, Freud ended his days in London.

Whatever his personal proclivities, Freud's theories are rich and subtle enough to offer provenance for a spectrum of political views ranging from conservative to far left. Undoubtedly it has been those representing the former who have prevailed in appropriating the father of psychoanalysis as a sybilline figure pronouncing the original sin of destructive instinct. Thus Freud's most explicitly conservative work, *Civilization and its Discontents*, is the one most widely read in American universities. His name is perhaps the one most widely appealed to by those who need to rationalize the injustices and inequalities of society by invoking 'human nature'.

On the other hand, Freud's essential materialism and his deeply critical attitude towards the established social order, which he recognized as incapable of bringing about happiness, have also provided an opening towards a left interpretation. This has developed the notion of instinctual drive by emphasizing its erotic rather than destructive aspect as essential, and has forged psychoanalysis into an emancipatory discourse which links Freud with Marx. The names of Wilhelm Reich and Herbert Marcuse are the best known of this minority.

See also

Adler, Reich, Marcuse.

Works

Totem and Taboo, 1913, in *The Standard Edition of the Complete Psychological Works of Sigmund Freud*, twenty-four volumes, ed. J. Strachey, London, Hogarth Press, 1953–73, XIII, pp. 1–68.
Group Psychology and the Analysis of the Ego, 1921, XVIII, pp. 65–144.
Future of an Illusion, 1927, XXI, pp. 1–56.
Civilization and its Discontents, 1930, XXI, pp. 57–146.

Other works

Herbert Marcuse, *Eros and Civilization*, Boston, Mass., Beacon Press, 1966.
Paul Ricoeur, *Freud and Philosophy*, New Haven, Conn., Yale University Press, 1970.
William McGrath, *Freud's Discovery of Psychoanalysis*, Ithaca, N.Y., Cornell University Press, 1986.
Peter Gay, *Freud: a Life for our Time*, New York, Norton, 1988.

Erich Fromm   1900–1980

Erich Fromm, who was born in Frankfurt, studied psychology, sociology and philosophy at the universities of Frankfurt and Heidelberg, receiving his Ph.D. from Frankfurt in 1922, and was trained in psychoanalysis at the Berlin Institute. In 1932 he published his first articles on social character, proposing the integration of Freud's theory of character with Marx's theory of social forces, thus explaining how people develop the motivation required by a particular economic system and why they are attracted to particular ideas, ideals and ideologies.

From 1928 to 1938 Fromm was associated with the Institute for Social Research, first at the University of Frankfurt, then at its residence in exile, Columbia University. In 1934 Fromm emigrated to the United States to escape the Nazis and lectured at the New School for Social Research, Yale University, Columbia University and Bennington College. He later served as chairman of the faculty of the William Alanson White Institute of Psychiatry, Psychoanalysis and Psychology.

In 1951 Fromm became a professor at the National University of Mexico, where he founded the Mexican Institute of Psychoanalysis. There he initiated a study of peasant social character and argued that development required not only economic opportunities but also education to overcome submissiveness and hopelessness and deeply rooted unproductive attitudes. For the next twenty years he spent most of his time in Mexico, travelling regularly to the United States to lecture and give seminars. In 1971 he moved to Locarno, in Switzerland, where he died.

Fromm first experimented with a new method of studying social character in 1931 at the Institute for Social Research at the University of Frankfurt. His immediate interest was knowing how many German workers and employees were reliable fighters against Nazism. In their political opinions respondents were all anti-Nazis. However, a different picture emerged when Fromm and his co-workers distinguished opinions from convictions rooted in the character structure. Only 15 per cent had deep-rooted democratic emotional attitudes, while 10 per cent expressed a strong authoritarian character. The majority, despite socialist or communist ideology and anti-Nazi views, had enough authoritarian traits for Fromm to believe that they would not actively oppose the Nazis once they were in power. These early studies resulted in *Escape from Freedom*, which explained man's unconscious fear of freedom and the appeal of authoritarian political systems. This book, the first to gain Fromm a large general readership, influenced generations of college students and helped to shape intellectual consciousness in America.

Fromm evaluated society according to whether or not its institutions stimulate healthy character development. From this point of view the normal is not the ideal, since normality may describe a social character with pathological elements, as in the authoritarian character. In a number of his books, especially *The Sane Society*, Fromm analyses modern industrial society – both its capitalistic and its socialistic versions – and concludes that bureaucratic mechanistic institutions cause dehumanization and alienation from the self.

For Fromm the total practice of life – at work, in the family, as a citizen and in cultural activity – influences character development. Human development requires above all a society that satisfies the need for security, justice and freedom – not only freedom from exploitation and tyranny but also freedom to participate actively and responsibly, to create and construct.

In 1959 Fromm wrote a manifesto for the Socialist Party of the United States, and in 1965 he edited a collection of papers by sociologists and philosophers on socialist humanism. He viewed Marx as a humanist and believed that Marx's concept of man and society was misinterpreted both by those who felt threatened by his programme and by many socialists, led by those in the Soviet Union, who believed that his goal was exclusively material affluence for all and that Marxism differed from capitalism only in its methods, which were supposedly more efficient and could be initiated by the working class.

Along with criticizing the industrial–bureaucratic system in both the West and the communist world, Fromm was active as a leader of the peace movement. In the early 1960s he spoke out for arms control and disarmament and opposed the war in Vietnam.

Fromm was criticized (Schaar, 1961) as a utopian whose view of human nature was overly benign and who did not take sufficient account of the realities of power. In fact, while optimistic about human nature and its capacity for creative growth, Fromm, as much as or more than any other psychologist of his time, focused on destructiveness and the potential for ending human life on this planet. Although his concept of health was demanding, and his view of the good society seemed sketchy at times, Fromm supported positive moves in the direction of health and sanity, particularly reforms in work and education that stimulated active participation. However, he believed that in an age of nuclear weapons and dehumanizing bureaucratic organization the danger of destruction from detached and over-intellectualized leaders was great. Preserving the world would ultimately require radical changes in the social system to increase economic democracy and affirm a human ideal based on 'being' rather than 'having'.

Works

'The method and function of an analytic social psychology', 1932, in *The Crisis of Psychoanalysis*, New York, Holt, 1970, pp. 110–34.
'Psychoanalytic characterology and its relevance for social psychology', 1932, in *The Crisis of Psychoanalysis*, New York, Holt, 1970, pp. 135–59.
Escape from Freedom, 1941, reprinted New York, Holt, 1960.
Man for Himself: an Inquiry into the Psychology of Ethics, New York, Rinehart, 1947.

The Sane Society, 1955, reprinted New York, Holt, 1962.
(ed.) *Marx's Concept of Man*, 1961, reprinted New York, Ungar, 1966.
May Man Prevail? An Inquiry into the Facts and Fictions of Foreign Policy, Garden City, N.Y., Doubleday, 1961.
(ed.) *Socialist Humanism: an International Symposium*, Garden City, N.Y., Doubleday, 1965.
Social Character in a Mexican Village: a Sociopsychoanalytic Study (with Michael Maccoby), Englewood Cliffs, N.J., Prentice-Hall, 1970.
The Anatomy of Human Destructiveness, New York, Holt, 1973.
To Have or to Be? New York, Harper, 1976.
The Working Class in Weimar Germany, Cambridge, Mass., Harvard University Press, 1984.

A paperback edition of Fromm's major works was published by Fawcett, New York, 1977.

Other works

John H. Schaar, *Escape from Authority: the Perspectives of Erich Fromm*, New York, Basic, 1961.

John Kenneth Galbraith 1908–

Born in Ontario, Galbraith made his most distinctive mark as a critic of American society. A pillar of the liberal wing of the Democratic Party, he is the most widely read (and viewed) social scientist of his time. Unlike his counterpart and adversary Milton Friedman (whose television series *Free to Choose* was a less successful response to Galbraith's own *The Age of Uncertainty*), Galbraith is not greatly respected by his professional peers for any technical accomplishment; an unsurprising circumstance, in that his work implicitly or explicitly, and with mordant wit, criticizes his fellow economists for their reliance on an individualistic, rationalistic, free-market model of economic decision-making that falsifies social reality.

Galbraith's work is best understood as a culmination of the American legal realist tradition which, whether in the form of Oliver Wendell Holmes's or Jerome K. Frank's jurisprudential theories, or in the institutional analyses of Adolph A. Berle and Thurman Arnold, always insisted on the mythological underpinnings of (in Galbraith's famous phrase) 'the conventional wisdom'. Berle, in *The Modern Corporation and Private Property* (with Gardiner C. Means), had introduced the notion of 'the separation of ownership and control', arguing that most modern corporations were controlled by professional managers rather than by founding families or other major shareholders. Arnold, in *The Folklore of Capitalism* (and in *Symbols of Government*), ridiculed the small-business or agrarian orientation of American populism, especially its fixation on anti-trust policies, pointing out that the most important source of American economic productivity was organized, big business. Trust-busting could only be an exercise in political obfuscation; in the end monopolies or oligopolies, regulated by government, would always be called on to do the essential work of society.

Galbraith's first major work, *American Capitalism*, built upon and extended the acceptance of bigness by these and other theorists of the New Deal. In it he argued that large-scale organizations – the giant firm, the trade union, the retailing chain, the factory farm – had effectively replaced the (now largely mythical) perfectly competitive individual firm of economics textbooks. However, the economic and political dangers of monopoly and oligopoly could be avoided, because bigness checked bigness: 'countervailing power' – a phrase that has become common currency – would prevent political domination by any one sector. Together with the work of other contemporary political scientists, especially Earl Latham, David Truman and Robert Dahl, *American Capitalism* helped set a pluralist agenda for American social science that was to last into the 1960s.

Galbraith's next major intervention, *The Affluent Society*, suggested a different but equally influential analysis. In this widely read work Galbraith asserted that American capitalism had 'solved' the age-old problem of poverty, in the sense that traditional mass poverty had been replaced by mass affluence (even if pockets of real poverty remained).

The real problem, and the real agenda for action, was public squalor in the midst of private affluence: an impoverished and run-down public sector that left important components of the good life unrealizable and thus vitiated the material accomplishments of private enterprise. At the same time Galbraith attacked free-market theory at its root by arguing that the wants which fuel privatized consumption are formed not endogenously but exogenously, via the efforts of advertising and public relations.

By calling liberalism away from its traditional redistributive emphasis Galbraith again, as in *American Capitalism*, masked a potentially radical programme with what looked like complacency. In fact, though, his attack on advertising is at the heart of recent critiques of consumer culture; and the analysis of contemporary poverty as insular and parochial rather than endemic was not strikingly different from that of the socialist Michael Harrington in his equally influential *The Other America*. Indeed, Galbraith and Harrington together were the most important intellectual influences on Lyndon Johnson's 'Great Society', and Galbraith was a speech writer for the President until his criticism of the Vietnam War became unacceptable.

In *The New Industrial Society* Galbraith extended the analysis of *American Capitalism*, but now the somewhat Pollyanna-ish pluralism of the earlier work was replaced by evident cynicism about the power and performance of big business. Building on the work of Berle and Means (which, although greatly overstated, remains central to any understanding of the modern corporate world), he repeated his earlier argument about the centrality of bigness, then advanced a new postulate about the technologically advanced industrial corporation: that, far from being a market competitor driven by the profit-seeking orientation of its owners, it is actually a miniature planned economy oriented around the search for organizational stability and longevity. Policy-making, whether in the corporation or in the government, is thus dominated by what he calls 'the technostructure', the managers, engineers and other experts in both the public and the private sectors. Democratic control and accountability of the technostructure are largely a myth, as, given the purposive (if not conspiratorial) and self-centred behaviour of corporate managers, is any notion of a benign 'invisible hand'. Although Galbraith has since acknowledged that he understated the persistence and contribution of small business to the modern economy, he has not retreated from the essentials of this analysis.

Galbraith has never called himself a 'socialist'; he is considered the doyen of American liberalism. His analysis of the relationship between business and government, however, fits well with Harrington's remark that in practice capitalism means 'socialism for the few, free enterprise for the many'; Galbraithian demystification of free-market pretensions marks the boundary where classical liberalism begins to desert its attachment to private enterprise for a serious flirtation with the idea of public regulation and control of the economy. Together with the commitment to enriching rather than impoverishing the public sector, this probably defines the attainable limit of social democracy in the late twentieth century. Only a lack of any visionary insight beyond his scathing cynicism (and, perhaps, a level of literate wit unparalleled in a social scientist) has kept Galbraith from being acknowledged as a political thinker of the first rank.

See also

Arnold, Berle, Dahl, Harrington.

Works

American Capitalism, Boston, Mass., Houghton Mifflin, 1952.
The Affluent Society, Boston, Mass., Houghton Mifflin, 1958.
The Liberal Hour, Boston, Mass., Houghton Mifflin, 1960.
The New Industrial State, Boston, Mass., Houghton Mifflin, 1967.

Economics and the Public Purpose, Boston, Mass., Houghton Mifflin, 1973.
Almost Everyone's Guide to Economics (with Nicole Salinger), Boston, Mass., Houghton Mifflin, 1978.
The Culture of Contentment, Boston, Mass., Houghton Mifflin, 1992.
The Good Society: the Humane Agenda, Boston, Mass., Houghton Mifflin, 1996.

Other works

Charles Henry Hession, *John Kenneth Galbraith and his Critics*, New York, New American Library, 1972.

Mohandas Karamchand Gandhi 1869–1948

M. K. Gandhi, also known as the Mahatma (Great Soul), was born in Porbander, India, into a political family, both his father and grandfather having been Prime Ministers to the rulers of two adjacent and tiny princely states. After a mediocre career at school he went to London to train as a lawyer. He returned to India three years later not only legally qualified but also better informed about and more critical of his religion. After an indifferent legal practice he left for South Africa in 1893 as legal adviser to an Indian firm. During his stay there of twenty years he conducted several partially successful campaigns against racist laws and developed his well-known method of *satyāgraha* or non-violent resistance.

Within five years of his return to India he had become the unquestioned leader of the independence movement. Almost single-handed, he transformed the middle and upper-class Indian National Congress into a powerful national organization, bringing in large sections of such hitherto excluded groups as women, traders, merchants, the upper and middle peasantry and youth. Convinced that independence had no meaning without a radical moral and social transformation, Gandhi launched a comprehensive programme of national regeneration. He declared war on many an ugly social practice, especially untouchability. He fostered among his countrymen the much-needed qualities of courage, self-respect, compassion, social justice and truthfulness. He gave Hinduism a long overdue activist and social orientation, generously borrowed from other religious and cultural traditions and became an inspiring example of a genuine inter-faith and inter-civilizational dialogue. Realizing that reason was often impotent in political life and that violence was fraught with horrendous consequences and subject to an inflationary spiral, he developed a new 'science of non-violence' involving moral conversion of the opponent by a delicate 'surgery of the soul'.

While fighting simultaneously on the social, economic, religious and political fronts, Gandhi carried on an even fiercer battle at the personal level. Determined to become as perfect as any human being could be, he set about mastering all his senses and desires. He conquered love of food, even hunger, anger, greed, possessiveness, ill will, jealousy, pettiness and so on, and felt literally sick at anything base and dishonourable. From 1901 onward he embarked on daring experiments in sexual self-control. Rejecting the 'cowardly' celibacy of traditional religions, he lived among and later slept naked with women both to probe the outermost limits of sexuality and to show that it was possible to attain 'absolute' and childlike innocence. His moral courage, candour and experimental vitality have few if any parallels in history.

Though born a *bania*, there was a powerful and endearing streak of the gambler and outlaw in him. When Hindus and Muslims were busy butchering one another in 1947 he moved among them alone and unprotected, dared them to do their worst, and by sheer force of personality consoled the inconsolable, dissolved hatred and restored a climate of humanity. When a bomb was dropped at one of his prayer meetings a few weeks later he did not bat an eyelid, continued his discourse and chided the audience for being scared of a 'mere bomb'. When the government of independent India decided, with popular support, to renege on its promise to

transfer to Pakistan its share of assets, he took on the entire country and successfully fasted to awaken its sense of honour and moral obligation. This deeply angered a section of Hindu nationalists, one of whom, after respectfully bowing to him, shot him dead at a prayer meeting.

Gandhi's moral and political thought was based on a relatively simple metaphysic. For him the universe was regulated by a Supreme Intelligence or Principle which he preferred to call *satya* (Truth) and, as a concession to convention, God. It was embodied in all living beings, above all men, in the form of self-conscious soul or spirit.

Since all men partook of divine essence, they were all 'ultimately one'. They were not merely equal but 'identical'. As such, love was the only proper form of relation between them; it was 'the law of our being', of 'our species'. Positively love implied care and concern for others and total dedication to the cause of 'wiping away every tear from every eye'. Negatively it implied *ahimsa*, or non-violence. Gandhi's entire social and political thought was an attempt to work out the implications of the principle of love in all areas of life.

For Gandhi the state 'represented violence in a concentrated form'. It spoke in the language of compulsion and uniformity, sapped its subjects' spirit of initiative and self-help, and 'unmanned' them. Since men were not yet morally developed and capable of acting in a socially responsible manner, the state was necessary. However, if it was not to hinder their growth it had to be so organized that it used as little coercion as possible and left as large an area of human life as possible to voluntary efforts.

As Gandhi imagined it, a truly non-violent society was federally constituted and composed of small, self-governing and relatively self-sufficient village communities relying largely on moral and social pressure. The police were basically social workers, enjoying the confidence and support of the local community and relying on moral suasion and public opinion to enforce the law. Crime was treated as a disease, requiring not punishment but understanding and help. The standing army was not necessary, either, as a determined people could be relied upon to mount non-violent resistance against an invader and die rather than lose their freedom.

Since majority rule violated the moral integrity of the minority and 'savoured of violence', and since unanimity was often impossible, all decisions in a non-violent society were based on a consensus arrived at by rational discussion in which each strove to look at the subject in question from the standpoint of others. For Gandhi rational discussion was not just an exchange of arguments but a process of deepening and expanding consciousness and widening the intellectual and moral parameters of one's world. When it was at its best, those involved reconstituted each other's being and were reborn as a result of the encounter. In extreme cases, when no consensus was possible, the majority decided the matter, not because it was more likely to be right but for administrative and pragmatic reasons. If a citizen felt morally troubled by a majority decision he was entitled to claim exemption from and even to disobey it. Civil disobedience was a 'moral' right. To surrender it was to forfeit one's 'self-respect' and integrity.

A non-violent society was committed to *sarvodaya*, the growth or uplift of all its citizens. Private property denied the 'identity' or 'oneness' of all men, and was immoral. In Gandhi's view it was a 'sin against humanity' to possess superfluous wealth when others could not even meet their basic needs. Since the institution of private property already existed, and men were attached to it, he suggested that the rich should take only what they needed and hold the rest in trust for the community. Increasingly he came to appreciate that the idea of trusteeship was too important to be left to the precarious goodwill of the rich, and suggested that it could be enforced by law on the recalcitrant. He advocated heavy taxes, limited rights of

inheritance, state ownership of land and heavy industry, and nationalization without compensation as a way of creating a just and equal society.

Gandhi's intellectual influence on his countrymen was considerable. Though none accepted all his ideas, none rejected them all, either. Some were attracted by his emphasis on political and economic decentralization; others by his insistence on individual freedom, moral integrity, the unity of means and ends and social service; yet others by his *satyāgraha* and political activism. Not even such ardent Marxists as M. N. Roy, J. P. Narayan and Jawaharlal Nehru could resist the appeal of some of his ideas. For some students of India Gandhi's influence is responsible for the emasculation of the left and a source of the country's misfortune. For others it successfully inoculated India against collectivism, violence, uncritical obedience to the law and excessive reliance on the state, and accounts for its political vitality, moderation and democratic government.

See also

Narayan, Roy.

Works

The Collected Works of Mahatma Gandhi, Ahmedabad, Navajivan, 1958.
The Moral and Political Writings of Mahatma Gandhi, ed. R. Iyer, three volumes, Oxford, Clarendon Press, 1986.

Other works

J. Bondurant, *Conquest of Violence: The Gandhian Philosophy of Conflict*, Berkeley, Cal., University of California Press, 1965.
B. Parekh, *Gandhi's Political Philosophy: a Critical Examination*, London, Macmillan, 1989.
B. Parekh, *Colonialism, Tradition and Reform: an Analysis of Gandhi's Political Discourse*, London, Sage, 1989.

Marcus Garvey   1887–1940

In the decade before the First World War the United States was extremely hostile to most

African-Americans. By that date the failure of the promise of Reconstruction was evident. The passage of the Thirteenth, Fourteenth and Fifteenth Amendments had not extended citizenship or, in any real way, political and economic rights to blacks. In the wake of increased lynchings in the 1880s, blacks began to flee the south. Some went to the Mid-west, others considered Africa, still others went to northern urban communities. In the northern urban communities blacks faced hostility from the white power structure and from recent immigrants from Europe. Each ethnic group formed its respective communities, or 'ghettos'; however, blacks were never integrated into the larger white society. In response to such racial discrimination, blacks formed the National Association for the Advancement of Colored People, which had some effect in bringing about legal changes. However, millions of others were outside the scope of the NAACP.

It was in this climate that Jamaican-born Marcus Garvey arrived in the United States in 1916. Ironically, he had hoped to meet Booker T. Washington; unfortunately, Washington had died the previous year. Assessing the black ghettos and the plight of their inhabitants, Garvey founded the Universal Negro Improvement Association. The UNIA was founded on pride in Africa, its culture, its history, and pride in the Negro race. Additionally, Garvey believed in a variation of Booker T. Washington's self-help programme, namely that blacks should establish their own businesses, become self-sufficient within New York's Harlem and other urban and rural communities throughout the United States.

Like Washington, Garvey was an orator: 'Education is the medium by which a people are prepared for the creation of their own particular civilization, and the advancement and glory of their own race. . . . Let Africa be our guiding Star – OUR STAR OF DESTINY. . . . We of the Negro Race are moving from one state of organization to another, and we shall so continue until we have thoroughly lifted ourselves into the organization of GOVERNMENT.' Philosophically, Garvey believed that blacks should segregate themselves, create their own internal government, that they might find equality. He believed in self-segregation as a means of achieving equality.

During the 1920s Garvey's UNIA was the largest mass organization for blacks in the United States, larger than the NAACP, with chapters in over thirty states. In the 1960s manifestation of Garvey's philosophies could be seen in the cries that 'Black is beautiful', 'Africa for Africans' and the Nation of Islam's call for a separate state.

See also

Washington.

Works

Philosophy and Opinions of Marcus Garvey, or, Africa for the Africans, ed. Amy Jacques-Garvey, New York, Atheneum Press, 1969.

Other works

David E. Cronon, *Black Moses: the Story of Marcus Garvey and the Universal Negro Improvement Association*, Madison, Wis., University of Wisconsin Press, 1955.
C. Eric Lincoln, *The Black Muslims in America*, Boston, Mass., Beacon Press, 1961.
E. V. Essien-Udom, *Black Nationalism: a Search for an Identity in America*, Chicago, University of Chicago Press, 1972.

Giovanni Gentile   1875–1944

Best known as the philosopher of Italian fascism, Gentile first came to prominence as the chief collaborator of Croce on the latter's cultural journal *La critica*. Born in Sicily in 1875, Gentile sought to continue the tradition of the southern Italian Hegelians. His idealist views inhibited his academic career at first, owing to the predominantly positivist philosophical climate at that time. However, together with Croce he succeeded in making idealism the dominant school of thought in

Italy and he ultimately held Chairs at Palermo, Pisa, Rome and Florence. Gentile's 'actualism' represented the subjective extreme of idealism and was arrived at through Hegelian reinterpretation of Marx – particularly the 'Theses on Feuerbach', which he translated into Italian for the first time. He aimed to integrate our consciousness of experience with its creation by uniting thought and will in the self-constitution or *autoctisi* of reality. The 'pure act' of spirit constituted the true *synthesis a priori* of self and world which made objective knowledge possible. He claimed that his theory explained the phenomenological development of self-consciousness within both the individual and Western thought as a whole. To illustrate the first thesis, he wrote a number of influential books on education. Later on he was to put his ideas into practice in the Gentile Reform of 1923 when Minister of Public Instruction under Mussolini. Demonstrating his second claim led him to write a detailed history of modern Italian philosophy in order to show how the ideas of the German thinkers that he admired were adopted or independently conceived by Italian philosophers as part of a single European tradition reflecting the unity of spirit or human consciousness.

On the political level, Gentile's theory of spirit as 'pure act' was so radically subjective that it could lead only to anarchism, in which each person's will battles it out with everyone else's, or totalitarianism, in which all wills are subordinated to the will of the ruler. Gentile's conservative sympathies resulted in him taking the latter option, and he joined the Fascist Party in 1923. Gentile became the official ideologist of fascism. In 1924 he wrote a 'Manifesto of fascist intellectuals', to which Croce penned a 'Counter-manifesto of anti-intellectual fascists', obtaining far greater support, and Mussolini was happy to put his name to Gentile's article on the party's philosophy in the *Enciclopedia Italiana*. Gentile argued that all force was moral force. By obliging all its citizens to adhere to its demands the state demonstrated its truly eth-

ical nature. He attempted to show how individuals could come voluntarily to accept the discipline of the state as an expression of their inner will, a process deriving from humanity's essentially social nature. His most successful work on the problem was his last, the *Genesis and Structure of Society*. Written in 1943 at a time when Italy was divided between the allied-occupied south and Mussolini's German puppet Fascist Social Republic in the north, which Gentile supported, he was forced perhaps to take the problem of dissent and uncoerced dialogue more seriously than in his earlier works. He was assassinated by communist partisans in Florence.

Gentile's pedagogical studies are still read by educationalists, and his history of Italian philosophy remains useful. His school and university reforms had a profound influence on the Italian education system until quite recently, and the *Enciclopedia Italiana*, which he edited, is an indispensable work of reference, constantly updated. Although after Gentile's turn to fascism they were loath to admit it, thinkers of the stature of Gramsci and Collingwood were in many respects more indebted to Gentile than to Croce, as their early writings attest.

See also

Croce, Gramsci.

Works

The Theory of Mind as Pure Act, London, Macmillan, 1922.
The Reform of Education, London, Benn, 1922.
Genesis and Stucture of Society, Urbana, Ill., University of Illinois Press, 1960.

Other works

Hugh S. Harris, *The Social Philosophy of Giovanni Gentile*, Urbana, Ill., University of Illinois Press, 1960.
Richard P. Bellamy, *Modern Italian Social Theory: Ideology and Politics from Pareto to the Present*, Cambridge, Polity Press, 1987.

Charlotte Perkins Gilman 1860–1933

Born in Hartford, Connecticut, Charlotte Perkins Gilman achieved international fame as a feminist socialist theorist with the publication in 1898 of her book *Women and Economics*, which was soon translated into seven languages. Today she is better known as the author of the chilling short story of a woman's descent into madness, 'The yellow wallpaper', published in 1892, and the witty and trenchant utopian novel *Herland*, serialized monthly in *The Forerunner* – a monthly magazine Gilman wrote and edited between 1909 and 1916 – and published as a novel in 1979.

A major critic of history and society, whose intriguing ideas have yet to be fully understood and appreciated, she sought to create a cohesive, integrated body of thought that combined socialism (she was an anti-Marxist collectivist ideologically close to the Fabians) and feminism (although she described herself not as a feminist but as a humanist, arguing that the world was masculinist and she wished to redress the balance).

In her vast body of work she tried to define a humane social order built upon values she identified as female, life-giving and nurturing. In her book-length studies in history, sociology, philosophy and ethics, as well as in her novels, poetry and short stories, she constructed a world view to explain human behaviour, past and present, and to project the outlines of her vision of the future. Her sociological and historical works analyse the past from her gender perspective, and in the fiction she illustrates the human drama and suggests the kind of world we could have if we were persuaded to remake it. She saw the first step towards resolving the world's distortions in the ideological sphere, and she saw herself engaged in a fierce struggle for the minds of women.

Gilman argued that women's subordination, which began with the expropriation by men of the agricultural surplus women produced, limited women's autonomy and therefore dehumanized them. Beginning with recorded history, women were forced to depend economically on male authority, so that it came to be believed that one entire sex should function as the domestic servants of the other. Future progress, she insisted, now required the restoration of the original balance. Subordination would end only when women led the struggle for their own autonomy and equality, thereby freeing themselves from bondage and freeing men from the distortions that come from dominance.

Gilman's own life was filled with the kinds of struggle and trauma that fed her writing, for she lived with chronic poverty and emotional instability. Soon after she had divorced her first husband she gave him and his second wife their child to rear, calling down upon herself vigorous attacks from the press and pulpit for being an unnatural mother. Eventually she was able to establish a long and enduring marriage with her first cousin, George Houghton Gilman, and to create a large and significant body of important work, attesting to her ultimate triumph over the crises that plagued her early years. In 1933 Gilman learned that she was dying of cancer. She rushed to complete her autobiography. She finished the manuscript and selected the cover but did not wait for publication before she ended her life, leaving behind a note explaining that her life's work was done, there was nothing ahead but increasing pain, she wished a dignified death and that chloroform was preferable to cancer.

Works

'The yellow wallpaper', 1892, in *The Charlotte Perkins Gilman Reader*, ed. Ann J. Lane, New York, Pantheon, 1980.

In this our World, Oakland, Cal., McCombs & Vaughn, 1893, a book of verse.

Women and Economics: a Study of the Economic Relation between Men and Women as a Factor in Social Evolution, Boston, Mass., Small Maynard, 1898, reprinted, New York, Gordon Press, 1975.

Concerning Children, Boston, Mass., Small Maynard, 1900.

The Home: its Work and Influence, New York, McClure Phillips, 1903.

Human Work, New York, McClure Phillips, 1904.
The Man-made World, or, Our Androcentric Culture, New York, Charlton, 1911.
His Religion and Hers: a Study of the Faith of our Fathers and the Work of our Mothers, New York and London, Century, 1923.
The Living of Charlotte Perkins Gilman: an Autobiography, New York and London, Appleton-Century, 1935, reprint Madison, Wis., University of Wisconsin Press, forthcoming.
Herland, ed. Ann J. Lane, New York, Pantheon, 1979.

Other works

Mary A. Hill, *Charlotte Perkins Gilman: the Making of a Radical Feminist, 1860–96*, Philadelphia, Pa, Temple University Press, 1980.
Gary Schnarnhorst, *Charlotte Perkins Gilman: a Bibliography*, Metuchen, N.J., and London, Scarecrow Press, 1985.
Polly Wynn Allen, *Building Domestic Liberty: Charlotte Perkins Gilman's Architectural Feminism*, Amherst, Mass., University of Massachusetts Press, 1988.
Ann J. Lane, *To Herland and Beyond: the Life and Work of Charlotte Perkins Gilman*, New York, Pantheon, 1990.

Emma Goldman   1869–1940

The most famous anarchist in the United States for nearly three decades prior to the First World War, Emma Goldman captured popular imagination as a symbol of working-class militance and female revolt. Born in Kovno, Lithuania, she grew up in a precariously petty-bourgeois, patriarchal Jewish family in a world bounded by Russian antisemitism, a growing revolutionary movement against tsarism and the first stirrings of Russian feminism. After attending school in Königsberg and St Petersburg, she emigrated in 1885 with an elder half-sister to Rochester, New York. Here she was radicalized by the harsh conditions of industrial capitalism and by the Haymarket tragedy (a fatal bombing at a May Day demonstration in Chicago in 1886 for which several anarchists were executed). Within a few years Goldman had emerged as one of the most charismatic and controversial speakers in the international anarchist movement, a branch of the left committed to anti-statist, anti-parliamentary, decentralized forms of socialism. Harassed by police and frequently arrested, at first because of her

association with Alexander Berkman – who had attempted to assassinate the anti-labour steel magnate Henry Clay Frick in 1892 – Goldman criss-crossed the country on spectacular annual lecture tours interrupted by several extended prison terms.

Goldman's iconoclastic anarchist vision owed much to the communist anarchism of Petr Kropotkin, which she attempted to integrate with the individualism of Nietzsche, Max Stirner, Ibsen and the American 'free lovers'. She set forth her ideas in two collections of lectures – *Anarchism and other Essays* and *The Social Significance of the Modern Drama* – and in *Mother Earth*, the monthly 'little magazine' she published between 1906 and 1918. A trenchant critic of conventional morality, Goldman denounced marriage, monogamy and the sexual double standard as inimical to women, attacking the patriarchal family as a source of female dependence and inequality. She campaigned for freely available birth control, called for freer relations between the sexes and defended the rights of homosexuals. Insisting that political and economic freedom was incomplete without sexual and social freedom as well, she urged women to free themselves from the 'internal tyrants' of repressive morality and public opinion, using lectures on literature and theatre to dramatize her arguments. She aroused further scandal by throwing herself into a tumultuous nine-year love affair with a Chicago physician, Dr Ben L. Reitman, who campaigned with her as her manager. Though she belonged only to her own *Mother Earth* group, Goldman also supported the Industrial Workers of the World in numerous strikes and free-speech fights.

Deported with Berkman in 1919 to the Soviet Union, she soon became disillusioned with the Bolsheviks. Along with many Russian anarchists, she and Berkman voluntarily left Russia in late 1921 to become ardent anti-Soviet agitators. Goldman's 1923 book *My Disillusionment in Russia* offered an emotional portrait of the civil war and early NEP period, emphasizing Bolshevik repression of dissent and the ambivalent response of Soviet Jews to Bolshevism, particularly in the Ukraine.

Goldman found herself increasingly marginalized in Great Britain and later in Canada, where she spent much of the 1920s attempting to publicize the plight of Russian political prisoners and to mobilize liberals and radicals against Soviet political repression. Despite considerable sympathy for her critique even on the left, her fierce anti-communism, her preoccupation with oppression in Russia and her relative indifference to capitalist and colonialist forms of injustice alienated potential allies outside the tiny circles of anarchists. In 1928 she withdrew to Saint-Tropez to write her autobiography, *Living my Life*, published to critical acclaim in 1931.

Though she clung to her sense of identity as a revolutionary, Goldman shared the growing post-war trend towards liberalism of many anarchists, abandoning her earlier faith in revolution in favour of a gradualist programme of 'educating the individual'. Still, inspired by the Spanish revolution of 1936, she served as agent and publicist in England for the Spanish anarcho-syndicalists during the Spanish Civil War. Following their defeat, which she blamed primarily on the communists, she travelled to Toronto in the spring of 1939 to raise money for Spanish and other refugees from fascism. After her death in May 1940 she was buried near the Haymarket martyrs in Chicago, in the country she still considered her home.

Despite her commitment to communist anarchism, Emma Goldman remained fundamentally a moralist and an individualist, proud of her identity as a 'free lance'. She oscillated between a Kropotkinite enthusiasm for the masses and a Nietzschean disdain for the 'mob', insisting on the power of ideals to motivate change and lamenting the loss of heroic values which had inspired earlier generations of revolutionaries. Although generally admired more for her courageous militance than for the originality of her ideas, Goldman synthesized many strands of European and American anarchism, feminism and sexual modernism, anticipating the concern of late twentieth-century feminists with sexuality and gender identity. Extending her analysis of domination to schools and churches, prisons, prostitution and the patriarchal family, conventional moral values and bourgeois aesthetics, she offered the broadest anarchist critique of any militant of her generation.

See also

Kropotkin.

Works

Anarchism and other Essays, New York, Mother Earth, 1911.
The Social Significance of the Modern Drama, New York, Applause Theatre, 1914.
Living my Life, New York, Da Capo Press, 1931.

Other works

Richard Drinnon, *Rebel in Paradise*, New York, Bantam, 1961.
Richard Drinnon, *Nowhere at Home: Letters from Exile of Emma Goldman and Alexander Berkman*, New York, Bantam, 1975.
David Porter, *Vision on Fire: Emma Goldman on the Spanish Revolution*, New Paltz, N.Y., Commonground Press, 1983.
Alice Wexler, *Emma Goldman in America*, Boston, Mass., Beacon Press, 1984.
Alice Wexler, *Emma Goldman in Exile*, New York, Bantam, 1989.

Paul Goodman 1911–1972

Paul Goodman leapt from obscurity to fame in 1960 with the publication of *Growing up Absurd*, a critique of American society that focused on the problems of the young and soon became a kind of handbook of the youth movement. Goodman's own political heroes were the communitarian anarchist Petr Kropotkin, the agrarian revolutionary Thomas Jefferson and Gandhi, the apostle of non-violence. Translated into contemporary

American terms and tactics, this amalgam was precisely the programme of the New Left. Although as the 1960s unfolded Leninist influences which also loomed large in the New Left, Goodman's appeal was not to this romantic vanguardism but to the more traditional idealism of the young. As one reviewer of *Growing up Absurd* put it, what was remarkable in him was his willingness to speak 'unblushingly' of old-fashioned virtues like prudence, thrift, fortitude, patriotism, honour and magnanimity while other intellectuals, although in their hearts they might believe them, were 'too sophisticated' to say such things out loud.

Because Goodman was thoroughly at home in the high culture of the West, he never questioned his right to its fruits and was able to champion it without embarrassment. He also advocated a set of fundamental social changes that were, or ought to be, the legacy of modern times; these were causes still to be won, 'unfinished revolutions' which, because they had been missed or compromised, disrupted the traditional order without arriving at a new social balance. Rather than trying to seize power, he urged the young to work towards goals that were paid lip service but not yet realized. His list ranged from pacifism and participatory democracy to syndicalism and progressive education, from the scientific revolution to human solidarity. Because Goodman was giving them permission to take their own conventional allegiances seriously some of his readers were genuinely inspired, while others were left disturbed and angry. As he wrote in his journal, this strategy 'has the effect of making my radical rejection of the *status quo* seem spectacularly conservative'.

It was Goodman's belief in the common sense of ordinary Americans that lay behind his plea for local autonomy, grounded in face-to-face community, with a more liveable balance of rural and urban values. These aims in turn entailed the return of technological choice to the jurisdiction of moral philosophy (out of the hands of the corporations and the Pentagon), reform of the lockstep educational system and revulsion from the spirit-killing mass media, devoted to a wasteful and venal standard of living.

Goodman's fifty years before emerging into the limelight were similarly full of apparent contradictions and unsettling demands on society. Born into poverty, he made his way through the public schools of Manhattan, graduating from City College in the early years of the Depression. He was not a political type but an artist and a philosopher – the college yearbook named him 'best poet'. His elder sister supported him for a few years while he carried his stories from editor to editor on his bicycle, saving postage. In 1936 a former teacher invited him to study for his doctorate at the University of Chicago, where the 'great books' experiment was in progress. He met his first wife there, read more Aristotle and Kant, and wrote a dissertation on 'The formal analysis of poems'. After three years Goodman was suddenly dismissed from his instructorship because he would not agree to be discreet about his homosexual 'cruising'.

Returning from academia with his common-law wife and a new baby, he quickly found his feet in the bohemian world of New York, becoming film critic for the independent left journal *Partisan Review* and placing fiction, plays and poems in the 'little magazines' and *avant-garde* press. But no one would publish his dissertation, nor could he land a job in the colleges. After several busy and relatively happy years, his wife left him and a year's teaching at a progressive school ended in disaster when he was accused of seducing his teenage students. As an anarchist opposed to the Second World War he defended draft-dodging and the black market, and this, along with his continued defiance of sexual *mores*, got him in trouble even with the *avant-garde*, so that he found himself blacklisted in many quarters. He was definitely 'out of the swim', as he bitterly put it.

None the less, in addition to his steady output of *belles-lettres*, Goodman produced classics in two different professional disciplines during this period: *Communitas*, a study of city planning, written with his architect brother Percival, and *Gestalt Therapy*, a collaboration with Frederick S. Perls and Ralph Hefferline which became the cornerstone of a new school of psychotherapy. These works added to his prestige among a growing band of disciples but did not win him the popular audience or modest income he longed for. By the end of the 1940s he had remarried and had a second child to support (a third came in the 1960s) but was still living below the poverty line. Julian Beck and Judith Malina, pioneers of off-Broadway theatre, produced four of his plays at the Living Theatre, but they played to empty houses. Reduced to issuing his novels by subscription because he could not find a publisher, Goodman virtually gave up his artistic career and turned to psychotherapy, taking patients and offering training sessions as a member of the New York Institute for Gestalt Therapy. He kept a journal which he called 'Thoughts during a useless time'.

All along he had been writing for the radical press, and helped edit Dwight Macdonald's *Politics*, the anarchist groups' *Resistance*, the pacifists' *Liberation*. In the late 1950s a larger audience for social criticism had begun to develop as a result of the civil rights movement and protests against atomic testing. *Growing up Absurd* appeared at just the right moment to share, and help shape, the new thrust of political activism. Soon Goodman was travelling to dozens of colleges, where he might address graduate students of sociology in the morning, lead a seminar of urban planners in the afternoon and give the keynote speech to a conference of educators in the evening. The Institute for Policy Studies in Washington named him its first visiting fellow; he served as Distinguished Professor of Urban Affairs for a semester in Milwaukee; students at San Francisco State College appointed him an at-large faculty member, paid directly by student government. He wrote a syndicated column for campus newspapers, helped organize the New York support for draft resisters (among them his son

Mathew), and delivered a blistering 'Causerie at the military-industrial' to a conference of research and development bigwigs during the 1967 Pentagon protests. But as the war in Vietnam escalated, the youth movement lost its non-violent ethos, and Goodman became more and more estranged from his 'crazy young allies', whose heroes were Che Guevara and Mao Zedong rather than Gandhi or Jefferson. His son's death in a freak hiking accident left him inconsolable. Although he continued to make speeches and write essays on social issues, his heart was no longer in it; his last works took up more personal themes: his credo as a man of letters, reflections on his homosexual experience, theological speculations. He was culling his poems for a collected edition when he died.

Goodman believed that states and institutions interfered too much in people's lives, undermining their natural autonomy for the sake of factitious order and soulless material progress. Towards the end of his life he began referring to himself as a 'neolithic conservative' and a 'peasant anarchist'. In his last book he wrote, 'I want only that the children have bright eyes, the river be clean, food and sex be available, and nobody be pushed around.'

See also

Gandhi, Guevara, Kropotkin, Mao Zedong.

Works

Growing up Absurd, New York, Random House, 1960.
Communitas, New York, Vintage, 1960.
Utopian Essays and Practical Proposals, New York, Random House, 1962.
People or Personnel, New York, Random House, 1965.

André Gorz 1924–

André Gorz was born in Austria and has lived most of his life in France. The formative experiences of his early life are discussed in the autobiographical philosophical reflections which he wrote in 1956, translated as *The Traitor*. He was a founder of *Le Nouvel Observateur* and for many years edited *Les Temps Modernes*. Heavily influenced by the existentialism of Jean-Paul Sartre, like Sartre he sought to extend the philosophical commitment to freedom and autonomy into political theory. His work also owes much to Herbert Marcuse's writings on alienation in modern society.

His early political writings contained robust support for revolutionary working-class struggle, although he rejected the authoritarian regimes of Eastern Europe as a legitimate model for socialism in the West, and considered that the germs of that authoritarianism were to be found in the Bolshevik conception of the revolutionary party. In the 1960s, in *Strategy for Labor* and *Socialism and Revolution*, he identified and advocated the increased politicization of workers' struggles, which he believed could bring into question the very nature of capitalist power over the productive process. He supported the development of revolutionary politics by students and others outside the sphere of established party politics, and anticipated the development of worker–student links which exploded in the events in France in May 1968.

However, in articles in *Les Temps Modernes* (reprinted in *The Division of Labour*) in the early 1970s Gorz began to accept that the revolutionary potential of the working class could be effectively countered by the use of human relations management techniques. He then switched his attention to the significance of ecology as a movement which had the potential to question the whole logic on which modern capitalism was based. *Ecology as Politics* was written in the mid-1970s; it contained some exaggerated predictions but the stress it laid on the destruction of non-renewable resources, the exploitation of the Third World and the complicity of science and education are all themes which have since been taken up by radical social theorists. In *Farewell to the Working Class* he talked about the revolutionary potential of what he termed the new non-class of non-producers, spawned by labour-saving technology, and in *Paths to Paradise* he pointed to the decentralizing and re-empowering possibilities inherent in the new technological revolution. The forceful rejection of the present system was contrasted with a number of utopian models in much of his later work, but not until *Critique of Economic Reason* was he able to point to political action which might lead to the sort of transformation he desired. Returning to some of the themes from the 1960s, in particular the ideological power exercised in the control of work processes, he praised the campaigns to reduce the working week, and urged unions to link their struggle with other movements which sought to win the right of individuals to control their own lives.

See also

Marcuse, Sartre.

Works

Strategy for Labor: a Radical Proposal, Boston, Mass., Beacon Press, 1967.
Socialism and Revolution, London, Allen Lane, 1975.
The Division of Labour, Brighton, Harvester, 1976.
Farewell to the Working Class: an Essay on Post-industrial Socialism, London, Pluto Press, 1982.
Ecology as Politics, London, Pluto Press, 1983.
Paths to Paradise: on the Liberation from Work, London, Pluto Press, 1985.
The Traitor, London, Verso, 1989.
Critique of Economic Reason, London, Verso, 1989.

Other works

Boris Frankel, *The Post-industrial Utopians*, Cambridge, Polity, 1986.
Vincent Geoghegan, *Utopianism and Marxism*, London, Methuen, 1987.

Antonio Gramsci   1891–1937

Gramsci was one of the most original and innovative of the twentieth-century political theorists working within the Marxist tradition. Born in Sardinia, and suffering from a malformation of the spine and ill health which dogged him throughout his life, he won a scholarship to study in Turin, where he first made contact with the proletarian movement, and came under the influence of Benedetto Croce (the idealist philosopher of culture) and Labriola (a leading philosopher of Italian socialism). Joining the Italian Socialist Party (PSI), he became a full-time political journalist and organizer for the workers' movement in Turin, and during this time first met and became a collaborator of such leading figures in Italian socialist politics as Bordiga and Togliatti. His political writing covers an extremely wide range, including literature, drama, education, the question of the national language and other aspects of Italian national cultural life.

Gramsci played a leading role in the strike movements and factory occupations which racked Italy in the immediate post-First World War years. He founded the socialist weekly review *Ordine Nuovo* and became the principal theorist of the new 'factory council movement'. He was a founder member of the Italian Communist Party (PCI) after its break from the PSI (1921) and went to Moscow as PCI representative to the Comintern (1922–3). He was a major contributor to the debates on strategy which dominated Italian revolutionary politics in the 1920s (including such questions as strategy towards the masses, relations between communists and the socialists, disputes between the PCI and the Comintern). He led the PCI in the difficult years following Mussolini's march on Rome and the fascist seizure of power. In the mass arrests which followed, Gramsci was imprisoned in Turin in 1926. During his long confinement he did much of the writing now collected in his *Prison Notebooks*. He became seriously ill and was moved to clinics, first in Formia, then the Quisisana, near Rome, where he died while awaiting release, at the age of forty-six.

Gramsci was a revolutionary. He combined the qualities of the political strategist and organizer with those of the political theorist. This created a unique fusion of theory and practice in all his writing. Among the seminal questions of his time which he addressed were: the nature of the revolutionary party and its role in winning popular support among the masses and in securing a leading position in Italian political life and culture; the question of the independence of 'national' communist movements *vis-à-vis* the 'vanguard role' assumed by the Comintern and the Soviet Communist Party after the Russian revolution in 1917; the uneven social development between the north and the south of Italy and the problems it presented for constructing a genuinely 'national popular' Italian state; the distinctive social development of Western European societies and the consequences of these 'peculiarities' for socialist strategy; the problem of finding an adequate response by the left to the rise of European fascism.

Most of Gramsci's work was informed by, and addressed in the first instance to, the specific historical conjuncture of Italian politics in which he was writing. This attention to the necessarily limiting conditions of 'a conjuncture' characterizes all his work. Together with the circumstances of imprisonment and censorship in which most of his essays were produced, it gives his work a fragmentary, incomplete character. Paradoxically, this may have saved his ideas from becoming embalmed in doctrinal orthodoxy. His work is suggestive rather than definitive. His insights have to be developed and reworked as they are translated to new contexts. This accounts in part for his seminal and continuing influence beyond his own lifetime. But the significance of the 'Gramscian legacy' for the second half of the twentieth century must also be attributed to two other factors. First, his distinctive, original and dogma-free expansion of the categories of the Marxist theory of politics. Second, his unique and wide-ranging conception of 'the political', which he developed in the light of the very different circumstances prevailing in the Western capitalist democracies, which presented the left with a very different terrain of struggle, and a much more complex and lasting social system, and state, than those of the Russian tsarist state which was toppled in 1917.

Gramsci always located his work, broadly, in the Marxist schema, in which the 'economic base' ultimately determines, or sets the limiting conditions for, politics, ideology and the state. But the underlying thrust of his work is consistently away from this simple form of reductionism. What he centrally addressed was the extremely complicated nature of the relations between structure and superstructure, which, he argued, could never be reduced to a mere reflection of economic conditions. His real theoretical originality lay in the series of novel concepts which he used to expand and transform our understanding of politics and 'the political'. He was greatly preoccupied with the character of state and civil society which prevailed in modern societies, especially the capitalist democracies. He challenged the reductionist conception of the state as, exclusively, a 'class' state, an instrument of ruling-class coercion and domination. He insisted on the 'educative' role of the state, its significance in constructing those alliances which could win popular support from different social strata, and its role of cultural and moral 'leadership' in modern society. He rethought the state in terms of the balance between 'coercion' and 'consent'. Similarly, he gave considerable attention to the complex structures of civil society, which, in modern societies, he saw as key sites – the 'trenches and fortifications' – of the struggle for leadership and power in society.

More generally, he expanded the conception of politics to include spheres of life and culture far removed from the narrow ground of the governing regime or parliamentary politics. Though the economic structure may be, 'in the last instance', determinative, Gramsci gave much greater autonomy to the effects of the actual conduct of the struggle for leadership, across a wide front and on a variety of sites and institutions. The conjuncture, he argued, was determined by the strategic 'balance' in the relations between all the different social forces, operating in the different sites

and institutions of national political and cultural life. The role of the party was to engage and lead in this broad, multi-faceted struggle for what he called 'hegemony' (which he distinguished from the simple rule by force of 'domination'). The shift in political strategy, dictated by modern social development, from outright frontal assault on the state to the 'winning of strategic positions' on a number of fronts, he described as the historic advance from politics conceived as a 'war of manoeuvre' to politics as a 'war of position'.

In the conduct of this type of hegemonic politics, Gramsci saw the necessity for the working class and its party (which he called, after Machiavelli, 'The Prince') to build wider alliances among other social factions and strata, to construct what he called a 'historic bloc' which could then not simply seize power in the state but actually win popular consent in society at large. Its role was to become the 'leading force' in Italian national and cultural life, and – on the basis of this hegemonic position – to set in train a new, historic project, the construction of a new type of state, a new level of civilization. For Gramsci, though the proletariat remained the key agency of social change, and the party its vehicle, the domain of political action was defined more broadly, in 'national popular' terms. His attention to 'social forces' other than 'classes' as such saved his work from the worst excesses of class reductionism. The party, in its struggle to construct the proletariat as the 'leading class' of a new historical bloc, had to win key intellectuals over to its side, as well as engage directly with the cultural and moral life, the practical ideologies (including popular Catholicism) and 'common sense' of the popular classes, if it were ever to succeed in securing hegemony.

This concept of 'hegemony', which has acquired a wide theoretical resonance in subsequent years, is often misunderstood. Because Gramsci paid attention to the political, cultural, ideological, intellectual and moral dimensions of 'power' in modern societies he is sometimes understood to have argued that 'hegemony' was essentially a matter of winning the ideological struggle. In fact Gramsci always insisted that, if the 'economic nucleus' was not secured, hegemony could not be won. (He did not believe, either, that hegemony was ever total or finally achieved. It had to be continually secured and 'won' by an unceasing struggle to command the leading position.) But it is also true that he gave much greater weight to political, cultural and ideological factors (the so-called 'superstructural' aspects) and to the 'non-state' organizations of civil society (churches, schools, families, trade unions, media, voluntary associations) than is common in classical Marxist political theory. In so doing he was the first of the Marxist theorists seriously and consistently to attempt to construct a theory and strategy of politics free of class or economic reductionism.

It is undoubtedly the combination of a range of new and original concepts, a deep strategic political sense and a keen analytical awareness of changing historical conditions in the modern societies in which the left has to operate that has made his work so relevant to contemporary politics.

See also

Croce.

Works

Selections from the Prison Notebooks, ed. and trans. Q. Hoare and G. N. Smith, London, Lawrence & Wishart, 1971.
The Modern Prince and other Writings, New York, International, 1957.
Selections from Political Writings, ed. Q. Hoare, trans. J. Mathews, London, Lawrence & Wishart, 2 volumes, 1977–9.
A Gramsci Reader: Selected Writings, 1916–35, ed. D. Forgacs, London, Lawrence & Wishart, 1985.

Other works

W. L. Adamson, *Hegemony and Revolution*, Berkeley, Cal., and London, University of California Press, 1980.
Joseph V. Femia, *Gramsci's Political Thought*, Oxford, Clarendon Press, 1981.

Anne Sassoon Showstack, *Gramsci's Politics*, second edition, London, Hutchinson, 1987.
Maurice A. Finocchiaro, *Gramsci and the History of Dialectical Thought*, Cambridge, Cambridge University Press, 1988.
Esteve Morera, *Gramsci's Historicism*, London, Routledge, 1990.

Susan Griffin   1943–

In her several books and collections of essays the feminist theorist and poet Susan Griffin explores the logic of patriarchy by describing the relation between Western representations of reason as masculine and depictions of nature as feminine. In so far as women's primary caretaking duties have historically associated them with the body and nature, women have been 'reputed to be more corporeal and therefore agents of the devil'. Griffin believes that women, by reminding men of their own bodies, call men's attention to their own connection with nature, and thus to a frailty that they would like to deny. Men have traditionally responded to their anxiety over their dependence on women and nature by doing violence to both, Griffin argues. Witch-burning, pornography and rape, she states, are practices linked in the misogynist mind with a self-hatred of its own feminine side.

Griffin's most important work, *Woman and Nature*, uses distinct masculine and feminine voices (the latter in italics) to describe and mimic Western civilization's tension between scientific reason and nature, attempting to show how scientific paradigms that assume the need to conquer nature coincide, historically and ideologically, with patriarchal customs that depend on the oppression of women.

Works

Rape: the Power of Consciousness, San Francisco, Harper & Row, 1979.
Women and Nature: the Roaring inside Her, New York, Harper, 1980.
A Chorus of Stones: the Private Life of War, New York, Doubleday, 1992.
The Eros of Everyday Life: Essays on Ecology, Gender and Society, New York, Doubleday, 1995.

Ernesto 'Che' Guevara
1928–1967

Che Guevara himself gave this simple summary of his life: 'I was born in Argentina, I fought in Cuba, and I began to be a revolutionary in Guatemala.' Perhaps some elaboration is needed. Guevara was born in Alta Gracia and died at the age of thirty-nine in Bolivia, murdered by special forces under the supervision of the CIA agent Felix Rodriguez (a Cuban exile who was to figure prominently two decades later in the 'Contragate' affair).

During his lifetime Guevara played a crucial role as the only non-Cuban participant in, and the major chronicler of, the Cuban revolutionary insurgence led by Fidel Castro. Upon the accession of Castro's movement to power in January 1959, Guevara held a series of key posts in the Cuban government related to industrial development and the economy. In 1965 Guevara disappeared from the public stage, first to join a revolutionary insurgence in the Congo, then to initiate a guerrilla movement in the heart of the Andes mountains in Bolivia.

Guevara, more than any other individual, charted in theoretical terms the development and direction of the Cuban revolution in its first crucial decade, just as he gave voice to the Cuban understanding of how revolution would occur elsewhere in the Third World in general and in Latin America in particular. In both these arenas, his emphasis on voluntarism and on the responsibility of the individual revolutionary as an historical actor gave new impetus to the Marxist revolutionary movement, particularly in Latin America. He was the most theoretically sophisticated of the revolutionary leadership: he was influenced by a wide and eclectic range of thinkers and activists, from Gramsci to Mariátegui to Fanon, Sandino and Jose Martí. During the years directly following the 1959 victory he found the writings of the young Marx particularly congenial to his thinking. Guevara kept as a constant a kind of humanist Marxism whose stress was upon the elimination of alienation and upon the fulfilment of individual human potential, which he gave voice to in various essays, perhaps most prominently 'Man and socialism in Cuba'. Despite the failure of many of his ideas in practice during his lifetime (witnessed most directly by his own death), Guevara's vision and his theoretical conclusions continue in various forms to reverberate beyond the decade of the 1960s, during which he became a virtual icon of the left, in both the industrialized and the 'wrongly developed' (his term) world. Thus his stress on individual responsibility and conscience helped directly to shape the terrain for the reconciliation between Marxism and Christianity embodied in liberation theology. His inherent internationalism informed a major vein in Cuban foreign policy, leading it, among other places, to Angola.

Further, he continues to represent one side of an ongoing debate concerning planning, incentives and industrialization in under-developed socialist economies. In multiple speeches and articles written from 1962 to 1965 he sought to counter European (and Cuban) Marxists who argued, along conventional lines, that economic and social structure had to reflect the material base in which they were rooted, and therefore, as long as scarcity existed, the law of value governed economic interactions, much as it did under capitalism. For Guevara this was a completely unacceptable set of concepts. He responded, 'I am not interested in dry economic socialism. We are fighting against misery, but we are also fighting against alienation . . . Marx was preoccupied both with economic factors and with their repercussions on the spirit. If communism isn't interested in this, too, it may be a method of distributing goods, but it will never be a revolutionary way of life.'

Guevara argued for a system which relied upon socialist consciousness to overcome economic scarcity: the capitalist law of value, for him, had no place in socialist society. He emphasized a high level of centralized planning and reliance largely on moral rather than material incentives. These ideas were to form the underpinning of the 1966–70 Cuban 'heresy': its attempt to create socialism and communism simultaneously. The Cuban experiment in simultaneous construction began after Guevara had left Cuba; it ended in failure three years after his death. In the decade of the 1970s, when Cuba turned to a more orthodox, Soviet-patterned transition, Guevara's ideas were all but forgotten. School-children ritually chanted, 'Seremos como Che', 'We will be like Che', and his image remained, but his writings were largely ignored. In the mid-1980s, in the midst of political and economic crisis, escalating scarcity and the declaration of the 'rectification campaign', Guevara's economic ideas have been resuscitated, and represent one end of the spectrum of discussion at present under way in Cuban leadership circles.

Finally, Guevara's ideas on guerrilla organization and warfare have had an enduring resonance among those engaged in such combat, particularly in Latin America. The path that led him to Bolivia was shaped by his experience with the rebel guerrillas in Cuba and his reflections upon this experience in numerous texts and essays. In its most developed form, he put forth the notion of the revolutionary *foco*, or guerrilla nucleus, as the force which would serve, in the Third World, to initiate revolution. In the *'foco* theory' Guevara found the means by which the established, orthodox and to his mind anti-revolutionary communist parties of Latin America could be circumvented, and the peasantry mobilized and transformed into a revolutionary force. His notion was to see *focos* set up throughout continental South America as part of a drive to, in his words, create 'two, three, many Vietnams', which would eventually, simply in their scope, defeat US imperialism. His failure in Bolivia marked the end of a decade of aggressively singleminded revolutionary foreign policy in Cuba: Castro now moved in far more diversified directions. It marked, as well, a rethinking of strategy and a widening of approaches on the part of guerrilla groups modelled upon his notion of the *foco*.

Guevara's last image of himself was aptly captured in a letter to his parents. He writes of himself, in September 1967, as Don Quixote, 'return[ing] to the road with my lance under my arm . . . Many will call me an adventurer, and I am, but of a different type, one of those who risks his skin to demonstrate his truths.' That, too, is part of his legacy.

See also

Castro, Fanon, Gramsci, Mariátegui.

Works

Rolando Bonachea and Nelson Valdes (eds.), *Che: Selected Works of Ernesto Guevara*, Cambridge, Mass., MIT Press, 1969.
Michael Lowy, *The Marxism of Che Guevara*, New York, Monthly Review Press, 1973.
Bertram Silverman (ed.), *Man and Socialism in Cuba: the Great Debate*, New York, Atheneum Press, 1973.
Carlos Tablada Perez, *El pensamiento economico de Ernesto Che Guevara*, Havana, Casa de las Americas, 1987.
Fernando Martinez Heredia, *Che, el socialismo y el communismo*, Havana, Casa de las Americas, 1989.

Gustavo Gutiérrez   1928–

Born in Lima, Peru, and ordained a priest in 1959, Gustavo Gutiérrez has become the progenitor and best-known advocate of liberation theology. During the past two decades, under Gutiérrez's influence, liberation theology has evolved into a unique and permanent political movement throughout much of the Third World. It consists of radical members of the clergy as well as lay members of the Church, both Protestant and Catholic, who use their religious convictions as a standard by which to gauge and criticize the effectiveness of contemporary societies in meeting the basic needs of the citizenry, and to participate in efforts towards social change.

Gutiérrez occupies a professorship in both theology and the social sciences at the Catholic Pontifical University in Lima. Earlier, after initiating studies in medicine, philosophy and theology at the National University in

Lima, he had travelled to Europe, where he continued and completed studies in philosophy, at the University of Louvain, Belgium, and theology, in Lyons, France, and at the Gregorian University in Rome.

Today Gutiérrez actively participates in various theological study groups, journals and conferences, and lectures frequently throughout the world on political theology. He has written numerous articles and books focusing on theology and the Third World. His most widely acclaimed work appeared in 1971: *Teología de la liberación* (*A Theology of Liberation*). This work set the tone for the emerging movement of Latin American liberation theology and the movement's development of a genuine political theory.

Gutiérrez maintains that the social context of human existence plays an important, if not the primary, role in mediating the will of God to humankind and thus in influencing the development of symbols, myths, rituals and practices that surround and give meaning to the religious experience. Furthermore, the will of God itself is not understood as a set of absolute proclamations to delineate proper human behaviour; God expresses only a constant commitment to respect for the value of human existence under fluctuating social conditions. Consequently, not only does change in social conditions influence interpretations of religious meaning, but, for religious meaning itself to be adequately expressed, the social context must be properly understood.

While Gutiérrez's political theory derives its normative commitment to helping the poor and oppressed from the morals of biblical stories, its approach to social analysis must be capable of revealing the origins of poverty and to suggest paths for its eradication. Consequently Gutiérrez argues for incorporating selected social science methodologies as a necessary ingredient in any attempt to develop a theological response to poverty and oppression. To this end, he finds the use of Marxist class analysis most appropriate.

Perhaps not unexpectedly, Gutiérrez typically reserves his harshest ethical criticism for the detrimental consequences of capitalism – primarily with regard to imperialism and economic dependence. Capitalism sets the stage for the emergence of elitist industrial economies in the First World, authoritarian political regimes in the Third World and an unjust international market economy. Multinational corporations dominate the international economy to link the First and Third World nations in a lopsided and destructive arrangement. This arrangement stimulates the development of particular political and economic institutions in the Third World to serve First World interests, and this in turn creates the conditions, impetus and structural support for mass suffering. According to Gutiérrez, these institutions are sinful and violent; they hurt the vast majority of the world's population with policies of terror and deprivation that result in human rights violations and massive poverty.

Furthermore, Gutiérrez maintains that unacceptable social conditions are manifestations of a deeper disequilibrium between the ethics of modern, individualistic liberalism and the older traditions of community and obligation. Yet he also recognizes the need to retain the liberal concept of individual rights as well as the material benefits of industrialization. Thus he argues in favour of change in most existing social, economic and political structures in Latin America compatible with a commitment to participatory democracy and socialist economics.

In an attempt to refine and clarify his position, Gutiérrez has written several works. He handles well critiques from other Latin American clergy, such as Bishop Alfonso López Trujillo and Father Juan Gutiérrez, involving philosophical issues of theory construction in his attempt to merge aspects of Marxist ideology with Christian theology. He demonstrates persuasively how Marxist class analysis can be effectively used as an analytical tool for socio-economic assessment while avoiding the orthodox Marxist position on the primacy of materialism and atheism. However,

Gutiérrez is on shakier ground in his assessment of the dynamics of economic development. While providing a powerful religious critique of the social consequences of capitalism, his writings are weak in the area of economic explanations of the origins and production of wealth, especially as they relate to market forces and subsequent problems of economic redistribution.

With regard to his political ethics, Gutiérrez uses Marxist class analysis in conjunction with his biblical commitment to the poor to justify engagement in a variety of reformist and revolutionary causes. Consequently the economic and political critique as well as the moral judgement of Gutiérrez and other liberation theologians, such as Clodovis Boff, Leonardo Boff, Ignacio Ellacuría, José Míguez Bonino, José Porfirio Miranda, Juan Luis Segundo and Jon Sobrino, has often found compatibility with and appeal to the sentiments of many social revolutionary movements, such as the Sandinistas in Nicaragua.

But, despite his academic training and the erudition of his writings, Gutiérrez desires that his life should evince the only identifying characteristic crucial to an understanding of liberation theology: reflection on praxis, reflection on the moral life of the Christian in an unjust world. Indeed, as founder and director of the Bartolomé de las Casas Centre in Rimac, Peru, Gutiérrez claims his most important work and learning experiences to be his pastoral duties with the poor in the slums of Lima – not his scholarly treatises exported to the First World.

See also

Boff.

Works

A Theology of Liberation, Maryknoll, N.Y., Orbis, 1973.
The Power of the Poor in History, Maryknoll, N.Y., Orbis, 1983.
We Drink from our own Wells, Maryknoll, N.Y., Orbis, 1984.

The Poor and the Church in Latin America, New York, State Mutual, 1984.
On Job: God-talk and the Suffering of the Poor, Maryknoll, N.Y., Orbis, 1987.

Other works

A. López Trujillo, *Liberation or Revolution? An Examination of the Priest's Role in the Socioeconomic Class Struggle in Latin America*, Huntington, Ind., Our Sunday Visitor, 1975.
J. Gutiérrez, *The New Liberation Gospel: Pitfalls of the Theology of Liberation*, Chicago, Franciscan Herald Press, 1977.
Ruth Martin Brown, *Gustavo Gutiérrez*, Atlanta, Ga, John Knox Press, 1980.
John R. Pottenger, *The Political Theory of Liberation Theology*, Albany, N.Y., State University of New York Press, 1989.

Jürgen Habermas   1929–

Jürgen Habermas, born in the German town of Gummersbach, is the leading thinker of the 'second generation' of the Frankfurt school. The philosophical and sociological approach of the Frankfurt school, generally known as 'critical theory', took shape in the 1930s, first at a research institute in Germany, then in exile in the United States, and has probably been the most influential current within the tradition of 'Western Marxism', which derives from the early work of Georg Lukács. Habermas's predecessors in this tradition are figures of the stature of Theodor Adorno, Walter Benjamin, Max Horkheimer and Herbert Marcuse.

The thought of the early Frankfurt school, developed in the shadow of European fascism, tended towards the assumption that the 'totally administered' society, supplanting the relative freedom of the era of liberal capitalism with comprehensive social and psychological controls, was the logical culmination of capitalist development. Even after their return to Germany in the post-war period, for example, Adorno and Horkheimer never fully came to terms with the historical achievement of the constitutional democracy, or ever considered the formal features of bourgeois legal and political systems – in their fundamental normative intentions, at least – as potential sources of social resistance.

It is on this crucial point that Habermas's basic outlook differs from that of his predecessors. Habermas's political and philosophical views were decisively shaped not only by the catastrophe of Nazism, which he lived through as a youth, but also by the emergence of a stable constitutional and democratic polity on German soil in the form of the Federal Republic. In consequence, while Habermas inherits a central concern with the distorting predominance of 'instrumental reason' in modern society from the earlier Frankfurt school, his account of the harm which this predominance causes, and of the appropriate remedies, implies a completely new theoretical foundation for critical theory.

This new approach is apparent in his early work *The Structural Transformation of the Public Sphere*, on the emergence, development and fate of the 'public sphere' in capitalist societies since the eighteenth century. The 'public sphere' is Habermas's term for the social arena in which communicating and reasoning private individuals form the normative orientations which exert a monitoring and rationalizing influence on the exercise of state power. 'Public opinion', in its classical bourgeois form, mediates between the abstract principles of natural law and the sovereign enactment of legislation. In Habermas's view, however, the classical conception of the 'public sphere' was fatally vitiated by its tacit equation of bourgeois (i.e. property owner) and human being: in the course of the nineteenth century this elision became apparent, as the conflict between capital and labour erupted into the sphere of supposedly free and equal exchange. Furthermore the public sphere has since been dangerously eroded by the modern technical apparatuses of mass communication, advertising and 'public relations', and by the reduction of democratic expectations to the periodic endorsement of political elites. Whereas the human needs and concerns discovered in the new intimate sphere of the family were once brought into the domain of literary communication, now that sphere is itself increasingly invaded and hollowed out by modern forms of media influence and manipulation.

In his account of the deformation of the public sphere, and of the progressive 're-feudalization' of society through the intertwining of state and private domains, Habermas is building on the powerful analysis of the modern 'culture industry' developed by his predecessors. The points of divergence, however, are also significant. Habermas is concerned to preserve what he takes to be the normative democratic potential of the notion of an arena of debate equally open to all – unlike so many contemporary European thinkers, who follow Nietzsche and Heidegger, he does not interpret modernity exclusively in terms of the objectification of the natural and social worlds by instrumental reason. Even the earlier Frankfurt school tended to adopt this account, building on Weber's analysis of the rationalization process. Habermas, however, does not see such dehumanization as a necessary consequence of the rise of the modern social and political sciences, nor does he believe it possible to abandon their cognitive achievements in favour of a pre-modern conception of political philosophy as practical wisdom. Rather, modern social science must become self-reflexive, as a medium through which the needs and interests of social groups can be clarified and connected with politically realizable goals.

During the 1970s Habermas worked intensively on the deep philosophical foundations of his conception of democratic legitimation. He sought to show that commitments to truth, sincerity and rightness are normative presuppositions of human communication. We cannot help but suppose that the conditions under which a non-coerced aggrement could be reached are already in force when we seek to resolve a dispute through discussion, otherwise the discussion would lose its point. These conditions, Habermas believes, can be defined in terms of a structure of equal and reciprocal access to dialogue, which he terms the 'ideal speech situation'. However counterfactual this situation may be, Habermas argues, it exerts a guiding force over modern moral consciousness.

Simultaneously, in *Legitimation Crisis*, Habermas sought to trace the concrete social consequences of these moral intuitions through a reformulation of the Marxist theory of capitalist crisis. In his view, advanced capitalism no longer produces 'pure' economic or system crises, since the state has taken over many regulative functions in relation to the economy. However, even state intervention is unable to balance the conflicting imperatives which arise from the fundamental contradictions of an economy whose operation is increasingly socialized but which continues to serve private interests. The resulting adminstrative 'rationality crisis' may itself become a 'legitimation crisis' if the values and meanings of the socio-cultural system begin to challenge the norms of civic privatism and the depoliticized public sphere. Hence, for Habermas, the fundamental crisis tendencies of the capitalist mode of production, analysed by Marx, remain in force. But, through a series of displacements, the ultimate points of resistance, and precipitators of crisis, are to be found in the emerging normative structures of a communicative universalism.

Habermas's work on the communicative foundations of language culminated in the publication of *The Theory of Communicative Action*, the most comprehensive statement of his social theory. Here he argues that the dynamics of modern society can be understood in terms of the differentiation of 'systems' which operate through the impersonal media of money and power (the market and government) from the 'lifeworld' (those domains of social existence which are communicatively structured). The pathologies of modern society can now be understood in terms of the 'colonization' of the lifeworld by the systems – the commodification and bureaucratization of areas of life which are essentially dependent on solidarity and mutual

recognition. With this formulation Habermas definitively abandons one of the strands of the Marxist tradition, the belief that the 'systems' in themselves are forms of 'alienation' ultimately to be overcome. The goal of democratization is now understood in terms of the organization of centres of concentrated communication which arise out of everyday practice, and which can monitor and restrain the encroachment of the systems without either being absorbed by them or seeking to abolish them.

Throughout his work Habermas has sought to reconcile respect for the achievements of the modern constitutional state with the Marxist critique of the socially destructive and anti-democratic dynamics of capitalist development – in other words, to sustain a dialectical conception of modernity. In his mature account, socialism cannot be defined *a priori* as a concrete form of life but is, rather, understood as the progressive limitation of these harmful effects through the expanding implantation, both formal and informal, of a communicative universalism.

See also

Adorno, Heidegger, Horkheimer, Lukács, Marcuse, Weber.

Works

Theory and Practice, London, Heinemann, 1974.
Legitimation Crisis, London, Heinemann, 1976.
The Theory of Communicative Action I *Reason and the Rationalization of Society* II *Lifeworld and System: A Critique of Functionalist Reason*, Cambridge, Polity Press, vol. I (1984), vol. II (1987).
Post-metaphysical Thinking, Cambridge, Mass., Polity Press, 1992.

Other works

Thomas A. McCarthy, *The Critical Theory of Jürgen Habermas*, London, MIT Press, 1978.
John B. Thompson and David Held (eds.), *Habermas: Critical Debates*, London, Macmillan, 1982.
Richard J. Bernstein (ed.), *Habermas and Modernity*, Cambridge, Polity Press, 1985.
Steven Leidman (ed.), *Jürgen Habermas on Society and Politics: a Reader*, Boston, Mass., Beacon Press, 1989.

Stuart Hall   1932–

Stuart Hall is closely identified with what has come to be known as 'cultural studies'. His work is regarded by many as decisive in the creation of an enormously influential, non-economistic, Marxian-inspired approach to the study of culture, media and subjectivity.

Born in Jamaica, Hall attended Oxford as a Rhodes Scholar in 1951 and since that time has remained an important public intellectual of the independent left in Britain. A founding member of the revived Socialist Club and soon after of the New Left Club, he became the first editor of *New Left Review* in 1959. In 1968 he was appointed Acting Director (then Director) of the Centre for Contemporary Cultural Studies (CCCS) at the University of Birmingham. Under Hall, the CCCS was the locus for a sustained effort, institutionally unmatched since, at retheorizing culture from the perspective of Western Marxism. In 1979 Hall moved to the Open University as Professor of Sociology in an attempt to move the 'high paradigm of cultural studies . . . to a popular level'.

'Cultural studies' emerged at a moment of profound cultural transformation in Britain. A decaying imperial culture was being radically redefined by economic decline and – as the empire came home to roost – by black and Asian migration into the heart of its urban centres. Hall's focus has always been on what he calls the 'dirty semiotic world' of everyday existence where knowledge and power intersect, set within the context of broader social and political structures. The CCCS attempt to rethink classical Marxism's base–superstructure metaphor from this perspective involved an intense dialogue with two European thinkers whose work was just becoming available in translation – Louis Althusser and Antonio Gramsci. From this interchange the central concepts of 'overdetermination' and 'hegemony' would produce the political discourse of the British left.

The CCCS produced many important works in the 1970s. The most prominent involved a focus on the highly visible and spectacular youth subcultures of postwar Britain (*Resistance through Rituals*), as well as a pathbreaking study (*Policing the Crisis*) detailing how the concept of 'mugging' was generated in a society undergoing a crisis of hegemony, to create folk-devils and scapegoats (young black men) on whom the ills of society could be pinned.

Policing the Crisis was highly prescient in its analysis of the emergence of 'a law-and-order society' that would reach fruition in the 1980s under Conservative governments led by Margaret Thatcher. It is widely claimed that Hall coined the term 'Thatcherism' to describe these new social and economic contours of British culture that would alter the political field on which the left would have to operate. He called attention particularly to the cultural component of Thatcherism, of how it was not simply an old ruling-class game of ideology and false consciousness but a new game of identity, ethnicity and subjectivity. His collection of essays on Thatcherism, *The Hard Road to Renewal*, is a call for the left to integrate culture as a constitutive force into its analysis and practice.

Hall was also closely associated in the 1980s with the periodical *Marxism Today* and the discussion it inaugurated around 'New Times'. This was an attempt to show that the social, cultural and political contours of the world had changed at the end of the twentieth century, and that for the left to survive it needed to recognize this transformed terrain on which its own practice would be conducted. Hall argued that Thatcherism presented itself as the only natural political form of these new conditions. The 'New Times' project was an attempt to pry apart this seemingly natural connection between Thatcherism and the world, and to create a space for a progressive and liberatory practice and politics.

At the theoretical level this insistence upon the multi-layered and practice-centred nature of social existence was reflected in Hall's development of the theory of 'articulation' of identities through human activity as an answer to the Marxian problematic of purely structural 'determination'. Similarly, Hall's later work has been characterized by addressing the issue of ideology through questions of identity and subjectivity, especially with reference to race and ethnicity.

The notion of 'dialogue' accurately describes Hall's mode of thinking and operating. He has been involved in a lifelong dialogue with various intellectual traditions (Marxist, post-structuralist, postmodern, post-colonial), never fully identifying with them, but engaging with them in the spirit of generosity and modesty to keep theory 'moving on'. His twin concerns have always been (1) for the most rigorous, analytical and 'objective' understanding of our present conditions, and (2) for the intellectual class to transmit such findings to the broader public. An inspirational teacher and public speaker, Hall has led an exemplary intellectual life.

See also

Althusser, Gramsci, Williams.

Works

Resistance through Rituals: Youth Subcultures in Post-war Britain (ed. with T. Jefferson), London, Hutchinson, 1976.
Policing the Crisis: 'Mugging', the State and Law and Order (with C. Critcher, T. Jefferson, J. Clarke and B. Roberts), London, Macmillan, 1978.
'The problem of ideology: Marxism without guarantees', in B. Matthews (ed.), *Marx 100 Years On*, London, Lawrence & Wishart, 1983.
The Hard Road to Renewal: Thatcherism and the Crisis of the Left, London, Verso, 1988.
New Times: the Changing Face of Politics in the 1990s (ed. with M. Jacques), London, Lawrence & Wishart, 1989.

Other works

Stuart Hall: Critical Dialogues in Cultural Studies (ed. D. Morley and K.-H. Chen), London, Routledge, 1996.

Michael Harrington
1928–1989

Michael Harrington, the best-known socialist writer and activist of his generation, achieved national prominence in 1962 with the publication of *The Other America*, a study of poverty in the United States. Harrington argued that poverty was far more widespread in the United States than was commonly assumed, and that the poor were trapped in their condition by a 'culture of poverty'. *The Other America* helped persuade John F. Kennedy to launch the 'war on poverty', and its assumptions shaped many of the programmes devised by the Johnson administration to cope with the problem. For the next quarter of a century Harrington remained a prominent commentator on social policy in the United States. Influential among liberal political circles and in the labour movement in the 1970s and 1980s for his criticism of the increasingly conservative domestic policies of the federal government under Jimmy Carter and Ronald Reagan, Harrington was none the less unable to win many converts to democratic socialism, the cause to which he devoted most of his adult life.

Born into a devoutly Catholic middle-class family in St Louis, Missouri, Harrington was educated in parochial schools. At the precocious age of sixteen he enrolled as an undergraduate at Holy Cross College in Worcester, Massachusetts, receiving his A.B. three years later. After a year at Yale University law school he enrolled in a graduate programme in English literature at the University of Chicago, receiving an M.A. in 1949.

Harrington moved to New York, determined to become both a writer and a political activist. He found an outlet for both ambitions in the radical Catholic Worker movement. He edited the group's newspaper, marched on pacifist picket lines, and spent his evenings socializing in bohemian haunts in Greenwich Village. Troubled by religious doubts, Harrington left the Church and the Catholic Worker movement in 1953 for the more secular radicalism of the Young People's Socialist League, the youth group of the Socialist Party, and then in 1954 for the even more obscure Young Socialist League, the youth affiliate of the 'Shachtmanites'. (Max Shachtman, a prominent figure in the Trotskyist movement in the 1930s, led a succession of small anti-Stalinist radical groups in the years that followed.) During the 1950s Harrington supported himself with a variety of odd jobs, including a stint as researcher for the Fund for the Republic. He also criss-crossed the country on speaking tours on behalf of the Young Socialist League. Despite the sectarian schooling he received among the Shachtmanites, he became a keen observer of American political and social life, developing an effective prose and an inspirational speaking style. He contributed articles on political and cultural topics to *Partisan Review*, *Dissent* and *Commonweal*: the articles he wrote for *Commentary* in the late 1950s on poverty led him to write *The Other America*.

In 1958 the Shachtmanites rejoined the Socialist Party. The party, a shadow of a once influential movement, no longer ran candidates in its own name, hoping instead to spark a 'realignment' of liberal forces within the Democratic Party. Harrington developed a close relationship with the Socialist Party's venerable leader, Norman Thomas, who came to regard him as his successor. With a decade's experience of radical politics behind him and links with key civil rights activists, including Martin Luther King, and respected by the student activists of the early New Left, Harrington seemed well suited to take advantage of the political opportunities opening up on the left in the 1960s.

But the 1960s proved a frustrating decade for him. At the founding convention of Students for a Democratic Society at Port Huron, Michigan, in 1962 Harrington alienated SDS leaders by denouncing them for insufficient anti-communism. (Harrington would later rue the 'rude insensitivity' he had displayed at the meeting.) Allied with the increasingly rightward-leaning Max Shachtman in the Socialist Party's factional battles, Harrington refused to call for support for an unconditional American withdrawal from Vietnam, alienating other potential allies. His political liabilities were magnified by the personal crisis of a nervous breakdown that made it difficult for him to speak in public for several years in the mid-1960s.

By the late 1960s Harrington was finding himself increasingly at odds with his right-wing socialist allies, who had thrown in their lot with the pro-Cold War wing of the Democratic Party. Finally, in 1973, he led a few hundred of his own followers into a new organization, the Democratic Socialist Organizing Committee. Determined to be the 'left wing of the possible', the DSOC launched an ambitious programme called the Democratic Agenda to woo the Democratic Party back to its fading New Deal liberal ideals.

In 1972 Harrington gained a measure of economic security when he was appointed Professor of Political Science at Queen's College. Throughout these years he remained a prolific author, publishing books on left-wing strategy, on the international economy and on religion as well as two autobiographical memoirs. Perhaps his most important work after *The Other America* was *Socialism*. A wide-ranging survey of socialist history and theory, *Socialism* argued that at the core of classical Marxism lay a deep commitment to working-class democracy, which had been perverted in the twentieth century by communist totalitarianism. The 'socialist vision', Harrington insisted, could still 'be made relevant to the twenty-first century' by restoring its democratic content.

In 1983 the DSOC merged with another radical group called the New American Movement, which had its roots in the New Left. Harrington served as co-chair of the resulting organization, Democratic Socialists of America, which had 5,000 members at its founding. Democratic Socialists of America continued the DSOC strategy of working within the Democratic Party, with limited success. Harrington grew increasingly involved with the Socialist International in the 1980s, attending many of its conferences and drafting its resolutions. Diagnosed with cancer of the oesophagus in 1985, he continued to speak and write as long as he could. His final book, *Socialism: Past and Future*, was published in July 1989, the month he died.

See also

King.

Works

The Other America: Poverty in the United States, New York, Macmillan, 1962.
The Accidental Century, New York, Macmillan, 1965.
Toward a Democratic Left: a Radical Program for a New Majority, Baltimore, Md, Penguin, 1969.
Socialism, New York, Saturday Review Press, 1972.
The Next Left: the History of a Future, New York, Holt, 1986.
The Long-distance Runner: an Autobiography, New York, Holt, 1988.
Socialism: Past and Future, New York, Arcade, 1989.

Friedrich August von Hayek
1899–1992

Hayek studied at the University of Vienna and became a doctor of both law and political science. After a period as a civil servant he became the first director of the Austrian Institute of Economic Research. In 1931 he took up a Chair in economics at the London School of Economics. In 1950 he became Professor of Social and Moral Science at the University of Chicago. Subsequently he became Professor of Economics at the University of Freiburg, from which he retired in 1967. In 1974 Hayek won the Nobel Prize for Economics.

Most of the main themes in his social and political thought had their roots in his early contributions to the philosophical basis of economics. In these, first of all, he rejected any attempt either to uncover the essential nature of social or economic ideas or practices or to develop general laws which purport to reveal their objective nature. He rejected both the idealist and the empiricist forms which such objectivism or rationalism can take. In the case of the empiricist approach he rejected the idea central to the logical positivism of the Vienna Circle that there is an incorrigible 'givenness' about our sensations and our perceptual judgements which is not contaminated by conceptual thought or judgement; and that we can build up wholly scientific or empirical concepts in the social sciences from such primitive epistemic data. Hayek, following the Austrian school of economics, which had regarded value as a subjective phenomenon, took the view that all social objects such as capital or money have an essentially subjective element in that what they are is bound up with human beliefs and attitudes, which in turn are part and parcel of particular communities and their ways of life. This led him to see the social sciences as being concerned with the principles which underlie or govern particular patterns of social life.

However, he believed that there is a limit to the extent to which such rules and principles are capable of elaboration. This led him to draw a normative conclusion relevant to social and political thought. Because we cannot specify all the rules which underlie our ways of life, we all exist in relative ignorance, which in turn produces an argument in favour of liberty, namely that liberty gives the opportunity for alternative experiments in ways of living. He argued that we could not examine a culture other than within the context of that culture. There is no external or transcendental standpoint from which the basic rules of social life can be derived. What is important is not the dream of a rational reconstruction of the social order from such an external standpoint, but rather the grounds which the ideas that form a particular culture have within a particular tradition. Traditions provide the basic constitutive presuppositions of social life, and it is with these that critical thought must stop. The social order, then, is not the product of some directing intelligence, and equally it cannot be rationally redirected through some kind of comprehensive rationalism. Social orders and traditions are spontaneous outcomes of individual action, but not of individual design.

Hayek's economic theories thus have a direct relevance to his social and political thought. The issues which preoccupied him in these areas were first set out in *The Road to Serfdom*, which contains an attack on the idea of planning and the political and economic machinery which accompanies the attempt to plan the economy. His first objection to planning followed directly from his writings on the epistemological foundations of economics. He argued that centralized planning was impossible, for epistemological reasons to do with the fragmentary nature of human knowledge and its tacit and non-propositional form. Centralized planning assumes that the knowledge to make inputs into a central plan for economic efficiency is available, whereas Hayek denied this. When ordinary individuals in a free society make economic choices they draw upon whatever knowledge they have, and it is likely to be very fragmented, yet it is crucial to economic decision-making at the individual level. This fragmentary knowledge cannot be brought together by central administrators to formulate an efficient plan for the economy.

This is not a contingent matter, having to do, for example, with the lack of computers able to process such knowledge; there are qualitative aspects to it as well. The knowledge which is used in everyday decision-making is not only fragmented among individuals but also tacit or implicit. That is to say, when we make individual choices we are not able to bring to mind or to put into propositions all the knowledge which is used as background to the decisions. It is as much a matter of knowing how as of knowing that. However, a centralized planning authority can make use only of propositional knowledge. Hence, in formulating a plan based upon knowing *that* rather than knowing *how*, a planner has to neglect many of those background conditions of human knowledge which are essential for economic efficiency.

There are moral as well as epistemological objections to planning, too. A plan presupposes that we have an agreed view on what we are planning for – what the aims of the plan are. However, in a free society in which individuals have their own conceptions of the good, planning means imposing on this diverse set of goals or ends some overriding purpose. This may be possible in an advanced society in time of war, when the whole of society is mobilized behind one overarching aim and when indeed many civil liberties may be restricted. However, in peacetime in an advanced society pluralism is likely to reassert itself and there will be no natural consensus over what the aims of a centralized plan are. In a diverse society committed to planning, such a consensus is likely to have to be manufactured or coerced.

In the post-war period one of the main purposes of planning in Western societies was to achieve a greater degree of social justice in the distribution of resources, and to diminish inequality. However, Hayek rejected this as a desirable political aim. He regarded social justice as an insidious mirage. Several arguments are employed here. First of all he argued that there are many diverse candidates for the principle of social justice. We could distribute resources according to need or according to deserts, for example, and these alternatives would lead to radically different distributions. In a morally diverse society we cannot get agreement on the appropriate criteria for the distribution of social goods. Even if we could agree, for example, to distribute according to deserts, it still remains the case that views about deserts will differ between those who belong to different moral communities. The secular person, the Christian, the Hindu, the Buddhist will all see deserts in different ways. Again moral diversity makes it impossible to agree on what are the appropriate criteria of deserts.

In the case of need the situation is similar and leads to baneful political results. Again we cannot reach an agreed view about what needs are and what is required to satisfy them.

However, if we pursue social or distributive justice without an agreed morality to underpin it we are led into a situation which is deeply incompatible with one of the central values of a liberal society, namely the rule of law. Law should be neutral between individuals and should be universalizable so that it covers all people in similar circumstances. However, that is impossible in the context of rules of social justice. Because we cannot agree what needs are, because they are incommensurable, and because they are subject to the limitations of resources, a principle of social justice cannot be turned into a universalizable rule of law. This also has the effect of conferring arbitrary power on bureaucrats who are charged with the duty of administering social justice. Because there cannot be rules governing the detailed distribution of resources, for example to meet medical needs, officials are required to act in discretionary ways. This means that a commitment of social justice puts inherently discretionary power into the hands of welfare bureaucracies in a way that is incompatible with one of the central ideas of a liberal society.

Hayek also rejected the idea that the free market produces social injustice in the distribution of income and wealth. Hayek regarded the idea of social justice as central to the socialist critique of capitalism in both its Marxist and its social democratic forms. What animates socialists, in Hayek's view, is that the free market, left to its own devices, produces an unjust degree of inequality. Social democrats believe that this injustice can be rectified within a mixed economy by political means, by the politically engineered redistribution of resources. Marxists believe that this is dealing with the symptoms of injustice and not its causes, which lie in the unequal distribution of property rights in the capitalist economy. Injustice can be rectified only by a complete change in property ownership, and that requires a revolution. Hayek, however, rejected the assumption that the market produces injustice. It cannot do so because injustice has to be caused by intentional action. Market outcomes, while being the product of individual actions of buying and selling, nevertheless produce outcomes which are not intended by anyone. They are the product of human action, not human design, and as such are not intended; therefore they cannot be characterized as unjust.

Another social democratic argument in favour of social justice has been to do with the nature of liberty. Many social democrats have been at least implicitly committed to a positive view of liberty. That liberty means not just the negative freedom of being free from interference of various sorts but also the power and capacity to act. If liberty is understood as power, then one can be free only if one has the resources to do what one chooses to do. Hayek recognized that this view of liberty would sanction a redistribution of resources. However, he rejected the argument, in favour of social justice. In *The Constitution of Liberty* Hayek defended a rigorously negative view of liberty. He argued that the positive view of freedom implies that one is free only when one is able to do what one wants to do. However, that would mean that one was free only if one were omnipotent, which is absurd. Also, if a more restricted view of positive liberty was taken, namely that one is free to act only if one has certain basic needs satisfied, then, in Hayek's view, this brings back into play the arguments about pluralism which have already been discussed in relation to needs. In addition, free markets cannot infringe liberty in terms of the distribution of resources. Market outcomes are not restrictions on liberty, since, for reasons given earlier, they are not intended by specific individuals. Hayek's methodological commitment to individualism meant that he rejected the idea that freedom can be infringed by anything other than identifiable individuals.

A regime committed to social justice is not confined in its consequences to the entrenching of the discretionary power of bureaucracies; it also gives rise to intolerable interest-group pressures. If government is seen as being in the business of distributing resources in the absence of an agreed morality of distribution, which is not available in a pluralistic society, then interest groups are bound to arise to claim what from their subjective point of view they see as their just share of the resources available. This is likely to mean that government will distribute resources to the most powerful groups in society when there is no agreement about the overall pattern of distribution. Social justice will become a camouflage for distribution to the most powerful interest groups in society.

Hayek argued that concern about poverty has underpinned the politics of social justice. However, he believed that such concern had to be handled carefully. In his view, if we understand poverty properly, then free markets improve the position of the poor more effectively than redistribution. They do so via the trickle-down effect: what is consumed by a few of the rich today is consumed by a wider and wider section of society, including the worst-off as time goes on. Hayek rejects the relative view of poverty which links it with inequality. Inequality is central to the incentives necessary for an effective free market economy, which in time will benefit the poor more than socialism will. Poverty is best understood as an absolute phenomenon, as destitution, rather than as the failure to consume on a more equal basis with the rest of society. What matters to the poor is not their position relative to other groups in society so much as whether their income is increasing on a year-by-year basis. The market does this in a way that socialism and social justice cannot.

Works

The Road to Serfdom, London, Routledge, 1944.
The Pure Theory of Capital, London, Macmillan, 1941; 1950.
The Sensory Order, London, Routledge, 1952.
The Constitution of Liberty, London, Routledge, 1960.
Studies in Philosophy, Politics and Economics, London, Routledge, 1967.
Law, Legislation and Liberty, London, Routledge, 3 volumes, 1973–9.

Other works

John Gray, Hayek on Liberty, Oxford, Blackwell, 1986.
Barbara M. Rowland, Ordered Liberty and the Constitutional Framework, New York, Greenwood Press, 1987.
Chandran Kukathas, Hayek and Modern Liberalism, Oxford, Clarendon Press, 1989.

Andras Hegedus 1928–

Born in Sopronfelsoszentmiklos, he is a Hungarian social democrat and a member of the Budapest Group, which hoped to produce an internal self-critique of Marxism, what he described as a 'critical Marxist social science' and 'a Marxist reformism'. His analysis was chiefly of the bureaucratic deformation of Stalinism. A Prime Minister in the 1950s, he eventually went into exile.

See also

Heller, Markovic.

Works include

Socialism and Bureaucracy, London, Allison & Busby, 1976.
The Humanisation of Socialism: Writings of the Budapest School (with others), London, Allison & Busby, 1976.

Other works

Donald Brown, Towards a Radical Democracy: the Political Economy of the Budapest School, London, Unwin Hyman, 1988.

Martin Heidegger 1889–1976

Martin Heidegger is widely recognized as one of the leading philosophers of the twentieth century for his contributions to the revival of ontology and for his reinterpretation of the Western tradition of metaphysics. He has exerted major influence on two divergent movements in European thought: phenomenology, through his existential analysis of being-in-the-world; and post-structuralism, through his anticipation of deconstruction as a means of critiquing metaphysics.

Heidegger, who taught that every genuine philosophical question involves all other philosophical questions, centred his thought on the *Seinsfrage*, the question of the meaning of Being, which he held to be the most fundamental philosophical query. He interpreted all other problems, including those of politics, within the context of his pursuit of Being, which was conducted against the background of nihilism. Heidegger believed that the history of Western metaphysics concealed a nihilistic tendency which culminated in the rule of technology and its 'heralds', the positive sciences. His project was an effort to overcome nihilism through forms of thinking, other than the circumspective calculation of technology, that would permit Being to reveal itself afresh to its questioner (*Dasein*).

Heidegger's political philosophy is integral to his efforts to find a way out of the nihilism of technology. Considered as a practical pursuit, politics is not philosophically privileged over any other human activity, but it had, for Heidegger, special relevance for ontology because of its potential for essential involvement with history, which is the medium through which Being reveals and conceals itself. In *An Introduction to Metaphysics* he interpreted the political community, the *polis*, as the historical place '*in* which, *out of* which, and *for* which history happens', bestowing on it an ontological significance which he denied to other associations. The *polis* is not simply an existing community that takes on a relation of ruler and ruled; rather, community itself is created politically by authentic rulers who give laws and set limits, structuring and ordering a form of life. The creative politics of the genuine statesman or ruler establishes the political space in which ordinary politicians pursue their circumspective competition, and the order of life in which Being is disclosed. The ruler, along with the poet, priest and philosopher, is concerned directly with the whole. Other, more specialized, vocations are at a greater remove from Being.

Heidegger's emphasis on creative politics and the primacy of the ruler places him within the conservative tradition of German romanticism. His political thought was directly influenced by Ernst Junger's conservative critique of technology, which he expanded on and grounded ontologically in the claim that the present moment of Western history is configured by the revelation of Being which is challenged forth by the will to order the world in terms of calculable consequences. Under the rule of technology only that is disclosed which can be placed at the behest of the nihilistic and uncreative will to will. All other possible revelations of Being are veiled by technological nihilism, which draws human beings into believing that the world is made in their image as a field for their mastery, whereas they are actually being made into human resources for technical schemes. The delusion of humanism, which substitutes a specious human dignity for the dignity of Being, was the critical target of Heidegger's politics and the spur to his persistent quest for other ways of thinking Being. The appeal to creative politics was one of his efforts to dispel humanism and to overcome technological nihilism.

During the 1930s, when Heidegger worked out his ontological interpretation of politics, he also became affiliated with National Socialism. The question of the meaning of Heidegger's Nazism has persistently overshadowed any other themes in commentary on his political thought, dividing critics, who claim that he provides a philosophical foundation or at least permission for National Socialism, from advocates, who argue for the independence of his questioning of Being from whatever political commitments he might have made. In his own account of his engagement with and disengagement from National Socialism, 'The rectorate, 1933–34: facts and thoughts', Heidegger rejected the idea that his National Socialism was gratuitous to his philosophy. He stated that he saw in the Nazi movement a possibility of the German people's 'inner recollection and renewal' and a path for that people to discover its 'historical vocation' in the West.

Heidegger's National Socialism, however, was not Hitler's Nazism. Criticized by a Nazi official for his 'private Nazism', Heidegger did not defend doctrines of racism or racial supremacy but held, in *The Introduction to Metaphysics*, that National Socialism had an 'inner truth and greatness' that had been obscured by propagandists. That truth, he added after the Second World War, involved the encounter between global technology and modern man. As a political thinker Heidegger interpreted the meaning of National Socialism through the lens of his romantic conservatism. After his resignation as Rector of the University of Freiburg in 1934 he progressively distanced himself from the Nazis until he reached the position that rather than an opportunity for overcoming technological nihilism through the creation of a *polis* they were a manifestation of nihilism. As he became disabused of National Socialism he turned away from appeals to creative politics and the genuine ruler.

Heidegger's late work, particularly after the Second World War, turned towards non-political responses to nihilism. In 'The question concerning technology' and 'The turning' he identified technology with denial of the world, in the form of 'injurious neglect of the thing'. Technology reveals Being as a 'standing reserve' or inventory to be ordered into calculable processes. Systems of order can be directed to 'the manufacture of corpses', as Heidegger stated in a remark on the death camps, or to such seemingly more benign activities as mechanized agriculture. In both cases, however, there is injurious neglect – the passing over of the otherness, objectivity and independent integrity of the thing or being. Technology is a global enframing of man for which politics offers no solutions but only evidence. At the end, poetry and meditation were Heidegger's resort as he struggled through technology, not over and against it.

Works

An Introduction to Metaphysics, New Haven, Conn., Yale University Press, 1959.
The Question concerning Technology and other Essays, New York, Garland, 1977.

Other works

Karsten Harries, 'Heidegger as a political thinker', *Review of Metaphysics* 29 (June 1976), pp. 642–69.
Thomas Sheehan, *Heidegger: the Man and the Thinker*, Chicago, Precedent, 1981.
Victor Farias, *Heidegger et le Nazisme*, Paris, Verdier, 1987.
Arnold I. Davidson (ed.), 'Symposium on Heidegger and Nazism', *Critical Inquiry* 15 (Winter 1989), pp. 407–88.

Agnes Heller

Born in Budapest. Perhaps the best known of the East European humanistic Marxist philosophers, attempting to make Marxism compatible with humanism. She was to become more humanist than Marxist and, like Hegedus, went into exile.

See also

Hegedus, Markovic.

Works include

The Theory of Need in Marx, London, Allison & Busby, 1976.
Beyond Justice, Oxford, Blackwell, 1989.
The Grandeur and Twilight of Radical Universalism, New Brunswick, N.J., Rutgers University, Transaction Publishers, 1990.
A Philosophy of Morals, Oxford, and Cambridge, Mass., Blackwell, 1990.

Other works

Donald Brown, *Towards a Radical Democracy: the Political Economy of the Budapest School*, London, Unwin Hyman, 1988

Rudolf Hilferding   1877–1941

Rudolf Hilferding was born in Vienna. After completing his medical studies at the university in 1901 he practised as a doctor until

1906 (and again during his military service from 1915 to 1918), but from his high-school days he became deeply interested in Marxist theory and began to write on economic and social questions while still at university. Some of his earliest articles appeared in *Le Mouvement Socialiste* (Paris) and from 1902 he was a frequent contributor to *Die Neue Zeit* (edited by Kautsky). In 1904 he published his rejoinder to Böhm-Bawerk's criticism (made from the standpoint of Austrian marginal utility theory) of Marx's economic theory, and in the same year founded and edited, with Max Adler, the *Marx-Studien*, a series of theoretical and political studies published intermittently from 1904 to 1923, which diffused the ideas of the new Austro-Marxist school. Soon afterwards, in 1906, Hilferding moved to Berlin to teach in the German Social Democratic Party (SPD) school, and then became foreign editor of the party journal, *Vorwärts*. By this time he had virtually completed his major study of the recent development of capitalism, published in 1910 as *Finance Capital*. On the outbreak of war in 1914 he joined the left wing of the SPD in opposing the voting of war credits, and after the war he edited the journal of the Independent Social Democratic Party (USPD), *Freiheit*, until he rejoined the SPD after its reunification in 1922.

Hilferding also had a directly political role in the post-war period. Having acquired Prussian citizenship in 1920, he became a member of the Reich Economic Council, and was elected to the Reichstag in 1924, remaining a member until 1933. On two occasions he was Minister of Finance, from August to October 1923 in the government of Gustav Stresemann, and from June 1928 to December 1929 in the government of Hermann Müller. During this period he also edited the journal *Die Gesellschaft*, to which he contributed many articles, and was active in the leadership of the SPD.

After Hitler's accession to power Hilferding was obliged to flee abroad, first to Denmark, then to Zurich, but he continued to participate actively in the work of the SPD while it

was in exile in Czechoslovakia and contributed frequently to the socialist press. In 1938 he moved to Paris, and after the collapse of France in 1940 went to the unoccupied zone, living at the Hôtel Forum in Arles. There he began to write his last major work, a reassessment of the Marxist theory of history entitled *Das historische Problem* (1941), the unfinished manuscript of which was published in 1954. But in February 1941 the Pétain government handed Hilferding over to the German authorities and he was taken by the Gestapo to Paris, where he probably committed suicide on 10 February.

Hilferding made a substantial and influential contribution to Marxist economic and social theory. His first major work was directed against Böhm-Bawerk as a representative of the psychological school of political economy (Austrian marginalism) and argued that the Marxist theory, which analyses the commodity as an expression of the social relationships among human beings, is superior to one which begins from a subjective value theory and ignores the social nexus. This argument retains much of its importance in relation to later debates about methodological individualism and rational action.

But it was in *Finance Capital* that Hilferding made his major contribution to Marxist theory. Here he analysed, in the light of recent changes in the capitalist economy, several questions which had been treated very briefly, or only mentioned, by Marx in the second and third volumes of *Capital*: the development of credit, the growth of joint-stock companies and cartels, economic crises and imperialism. His analysis of credit money is a preliminary to the main themes of his study, which are the increasing concentration and centralization of capital in large corporations, the dominant role of the banks in this process and the social and political consequences of these economic changes. The growth of corporations and the role of bank capital represented, for Hilferding, a further stage in the socialization of the economy, leading to a situation in which, as he argued, the most important spheres of large-scale industry could be taken into public ownership by taking possession of six large Berlin banks. Subsequently, in articles written during the war and in the 1920s, Hilferding developed and to some extent qualified this argument in his theory of 'organized capitalism' as a partially planned economy – a conception which has continued to influence more recent discussions of the capitalist economy. Equally, his view of the role of bank capital, though widely criticized, has remained influential, especially with regard to comparisons between capitalist economies.

The theory of imperialism which Hilferding expounded in the later chapters of his book initially attracted most attention and provided the starting point of the studies by Bukharin and Lenin, although Hilferding reached very different conclusions about the significance of imperialism for a transition to socialism, emphasizing the importance of the socialization of the economy, increasing state intervention and the various forces opposed to militarism and war, rather than the sequence of imperialism, war and revolution suggested by the Bolshevik theorists. In the event the socialist movement was unable to prevent the outbreak of war, but the eventual consequences of war and revolution did not conform very closely with the Bolshevik model either. Hilferding's main argument was that the development of monopolies and cartels leads to a new form of protectionism to defend the domestic market, and at the same time to a new form of expansionism through the export of capital to areas of cheap labour; and the maintenance of control over the new economic areas requires the active intervention of the state, which also leads to an intensification of conflict among the major capitalist states. Nationalism is transformed from a doctrine of national independence and cultural autonomy into an ideology of imperialism and world domination. Schumpeter attached great importance to this Austro-Marxist theory while criticizing the view that imperialism is a necessary stage of capitalism.

In his last major writings, in the light of experience of National Socialism in Germany and of Stalinism in the Soviet Union, Hilferding embarked on an analysis of totalitarianism and a revision of the Marxist theory of the state. He now argued that the growth of state power has accompanied the development of the modern economy, and that a significant change in the relation of the state to society has been brought about by the subordination of the economy to the coercive power of the state. In the case of the Soviet Union in particular he observed that, notwithstanding Engels's expectations, history had shown that the administration of things may become an unlimited domination over human beings. This radical reassessment of Marxist political theory, which suggests, like other Austro-Marxist writing on the state, a latent *rapprochement* with other conceptions of political power such as that of Max Weber, was not pursued in any systematic way after Hilferding's death, and recent debates about the 'relative autonomy' of the state have as yet brought little advance towards a more realistic theoretical scheme.

Hilferding was one of the founders of the Austro-Marxist school and remained closely associated with it throughout his life, even though he was resident, and politically active, in Germany for much of the time. The principal members of the school developed, in a neo-Kantian and positivist form, a conception of Marxism as a social theory, and more specifically as a sociological system, which by virtue of its scientific character was corrigible and had to engage in debate with rival theories. Hence Hilferding's critique of Austrian marginalist theory, various economic studies (of crises and of post-war capitalist rationalization) by Otto Bauer, and the analysis of imperialism by both Hilferding and Bauer. The philosophy of science which shaped Austro-Marxism was expounded primarily by Max Adler, whose methodological writings dealt with many of the same issues which preoccupied Weber, and have an affinity with modern scientific realism. This outlook also led the Austro-Marxists to extend Marxist research to new fields, notably in major studies of nationalism by Karl Renner and especially Bauer, in Renner's pioneering study of the social functions of law and in Hilferding's studies of finance capital, organized capitalism and the totalitarian state.

The theoretical stance, positivist and empirical, of the Austro-Marxists was reflected in their political practice, which conceived the transition to socialism as a democratic, gradual and largely peaceful process, a 'slow revolution', exemplified by their post-war achievements in Vienna in providing working-class housing, health and welfare services, and cultural and leisure activities, and in implementing major educational reforms, which made the city a showplace of social democracy. But they never obtained the majority support in Austria as a whole which would have enabled them to extend these social policies, or to promote the socialization of the economy in a socialist form, and they were finally overwhelmed in the civil war of 1934 provoked by the rising fascist movements. From the mid-1930s to the late 1960s, as a consequence first of fascist rule and then the dominance of Soviet Marxism, the Austro-Marxist school languished in obscurity, but since then it has attracted renewed attention, and with the final disintegration, following the radical changes in Eastern Europe, of the dogmatic Marxism inherited from the Stalinist era Austro-Marxism may well resume its development as the most viable and fruitful form of Marxist social theory.

See also

Adler, Bauer, Bukharin, Kautsky, Lenin, Renner, Schumpeter, Weber.

Works

Böhm-Bawerks Marx-Kritik, Vienna, Wiener Volksbuchhandlung, 1904, trans. Paul Sweezy as *Böhm-Bawerk: Karl Marx and the Close of his System*, New York, Kelley, 1949.
Finance Capital: a Study of the Latest Phase of Capitalist Development, 1910, London, Routledge, 1981.
'State capitalism or totalitarian state economy', *Socialist Courier* (New York), 1940.
Das historische Problem, new series, I, 1954, trans. in part in Tom Bottomore, *Interpretations of Marx*, Oxford, Blackwell, 1988.

Other works

Tom Bottomore, (ed.), *Austro-Marxism* (with Patrick Goode), Oxford, Clarendon Press, 1978.
Anthony Brewer, *Marxist Theories of Imperialism*, London, Routledge, 1980.
Laurence Harris, 'Finance capital', in *A Dictionary of Marxist Thought*, ed. Tom Bottomore, Oxford, Blackwell, 1983.
Tom Bottomore, *Theories of Modern Capitalism*, London, Allen & Unwin, 1985.

Adolf Hitler   1889–1945

Adolf Hitler was dictator of Germany from 1934 to 1945 and was the author of *Mein Kampf* (My Struggle), which became the affirmation of the Nazi movement. While in prison following the abortive beer-hall *Putsch* of 1923 Hitler wrote his political testament, which was first published in two volumes in 1925–6 and translated into English in 1933. It is not difficult to understand why *Mein Kampf* was more displayed than read, given its turgid prose, unsupported assertions and disjointed discourse. Indeed, Hitler argued that great world events were brought about by the spoken rather than the written word and in what was to be an accurate assessment of his own abilities declared that the success of a speech is measured not by its impression on a university professor but by its impact on the people. Simply to dismiss *Mein Kampf* as anti-intellectual and incoherent, however, is to overlook the blueprint of an astute politician for dictatorship, dominance and ultimately the crudest of crimes against humanity. To search *Mein Kampf* solely to discover Hitler's aggressive foreign-policy intentions is to neglect the ideological underpinnings of a racial nation state.

Hitler's political ideas were derived from a racial theory that combined vulgar Social Darwinism with virulent antisemitism. History was interpreted as a struggle between

Aryan superiority, which would be expressed through a German *Volk*, and the Jewish people as the evil detractors and carriers of corrupt culture. The achievement of racial purity was an imperative of the highest order. Everything else followed. Hitler wrote in *Mein Kampf*, 'We all sense that in the distant future humanity must be faced by problems which only a highest race, become master people and supported by the means and possibilities of an entire globe, will be equipped to overcome.' This was the mission of the Nazi movement, and the state was to be the means. Leadership provided the understanding, the inspiration and the will to make it happen. It was a sure-fire recipe for destruction which still inspires fringe (and sometimes not so fringe) political movements of antisemites and white suprem-acists in industrial and industrializing societies.

Works

Mein Kampf, D. W. Watt (ed.), trans. Ralph Manheim, London, Pimlico, 1992.
The Speeches of Adolf Hitler, April 1922–August 1939, ed. Norman H. Baines, two volumes, London, Oxford University Press, 1942.

Other works

Franz L. Neumann, *Behemoth: the Structure and Practice of German Socialism, 1933–44*, New York, Oxford University Press, 1942.
Alan Bullock, *Hitler: a Study in Tyranny*, London, Odhams Press, 1952.
Walter Laqueur (ed.), *Fascism: a Reader's Guide*, London, Wildwood House, 1988.
Stanley G. Payne, *A History of Facism*, Madison, University of Wisconsin Press, 1996.

Leonard Trelawney Hobhouse 1864–1929

British social philosopher and liberal political theorist. Hobhouse developed a view of social evolution which underpinned a positive role for the state in preserving individual freedom while promoting the common good.

Works

Liberalism, 1911, reprinted New York, Oxford University Press, 1964.
Development and Purpose, London, Macmillan, 1913.
The Metaphysical Theory of the State, 1918, reprinted London, Allen & Unwin, 1960.
The Elements of Social Justice, 1922, reprinted London, Allen & Unwin, 1965.
Social Development: its Nature and Conditions, London, Allen & Unwin, 1924.

Other works

P. Clarke, *Liberals and Social Democrats*, Cambridge, Cambridge University Press, 1978.
S. Collini, *Liberalism and Sociology: L. T. Hobhouse and Political Argument in England, 1880–1914*, Cambridge, Cambridge University Press, 1979.

John Atkinson Hobson 1858–1940

Author of more than fifty books, Hobson is best known as a precursor of Lenin's theory of imperialism and Keynes's concept of effective demand. Imperialism was a consequence of the need for an outlet for over-saving by capitalists. His analysis, however, differed from Lenin's in rejecting imperialism as an historical necessity, advocating reformist measures.

See also

Keynes, Lenin.

Works include

The Physiology of Industry (with A. F. Mummery), London, Murray, 1889.
Imperialism: a Study, London, Nisbet, 1902.
The Crisis of Liberalism, 1909, reprinted Brighton, Harvester, 1974.
The Industrial System, London, Longman, 1909.

Other works

Jules Townshend, *J. A. Hobson*, Manchester, Manchester University Press, 1990.

Max Horkheimer 1895–1973

Max Horkheimer, a primary exponent of 'critical theory' and the most influential director of the Institute for Social Research at the University of Frankfurt, was born in the vicinity of Stuttgart. The son of a wealthy Jewish industrialist, Horkheimer finished high school after the First World War and studied a variety of subjects at the University of Frankfurt, where he ultimately wrote a dissertation on Kant's *Critique of Judgement*.

It was in 1923 that Horkheimer's friend, Felix Weil, decided to found the Institute for Social Research; Horkheimer took over as the institute's director in 1930. Before then he had published very little of note. But during the early 1930s he articulated a new interdisciplinary perspective for the 'Frankfurt school'. With essays like 'Traditional and critical theory', which rejected both positivism and ontology, he began the formulation of a non-systemic and inherently 'critical' stance capable of situating phenomena empirically while still retaining an emancipatory interest in transforming all repressive conditions. Indeed, with this new critical perspective Horkheimer and his colleagues tried to explore the non-economic institutions and cultural forces that had subverted the revolutionary mission of the proletariat and led so many to the right.

The triumph of Hitler forced the Frankfurt school into exile. Horkheimer, for his part, was engaged in relocating the institute first in Geneva, then in Paris and finally at Columbia University. It was thus under difficult conditions that, in collaboration with Erich Fromm, he completed *Studies on Authority and the Family* (1936) as well as a number of seminal essays like 'The Jews and Europe' (1938) and 'The authoritarian state' (1940), all of which expose the manner in which liberal capitalism betrayed its emancipatory promise and laid the psychological, racial and political foundations of totalitarianism.

Dialectic of Enlightenment, co-authored with Theodor Adorno, and *The Eclipse of Reason* drew the implications. These works argued that the Enlightenment notion of progress – inherited by Marxism – was illusory, since a 'mass society' has come into existence wherein old ideological divisions hardly matter and the freedom of the individual is pitted against all objective social relations. Commodity production has rendered individuals interchangeable, nature has become a mere object of utilitarian domination, the capacity for ethical judgement is undercut by instrumental rationality, and conformism is reinforced by a profit-driven 'culture industry' that seeks only the lowest common denominator for its products and threatens the very possibility of reflection. Such are the results of Enlightenment thought which, intent upon attacking religious dogma in the name of scientific truth, would ultimately reject all forms of non-technical thinking as irrational.

After the return of the institute to Germany in 1949, Horkheimer and Adorno decided to publish the *Frankfurt Contributions to Sociology* (1955), which made popular many of the previously unknown publications of its *Journal for Social Research*. The two became major intellectual figures, with a coterie of outstanding students that included Jürgen Habermas and Alfred Schmidt. Horkheimer even served as Rector of the University of Frankfurt from 1951 to 1953.

He had relinquished his faith in philosophical idealism and Marxism, rejected the certainties of ontology, and – by 1968 – decried the possibility of cultural or political liberation. The only way to keep alive the idea of an emancipatory alternative, an order 'totally different' from the present, was through religion. Horkheimer thus looked to the Old Testament, which taught that, just as the attempt to portray God is prohibited, so is it necessary to admit that we cannot know the true or the good; happiness must remain always incomplete. The last essays, crucially influenced by critics of the Enlightenment like Schopenhauer and Nietzsche, thus combine utopianism with a profound pessimism.

Just as Horkheimer and Adorno never bothered to note earlier that the great thinkers of the Enlightenment were generally adherents of liberalism, and that its entire political thrust was anti-totalitarian, so did the elder theorist of the Frankfurt school forget that an affirmation of the absolute is not the prerequisite of judgement and that the sacred may not prove useful in making sense of the profane. The time for a critique of critical theory had come. Indeed, far more than Enlightenment philosophy, the whole philosophical enterprise stood perilously close to jettisoning its emancipatory character when Max Horkheimer died at the age of seventy-eight.

See also

Adorno, Fromm, Habermas.

Works

Dialectic of Enlightenment (with Theodor Adorno), 1944, New York, Herder, 1972.
Critical Theory, New York, Seabury Press, 1972.
The Eclipse of Reason, New York, Seabury Press, 1974.
Dawn and Decline: Notes, 1926–31, 1950–69, New York, Seabury Press, 1978.

Other works

Martin Jay, *The Dialectical Imagination: a History of the Frankfurt School and the Institute of Social Research, 1923–50*, Boston, Mass., Little Brown, 1973.
David Held, *An Introduction to Critical Theory*, Berkeley, Cal., University of California Press, 1980.
Helmut Dubiel, *Theory and Politics*, Cambridge, Mass., MIT Press, 1985.
Douglas Kellner, *Critical Theory, Marxism and Modernity*, Baltimore, Md, Johns Hopkins University Press, 1989.

There is still no major biography in English.

Branko Horvat   1928–

Born in Petrinja, Yugoslavia. Principal theorist of self-governing socialism based on the former Yugoslav model and a major proponent of participatory democracy rooted in the workplace. Went into exile.

See also

Markovic.

Works include

Self-governing Socialism, White Plains, N.Y., International Arts and Sciences, 1975.

Ivan Illich   1926–1997

The pace of change in the latter part of the twentieth century has been its own forcing frame for fresh assessments of the working of political and social institutions, and if the name of Ivan Illich stands out as one of a select company of innovators in the realm of ideas it does so on the basis of a remarkable range of books, each of which has expressed the spirit of this change as much as it has helped to fashion and stimulate it. A Viennese-born seminarian, he was ordained a Catholic priest at twenty-five and made a monsignor at thirty-three. His pre-ordination studies in the natural sciences, history, philosophy and theology took him to Florence, Rome, Munich and to Salzburg, where he received his doctorate. He regarded his clerical office and his academic distinction as a means of pursuing truth rather than of affirming a received faith. When the inevitable clash with his superiors came it was their authority he disclaimed rather than his quest or his essential faith.

Illich burst upon the intellectual scene two years after his resignation from the priesthood, with *Celebration of Awareness* in 1970, and it set the tone for the decade of work that was to follow. Combining a feisty faith in individual authority and a distrust of hierarchy and 'expertise', he criticized and exposed most of the institutions of the modern world and called instead for a world emphasizing the liberty – and, more, the sovereignty – of the individual citizen. This book was followed the very next year by the work that made him famous, *De-schooling Society*, whose simple and amply proven message was that 'most learning happens casually and even most intentional learning is not the result of programmed instruction'; from that premise comes the conclusion that the home environment is most important in all children's development and that neither formal teaching nor authorized teachers are necessary for effective learning. In 1976 a similar analysis, *Medical Nemesis*, challenged the idea that 'what medical schools produce in any way contributes to health' and showed that the medical establishment in fact largely results in 'iatrogenesis' – the creation of ill health by those who are supposed to eliminate it.

This same sagacious critique of contemporary society, and particularly of its establishment, continued in several other works of the period: *Tools for Conviviality* and *Energy and Equity* attacked the 'manipulative technologies' of industrial nations for failing to deliver their promised liberation and happiness; *The Disabling Professions, Toward a History of Needs* and especially *Shadow Work* were merciless onslaughts on modernity itself and the multiple ways in which it expropriates, alienates, manipulates and degrades its human components. Naturally enough, most conventional critics found such approaches uncongenial, and Illich was taken to task for his failure to appreciate the 'beneficial effects' of modern technology. Consequently his work had a harder time finding a larger audience.

Undaunted, Illich in the 1980s produced several works, particularly *Gender* and *H(2)0 and the Waters of Forgetfulness*, that continue to demonstrate this disenchantment with the contemporary world, criticizing even such bedrock concepts as the way we think about sex roles, sexuality, language and liberation itself. And in response to those who continued to challenge his all-out assault, demanding that he come up with the constructs of an alternative, Illich publicly disdained any such palliative, arguing instead that 'I want to provide a method which allows people to distinguish the feasible from the infeasible utopia.'

Whatever the final judgement on his two decades of critique, it is clear that he must be regarded as one of the main intellectual forces that led the widespread reassessment of industrial society in the mid-twentieth century. His frequently vituperative onslaughts appeared at a time when 'welfare statism' was riding high. The idea that it was not delivering the goods and that it was institutionally incapable of doing so seemed to many a form of intellectual aberrance and social heresy.

According to Illich, doctors, hospitals and specialized and expensive forms of treatment were not curing illness, they were causing it; educationalists, schools and specialized techniques of teaching were not educating children so much as misinforming them and blunting their natural disposition to learn in order to mould them into the consumerist society. In the same way machines, whether in industry, in the home or for transport, were not widening human horizons but enslaving humankind in a mechanized pattern of life the keynotes of which were uniformity of experience, mediocrity of response and a deadening of the creative capacity.

For all the startling novelty of much of his thinking there is a traditionalist streak of utopianism running through his work, with echoes of William Morris, Bernard Shaw, Chesterton, Tolstoy and Gandhi as well as of some of the moderns, Mumford, Goodman, Schumacher and Kohr.

Until recently it might not have been too difficult to dismiss Illich as a man before his time, out of touch with current reality. Opinion has become transformed in so many ways, however, that some aspects of his work are even beginning to appear dated, despite the fact that his writings have been a major causative factor in the transformation.

See also

Gandhi, Goodman, Kohr, Schumacher, Shaw.

Works

Celebration of Awareness: a Call for Institutional Awareness, New York, Doubleday, 1970; London, Calder & Boyars, 1971.

De-schooling Society, New York, Harper, 1971; London, Calder & Boyars, 1972.

Tools for Conviviality, New York, Harper; London, Calder & Boyars, 1973.

Energy and Equity, New York, Harper; London, Calder & Boyars, 1974.

Medical Nemesis: the Expropriation of Health, London, Calder & Boyars, 1975.

Toward a History of Needs, New York, Pantheon, 1978.

Shadow Work, London, Boyars, 1981.

Gender, New York, Pantheon, 1983; London, Boyars, 1982.

H(2)0 and the Waters of Forgetfulness, Berkeley, Cal., Heyday, 1987; London, Boyars, 1986.

Other works

John L. Elias, *Conscientization and Deschooling: Freire's and Illich's Proposals for Reshaping Society*, Philadelphia, Pa, Westminster, 1976.

David F. Horrobin, *Medical Hubris: a Reply to Ivan Illich*, Montreal, Eden, n.d.

Peter Lund, *Ivan Illich and his Antics*, Denby Dale, England, SLD, 1978.

Muhammad Iqbal   1877–1938

Muhammad Iqbal was the most outstanding poet and philosopher of modern South Asia. Born at Sialkot, he obtained his early education in Lahore under Sir Thomas Arnold. In 1905 he went to Cambridge to read philosophy with the neo-Hegelian McTaggart. Later he was called to the bar. For his doctorate he worked on the 'Development of Metaphysics in Persia' at Munich University. In 1922 he was knighted.

For Iqbal, who wrote both in Urdu and in Persian, poetry was a vehicle for conveying a social and political message. His major work in prose, *Six Lectures on the Reconstruction of Religious Thought in Islam*, was characterized by an impassioned call for rejuvenating classical thought by recourse to *ijtihad* (reinterpretation). Although he has been described as both a philosopher and a religious scholar, he was neither a systematic thinker nor a trained theologian but a poet whose writing often conveys deep philosophical ideas, is imbued with religious imagery and vocabulary and draws heavily upon the cumulative history of the Muslim community, extolling and inspiring it to attain new heights of glory.

Iqbal practised law in Lahore and engaged in political activity. From 1925 to 1928 he was a member of the Punjab Legislative Assembly. In 1930 he presided over the Allahabad session of the Muslim League and made history by calling for the amalgamation of the Punjab, North West Frontier Provinces, Sindh and Baluchistan into a single state within or outside the British Empire. During 1937, in correspondence with M. A. Jinnah, the leader of the Muslim League, Iqbal expressed dissatisfaction with the effects the Government of India Act of 1935 had on Muslims and called for self-determination for the Muslim-majority provinces. This has been viewed by some as the first call for the creation of Pakistan. In 1931 and 1932 Iqbal represented the Muslim League at the Round Table conferences in London.

Iqbal's intellectual genealogy has been traced back to different sources. Some have seen in him the influence of Hegel, Nietzsche and Bergson. While not denying his familiarity with the Western philosophical tradition, it must be emphasized that his ideas are rooted in his own understanding of the Qur'an, the work of the great sufi master Jalaluddin Rumi, the lessons of Islamic history and the realities, as he perceived them, of the age in which he lived.

Iqbal's political ideas cannot be separated from the rest of his thought. He lays great emphasis on *Khudi*, translated by some as ego, and used it to develop the concept of *Insan i Kamil*, the Perfect Man who is exhorted to fulfil God's mission on earth. This is not Nietzsche's superman at work but rather a personality inspired by the ideals of the Qur'an and the example of the Prophet. Similarly, the Islamic belief in the unity of God *(tauhid)* served for Iqbal a concrete social and political function: it leads to the unity of mankind and the dismantling of distinctions based on race, religion or birth.

Before his departure for Europe, Iqbal's poetry focused on Indian themes and was not critical of nationalism. The outstanding examples of this phase are the two poems *National Anthem* and *New Temple*, which in the wake of Hindu–Muslim conflict advocated coexistence and human solidarity. Condemnation of communal strife, oppression and untouchability and advocacy of freedom remain important themes in his work.

By the time Iqbal returned from Europe he had undergone a profound change, best epitomized perhaps in *Anthem of the Community*, where his main concern becomes the international Islamic *ummah* (community). In 1908, as his ship passed Sicily, he yearned for the Muslim rule of the island. The Balkan wars and the battle of Tripoli in 1910 shook him profoundly and resulted in his major poem, *Shikwa* (Complaint), and the *Jawab-i-Shikwa* (Reply to the Complaint) which outlined the lost glories of the Muslim past and offered a panacea for the future.

The early decades of the twentieth century saw large parts of the Muslim world become subservient to the West. Iqbal was greatly touched by these events, as is reflected in poems such as the *Land of Islam, Muslim, Modern Civilization.* He exhorted his people to go back to the pristine purity of the faith, to the spirit and enthusiasm which had fired the early Muslims. As Iqbal's subject and perspective enlarged from the regional to the global, his language changed from Urdu to Persian. In 1915 *Asrar-i-Khudi* (Secrets of the Self) appeared, with its powerful appeal for action and realization of man's goal in life. R. A. Nicholson, who translated the *Asrar* in 1920, summed Iqbal up: 'Iqbal is a man of his age and a man in advance of his age; he is also a man in disagreement with his age.'

The *Rumuz-i-Bikhudi* (Mysteries of Selflessness), the other major work in Persian, advocated development of a morally autonomous personality of the individual as the quintessence of an Islamic society.

Iqbal provided a powerful indictment of territorial nationalism with its concomitant regard for race and regionalism. He considered it the cause of rivalry between people and wars. Rejecting the separation of church and state, he argued that community in Islam, despite geographical differences, was held together by faith in the unity of God. The externalization of this basic belief is found in the human solidarity of Islam, which as a social force is grounded in the Qur'an and Sunna. The obvious contradiction between this call for a transnational Muslim confederation and the call for a Muslim nation state in South Asia perhaps never occurred to him.

While exhorting Muslims to action, Iqbal denounced the otherworldliness of the sufis. He was critical of godless Western life and thought and argued that materialism and irreligiosity would inevitably bring about the decline of the West. Conceding that the West was 'dazzling', he went on to remark that its 'jewels' were like 'broken shells'. He severely criticized Western-style emancipation of women and regarded democracy as autocracy in disguise. In it, men are counted, not weighed. Legislative bodies serve as camouflage for rich capitalists exploiting the poor. Even the League of Nations did not escape his ridicule.

There is praise for socialism and its struggle against capitalism, exploitation of the peasantry and unemployment, but communism is rejected as an ideal. For Iqbal communism had got bogged down in destruction and did not move on to a creative and positive stage as does Islam. The early Islamic polity as developed in the time of the Prophet and the early Caliphs, which brought together the existential and spiritual needs of mankind, remained his ideal.

Iqbal has been claimed by people from different backgrounds. His verses have been cited to justify different spiritual, political or social positions. He has commanded tremendous affection and reverence and his poetry continues to have a wide appeal.

Works

Secrets of the Self, trans. R. A. Nicholson, London, Macmillan, 1920.
The Reconstruction of Religious Thought in Islam, London, Oxford University Press, 1934.
Persian Psalms, trans. A. J. Arberry, Lahore, Ashraf, 1948.
Mysteries of Selflessness, trans. A. J. Arberry, London, Murray, 1953.
Javid Nama, trans. A. J. Arberry, London, Allen & Unwin, 1966.

Other works

S. Abdul Valid, *Iqbal: his Art and Thought*, London, Murray, 1959.
A. Schimmel, *Gabriel's Wing*, Leiden, Brill, 1963.
Aziz Ahmad, *Islamic Modernism in India and Pakistan, 1857–1964*, London, Oxford University Press, 1967.
S. A. A. Nadwi, *The Glory of Iqbal*, trans. A. Kidwai, Lucknow, Academy of Islamic Research and Publications, 1973.

Vladimir Jabotinsky
1880–1940

Vladimir Jabotinsky was born in Odessa, a centre of Jewish intellectual life in Russia. He remained a powerful influence and a controversial figure in Zionist politics long after his death. His talents for language and literature were broadened by travel and study in Western Europe. He earned a law degree from the University of Rome. A renowned orator, Jabotinsky was also a prolific writer who published essays, novels, poems and plays. Calling himself an authentic follower of Theodor Herzl, the founder of Zionism, Jabotinsky postulated the establishment of Palestine as a Jewish state as Zionism's only significant long and short-term goal. Prior to the institution of British rule in Palestine, Jabotinsky's political positions were indistinguishable from the mainstream Zionist agenda: support for economic and cultural projects in Palestine and the organization of self-defence units.

The First World War altered the international balance of forces and left its imprint on Jabotinsky's political philosophy. He became known for his opposition to the Zionist leadership and to the strategy of modifying Zionist political aims. Jabotinsky's adversarial stance split the World Zionist Organization in 1935. British sponsorship of a Jewish national home had offered Jews the opportunity to expand their domain in Palestine, but only if they asserted their autonomy and aggressively pressed their demands for sovereignty. The Zionist programme could not be overly ambitious, and Jabotinsky identified a Jewish army and police force as absolute priorities. There ought not to be immigration quotas in Palestine for Jews. Jewish political independence could be won if the state-building process was rapid. A Jewish majority and army were essential prerequisites of sovereignty because independence could not be achieved without combat. An army would also instil a sense of discipline, self-esteem and an etiquette supportive of a national liberation struggle. A Jewish state on both sides of the river Jordan was indispensable, not on religious or historical grounds but rather for the sake of power politics. The British must be held to their promises.

Jabotinsky emphasized that Arabs and Jews were locked in competition for control over Palestine, and that only force would check Arab efforts to secure independence. Jews must build an 'iron wall' in Palestine before they could create a state and thereby generate the conditions for coexistence with the Arabs. A clarion call for a Jewish state must be issued. Demands ought not to be subdued for fear of inciting Arab opposition or widening the breach between Zionist and British interests.

Prompted by the boldness of Jabotinsky's romantic passion for the military, many of his followers formed secret militias and terrorist organizations which attacked the British and the Arabs. Jabotinsky never authorized these attacks, nor did he condemn them. He based his hopes for the future on the possibility of creating a dedicated corps of young people capable of fighting for a Jewish state. Betar, the youth movement, moulded under his inspiration, gravitated to displays of martial arts. Among Zionist theoreticians Jabotinsky was unique in his self-conscious reflections on the nature of leadership, which seemed more congenial to authoritarian than to democratic political principles.

Works

Samson the Nazirite, London, Basic, 1930.

Other works

Joseph B. Schechtman, *The Vladimir Jabotinsky Story*, New York, Yoseloff, 1956.
Arthur Hertzberg (ed.), *The Zionist Idea*, New York, Atheneum Press, 1959.
Rael Isaac, *Israel Divided: Ideological Politics in the Jewish State*, Baltimore, Md, Johns Hopkins University Press, 1976.
Shlomo Avineri, *The Making of Modern Zionism*, New York, Basic, 1981.

C. L. R. James   1901–1989

Born in Trinidad, Cyril Lionel Robert James was a many-sided social and cultural theorist, revolutionary activist and influential mentor of Afro-Caribbean origin. For over half a century he made a distinctive contribution to the history and analysis of slave revolts, anti-colonial revolutions, popular culture and post-Trotskyist Marxism. Although called, late in life, to a Chair at an inner-city university in Washington, D.C. – and the recipient of honorary doctorates from the Universities of the West Indies and Hull – he received no formal university education himself, tending to be highly critical of academicized knowledge and its associated careerist life style. His life and work were marked by a passionate didacticism which took as axiomatic Marx's dictum that the aim of attempting to interpret the world was to change it.

Despite the strength of his revolutionary commitment, James possessed both a highly cultivated and a cosmopolitan outlook. The former had its origin in the *entrée* which a few outstanding 'native' pupils could obtain to a high-powered classical education through scholarships to the elite British secondary school in colonial Port of Spain; while his wide cultural sympathies, completely immune from racial or ethnic prejudices of any kind, were shaped by a radical creole nationalist ideology endemic to the vibrant, polyglot island on which he was born and lived until the age of thirty. Unmistakably black in appearance – and affirmatively matter-of-fact about his personal racial identity – he dedicated a major part of his life's work to the advancement of black freedom movements while always regarding them as subsumed in a process of universal emancipation.

Departing from the West Indies for England in 1932 as a provincial *littérateur*, teacher and cricketing enthusiast, he obtained employment as a freelance cricket correspondent for the *Manchester Guardian*; he became deeply embroiled in the revolutionary socialist ferment of the Depression years, quickly rising – by virtue of his natural intellectual and oratorical gifts – to a position of leadership in the Marxist group within the Independent Labour Party. His publications during this initial sojourn in Britain included a major Trotskyist polemic, *World Revolution, 1917–36: Rise and Fall of the Communist International* and a translation of Boris Souvarine's *Stalin*

His Trinidad-acquired fluency in French also enabled him to conduct historical research in France on the Haitian extension of the French revolution, an epic struggle narrated in his best-known work, *The Black Jacobins*, which was supplemented by his pioneering comparative study, *A History of Negro Revolt*. At the same time he was active in the early African anti-colonial struggle, collaborating in London with an old Trinidad friend, George Padmore, in forming the International African Service Bureau, editing its periodical *International African Opinion*, while also providing yet another Trinidadian, Eric Williams, then a student at Oxford, with ideas for the latter's classic study *Capitalism and Slavery*. In 1936 James's play *Toussaint l'Ouverture*, with his friend, the black American singer Paul Robeson in the lead, was performed in London.

In 1938 James left Britain for the United States as an established historian and Trotskyist ideologue. Invited to Mexico to discuss with Trotsky the dwindling movement's position on the hitherto neglected Negro question, James stressed the revolutionary potential of the black masses and became the party's authority on the issue through articles written for its newspaper under the name 'J. R. Johnson'.

In 1940 he left the official Trotskyist organization and founded, with Raya Dunayevskaya and others, the 'Johnson–Forrest Tendency', representing a radical break not only with Trotskyism but with all versions of a revolutionary vanguard. The 'Johnsonites' consigned the previously privileged Marxist intellectual vanguard to a mere technical, facilitating role in relation to the autonomous working-class movements which would arise in surprising and unpredictable forms out of structural contradictions central to both Western capitalist and Stalinist societies. Such movements, when they appeared, would themselves constitute the only viable, creative centres of social transformation.

This theory, which anticipated by over a generation key aspects in the dismantling of Stalinism begun by the workers of Solidarity in Poland – the initial stages of which James would live to witness and comment on – was based not only on an historical analysis of class struggle but on a critique of vanguardist thinking arising from an intensive study of the obscured Hegelian roots of Marxism. James's *Notes on Dialectics*, which circulated in mimeographed form within his political circle for many years prior to publication, employed a lively exposition of Hegel's *Logic* to demolish orthodox Leninist organizational principles, and claimed to expose the origins of the conceptual errors in the thought of other Marxists.

While a radical democratic metaphysics characterized all James's mature work, it was far removed from a vulgar socialist populism. James was fascinated by outstanding individual achievement in all fields, whether in the Renaissance art of Michelangelo, the cricketing technique of W. G. Grace – James's *Beyond a Boundary* is a recognized classic on the social origins of the sport – or in the calypsos of Mighty Sparrow. His approach to both cultural and political analysis was essentially the same: he embraced a speculative approach and always insisted, in true Hegelian style, that valid knowledge was a total process based on the dialectical interdependence of empirical fact, generalization and theoretical interpretation. This was the sophisticated, European, philosophical foundation of his cultural and political critiques which was, understandably, scarcely acknowledged, let alone understood, by admirers who saw him primarily in the context of his contributions to black liberation and Caribbean history and politics.

In 1952 James was expelled from the United States, penning *Mariners, Renegades and Castaways*, his brilliant study of Melville's *Moby Dick*, while awaiting deportation on Ellis Island. His old pupil Eric Williams summoned him to assist in the independence movement in Trinidad in 1958 and for the next thirty years – based variously in Trinidad, the United States and the black ghetto district of Brixton in south London – to the end of his life C. L. R. James was widely regarded as the most important radical philosopher which the English-speaking Caribbean had produced – a champion of pan-Caribbean political union – and even as a humanist genius of world stature.

Personally approachable, and intellectually acute to the end of his life, 'Nello' James became a venerable institution with an enormous influence on the rising generation of West Indians, serving as an important adviser to black political activists in Britain, eventually making appearances as commentator and lecturer on British television. He was finally interred, appropriately, in his native Trinidad by the island's leading industrial trade union.

Works

The Black Jacobins: Toussaint l'Ouverture and the San Domingo Revolution, 1938, reprinted London, Allison & Busby, 1980.
Notes on Dialectics: Hegel, Marx, Lenin, London, 1948, Allison & Busby, 1980.
Beyond a Boundary, London, Hutchinson, 1963.
At the Rendezvous of Victory, London, Allison & Busby, 1984.

Other works

I. Oxaal, Black Intellectuals come to Power: the Rise of Creole Nationalism in Trinidad, Cambridge, Mass., Schenkman, 1968.
C. J. Robinson, Black Marxism: the Making of the Black Radical Tradition, London, Zed Press, 1983.
P. Buhle (ed.), C. L. R. James: his Life and Work, London, Allison & Busby, 1986.
P. Buhle, C. L. R. James: the Artist as Revolutionary, London & New York, Verso, 1988; contains extensive bibliography.
Anna Grimshaw (ed.), The C. L. R. James Reader, Cambridge, Mass., Blackwell, 1992.

Karl Kautsky   1854–1938

Karl Kautsky was the pre-eminent theorist of the social democratic workers' movement and of what would come to be known as 'orthodox Marxism'. Born in Prague, he left for Vienna in 1874 to enter the university, where he studied history, economics and philosophy. The following year he joined the Social Democratic Party and gradually came to know the leaders of Austrian and German socialism, Viktor Adler, August Bebel and Wilhelm Liebknecht. In 1880 Kautsky went to Zurich, where he became a close friend of Eduard Bernstein, then a committed Marxist and editor of The Social Democrat. Nevertheless, when he got the chance to meet Marx and Engels he moved to London in 1881 and served briefly as the latter's private secretary.

Only in 1883 did he return to Vienna to found Die Neue Zeit (New Age) which until 1917 served as the major organ of Marxist thought. For seven years it was published in London, owing to the repressive 'anti-socialist laws' initiated by Bismarck's authoritarian regime. During that time Kautsky published an enormously popular summary of the first volume of Capital entitled The Economic Doctrines of Karl Marx (1887) and a slew of historical enquiries which included Thomas More and his Utopia (1887) as well as The Class Contradictions of 1789 (1889). These, along with later works, such as The Precursors of Modern Socialism (1894) and Foundations of Christianity (1908), would not only employ a class perspective to analyse political and ideological events but also help place the workers' movement of his time in historical and philosophical context. Indeed, Kautsky was already a well-known figure when he returned to Germany in 1890 to co-author – with Bernstein – the Erfurt Programme, which would serve as the guiding document of that country's Social Democratic Party (SPD) and as an inspiration to virtually every other European socialist organization.

Anticipating the modern welfare state with a set of proposed reforms ranging from better working conditions to free funerals, this programme was predicated on an orthodox Marxism that foretold the 'inevitable' collapse of capitalism through 'natural necessity'. Following Marx, Kautsky believed that capitalist development demanded an increasing supply of workers forced to sell their time, or 'labour power', on the market. Even so, in order to minimize costs and maximize profits, the bourgeoisie would constantly seek to introduce new technology to supplant this 'living labour'. As more was produced, ever fewer would be able to buy the goods in question. Overproduction, and a 'falling rate of profit', would subsequently lead to one 'crisis' after another of ever-increasing severity. The future collapse of capitalism could thus be argued in 'objective' terms.

This made it possible for Marxism to dispense with a purely normative justification and rely on the truth criteria of the natural sciences. Always closer to positivism than idealist dialectics, Kautsky could understand ideologies and political events as direct responses to concrete economic class interests that were themselves open to empirical investigation. Throughout his life he maintained that both the natural and the social world could be encompassed within a single overriding theory. Indeed, this stance was only buttressed by the publication of his *Ethics and the Materialist Conception of History* (1906), which provided an anthropological basis for class struggle.

Because capitalist development demanded an ever-expanding working class, an 'objective' foundation appeared for the socialist commitment to republicanism and electoral politics. And, in terms of his allegiance to the goal of a republican order, Kautsky never wavered. If the year 1898 witnessed a break with the right wing of the socialist movement and with Bernstein, who was attempting to 'revise' Marxism and supplant an emphasis on political transformation with a strategy of class compromise to further incremental economic gains, the Russian events of 1905 brought Kautsky into conflict with the left wing of the SPD and his one-time protégé, Rosa Luxemburg, who called upon German workers basically to forgo elections and initiate an 'offensive' mass strike. Then too, with the outbreak of the Russian revolution, Kautsky was adamant in his condemnation of bolshevik authoritarianism in works like *The Dictatorship of the Proletariat* (1918).

However, Kautsky's 'centrist' stance – articulated in *The Road to Power* (1909) – was content to call upon the SPD to remain in 'opposition' to the existing order and wait for the 'laws' of capitalist development to realize themselves in its favour it seemed, after all, that the mass party was too small to rule democratically and too large to embark on a revolutionary adventure. Even *The Social Revolution* (1902), Kautsky's most radical attempt to provide a framework for the new society, never dealt with the political means necessary for transforming the existing one. Indeed, this inability to formulate a positive political tactic is precisely what highlighted the 'deterministic' and 'economistic' aspects of orthodox Marxism.

Such inadequacies came to a head in 1914. Though committed to the traditional pacifism of pre-war social democracy, Kautsky found himself faced with a party majority in favour of war and the sudden inflation of chauvinist sentiments among the workers themselves. He obeyed party discipline and voted to grant the Kaiser's request for war credits – thereby earning the condemnation of Lenin in *The Proletarian Revolution and the Renegade Kautsky*. But by 1916 the politics of the SPD had become too conciliatory and its discipline too constraining. Kautsky, along with Bernstein and many others of their generation, thus made the painful decision to split and constitute the Independent Social Democratic Party (USPD). They were to rejoin the parent organization only in 1922 when the new party was ready to dissolve and it had become necessary to choose between the nascent Weimar Republic and Lenin's Communist International. Indeed, given Kautsky's democratic commitments, his decision was a foregone conclusion.

According to Kautsky, the existence of a republic invalidated the theoretical need for further revolution. But this left the SPD with an identity deficit – and so he was asked to draw up a new programme for the 1925 socialist party congress in Heidelberg. The result, however, was little more than stale remake of the Erfurt Programme. And the publication of *The Materialist Conception of History* (1927), a last attempt to systematize his world view, did not help matters. Especially with the Nazi triumph, it became ever more difficult to sustain the old thinking in a new period. If Kautsky's 'orthodox' was to prove increasingly irrelevant to socialist reformists the commitment to democracy made it positively threatening to communist authoritarians. That is why, today, his importance is primarily historical. Nevertheless, in that respect Kautsky remains the outstanding symbol of a time when socialism was infused with a radical democratic ethos and a unified workers' movement believed it incarnated humanity's future.

See also

Bernstein, Lenin, Luxemburg.

Works

The Agrarian Question, 1899, reprinted London, Zwan, 1988.
The Social Revolution, Chicago, Kerr, 1902.
The Class Struggle, Chicago, Kerr, 1910.
The Dictatorship of the Proletariat, 1918, reprinted Ann Arbor, University of Michigan Press, 1964.
The Materialist Conception of History, 1927, reprinted New Haven, Conn., Yale University Press, 1988.

Other works

Kolakowski Leszek, 'German Orthodoxy: Karl Kautsky', *Main Currents of Marxism*, Oxford, Oxford University Press, 1978.
Massimo Salvadori, *Karl Kautsky and the Socialist Revolution*, London, Lawrence & Wishart, 1979.
Stephen Eric Bronner, 'Karl Kautsky: the Rise and Fall of Orthodox Marxism', in *Socialism Unbound*, New York, Routledge, 1990.

Hans Kelsen   1881–1973

Primarily a legal theorist, Kelsen studied law at the University of Vienna and later became professor of law there (1911–30). He then moved to Cologne where he stayed for only three years (1930–3). The rise of National Socialism drove him as a Jew first to Prague (1933–8) and eventually to the University of California in Berkeley.

To understand Kelsen's contribution to political philosophy, one must first come to grips with certain aspects of his legal theory. In jurisprudential thought, at least three schools can be identified, namely natural law, legal realism and legal positivism. Of the last, Kelsen is commonly acknowledged as the most systematic and outstanding theorist in the twentieth century.

However, legal positivism itself is a complex doctrine of law and includes theorists as diverse as Jeremy Bentham and Thomas Hobbes. Epistemologically, Kelsen constructs his science of law by presupposing a basic norm (or *grundnorm*) from which ultimately may be derived all the valid norms of the legal system. Methodologically, this basic norm is

the same in all systems and may be formulated as 'the constitution ought to be obeyed', or more precisely, 'coercive acts ought to be performed only in accordance with the constitution'. For instance, in the English legal system the basic norm would be 'what the Queen in Parliament says is law'. Any legal norm created by a legal organ in England is valid only if it could be derived from that basic norm itself. The basic norm acts as a unifying framework, giving a particular legal system its identity as well as guaranteeing the validity of legal decisions, rules and norms. The basic norm validates the constitution, the constitution validates the general norms (e.g. statutes) and in turn the general norms validate the individual judicial decisions.

Like other forms of legal positivism, the Kelsenian variety crucially distinguishes between the validity and the morality of a legal rule. To say that a rule is valid is not to say that it is morally proper or desirable (and vice versa). Furthermore, its validity, not its morality, establishes the citizen's obligation to obey it. This is the so-called separation-of-law-and-morals thesis which all forms of legal positivism uphold as central. However, Kelsen differs from Bentham in his account of the epistemological status of moral decisions and rules.

Bentham holds that an objective principle – namely, the overarching principle of utility – exists to determine correctness or otherwise. For Bentham, utilitarian considerations demand that the citizen should obey a valid legal rule even if the rule is shown to be morally inappropriate, as greater utility will on the whole be generated through obedience. However, obedience does not and ought not to preclude the citizen from campaigning to change the rule; but, until the rule is rescinded, one ought to obey. Hence, Bentham's dictum: 'obey punctually, criticize freely'. Furthermore, it is Parliament's function to create valid pieces of legislation; it is the judiciary's function to uphold them, no matter how morally undesirable they may be, so long as they have not been rescinded.

But, according to Kelsen, influenced by neo-Kantianism and at one with the Weberian perspective, moral norms are irrational and arbitrary. There are no objective, rational principles or guidelines for determining their correctness or otherwise. Even should a consensus exist, it would be entirely a contingent matter. Given that in principle there are as many conceptions of a good or just law as there may be individual citizens, the notion of 'good' or 'bad', 'just' or 'unjust' laws is an empty one. The only non-empty notion is that of legal validity; it constitutes the sole ground for civil obedience. This means that moral disapproval of a law is not a justification for disobeying it. That is why Kelsen's account of legal positivism has been charged with providing the philosophical foundation for law during the Nazi regime in Germany. Paradoxically, Kelsen's attempt to banish political and ideological commitments from his so-called pure theory of law has led to the very allegation of lending (unwitting) intellectual support to Nazi law itself in spite of his own personal total opposition to it. Kelsen thought that, by making the law ideologically neutral, he would make the law safe for liberal values; but, ironically, he made it possible for it to serve the ideology of those in power.

This critical difference in the respective meta-ethics of Kelsen and Bentham not only informs their respective philosophies of law but also explains Kelsen's theoretical justification of democracy and of liberalism in the twentieth century. Classical liberalism of the J. S. Mill kind upholds the possibility of sifting truth from error in moral beliefs and calls for toleration of diverse opinions to enable truth to emerge eventually in such a competition. Although his compatriots might not be ready for democracy, nevertheless Mill argued that in principle all adults are capable of rational thought and decision-making. For him, democracy is that form of government which is most compatible with the recognition of such a faculty. In contrast, democracy, in the Kelsenian view, is to be understood as simple majority rule; since consensus, should it emerge, is only a happy coincidence which has nothing to do with reasoned thought. Liberalism and democracy tolerate diversity of opinions not as testing grounds for truth to appear but because there is no truth to be found. Furthermore, liberal values could, in theory, be superseded by an electoral majority will which chooses no longer to tolerate them.

In other words, Kelsen's political and jurisprudential thoughts may be said to follow from his meta-ethical stance, each reinforcing the other. Democracy as simple majoritarian rule is an attempt to enforce political or social order, just as legal validity as the sole grounds for civil obedience is an attempt to secure order in a context of value irrationalism. While anarchy is considered by all forms of legal positivism to be the greatest social evil and order the greatest social good, the Kelsenian variety alone focuses on procuring order, not good or just order, as goodness and justice are ultimately empty of content – what is good or just is whatever is deemed to be good or just by the individual.

All forms of legal positivism uphold the tenet that law and the physical sanction go together. But in the Kelsenian variety, law and order come into focus in a much harsher light. The fear of violating valid legislation and the fear of the physical sanction entailed by such violation coalesce. It is ironic then that Kelsenian legal theory should turn out to be more Hobbesian in character than Hobbes's own variety of legal positivist thought.

See also

Weber.

Works

General Theory of Law and State, trans. M. Knight, Berkeley, University of California Press, 1945.
What is Justice? Berkeley, University of California Press, 1957.
The Pure Theory of Law, trans. M. Knight, Berkeley, University of California Press, 1967.
Essays in Legal and Moral Philosophy, selected by O. Weinberger, Dordrecht and Boston, Mass., D. Reidel Publishing Co., 1973.

General Theory of Norms, trans. M. Hartney, Oxford, Clarendon Press, 1991.

Other works

S. Engel and R. A. Metall (eds.), *Law, State and International Legal Order: Essays in Honour of Hans Kelsen*, Knoxville, Tenn., University of Tennessee Press, 1964.

Essays in Honour of Hans Kelsen, California Law Review, 59, 1971.

R. Moore, *Legal Norms and Legal Science: a Critical Study of Kelsen's Pure Theory of Law*, Honolulu, University of Hawaii Press, 1978.

Richard H. Tur and William Twining (eds.), *Essays on Kelsen*, Oxford, Clarendon Press, 1986.

Keekok Lee, *The Legal-Rational State; a Comparison of Hobbes, Bentham and Kelsen*, Aldershot, Avebury Press, 1990.

I. Stewart, 'The critical legal science of Hans Kelsen', *Journal of Law and Society*, 17 (1990), pp. 273–308.

John Maynard Keynes
1883–1946

Known primarily as an economist, Keynes was to have a considerable influence on the political agenda in the inter-war and post-war eras and on the theory and practice of liberalism. He was the son of John Neville Keynes, a Cambridge don and author of *The Scope and Method of Political Economy* (1891). The young Keynes was very much a product of the Cambridge academic world. He was the pupil of two of the greatest English economists, Alfred Marshall and Arthur Pigou. His first degree was actually in mathematics, his formal economics education being the result of a further year's study. The key to understanding the philosophy and attitudes which underpinned his work as an economist is to be found in his relationship with G. E. Moore and the Cambridge secret society, the Apostles. (This is recounted in his essay *My Early Beliefs.*) After coming down from Cambridge he became a civil servant in the India Office. Whilst there he developed considerable expertise in the field of Indian currency reform. As a result of the fame which he achieved through his *Indian Currency and Finance* (1913) he was appointed to the Royal Commission on Indian Finance (1913–14). But the main turning point in his career as a public figure came with the period he spent in the Treasury and his subsequent involvement in the Versailles peace conference.

Keynes soon found himself at odds with the proceedings and was deeply disillusioned by the politics of the conference. He therefore resigned from government service to write *The Economic Consequences of the Peace* (1919). The book launched him on a new career as a publicist and economic journalist – most notably through his editorship of the *Manchester Guardian*'s reconstruction supplements (1922–4). Thereafter Keynes was a very public economist indeed, in contrast to Marshall and Pigou, who believed that economists should not intervene in public debate and political argument. In the following years he campaigned for a revision of the Versailles treaty and when in 1923 bank rate was raised he began to criticize the dominance of what he argued was an erroneous theory of money. In 1924 he published his *Tract on Monetary Reform* and in 1925 an attack on *The Economic Consequences of Mr Churchill.* These pamphlets were followed by two volumes on monetary theory *(A Treatise on Money*, 1930).

The early economic writings reveal his political method: public argument to win over economic opinion, followed by an academic theory aimed at converting his fellow economists. This pattern was also to be followed in his campaign on unemployment and public spending. *Can Lloyd George do it?* (1929), *The Means of Prosperity* (1933) and numerous articles in the *Nation* and *Athenaeum* were followed in 1936 by *The General Theory of Employment, Interest and Money.* By this time it had become apparent to Keynes that a more coherent theoretical argument was needed to support the political case for government action. *The General Theory* was therefore both a tract for the times, aimed at influencing 'men in authority', and a theoretical work designed to persuade economists to his point of view. For Keynes persuading and theorizing were all part and parcel of the same activity. Above all, he wrote to change people's minds.

Economists are naturally given to discussing what Keynes really meant in *The General Theory*, but as far as its political dimension is concerned there is, perhaps, less controversy. An understanding of Keynes's political thought requires that *The General Theory* be read in conjunction with his essay *An End to Laissez-faire* (1926). Taken together, these works show Keynes arguing that the two alternatives – socialism and capitalism – were no longer satisfactory solutions to the problems faced by forms of social, economic and political organization in the twentieth century. There was, he maintained, a middle way: an economic arrangement where the state took upon itself the task of regulating the levels of saving and investment. Capitalism and individualism would be left intact, while the chief defects of the market place – such as unemployment – would be corrected.

In so arguing Keynes was to provide, more than any other social scientist, one of the most potent political ideas of the second half of the twentieth century: that the application of certain techniques of economic management could reconcile a more extensive state with the principles and practice of liberal democracy. Had he lived longer it may well be that Keynes would have made the relationship between economics and political liberalism clearer. However, the nearest he came to such an analysis after the publication of *The General Theory* is contained in some comments on Hayek's *Road to Serfdom*, wherein he confesses that he is in sympathy with Hayek's position but nevertheless concludes that moderate planning will be safe if those carrying it out are 'rightly orientated in their own minds'. Many commentators have interpreted this argument, and the assertion in the closing pages of *The General Theory* that it was economic ideas and not vested interests which ultimately ruled and shaped the thoughts of policy-makers, as simply revealing his essential belief in an intellectual aristocracy and an overriding idealistic naivety.

Keynes's writing and a life which encompassed the arts, book collecting and the theatre, as well as economics and public service, continue to be a source of critical scholarship. Nevertheless, as a political idea Keynesianism has become synonymous with so-called 'deficit spending' and 'spending your way out of recession'. Thus it was that Keynes and his followers came to be the main target of conservative critics of economic management. Whether Keynes was himself a 'Keynesian' in this sense is, of course, another matter. Unquestionably, however, his reluctance to tackle the issue of the relationship between economic organization and liberalism left him open to criticism. It is not always the people who 'think and feel right' who come to exercise power. In this respect Keynes the economist fundamentally ignored the political implications of this theory and the political context of economic policy.

During the war he was very active in government as economic adviser to the Chancellor. He was a central figure in the Anglo-American economic discussions which led to the policy of Lend–Lease and the Bretton Woods agreement (1944). In the end it may be that his role in establishing economics and economists as having a major part to play in public policy was his main contribution to the politics of economics.

Works

The Collected Writings of John Maynard Keynes, twenty-nine volumes, London, Macmillan, for the Royal Economic Society, 1971–8.

Other works

Peter Clarke, *The Keynesian Revolution in the Making, 1924–1936*, Oxford, Clarendon Press, 1988.

Robert Skidelsky, *John Maynard Keynes: a Biography*, vol. 1: *Hopes Betrayed, 1883–1920*, London, Macmillan, 1983; vol. 2: *The Economist as Saviour, 1920–1937*, London, Macmillan, 1992.

W. Parsons, 'Keynes and the politics of ideas', *History of Political Thought* 4, 2 (1983).

Ayatollah Rohallah Khomeini 1902–1989

Born in Khomein, near Arak, in central Iran, to a family of merchants, small landowners and clerics. He studied at the Fayzieh *madrasa* in Qom, under leading theologians of the time. On graduating he was appointed at the same institution to teach philosophy and jurisprudence. At the same time he acted as secretary to Ayatollah Boroujourdi, the chief cleric in Iran until his death in 1961, a political conservative with connections with the court. This explains, in part, Khomeini's aloofness from politics till after Boroujourdi's death. He emerged on the political stage in 1961–3, in the context of widespread agitation against the Shah's 'white revolution', which included land reforms, led by clergy and bazaar merchants. Khomeini spoke with a distinctive voice, avoiding the land reform issue but denouncing the government for extending the franchise in local elections to women and religious minorities, for granting legal exemptions to American service personnel, for selling oil to Israel and for tyranny and corruption. His forthright denunciation of the Shah and his radical stance earned him widespread support but also imprisonment, then exile, to Turkey, then Iraq. There Khomeini resided and taught at the famous seminary of Najaf, a Shi'i holy shrine. It was there that he delivered his lectures on Islamic government, *velayat-e faqih* (the guardianship of the jurist), which laid down his particular theory of government, and was to become part of the constitution of the Islamic Republic. The agitation against the Shah which started in 1977 brought Khomeini to the centre of the stage again. He spoke from exile, again with a forthright voice, demanding the abdication of the Shah and the institution of an Islamic republic. Iranian pressure led to his expulsion from Iraq, and into residence in a village outside Paris. There he assumed the leadership of the revolution. The success of the revolution in February 1979 saw his installation as the ruling *faqih*, as specified in his theory of government.

Khomeini's first book, *Kashfi-i Asrar* (1943), dealt with political matters only in small part. In it he called for Islamic government, but only in the sense of applying Islamic legal and ethical principles. His distinctive theory of Islamic government came in the lectures on the subject delivered in Najaf in the 1960s. The gist of this theory is that, in the absence of the Imam of the Age, the community of Islam is deprived of his infallible guidance, but must nevertheless regulate its affairs as best it can according to righteous principles. The person(s) best qualified to assume this regulation is the just and learned jurist (*faqih*), for he is versed in the law and the traditions of the Prophet and the imams, and experienced in reading and interpreting the esoteric meanings underlying those traditions. Khomeini cites many traditions of the Prophet and the Shi'i imams to corroborate his argument that the *ulama* are the guardians of the community.

There is nothing extraordinary about this argument. It is widely accepted in Shi'i and Sunni Islam that the *ulama* have a position of authority and a function of regulation in the community. The novelty of Khomeini's argument lay in the implicit identification of the state with the community. Traditional Islamic doctrine, Sunni and Shi'i, has accepted the necessity of government by kings and their military–administrative arms. They may claim authority over the people and their civil affairs, but not over the king and his government. All they could hope for was a just king who respected religion and enforced its provisions. It may be argued that Khomeini's identification of state and community is based on peculiarly modern assumptions on the model of the nation state and citizenship, although he does not enter into any modern discourses.

The principle of *velayet-e faqih* is enshrined in the constitution of the Islamic Republic of Iran, alongside the (incompatible) principle of popular sovereignty. In the decade of his tenure as the ruling *faqih* Khomeini exercised arbitrary power, and in a proclamation a few months before his death claimed the competence to overrule even the most basic Islamic requirements if necessary in the public interest of the Islamic community. It is difficult to see how his successors can claim the same authority. It remains to be seen whether the principle of *velayet-e faqih* died with its author.

Works

Islam and Revolution: Writings and Declarations of Imam Khomeini, trans. Hamid Algar, Berkeley, Cal., Mizan Press, 1981.

Other works

Nikki Keddie, *Roots of Revolution*, New Haven, Conn., and London, Yale University Press, 1981.

Gregory Rose, '*Velayat-e Faqih* and the recovery of Islamic identity in the thought of Ayatollah Khomeini', in *Religion and Politics in Iran*, ed. N. Keddie, New Haven, Conn., and London, Yale University Press, 1983.

Bager Moin Khomeini, *Sign of God*, London, I.B. Tauris, 1992.

Sami Zubaida, *Islam, the People and the State*, London, Routledge, 1989.

Martin Luther King, Junior
1929–1968

Martin Luther King, Jr, was born in Atlanta, Georgia, the second son of the Rev. Michael (later Martin) and Mrs Alberta Williams King. After attending city public and private schools, he matriculated at Morehouse College, graduating in 1948 at the age of nineteen, received a B.D. degree from Crozer Theological Seminary in Chester, Pennsylvania, and a Ph.D. in systematic theology from Boston University in 1955. The previous year he became pastor of Dexter Avenue Baptist Church in Montgomery, Alabama. His civil rights career may be divided into two major periods – before Selma, Alabama, and after.

The first began with the December 1955 Montgomery bus boycott and ended with the march from Selma to Montgomery in late March 1965. The second began with the Chicago demonstrations for jobs and housing during 1966 and ended with his assassination in Memphis on 4 April 1968. The goals of racial desegregation of the first period were largely achieved, but their relative realization merely accentuated the things that yet remained to be done before the poor, the powerless and the racially disadvantaged could begin to achieve real equality of opportunity in America. The second period of Dr King's life was marked by relative incompletion, and its goal of political power and economic well-being devolving upon the people themselves remains highly problematic.

The formula for non-violent civil rights campaigns was perfected in Montgomery. Fundamental to non-violent success were three elements, (1) meticulous planning, (2) irresolute or unintelligent local white opposition and (3) ultimate active support from the federal government. Birmingham, Alabama, in spring 1963, coming after the internal bickering, poor national press and stalemate of Albany, Georgia, the previous year, was an energizing triumph for King and his organization, the Southern Christian Leadership Conference. The mobilization of thousands of Afro-American citizens in Birmingham (using children for the first time) and the anticipated white reaction were intended to compel the federal government to implement vigorously the historic 1954 Supreme Court desegregation decision in Brown *v.* Topeka Board of Education.

In three documents coming at the beginning, middle and immediate aftermath of the Birmingham campaign the SCLC leader became the national embodiment of civil rights. The 'Birmingham Manifesto' spelled out the circumstances driving the people of that city to active civil defiance and the moral basis of that defiance. King's arrest and solitary confinement resulted in the second document, the magisterial 'Letter from Birmingham Jail', written in the margins of newspapers and on scraps of paper. Citing examples from the lives of Socrates and Gandhi, King justified his and his followers' so-called 'lawlessness' by arguing that the highest Judaeo-Christian principles commanded that only just laws had to be obeyed.

The March on Washington speech on 28 August 1963, from the Lincoln Memorial, the third splendid document, raised hopes that the demands presented at the White House later that day would move the President and the Congress to pass a comprehensive civil rights act, a strong federal employment practices act, extend an increased national minimum wage to domestic workers and others not covered, enact a massive federal programme to train unemployed and unskilled workers, enforce desegregation of all public schools by the end of the year, pass an open housing law and, finally, reduce the congressional representation of states disfranchising minority groups. Not the march on Washington but President John F. Kennedy's fateful trip to Dallas would cause some of these demands to be enacted into law. In 1964 *Time* magazine chose King as Man of the Year, the first Afro-American selected. The civil rights bill was finally signed into law in June after eighty-three days of Senate debate, and the year ended with the bestowal upon him of the Nobel Prize for Peace.

The passage of the Civil Rights Act of 1964 and the Voting Rights Act of 1965, however, only caused many Americans to wonder whether or not protest demonstrations any longer served a positive purpose. Such doubts found powerful confirmation in the explosion of the Los Angeles ghetto, Watts, in August 1965. The nation was also now well into a foreign war that would drain resources away from the improvement of social conditions. There was a growing national sentiment, shared by many in the National Association for the Advancement of Colored People and National Urban League, that the time was right for pause and consolidation. Instead Martin Luther King, Jr, elected to take his movement into the north, focusing on Chicago.

His foray was less than successful. Many northern white civil rights supporters – labour leaders, various liberals, prelates – gave only token support, while many Afro-Americans were disappointed with the August 1966 truce between King and the mayor of Chicago, Richard Daley, known as the Summit Agreement, a catalogue of extremely ambitious, loose concessions hastily conceived a few days before a massive civil rights march into white suburban enclaves was to take place. Weighing the significance of these reverses, King concluded that it was time for major changes. 'I think you've got to have a reconstruction of the entire society, a revolution of values', *Harper's* quoted him as saying. The cities had to be rebuilt so that the poor could live decently and work productively in them. 'Some of the nation's industries must be nationalized', and a guaranteed annual wage enacted. The country's foreign investments ought be reviewed (he had South Africa in mind). Given the single-issue politics of most of his Afro-American followers, the limited character of the liberal white allegiance and of the labour movement, and the certainty of federal animosity, King appeared to make all the wrong decisions in this last stage. It is now clear that another consideration, only guessed at then by a few, may have dissuaded him from his new path: the malevolence of J. Edgar Hoover's Federal Bureau of Investigation. Instead, he chose to merge civil rights with a larger, institutionally destabilizing crusade for human rights.

Gandhi, Marx, Rauschenbusch and Thoreau played a part in King's evolving ideas and programmes. In the final analysis, however, his seemingly rapid shift leftward was grounded in Christian morality, the black Church and common sense. 'Any religion,' he wrote emphatically in *Stride toward Freedom*, 'that professes to be concerned with the souls of men and is not concerned with the slums that damn them, the economic conditions that strangle them, and the social conditions that cripple them is a dry-as-dust religion.' Similarly, democracy with poverty was a cruelly unnecessary contradiction, he believed. 'The poor can stop being poor,' King was fond of saying, 'if the rich are willing to become even richer at a slower rate.' In *Where do we Go from Here* he criticized the black separatists because they gave 'priority to race precisely at a time when the impact of automation and other forces have made the economic question fundamental for blacks and whites alike'.

When King proclaimed for the first time, on 25 March 1967 at the Chicago coliseum, that 'we must combine the fervor of the civil rights movement with the peace movement', the outlines of his new non-violent populist movement were clear. During the following months he strove to address a larger, more varied audience than ever before, driving home statistics on poverty, repeating that the numerical majority living below the poverty line was white, not black or brown, that the whites of Appalachia were worse-off materially (and more powerless) than inner-city Afro-Americans and Hispanics, and that the Vietnam War was undermining social democracy at home. He summoned the politically weak, the economically deprived, the angry young of all races and the anti-war liberals to form together a community of action sufficiently powerful to command the enlightened attention of Washington and Wall Street. 'Our challenge,' King wrote in *Look* in 1968, 'is to organize the power we already have in our midsts': to create a force 'powerful enough, dramatic enough, morally appealing enough, so that people of goodwill, the churches, labor, liberals, intellectuals, students, poor people themselves' would begin to 'put pressure on congressmen'.

King's new approach – a Popular Front of the racially abused, economically deprived, working poor and politically outraged, cutting across race and class – was prospectively potent. It was also an approach that revealed him at his imaginative best as a leader, and demonstrated the pragmatist who calibrated his swing leftward the better to construct a basis for civilized, moderated, genuine social progress. In the presence of his key lieutenants, Ralph Abernathy, Andrew Young and Jesse Jackson, he was gunned down on the balcony of the Lorraine Motel shortly after returning to Memphis to lead a march of striking sanitation workers. His mausoleum is in the grounds of the Nonviolent Center for Social Change in Atlanta, of which his widow, Coretta, is president. By an Act of Congress 15 January is now a federal holiday.

See also

Gandhi.

Works

Stride toward Freedom: the Montgomery Story, New York, Harper & Row, 1958.
Strength to Love, New York, Harper & Row, 1963.
Why we can't Wait, New York, Harper & Row, 1964.
Where do we Go from Here: Chaos or Community? New York, Harper & Row, 1967.

Other works

Kenneth Lee Smith and Ira Zepp, *Search for the Beloved Community: the Thinking of Martin Luther King, Jr.*, Lanham, Md, University Press of America, 1974.
David J. Garrow, *Protest at Selma: Martin Luther King, Jr., and the Voting Rights Act of 1965*, New Haven, Conn., Yale University Press, 1978.
David L. Lewis, *King: a Biography*, New York, Praeger, 1978.
David J. Garrow, *The FBI and Martin Luther King, Jr.*, New York, Norton, 1981.
Stephen B. Oates, *Let the Trumpet Sound: the Life of Martin Luther King, Jr.*, New York, Harper & Row, 1982.
David J. Garrow, *Bearing the Cross: Martin Luther King, Jr., and the Southern Christian Leadership Conference*, New York, Morrow, 1986.
Taylor Branch, *Parting the Waters: America in the King Years*, New York, Simon & Schuster, 1988

Kita Ikki   1883–1937

Theoretician and strategist of Japan's national socialist movement in the pre-war period, Kita Ikki defies facile categorization in terms of the political left and right. Born Kita Terujirō into the household of a brewer in Niigata prefecture, as a young man Kita may have been influenced towards political activism by his father's service as a Jiyūtō (Liberal Party) member of the local assembly and town mayor. In 1901 Kita went to Tokyo, where the newly formed Social Democratic Party (Shakai Minshutō) was banned, and immediately took an interest in socialist thought. Kita audited courses at Waseda University, and began to publish articles in the *Morning Star* (*Myōjō*) literary magazine and in his home-town local, *Sado News*. In 1906 he published at his own expense *The National Polity and Pure Socialism*. The book was immediately banned. Meanwhile he became associated with Kōtoku Shūsui, Sakai Toshihiko and other Japanese revolutionary socialists, and in November the same year he became a member of the Revolutionary Review publishing society, and entered the Chinese Tongmenghui (Revolutionary Alliance) under the leadership of Sun Yat-sen. In 1911 he went to China to help in the Chinese Republican Revolution, but after the assassination of the liberal party leader Song Jiaoren he was ordered to leave China because of his efforts to publicize the facts of Song's death.

After returning to Japan in 1913 Kita published an account of the Chinese revolution under the title *The Chinese Revolutionary Party and the Chinese Revolution*. From the outline of his own concept of Asian nationalism in the preface of this work he quickly became known as a state or national socialist. In 1916 he returned to Shanghai, only to return home in the wake of the dramatic expression of anti-Japanese Chinese nationalism in the 1919 Fourth of May Movement. Nevertheless, while in China he penned the work for which he would become best known, *An Outline Plan for the Reconstruction of Japan*. This work, outlining a strategy to implement his principles of pan-Asian nationalism, soon drew the support of young army officers advocating a Shōwa restoration to restore Japan to the values of emperor-centred nationalism that had been implemented only partially in the 1866–8 Meiji restoration. This position was solidified when Kita joined the right-wing Yūzonsha and became a leading theorist of the nationalist movement in Japan. When the attempted *coup*

d'état by young military officers inspired by Kita's theory failed on 26 February 1936 Kita was arrested, convicted of involvement in the plot and executed the following year.

While Kita's nationalist proclivities would seem to reinforce the power of the existing state, state officials rightly viewed his views as critical of the existing regime. His *Outline for the Reconstruction of Japan* criticized the official mythology of the Japanese state, the *kokutai* (national polity) myth, which postulated the divinity of the emperor and argued that all Japanese were part of a single extended family, of which the emperor was patriarch. This official mythology, Kita argued, was a perversion of the true *kokutai*, which was actually social democratic, not autocratic as the purveyors of the official mythology insisted. In short, Kita sought to reinterpret the ideological basis of the Japanese polity to embrace a revolutionary vision of national socialism.

The foundation of his theory was a new formulation of the concept of revolution and its role in human progress. Revolution was not simply the outcome of violent change or conflict, but rather a war of ideas resulting in the transformation of the social values of a society. Modern revolutions were distinguished by their liberating character. They produced a 'citizen state', the political nature of which was social democratic, Kita insisted. Their agents, moreover, were not a specific class, and specifically Kita maintained that it was impossible for a ruling class to be the agent of revolution. That agent was, rather, a sort of vanguard elite that acted on behalf of the nation as a whole. In twentieth-century Japan it made sense that the most distinctive characteristic of this revolutionary elite would be its nationalism. Thus, while such an elite might be influenced by foreign ideas, it would above all be indigenous and create a revolution that could only be internal to the country in which it would occur. In Japan the purpose of such a revolution would be to end oligarchic rule and re-establish a genuine union between the emperor and the Japanese people.

Works

Kita Ikki chosakushū (Collected Writings of Kita Ikki), three volumes, Tokyo, Misuzu Shobō, 1959.
Kokutai ron oyobi junsui shakai-shugi (The Theory of the *Kokutai* and Pure Socialism), in *Kita Ikki chosakushū.*
Shina kakumeitō oyobi kakumei no Shina (The Chinese Revolutionary Party and the Chinese Revolution), in *Kita Ikki chosakushū.*
Nihon kaizō hōan taikō (An Outline Plan for the Reconstruction of Japan), in *Kita Ikki chosakushū.*

Other works

Kuno Osamu, 'Chōkokka-shugi no ichi genkei: Kita Ikki no baai' (One prototype of ultranationalism: the case of Kita Ikki), *Chishikijin no seisei to yakuwari* (The Formation and Role of Intellectuals), volume 6 of *Kindai Nihon shisō shi kōza* (Symposium on the History of Modern Japanese Thought), Tokyo, Chikuma Shobō, 1959, pp. 126–54.
Tanaka Sōgorō, *Kita Ikki: Nihon-teki fuashisuto no shōchō*, Tokyo, Mirai-sha, 1959.
George M. Wilson, 'Kita Ikki's theory of revolution', *Journal of Asian Studies* 26, 1 (November 1966), pp. 89–99.
George M. Wilson, *Radical Nationalist in Japan: Kita Ikki, 1883–1937*, Cambridge, Mass., Harvard University Press, 1969.

Note

Japanese names appear in the customary order, surname first.

Leopold Kohr   1909–

Leopold Kohr is one of those few prophets of political thought who are without deserved honour in the rest of the world but are duly and affectionately recognized in their own country. Kohr, who was born in Oberndorf, just outside Salzburg, always insisted that his love and appreciation of the small stemmed from his birthplace, a village of less than 2,000 people, and he has said, 'Everything that I have learned worth knowing I learned in that small town.' None the less, he went on to attend Gymnasium in Salzburg, earn a law degree from the University of Innsbruck in 1933 and a second degree in political science from the University of Vienna in 1935 before escaping from Europe in 1938 and taking up positions in North America, first at the

University of Toronto in 1939–40 and then at Rutgers University in 1952–5. Thereafter he taught at the University of Puerto Rico (1955–73) and the University College of Wales at Aberystwyth (1973–8), after which he retired to concentrate on writing, lecturing and travelling.

An economist by profession and for three decades a professor of economics and public administration in the United States, Puerto Rico and Britain, he has written half a dozen books that have set out and elaborated what he calls 'the theory of the small', most starkly enunciated in the opening pages of his first book, *The Breakdown of Nations.* 'There seems only one cause behind all forms of social misery: *bigness.* Oversimplified as this may seem, we shall find the idea more easily acceptable if we consider that bigness, or oversize, is really much more than just a social problem. It appears to be the one and only problem permeating all creation. Wherever something is wrong, something is too big.' *Breakdown* went on to buttress the theory in minute, and engaging, detail, providing arguments philosophic, political, cultural, economic and administrative to prove that small organizations, small cities and small states are more efficient, benevolent, creative and stable than their larger counterparts. It ended with a call for the transformation of big-state systems into a series of small, federated states largely on the model of Switzerland, with many equal and largely autonomous cantons operating in a small-state periphery.

These ideas were further spelled out in a series of books over the next thirty years: *Development without Aid*, arguing that Third World countries could provide more for their citizens by processes of self-sufficiency than by economic integration, by 'going it alone – unintegrated, unaffiliated, unco-ordinated' and small; *The Overdeveloped Nations*, showing how social and economic dysfunction results from the size of the modern state and that 'the larger the state, the worse off is the citizen'; *The City of Man*, demonstrating why small medieval cities were socially and culturally so effective and how a modern city might transform itself by adopting small-city principles; and *The Inner City*, a collection of columns on architecture and town planning maintaining that 'urban giantism' can be cured in only one way, 'by making large things smaller', a 'return to the human scale'.

Although he has always been influential among that circle of intellectuals critical of modernism – E. F. Schumacher (who called him 'a teacher from whom I have learned more than from anyone else'), Ivan Illich, Herbert Read, Danilo Dolci, John Papworth, Manfred Max-Neef, Edward Goldsmith – it was not until the late 1970s that he began to have any impact on a wider group of thinkers and activists. *Breakdown* was given its first paperback publication in the United States in 1977, followed by reprints of several other books. He was given a Right Livelihood Award (called 'the alternative Nobel Prize') in 1983, and he was invited to give the annual lecture by the British Schumacher Society in 1983 and the American Schumacher Society in 1989.

Still, Kohr never achieved the popularity or influence around the world of such social critics as his friend Schumacher, despite a writing style as accessible and a personal style as congenial. It is only back in Salzburg, Austria, the city in whose shadow he was born, that Kohr has been honoured. In 1982 he was given the 'key' to the province of Salzburg, and later that year the city was host to a 'Leopold Kohr Symposium on the Human Scale' that brought in scholars, activists and friends from all over the world for a week-long celebration of the man and his ideas. In 1985 he was made president of a new Leopold Kohr Academy established in a nearby national park and animal reserve, where courses and symposia on local crafts, village renewal and self-sufficiency are given year-round and an alternative technical centre provides a home for experiments.

Works

'Disunion now: a plea for a society based upon small autonomous units', *Commonweal*, 26 September 1941.
The Breakdown of Nations, London, Routledge; New York, Rinehart, 1957.
Development without Aid, Swansea, Davies, 1973.
The City of Man: the Duke of Buen Consejo, Puerto Rico, University of Puerto Rico, 1976.
The Overdeveloped Nations: the Diseconomies of Scale, Swansea, Davies, 1977.
The Inner City: from Mud to Marble, Talybont, Wales, Y Lolfa, 1989.

Alexandra Kollontai
1872–1952

Alexandra Kollontai, *née* Domontovich, was born in St Petersburg, Russia. Her parents, members of the nobility, educated their daughter at home in an atmosphere of comfort and political liberalism. At twenty-two she married her cousin Vladimir Kollontai; after the birth of a son in 1894 she became increasingly discontented with domestic life. In 1899, after a year of study in Switzerland, she embarked on a career as a revolutionary journalist, joining the illegal Russian Social Democratic Labour Party (the Marxists).

Kollontai's first publications were studies of the Finnish economy, notable only for demonstrating her mastery of Marxism. By 1905 she had found the issue that would occupy much of her career – the emancipation of women. Her first major work on the subject – *The Social Bases of the Woman Question* (1908) – was a lengthy attack on Russian feminism joined with a plea for the Social Democrats to make an effort to attract women to their ranks.

In 1908 Kollontai fled Russia to avoid arrest. She remained in Western Europe until 1917, lecturing and writing. Her most important publications during this period were articles exploring the psychology of women's oppression. She wrote that women had internalized 'an atavistic tendency' to become dependent on men, a tendency that would be overcome only when revolution had destroyed private property and thereby the basis of male power over women.

Kollontai returned to Russia in 1917, after the February revolution. She spent the year as a prominent, popular Bolshevik agitator. When the Bolsheviks seized power in the autumn she was appointed Commissar of Social Welfare. In that capacity she established public funding of maternity care and collaborated with other commissars in the drafting of protective labour legislation for women and of civil marriage and divorce laws. She resigned in March 1918 as a protest against the Treaty of Brest-Litovsk, which ended the war with Germany; when she returned to work later in the year she specialized in organizing women. In 1919 the party leadership established a department within the Communist Party, the Zhenotdel, devoted to women's issues; in 1920 Kollontai became its head. Over the next two years she continued to develop the organization's programme of organizing nurseries, day-care centres, maternity hospitals and restaurants to relieve women's domestic burden. Kollontai also instructed Zhenotdel workers to inform women of their rights, to protest against abusive male workers, and to push for the inclusion of women on decision-making bodies within the party, government and trade unions.

Kollontai's vision of the Zhenotdel as an advocate for women did not win widespread support among male communists, many of whom were suspicious of women's emancipation. Her involvement in 1921 in the Workers' Opposition, a party group critical of Lenin, further irritated the leadership. In early 1922 they dismissed her from the Zhenotdel, offering instead a post in diplomatic service. After two decades as a Soviet diplomat she retired in 1945 and died in Moscow in 1952.

Between 1918 and 1923 Kollontai wrote several articles and novellas that discussed the relationship between women and men that should prevail in a socialist society. True to her Marxist beliefs, she advocated the complete abolition of existing family structures. In their place would be created the 'Winged Eros', heterosexual love based on erotic attraction and shared commitment to the building of a new society. The 'Winged Eros' was monogamy purified, love between a man and a woman freed of economic considerations, of male domination, and even of child-rearing, for children would be cared for communally. Kollontai bemoaned the fact that such love had not yet arrived in the Soviet Union, that women continued to be burdened by their economic and psychological dependence on men, and she urged communists to pay more attention to the revolutionizing of the family. The Soviet press responded by condemning these works as trivial and feminist. In 1926, after she had made several speeches that were also denounced as feminist, Kollontai decided to fall silent on women's issues.

Kollontai was the leading Marxist feminist of her generation. In her writing she made the emancipation of women from subordination within marriage a central issue on the revolutionary agenda. In her work with the Zhenotdel she laid out the pattern of reform for women that became the model for communist governments the world over. Rediscovered by feminists in the 1970s, she has again become an important figure in the history of feminist thought.

See also

Lenin.

Works

The Autobiography of a Sexually Emancipated Woman, London, Herder, 1971.

Marxisme et révolution sexuelle, Maspéro, 1973.

The Love of Worker Bees, trans. Cathy Porter, Chicago, Academy Press, 1977.

Selected Writings, ed. Alix Holt, Westport, Conn., Hill, 1978.

Other works

Barbara Evans Clements, Bolshevik Feminist: the Life of Aleksandra Kollontai, Bloomington, Ind., Indiana University Press, 1979.

Beatrice Farnsworth, *Alexandra Kollontai*, Stanford, Cal., Stanford University Press, 1980.
Cathy Porter, *Alexandra Kollontai*, New York, Dial, 1980.

Julia Kristeva   1941–

Literary theorist and psychoanalyst, Kristeva left Bulgaria in 1966 to study in Paris, where she worked with the Marxist critic Lucien Goldmann and with Roland Barthes. During the next decade, she developed a psycho-ana-lytic theory of literary production, drawing on structuralist linguistics, Russian formal-ism, Freud's theories of the Oedipus complex and Lacan's emphasis on language as a mode of coercive acculturation. Throughout her career she stressed the unconscious as a source of resistance to social order, especially in the writing of the nineteenth- and twen-tieth-century *avant-garde*. Kristeva's rela-tionship to political activism, including the events of May 1968 and the rise of neo-feminism in France, was one of cautious distance. However, her interest in the ways experimental texts disrupt linguistic and social rules led to her acute critiques of Nazism, antisemitism and the excesses of nationalism, while her analysis of the re-pression of the maternal in Western culture made her work important for feminist theory.

From her first publications Kristeva argued that literary and social freedom coincided. One example is the mixture of verbal styles and speaking positions in early, pre-realist narratives of the kinds analysed by the Russian critic Mikhail Bakhtin. In 'Word, dialogue and novel', written in 1966, she summarizes Bakhtin's celebration of the free juxtaposition of elements from popular cul-ture and elite genres in carnivalesque writing, in contrast to the monolithic, rule-governed perspective of genres such as epic and the real-ist novel. Writing as rebellion remained a theme in her massive theoretical approach to *avant-garde* French writers, *The Revolution in Poetic Language* (1974), in which she added to structuralist linguistics a psychoanalytical concept of the speaking and writing subject. From infancy, Kristeva argues, human drives are contained by early childhood training, particularly by the entry into language, a pro-cess through which the child must give up pre-verbal fusion with the mother and submit to the Symbolic order, the system of rules and codes associated with the father as prohibitor of mother–child incest and the in-family rep-resentative of authority in the public world. The unconscious is formed through the repression of pre-verbal aggression and desires that must be given up as the child enters the social realm; but these drives remain active in what Kristeva calls the 'chora', a pool of instinctual energies capable of disturbing the abstract syntax of language. From the chora comes the 'semiotic', a com-plex of rhythmic, corporeal, pre-linguistic energies which work in tension with the Sym-bolic (the rules of formal language). In her analysis of the semiotic in *avant-garde* texts she stresses negativity (aggressiveness against others and the self) and heterogeneity, the linguistic instability symptomatic of a subject split between unconscious demand and com-municative codes.

By exploring such texts as instances of a radical new discourse, Kristeva privileges lit-erature as a site of struggle against oppressive structures. Using Marxist theory to argue for a parallel between commodity fetishism on the economic level and the demand for con-ventional realist representation on the literary level, she sets up an analogy between the demand for the finished, unvarying products of the assembly line and the requirement that language be used instrumentally, to refer to the outer world in fixed, repeatable forms. In contrast, the 'text in process', like the mobile, fluctuating subjectivity that generates it, refuses closure or transcendence. For Kristeva such writing has value as a practice of unconscious struggle in itself rather than as a means to ends beyond the text.

Whatever her claims for the homology between modernism as a revolutionary liter-ary mode and social revolution as a political mode, Kristeva showed that the parallel may not be so simple in the long third section of *The Revolution in Poetic Language*, 'L'Etat et le mystère' (The state and the sacred), in which she analyses the apolitical responses of her two major writers to their historical situations. Lautréamont, seeing no effective means of resisting the bourgeois hegemony and trivial poetry of the Second Empire, and dying a year before the revolutionary activity of the Paris Commune of 1871, took a position of anarchic individualism; Mallarmé, as indifferent to politics as many other writers repulsed by censorship and hypocrisy in the reign of Napoleon III, took refuge in a theory of art for art's sake and in isolated mysticism. Kristeva argues that both poets' unleashing of semiotic energies in their texts signals an attack on the bourgeois family, but she acknowledges that the risks implicit in racial semiotic experiment led both writers by compensation, into complicity with reactionary political positions. The chapters on the limits of semiotic liberation were cut from the American translation of *The Revolution in Poetic Language*, which presents Kristeva's work as ahistorical psychoanalytic theory. But in 'The state and the sacred' she raises important questions about the literary history of the *avant-garde* in relation to the political history of the late nineteenth century.

From 1976 to the mid-1980s, however, Kristeva's political thinking underwent changes shared by other members of the *Tel Quel* collective, the group of critics and writers who worked on a journal devoted to literary modernism. After the student–worker coalition and general strikes of 1968, strongly opposed by the French Communist Party, *Tel Quel* rejected its earlier alliance with the party and with Althusserian Marxism. One example of this rejection in Kristeva is her definition of practice as the mobilization of psychic energies preliminary to the actual production of a text, in contrast to Althusser's notion of practice as the public rituals through which ideology materially interpellates subjects. What for Althusser are the channels that state power

designs to shape the individual into a self-regulating subject obedient to laws is for Kristeva the private, non-teleological play of unconscious subjectivity against the laws of language. The *Tel Quel* group turned to China as a model, and to Maoist celebrations of cultural diversity and post-Foucauldian notions of 'molecular', local struggles rather than adherence to a general party platform, and began to align political pluralism with textual pluralism as its ideals. In 1977, after a trip to China had convinced three *Tel Quel* travellers that Mao's revolution had led merely to a Stalinist state, the journal began criticizing all large-scale political movements as totalitarian and celebrating literary dissidents such as Solzhenitsyn. One of Kristeva's articles from this period is 'A new type of intellectual; the dissident' (1977), in which she argues that *avant-garde* writing will always be more subversive than direct political action, which she believes entraps radicals in the discourses they attempt to resist. A later piece hostile to collective thinking of any kind is her 'Psychoanalysis and the polis', in which she dismisses recent political history as a series of disasters: 'The political interpretations of our century have produced two powerful and totalitarian results: fascism and Stalinism.' In a 1983 talk she remarked, 'I belong to a generation that no longer believes in the miraculous political solution . . . We try not to be political.'

This anti-political turn was a reaction to the triumph of the French right after 1968, but also to Kristeva's training in psychoanalysis (she became an analyst in 1979). She published psychoanalytic readings of writers and painters in *Polylogue* (1977), and she coedited an anthology of her seminars on the language and treatment of psychotic patients, *Folle vérité* (1979). She then published a study of Ferdinand Céline as writer and antisemite, *The Powers of Horror* (1980). Here she combines psychoanalytic and political issues, theorizing that the early process by which children turn away from their mother, violently *abjecting* her (repressing all elements of the self associated with her) in order to achieve a sense of autonomous selfhood, establishes hostility to the other as a basic element in the self-definition of cultures and nations. An example is extreme nationalism. Rivalry and hatred towards the father enter into the process of abjection, as well, which Kristeva sees typified in Céline's antisemitic pamphlets and his fascination with Nazism. In a later book, *Etrangers à nous-mêmes*, she extended her analysis of exile and nationalism, arguing that racism in France, like xenophobia throughout history, includes elements of abjection and therefore needs to be treated psychoanalytically as well as politically.

Throughout the 1970s Kristeva shared with certain other Frenchwomen a distrust of feminist politics as too imitative of men's organizations, as a repetition of bourgeois power plays inadequate to radical new concepts of subjectivity. She proposed instead a position of critical marginality, an outsider's stance ('That's not it, that's still not it') towards masculine identity and official systems ('La femme, ce n'est jamais ça,' 1974). Her work on femininity centres on the maternal as a challenge to the Symbolic, a challenge she suggested had been worked out in practical terms in the Chinese revolution *(About Chinese Women*, 1974). She also focused on the maternal as a substratum of desire in semiotic practice in the arts ('Giotto's joy', 1972; 'Motherhood according to Giovanni Bellini', 1975) and as an experience that calls conventional logic and notions of the self into question: to be a mother is to be both oneself and another, to be both passive and active, to engage in both self-forgetting and self-affirmation through the infant ('Héréthique d'amour', 1977). She suggests that this maternal lens gives women access to a different sense of time (cyclical and monumental rather than merely historical) and of ethics (responsibility without the hunger for power) and argues that a maternally inflected subjectivity has utopian and international dimensions crucial to change and survival in the post-modern era ('Women's time', 1979). Kristeva's suspicion of feminism as a

political movement gave her something in common in the 1970s with other psychoanalytically oriented Frenchwomen, such as members of the group Psych et Po (Psychoanalysis and Politics), and with academics such as Hélène Cixous and Luce Irigaray, also working within a critical psychoanalytic framework. As British and American historians of French feminism have pointed out, however, very different positions existed from the beginning in French feminism particularly the Marxist-inflected sociology of Catherine Clément and Christine Delphy, as typified in the journal *Questions féministes* (published in English as *Feminist Issues)*, and the lesbian separatism of Monique Wittig. Reading Kristeva in this larger context reveals how much she shares with other French theoreticians of language and the unconscious, as well as what is particular in her commitment to semiotic subversion.

See also

Althusser, Clément, Delphy, Foucault, Freud, Wittig.

Works

Revolution in Poetic Language: the Avant-garde at the End of the Nineteenth Century, Mallarmé and Lautréamont, trans. Margaret Waller, New York, Columbia University Press, 1974.

About Chinese Women, trans. A. Barrows, London, Boyars, 1977.

The Powers of Horror: an Essay on Abjection, trans. Leon Roudiez, New York, Columbia University Press, 1982.

Etrangers à nous-mêmes, Paris, Fayard, 1988.

Nations without Nationalism, trans. Leon Roudiez, New York, Columbia University Press, 1993.

Other works

Leon S. Roudiez (ed.), *Desire in Language: a Semiotic Approach to Literature and Art*, New York, Columbia University Press, 1980. (Includes 'Word, Dialogue, novel' and 'Motherhood according to Giovanni Bellini'.)

Petr Alekseevich Kropotkin
1842–1921

Kropotkin, born into the Russian nobility, and respected internationally as a physical geographer, was one of the founding theorists of social anarchism. His scientific travels in Siberia, northern Europe and Asia provided the data for a two-volume work on the orography of Asia and on the glacial period in Finland and Central Europe that established his reputation as a physical geographer. While presenting this work at a scientific conference in Russia, Kropotkin was arrested for antitsarist activities. He escaped, fled to France (where he was imprisoned again) and eventually settled in London, where he founded the anarchist journal *Freedom* (1886). There he remained until his return to Russia in 1917. Kropotkin attempted to establish a scientific basis for social anarchism – to prove, using the methods of natural science, the negative effects of authority in all its forms and the need for a total reorganization of society on the basis of the free co-operation of independent associations. Drawing on his observations of the relation of Russian peasants to their physical environment, he sought to demonstrate the possibilities of human co-operation in contexts free of centralist and authoritarian influence. In *Mutual Aid* (1917) and in *Ethics* (1924) Kropotkin took issue with Social Darwinism, affirming the predominance of mutual aid over competition in the quest for survival and human progress.

Mutual aid was not, however, everywhere in the ascendant. Kropotkin argued that certain modes of political, economic, social and spatial organization effectively discouraged its emergence. Capitalist divisions of labour and class inequality inhibited creative communal expression. Work environments which promote inequality, fragment work tasks and create pyramids of power transform work into a competitive struggle. Anticipating later theorists, Kropotkin also recognized the limitation of economies of scale, and the economic inefficiences that can result from over-concentration of economic activity in space (*Fields, Factories and Workshops*, 1898). He also criticized governments for creating and preserving authoritarian relationships that inhibit co-operation and further social privilege. His goal was a 'politics' which aimed at the direct participation of people in their daily lives through a system of complete workers' and citizens' control, and a redefinition of 'political economy' as a science devoted to the study of the needs of people and of the best means of satisfying those needs with the least possible waste of human energy (*The Conquest of Bread*, 1892). In the educational arena Kropotkin advocated a libertarian approach that would facilitate choice rather than mould character.

In developing his theory of mutual aid Kropotkin laid the conceptual foundation for a radical theory of human ecology. He viewed nature and people in nature as organic, interrelated wholes. To harmonize the relationship between people and nature, he saw the need to create a human community which lived in harmony with itself.

For Kropotkin the creation of alternative institutions and modes of behaviour was the essence of revolution. Revolutionary methods had, then, to embody the egalitarian, participatory relationships that the revolution aimed to create. This process would begin when people began to exercise responsibility over their lives and function without submitting to authority.

Throughout his life Kropotkin maintained a strong commitment to physical geographical research and education aimed at creating within people an awareness of the social forces acting upon them and a desire to resist manipulation. Rather than supporting imperialistic ventures, he argued, geography ought to promote the study of human interdependence and co-operation for the purpose of furthering the evolution of inventive, peace-loving people ('What geography ought to be', 1885).

Kropotkin combined his theory of mutual aid with 'decentralism', the general principles upon which an anarchist society would be based. The primary unit was to be the self-governing commune, where living, working and recreational activities were integrated in space. Anticipating later work by Ebenezer Howard, Lewis Mumford, Patrick Geddes and Paul and Percival Goodman, he argued against the dichotomization of city and country, and economic overspecialization. He advocated instead a form of regionalism which would promote the active interchange of information and products between areas through multiple federations. Decentralism was thus the revolutionary philosophy and mode of socio-spatial organization that would form the basis of a new co-operative mode of existence. It was the geography and sociology of anarchism.

Many of his suggestions for the decentralist reorganization of society were applied in Spain in the late nineteenth and early twentieth centuries, when anarchism emerged as a powerful movement for radical social change. Here, as he predicted, a revolution that began by changing social and economic relationships ended by creating a totally new environment. The contemporary relevance of Kropotkin's ideas is also apparent in his insistence on connecting means to ends in social change movements, and in his encouragement of grass-roots organizing where people transform themselves into active agents for change. Finally, in professional contexts, Kropotkin decried the dehumanizing effects of bureaucracy and institutional forms which, even inadvertently, cause the atrophy of people's desire to mould their environment.

Works

Memoirs of a Revolutionary, London, Smith Elder, 1899.
The Conquest of Bread, 1892, reprinted New York, Kraus, 1970.
Fields, Factories, and Workshops, 1898, reprinted New York, Harper & Row, 1974.
Mutual Aid: a Factor of Evolution, 1917, reprinted London, Freedom, 1987.

Other works

Caroline Cohen, Peter Kropotkin and the Rise of Revolutionary Anarchism, 1872–86, New York, Cambridge University Press, 1989.
George Woodcock and Ivan Avakumovic, The Anarchist Prince: a Biographical Study of Peter Kropotkin, New York, Schocken, 1950.
Martin Miller, Kropotkin, Chicago, University of Chicago Press, 1976.
David Stoddart, Geography, Ideology and Social Concern, Oxford, Oxford University Press, 1981.

Harold Laski   1893–1950

During his life Laski was a major influence over socialist and progressive movements. His writings were highly regarded in Britain, continental Europe, the United States and India; he was politically active in the British Labour Party, where he was an elected member of the National Executive Committee from 1937 until 1949, and also in the United States, where he was particularly well known during the New Deal era. Always a highly controversial figure, he was discredited in the West during the Cold War era and has been somewhat neglected since his death.

His earliest major writings – Studies in the Problem of Sovereignty and Authority in the Modern State – were completed during a six-year period as a lecturer in North America (he was at Harvard Law School from 1916 to 1920) and quickly established his reputation as a major pluralist critic of the sovereign state. However, his scholarly tone masked a burning political commitment, and Laski was soon to upset the Boston elite with his support for the police strike in 1919. This effectively ended his academic career in the United States and he returned to Britain as a lecturer at the London School of Economics (subsequently promoted to professor at the age of thirty-three), where he was to remain an unusually charismatic teacher for generations of political science students.

During the early 1920s his belief in decentralized participation was tempered by the growing conviction that firm state action was necessary to bring about fundamental socio-economic change. He tried to attain a synthesis between the pluralist and Fabian conceptions in his most influential book, *A Grammar of Politics* – an encyclopedic work which outlined a socialist approach to political theory, constitutional practice, economic organization and national sovereignty. However, the debacle of the second Labour government of 1929–31 and the growth of fascism in Europe undermined his confidence in the viability of peaceful change. He turned to an idiosyncratic form of Marxism and, in a series of books, argued that capitalism must accept socialist reform so as to preserve liberal civilization. He approached such issues historically (*Democracy in Crisis*), theoretically (*The State in Theory and Practice*) and constitutionally (*Parliamentary Government in England*). Ultimately his position was, no doubt, contradictory, but his exploration of the underlying tensions in liberal democracy was significant for socialists because it combined detailed empirical evidence with a passionate commitment to equality. However, Laski's loathing of fascism and pessimism about capitalist democracy led him to evaluate Stalinist Russia far higher than previously. In 1936 he thus became one of the key figures in the Left Book Club, which often promoted pro-Soviet propaganda in the attempt to bring about a popular front. Nevertheless, in September 1939 he immediately rallied to the war effort and played a major role in countering communist propaganda within the Labour Party.

Yet Laski did not see the war simply as a military struggle against Nazi Germany. Convinced that both fascism and war stemmed from capitalism, he argued that it was vital to use the situation to bring about a 'revolution by consent'. After the Nazi attack upon the Soviet Union he once again tended to play down the negative features of Stalinism and to insist that the continuation of the Grand Alliance,· and socialist–communist harmony, would be essential in the post-war era (*Reflections on the Revolution of our Time*). Such arguments alienated the Anglo-American political 'establishment' and the Labour Party leadership. During the 1945 general election campaign he thus served as the *bête noir* of the Conservatives, and was disavowed by Attlee. His isolation was reinforced when he lost a notorious libel action the next year in which his writings were used to sustain the claim that he had advocated violent revolution. It was a bitter blow to a man whose major preoccupation had been to avert conflict of that kind. In his last years he was a rather tragic figure, increasingly disillusioned with all his former beacons of hope – the United States, the Soviet Union, even the Labour Party. But his influence had by then diminished, partly because he refused to accept Western Cold War orthodoxies, which he criticized effectively in his posthumous work (*The Dilemma of our Times*).

Laski was a serious thinker who used his immense erudition in the history of ideas to search for a synthesis between liberty and equality. His attempt to define a democratic version of socialism – influenced by both Marxism and liberalism – and his insight into the failures and obsolescence of national sovereignty remain highly relevant in the late twentieth century. Convinced that the problems of his time were too urgent for leisurely, academic analysis, he wrote too much, overestimated his influence and sometimes failed to distinguish sufficiently between analysis and polemic. But he certainly deserves greater recognition than he has received in recent years.

Works

Studies in the Problem of Sovereignty, New Haven, Conn., Yale University Press, 1917.

Authority in the Modern State, New Haven, Conn., Yale University Press, 1919.

A Grammar of Politics, London, Allen & Unwin, 1925.

Democracy in Crisis, London, Allen & Unwin, 1933.

The State in Theory and Practice, London, Allen & Unwin, 1935.

Parliamentary Government in England, London, Allen & Unwin, 1938.

Reflections on the Revolution of our Time, London, Allen & Unwin, 1943.

The Dilemma of our Times, Allen & Unwin, 1952.

Other works

Kingsley Martin, *Harold Laski*, London, Gollancz, 1953.

H. A. Deane, *The Political Ideas of Harold J. Laski*, New York, Columbia University Press, 1955.

B. Zylstra, *From Pluralism to Collectivism: the Development of Harold Laski's Political Thought*, Assen, Van Gorcum, 1968.

Michael Newman, *Harold Laski: A Political Biography*, London, Macmillan, 1993.

V. I. Lenin   1870–1924

Lenin was the founder of modern communism. He gave it much of its theory, led its first successful revolution and created the Bolshevik Party (later the Communist Party) as an instrument of revolution and as the effective bearer of state power in Russia. Through the Communist International, which he inspired, his ideas and practices spread throughout the world as the ideology of communism committed to the overthrow of capitalism and imperialism. He has, arguably, had the largest impact upon the politics of the twentieth century of any single individual.

Vladimir Ilich Ulyanov was born into a well-to-do scholarly family in Simbirsk (later called Ulyanovsk). His father was a highly respected inspector of schools who died suddenly when Lenin was sixteen. In the following year his elder brother, Alexander, was hanged for participating in a plot to assassinate the Tsar. Lenin was admitted to Kazan University on the strength of his outstanding academic record and the reference of his headmaster (the father of Alexander Kerensky, whom he deposed in October 1917). After less than a term he was expelled for allegedly participating in a student demonstration. As the brother of a would-be regicide he was a marked man. By the age of eighteen he had begun a systematic study of the Russian radical tradition, had already read Marx's *Capital* (volume one) and was associating with revolutionary intelligentsia circles in Samara that embraced a broad spectrum of views – Jacobinism, Russian populism, anarchism and Marxism.

The psychological trauma of his brother's execution, his own expulsion from university and the influence of his early revolutionary associates combined, in the view of many commentators, to make an indelible imprint upon Lenin's subsequent political development. In the psycho-historical account Lenin's life is an odyssey of revenge for his executed brother and/or a voyage of atonement for failing to understand or respect his views. If the child is father of the man Lenin is the last and most illustrious of a long line of Russian Jacobins, tied to them by family linkage, personal inclination and early association. His later Marxism is here viewed as a thin intellectual veneer that overlies an imperious will to power and a consistently high estimation of the mission of a tightly disciplined group to impose itself upon a recalcitrant historical process. Conventionally Lenin is portrayed, therefore, as a thoroughgoing voluntarist or Jacobin, or else as a superbly adroit political opportunist able to extract from any situation the maximum advantage precisely because he is unconstrained by qualms of theoretical (or moral) propriety. It would be idle, therefore, to seek coherence in his ideas and misleading to presume that Marxism forms their guiding thread.

Plausible and seemingly consistent as these accounts might be, they fail to accommodate the evidence. Lenin's own voluminous writing (fifty volumes in the English *Collected Works*), the reflections and memoirs of associates, family and friends, all suggest an alternative intellectual biography. By the age of twenty-four Lenin had established himself as the spokesman of the most prominent group of Marxists in Russia and had written a lengthy programmatic statement of their opposition to the theory and practice of Russian populism (*What the 'Friends of the People' are . . .*). For the next two years he was active organizing workers' circles in St Petersburg. Arrested at the end of 1895, he was sentenced to administrative exile in Siberia and there began work on *The Development of*

Capitalism in Russia, published in March 1899. This work represented the culmination of almost ten years of statistical and theoretical enquiry into the socio-economic structure of contemporary Russia. It is the fullest account in Marxist literature of the development of capitalist economic and social formations out of feudalism or 'natural economy' and is, arguably, Lenin's most original contribution to Marxist theory. It was also to dictate the limits of his political strategy for its findings with regard to the uneven development of Russian capitalism, and the consequent relative immaturity of modern class formations (bourgeoisie and proletariat) dictated that the most the Russian Marxists could aspire to for the foreseeable future was a radical democratic, rather than socialist, revolution. It was to be the object of the party to agitate among and co-ordinate the revolutionary potential of all anti-autocratic and democratic forces in Russian society. In conditions of illegality and severe repression this required a vertically structured underground organization led by professional revolutionaries and organized around a newspaper. The strategy of the party was to prepare for the most radical realization of the economic and political programme of the democratic revolution, and its tactics were therefore to be directed above all at revealing the structural economic antagonisms of society, by seizing upon those political issues that most united industrial and rural wage workers in this opposition to the interests of landowners and capitalists. The latter would betray the interests of democracy and desert to the camp of the autocracy as soon as radical democracy threatened their economic interests. It was therefore imperative that the proletariat and its allies within the poor peasantry should retain its political independence and lay claim to the leadership of the anti-autocratic, anti-landlord revolution. This was Lenin's stance during his editorship of *Iskra* (The Spark). It was reiterated in *What is to be Done?*, where the role of the party in the democratic revolution is presented in detail, and it informed the strategy of the Bolsheviks during the revolution of 1905. Not until 1914 was the basic position altered.

The attitude of the European socialist parties to the outbreak of the Great War led Lenin to alter fundamentally the theoretical analysis upon which his political strategy had hitherto been based. His attention now focused upon the nature of international capitalism: what tendencies within it had led to international war? How had it so perverted the consciousness of socialist leaders as to turn them into supporters of their own countries' war effort rather than tribunes of an international proletarian assault on capitalism? In *Imperialism: the Highest Stage of Capitalism* Lenin (following Hilferding and Bukharin) concluded that capitalism had, by the turn of the century, fundamentally changed in character. It typically exported capital rather than manufactured goods and was consequently obliged to commit huge administrative, military and naval resources to protecting its investments (imperialism). Monopoly displaced competition in large sectors of the economy and, consequently, technological innovation suffered. The big banks assumed a cardinal role not only in financing and restructuring industry (finance capital) but in dominating the state as well (state monopoly capitalism). As an international system, capitalism was monopolistic, parasitic upon colonial exploitation, technologically retrogressive, committed to huge military expenditure and war to defend its interests externally and to political monolithism and state oppression internally in order to guarantee its profits and power structures. Finance capitalism, imperialism and state monopoly capitalism represented the last degenerate and brutal forms of an economic and political system that had forfeited its right to existence and had brought civilization to the unprecedented carnage of the Great War. Lenin concluded that the epoch of socialist revolution was at hand, requiring the unity of all anti-imperialist forces on a worldwide basis. Unlike other anti-war radicals (Luxemburg and Bukharin, for example) he aimed to combine movements for national liberation in the colonies and semi-colonies with the socialist revolution in the Western industrialized world, co-ordinated by a new and genuinely revolutionary International.

Following the successful overthrow of tsarism in February–March 1917 and the emergence of workers' and soldiers' soviets as the organizational focus of popular power, Lenin insisted that Russian socialists had an obligation to begin the worldwide revolutionary assault against state monopoly capitalism and to turn the world war into an international civil war for socialism. The radicalized soviets would displace the parliamentary constitutional forms that had everywhere served to mask bourgeois dictatorship and end the 'despicable prejudice' that only the rich and educated could rule. The soviets were to be governmental agencies that combined in one body legislative, executive, judicial and military powers exercised directly by the armed people. Their role (as with the Paris Commune that Marx had extolled) was to initiate the broad masses of the people into every aspect of their own government. Through their own self-administration, Lenin believed, the masses would ascend to properly socialist consciousness. These theories were elaborated in his *The State and Revolution*, written in 1917. As far as tactics were concerned, from April 1917 onwards (April Theses) Lenin urged the overthrow of Russia's provisional government and all power to the soviets, an end to the war, land to the peasants, freedom to the nationalities of the old empire, workers' control (but not ownership) of industry, and nationalization of the banks, through which control over the economy was to be exercised. A good summary of his position, written some weeks before the October revolution, is given in 'Can the Bolsheviks retain state power?'

After the October revolution the Bolshevik Party (which did not change its name to 'Communist' until March 1918) was faced by a succession of crises – the breakdown of the

transport system and consequent famine in the towns, fuel and raw material shortages, industrial dislocation, growing opposition, foreign intervention and civil war. As chairman of the Council of People's Commissars his preoccupations were to assure the most efficient mobilization of the regime's scarce resources, to instil firm discipline and to insist upon the authority of the centre. The emphasis now was upon the accountability of lower party (and state) organs to higher ones; a hierarchical and vertically structured system modelled on the so-called democratic centralism of the party was imposed on the whole of the administration. The soviets and the factory and regimental committees rapidly lost their autonomy and influence. One-man management and appointment from the centre displaced collegial administration and the elective principle. This harsher, tightly centralized state power, in which the party and the state were increasingly merged and opposition was put down by a rapidly expanding security police (or Cheka), was now held by Lenin to be the historically necessary form of state power appropriate to the transitional period between capitalism and communism. The necessity of the dictatorship of the proletariat exercised by the advance guard of the working class – the Communist Party – became a central tenet of the Communist International that Lenin inspired and founded in 1919. Its objective was to promote and co-ordinate the world revolution which would, in its turn, relieve the isolation of the Russian revolution and mitigate its economic and cultural backwardness.

In the event the Russian Communists found themselves in 1921 increasingly isolated internationally and internally. Industrial collapse, urban deprivation, peasant risings and workers' opposition culminated in the revolt of the Kronstadt naval base and a retreat from the austere 'war communism' of the civil war years. Concessions and incentives were introduced in the New Economic Policy to encourage the peasants to produce and to trade their surplus; the concessions were not, however, matched by political relaxation. Lenin insisted upon a ban on factions within the party and instituted a secretariat (headed by Stalin) to bolster party discipline.

Not until his last writings of late 1922 and 1923, after a second stroke had effectively forced him to retire from the leadership of the government, did Lenin have leisure to reflect upon what had been built in Russia and the future prospects of socialism. He was disturbed that the state apparatus had replicated many of the worst abuses of the tsarist regime – red tape, bureaucratic inertia and high-handedness typified its style, and its size was out of all proportion to the tasks it performed. It ought, he insisted, to be purged and drastically reduced in size ('Better fewer but better' and 'How we should reorganize the workers' and peasants' inspection'). The party itself was far from blameless, careerists had entered its ranks, the level of its culture was too low and its administrative incompetence everywhere manifest. Some of its leading members, Stalin in particular, were intolerably rude and over-mighty. ('Letter to the Congress', also known as Lenin's 'Testament'). He was even unsure whether the party was capable of preserving socialist values when the revolution was internationally isolated in a land where industry (and the working class) had suffered so severely from war, civil war and famine and where it was surrounded by a backward peasant mass. His final proposals were that the party and state should fuse their best personnel in one exemplary institution. Lenin's last writings were largely ignored by the Communist Party of the Soviet Union and by the Communist International. It was, paradoxically, Stalin who emerged immediately following Lenin's death in January 1924 with a codified and simplified account of *The Foundation of Leninism* that was to ossify into obligatory doctrine.

See also

Bukharin, Hilferding, Luxemburg, Stalin.

Works

Collected Works, forty-five volumes, Moscow, Foreign Languages Publishing House, 1960–70.

Other works

E. H. Carr, *The Bolshevik Revolution*, three volumes, Harmondsworth, Penguin, 1966.
D. Shub, *Lenin*, Harmondsworth, Penguin, 1966.
A. B. Ulam, *Lenin and the Bolsheviks*, London, 1966. Secker & Warburg,
M. Leyin, *Lenin's Last Struggle*, London, Pluto Press, 1975.
N. Harding, *Lenin's Political Thought*, two volumes, London, Macmillan, 1977, 1981.
A. J. Polan, *Lenin and the End of Politics*, London, Methuen, 1984.

Li Dazhao   1889–1927

Li Dazhao is esteemed as one of the most distinguished figures of the early Chinese communist movement. Highly patriotic, he sought means of national salvation since his youth, but with the October revolution of 1917 and the uprising of the Fourth of May Movement of 1919 he concluded that Marxism was the best way of solving the problems of Chinese society. His contributions to the communist movement in China can be summed up as follows: (1) his introduction of Marxism into China, which influenced a whole generation of followers; (2) he was the most influential among the founding members of the Chinese Communist Party, adapting Marxism–Leninism to Chinese conditions; (3) his death as a martyr set an example of self-sacrifice and moral integrity to members of the early communist movement.

Li Dazhao enthusiastically hailed the October revolution in his articles 'The victory of Bolshevism' (1918) and 'The victory of the masses' (1918). He advocated that the building of a new social system in China must be linked with the defeat of the imperialist power and war lords standing in the way. The social driving forces which must be relied on to carry out a new democratic revolution were the working class and peasantry, who made up the majority of the Chinese people, but the former must assume leadership of the revolution. Li attached great importance to armed struggle and the peasant movement, and undertook considerable practical work in setting up the Communist Party and mass organizations in vast areas of China. He also paid great attention to developing united front tactics and played an important role in the realization of the first period of co-operation between the Communist Party and the Kuomintang, led by Sun Yat-sen.

Li Dazhao was executed by a Chinese war lord in 1927. Since then he has been regarded as a martyr and hero by the party, though there was an unsuccessful attempt to belittle his historical role during the Cultural Revolution. In 1989 his centenary was celebrated in both China and the Soviet Union.

See also

Sun Yat-sen.

Works

Li Dazhao, *Wen Zi (Selected Writings of Li Dazhao)*, two volumes, Beijing, People's Publishing House, 1984.

Other works

Maurice Meisner, *Li Ta-Chao and the Origins of Chinese Marxism*, Cambridge, Mass., Harvard University Press, 1967.

Liang Qichao   1873–1929

Liang Qichao was an influential reformer, scholar and political thinker during an eventful period of Chinese history when the country was undergoing a radical transition from monarchy to a republic.

A patriot, Liang was concerned about the corrupt politics of the late Qing Dynasty, which had led to the accumulation of numerous national weaknesses. However, under the strong influence of his teacher, Kang Youwei, he was loyal to monarchism and dedicated himself to fostering China's constitutional movement. This set him apart from the revolution led by Sun Yat-sen. Although his political attitude underwent some change after the short-lived Hundred Days reform of 1898, when all his activities were banned by the Qing government manipulated by the dowager empress, he remained a reformist and never went over to the revolutionary camp. After a period of exile in Japan, Liang continued his political activities under the republican regime, founding a new political party to compete with Sun Yat-sen's Kuomintang in the National Assembly; he also assumed a high-ranking position in Yuan Shikai's government in 1913. Liang's cooperation with Yuan Shikai, however, alienated much of his public support. He spent the last decade of his life lecturing in various Chinese universities.

Through his interest in Western political philosophy and his travels abroad Liang surpassed the teachings of Kang Youwei in many ways. He advocated freedom of thought and denied Confucianism and Marxism alike, on the grounds that both doctrines would restrict such freedom. He advised the Chinese people not to be slaves to the past and to form their own judgements by the criteria of truth. In his thesis 'On the renewal of the people' (1902–4) he referred to the relationship between a nation and its people as a metaphor of the organs of the body. The nation is just like a human body, while people are its organs, so the renewal of the nation must be effected through the renewal of its people. Once the people have been renewed, there will be no question about having a new system, a new government and a new nation.

Through his prolific writings, covering many aspects of Western political thinking, Liang exerted a great influence on modern Chinese thought during the first two decades of this century.

See also

Sun Yat-sen.

Works

Liang Qichao Xuan Zi (The Selected Writings of Liang Qichao), Shanghai, People's Publishing House, 1984.

Other works

J. Levenson, *Laing Ch'i-ch'ao and the Mind of Modern China*, Cambridge, Mass., Harvard University Press, 1953.
H. Chang, *Liang Ch'i-ch'ao and the Intellectual Transition in China*, Cambridge, Mass., Harvard University Press, 1971.
P. Huang, *Liang Ch'i-ch'ao and Modern Chinese Liberalism*, Seattle, University of Washington Press, 1972.

Charles Edward Lindblom 1917–

Lindblom was co-author, with Robert A. Dahl, of *Politics, Economics, and Welfare*. He is also the author of *The Intelligence of Democracy* and *Politics and Markets*, a revisionist work from a founder of the pluralist school, which persuasively documents the inherent political power and privilege conferred by market power.

Works

Politics, Economics and Welfare, New York, Harper & Row, 1953.
The Intelligence of Democracy, New York, Free Press, 1965.
Politics and Markets, New York, Basic, 1977.

Walter Lippmann 1889–1974

Lippmann is remembered primarily as a journalist. After a precocious start as founding co-editor of the liberal *New Republic* in 1914, he quickly assumed the status of one of America's leading pundits. Moving on to Pulitzer's *New York World* in 1920, and later to other papers, he virtually invented the institution of the newspaper columnist. Lippmann was also, however, a political philosopher who regularly retreated from the daily grind of his column to reflect on deeper themes. A sensitive barometer of the public mood rather than a systematic thinker, he moved through many phases of thought but returned continually to the theme of the capacity or otherwise of human nature to sustain democratic government.

Following a brief period as assistant to the socialist mayor of Schenectady, New York, on graduation from Harvard in 1910, he soon put socialism and practical politics behind him. Out of this experience came *A Preface to Politics*, an amalgam of Freudian psychology and vitalist philosophy. Lippmann was the first, as Freud's biographer Ernest Jones pointed out, to apply Freud's ideas to the study of politics. He drew the conclusion that existing political institutions and the rational arguments which legitimized them were no more than forms that masked and ultimately repressed the real social forces which lay behind them. Sharing the views of many of his progressive contemporaries that radical changes were needed to accommodate the demands of trade unions, women and others, he thought of new social movements as feelings waiting to be expressed. The task of political leadership was to guide mass feelings into fruitful channels. His model for such leadership was former President Theodore Roosevelt.

Within a year, however, Lippmann had retreated from the anti-intellectualism of this first book, following it up in *Drift and Mastery* with a more measured liberalism which placed emphasis on the need for 'mastery' in the management of social change. Drawing now on the instrumentalism of John Dewey, Lippmann employed the method of science as his guiding concept. It offered a means of control, without which change would be mere 'drift'. The method of science, moreover, was in essence the method of democracy. 'As absolutism falls,' he wrote, 'science rises. It *is* self-government.' In short, the politics of ecstasy gave way to the politics of process in Lippmann's thought. He had arrived at a form of political pluralism, focusing on the role of interest groups, a concept which had been

145

given more systematic form by Arthur Bentley in *The Process of Government* (1908).

Lippmann's newly discovered respect for reason was enhanced by his dismay at the eruption of unreason in the First World War. A warm supporter of American intervention in 1917, he nevertheless shared the liberals' disillusionment with both the punitive peace imposed on Germany and the disturbing manifestations of war psychology in the United States. His writings of the 1920s display a growing mistrust of mass emotion which was to inform much of his subsequent thought. In his path-breaking study of the news media, *Public Opinion*, Lippmann explored the gap between the 'pictures in our heads' and the 'world outside', concluding that representative government itself risked foundering on the incapacity of the average voter to make rational decisions. *A Preface to Morals*, a powerful and best-selling meditation on a Western culture eaten into by the 'acids of modernity', betrayed a deepening philosophical scepticism. His answer was not a return to religious faith but an affirmation of civic humanism, informed by stoic detachment. Humanist ethics, not science, now provided the ballast of his social philosophy.

Lippmann's 1937 tract against Franklin Roosevelt's New Deal, *The Good Society*, seemed to represent a wholesale repudiation of his earlier liberal pluralism. The New Deal, he suggested, with its proliferation of centralized administrative agencies, betrayed a dangerous spirit of collectivism of the sort which had developed in Italy and Germany. In practice, however, Lippmann's proposals for reform were not so different from those of Roosevelt. They included public works, social insurance and income equalization through taxation, among others. His objection, he said, was to the pursuit of reform by administrative *fiat* rather than through a system of law. Arbitrary power, not power itself, was the danger.

Lippmann's growing concern with the role of law as the guarantor of the democratic polity found expression in his last full-length book, *The Public Philosophy*. Echoing the conclusions of many post-war social scientists about the instability and unformed character of mass opinion, he proposed that its influence on government had led to a 'morbid derangement of the functions of power'. Stronger executive power and a revival of the tradition of natural law were required to re-establish both the authority of government and the necessary restraints on its exercise. If the authoritarian emphasis of the argument was most in evidence at the time of publication, its liberal implications – resting on the need to limit governmental power – were there to be taken up.

The tension in Lippmann's career between the capacity to adapt to changed circumstances and his search for core values is clearly visible in the last decade of his life. Governmental authority now seemed more at risk from the actions of the government than from those of the people. Not only did he emerge as a powerful opponent of the war in Vietnam, he even swallowed his distaste for mass protest politics in professing to understand, if not entirely to endorse, the demonstrations of America's students against the war. The roots of Lippmann's position lay in the philosophy of foreign affairs which he had developed over the previous half-century. His watchword was 'realism', born of a distaste for America's long tradition of missionary diplomacy. His objections to American intervention in Vietnam did not, like those of left-wing critics, rest on moral grounds; nor was he opposed in principle to military intervention. He counselled, rather, a cold calculation of American interests, which should be determined on geopolitical grounds and on the basis of America's capacity to achieve its goals. On both counts, he felt, Vietnam was not worth the candle. Lippmann's priorities in foreign affairs – belief in the balance of power, as opposed to such notions as collective security, and emphasis on Europe as America's primary theatre of interest – are most clearly set out in *US Foreign Policy*. These priorities align Lippmann firmly with the 'realist' school of international relations theory, most prominently represented by Hans Morgenthau and Raymond Aron.

If the mature Lippmann is to be considered a conservative, then he was of that peculiarly American sort which sought to conserve liberal principles. His strong support for black civil rights legislation during the 1960s doubtless arose in part from fears of the danger which racial violence posed to social stability, but his columns in the mid-1960s also displayed a moral passion for minority rights such as he had not shown since his early years. Ultimately the liberal in Lippmann prevented the sceptic in him from breaking faith with democracy.

See also

Aron, Bentley, Dewey, Freud, Morgenthau.

Works

A Preface to Politics, 1913, reprinted Ann Arbor, University of Michigan Press, 1962.
Drift and Mastery, 1914, reprinted Englewood Cliffs, N.J., Prentice-Hall, 1961.
Public Opinion, New York, Harcourt Brace, 1922.
A Preface to Morals, New York, Macmillan, 1929.
The Good Society, Boston, Mass., Little Brown, 1937.
US Foreign Policy: Shield of the Republic, Boston, Mass., Little Brown, 1943.
The Public Philosophy: on the Decline and Revival of Western Society, Boston, Mass., Little Brown, 1955.

Other works

Marquis Childs and James Reston (eds.), *Walter Lippmann and his Times*, New York, Harcourt Brace, 1959.
Ronald Steel, *Walter Lippmann and the American Century*, Boston, Mass., Little Brown, 1980.
Dieter S. Blum, *Walter Lippmann: Cosmopolitanism and the Century of Total War*, Ithaca, N.Y., Cornell University Press, 1984.
John M. Blum (ed.), *Public Philosopher: Selected Letters of Walter Lippmann*, New York, Ticknor & Fields, 1985.

Audre Lorde   1934–1992

Audre Lorde, black American lesbian poet, was born in New York city. The youngest daughter of Grenadian immigrants, she began speaking very late, learning to read at about the same time and finding poetry – whether memorized or self-created – the best means of expressing her feelings. She writes about this, and other aspects of her early life, including the impact of racism and her erotic love for women, in the autobiographical *Zami*. In 1961 she received a master's degree in library science and worked for a time as a librarian, but publication of her first collection of poems, *The First Cities* (1968), led to a teaching stint at Tougaloo in Mississippi and to her realization that 'teaching was the work I needed to be doing'. She subsequently taught in New York high schools and at several American colleges, becoming Professor of English at Hunter College in 1981.

Although she identified herself primarily as a poet, not a theorist, her essays placed her at the forefront of a new, non-racist feminism. Modern feminist theory as it developed in the 1960s and 1970s tended towards a questionable universalism which assumed, from a white middle-class perspective, that all women shared the same experience of oppression. While never denying that sexism harms all women, Lorde always stressed the importance of difference, and warned of the dangers of either ignoring or simply tolerating difference, which should function as a source of creativity, in individuals as well as the whole society.

Whether writing poetry or prose Lorde drew on her feelings and experience, favouring more intuitive modes of knowledge over analytical reasoning. Without accepting a firm dichotomy between thinking and feeling, she believed people are taught to think in a certain way and to deny an area of humanity she likes to personify as 'the Black mother in each of us'. This 'Black mother' is the source of power which is repressed in a male-dominated society, being female, dark, chaotic and erotic. In one of her best-known essays, the controversial 'Uses of the erotic: the erotic as power', first delivered at the fourth Berkshire Conference on the History of Women at Mount Holyoke College in 1978, Lorde defines the erotic as the life force of women, which has been trivialized by being limited to sexual relationships instead of informing all aspects of life. She was accused by some of reviving old, anti-feminist stereotypes of the rational white male *v.* the intuitive dark female. Her response was that women have been taught to distrust themselves and to reject any insights not sanctioned by the ruling culture, and if anything is to change women must not model themselves on men but find and use their own strengths because (as the title of another Lorde speech declares) 'The master's tools will never dismantle the master's house'.

In 1978 she discovered a lump in her right breast which proved to be malignant. *The Cancer Journals* (1980) document how her life was changed by coming so close to death, a subject which grimly recurred a few years later when she was found to have cancer of the liver, an experience explored in *A Burst of Light*. The journal form and the subject matter of both are highly personal, yet also political, in the contemporary feminist meaning of the word: Lorde writes about her struggle with cancer to offer strength and hope to others, and, in addition, makes clear the political implications of diseases which have their source in unsafe working conditions and contaminated air and water.

Works

Zami: a new Spelling of my Name, Watertown, Persephone Press, 1982.
Sister Outsider, Trumansburg, N.Y., Crossing Press, 1984.
A Burst of Light, London, Sheba, 1988.

Other works

Mary DeShazer, *Inspiring Women: Reimagining the Muse*, Oxford, Pergamon, 1986.
Maggie Humm, *Feminist Criticism: Women as Contemporary Critics*, Brighton, Harvester, 1986.

Lu Xun   1881–1936

Lu Xun (born Zhou Shuren) is regarded as China's foremost essayist of the twentieth century. His writings are distinguished by an intense patriotism, advocacy of the cause of the down-trodden and a commitment to political and social change.

Lu Xun's patriotism led him to choose a medical career as a means of serving his country. While a medical student in Japan, he accidentally saw a lantern slide documentary of Japanese killing Chinese while other Chinese looked on, apparently undisturbed. The apathetic attitude of the Chinese onlookers shocked him so much that he soon gave up his studies for a writing career. He believed that medicine could save only his compatriots' bodies when it was important to save their spirit.

In his most famous works, *Diary of a Madman, The True Story of Ah Q, Kong Yiji* and *Medicine and the New Sacrifice*, as well as in others, he relentlessly attacked the evils of the decaying Chinese social system and the remnants of the feudal order. In particular, he criticized the disappointing results of the 1911 Revolution. In doing so he expressed his profound sympathy with the exploited and oppressed while exposing their weaknesses concealed in the depth of their spiritual world in order to 'uncover the pains and draw attention to treatment and rescue'.

Lu Xun's didactic approach aimed at inspiring his readers to seek social justice and to improve their lot through storming the social system. Not surprisingly, the polemical style and overt political intent of his works did not go unanswered from the left or from the right. The responses, however, had the effect of strengthening his political commitment and of sharpening his critique of his opponents as expressed in his famous couplet: 'Fierce-browed, I coolly defy a thousand pointing fingers; Head-bowed, like a willing ox I serve the children.'

Apart from his essays, short stories, translations and contributions to the development of wood-block printing in China, Lu Xun lent his support to the patriotic movements of the period. The first wave of these involved students including the May 4th (1919) Movement, May 30th (1925) Movement and March 18th (1926) Movement in which a number of young students were killed. Towards the end of his life when Japanese aggression was spreading in China, Lu Xun actively participated in a number of organizations dedicated to national salvation and was the acknowledged leader of left-wing writers. In the course of common struggles he became associated with the Chinese Communist Party, which he believed held the future hope of saving China. In sending a congratulatory telegram to the Central Committee on the successful completion of the Long March, Lu Xun identified himself with their cause. However, he never joined the Party. Lu Xun's works have been variously invoked by Mao Zedong; Red Guards; the Gang of Four; Deng Xiaoping's reformist leadership in denouncing the Gang of Four; and by Chinese dissidents.

See also

Mao Zedong.

Works

Selected Poems, trans. W. T. F. Jenner, Beijing, Foreign Language Press, 1981.
Selected Works (four vols), Beijing, Foreign Language Press, 1985.

Other works

Jonathan D. Spence, *The Gate of Heavenly Peace*, London, Faber, 1982.
Wang Shiqing, *Lu Xun: a Biography*, Beijing, Foreign Language Press, 1984.
Ruth F. Weiss, *Lu Xun: a Chinese Writer for All Times*, Beijing, New World Press, 1985.
Leo Ou-fan Lee, *Lu Hsun and his Legacy*, Berkeley, Los Angeles and London, University of California Press, 1985.
Lin Zhihao, *La Vie de Luxun* (two vols), Beijing, Editions en Langues Etrangères, 1990.

György (Georg) Lukács 1885–1971

A major figure of the Hungarian communist movement and one of the outstanding Marxist theoreticians of the century, Lukács was born and died in Budapest. He started to publish at a very early age (in 1902), but until 1918 his writings – under the influence of Plato, Kant, Hegel and Kierkegaard – touched upon politics only in relation to cultural and literary controversies (e.g. the significance of the great revolutionary poet, the contemporary Endre Ady, or the reasons behind the neglect of the poet and Bartók's librettist, Béla Balázs). All this radically changed after the Russian revolution, when Lukács (a former friend of Georg Simmel, Emil Lask, Max Scheler and Max Weber) enthusiastically embraced Marxism and became one of the founding members of the Hungarian Communist Party.

During the short-lived Hungarian Council Republic Lukács was People's Commissar for Education and Culture, and in the last weeks of armed struggle against the foreign interventionist forces he acted as the political commissar of the best military divisions. After the defeat he escaped from the country and settled in Vienna, returning to Hungary only for clandestine party work, defying the death sentence passed on him by the judges of Admiral Horty's dictatorship. After a short period of work at the Moscow Institute of Marxism–Leninism under the direction of the later executed Ryazanov, he spent some years in Berlin. Following Hitler's accession to power he had to flee again, moving to Moscow, where he spent the war years. Lukács returned to Hungary in 1945, to take up the Chair of aesthetics at the University of Budapest, and stayed there until his death in 1971.

Between 1919 and 1929 Lukács was one of the leaders of the Hungarian Communist Party, second in ranking in the majority Landler faction (named after the great Hungarian trade unionist Eugene Landler). The faction led by Béla Kún was its main antagonist within the party. Their conflict came to a head in

1928–9, by which time Landler was dead and Lukács was for a short period in charge of the majority faction. In this capacity he wrote the famous 'Blum Theses' in which he formulated what he considered to be the only viable political strategy for the party, in opposition to Kún's sectarian maximalism. Lukács's Blum Theses in many ways anticipated Georgi Dimitrov's advocacy of a Popular Front, which later became in fact official Comintern policy. However, the Blum Theses arrived seven years too early, and – as a result of the authoritarian intervention of the Comintern, where at the time the later liquidated Béla Kún was one of Stalin's favourite high-ranking functionaries – Lukács was forced to retire completely from politics. The Blum Theses were condemned as 'a half social democratic liquidationist theory', and their author was confined to literary and cultural work to the end of his life, with the exception of a brief interlude in 1956, when he was Minister of Culture during the uprising in Imre Nagy's government. In 1941 Lukács was arrested in Moscow and spent some time in Stalin's jail, accused of being a Trotskyite agent. Fortunately for him, Dimitrov was in charge of the Comintern in this period, and his direct intervention secured Lukács's release after a few months.

Lukács's most important political writings all date to the period 1919–29, collected in three volumes: *History and Class Consciousness*, *Lenin* and *Political Writings, 1919–29*. Among these, *History and Class Consciousness* exercised by far the greatest influence, on major intellectuals and political figures alike, from Karl Korsch to Gramsci and Walter Benjamin, and from Marcuse to Sartre, Lucien Goldmann and Merleau-Ponty. Equally, the work had an enormous impact during the later 1960s on the student movement, especially in Germany, France and Italy. Lukács's early political writings were likewise highly influential both in the 1920s and in the 1960s.

One of the most important theoretical contributions of *History and Class Consciousness*

to twentieth-century debate was Lukács's interpretation of *reification*. It provided a framework for analysing the conditions of capitalist development on lines very similar to Marx's theory of alienation several years before the publication of his *Economic and Philosophic Manuscripts of 1844*. Also, on the basis of the 'identical subject/object' postulated by Lukács, *History and Class Consciousness* put forward an idealized picture of the proletariat as the only true agent of history, with its 'standpoint of totality' and 'imputed' or 'ascribed' (as opposed to actually given psychological/empirical) class consciousness. At the same time Lukács argued that class consciousness was the 'ethics of the proletariat', embodied in the party. Thus he could define the role of the party itself in strict moral terms, criticizing the tendency to bureaucratization as a failure to live up to the 'moral mandate' of the proletarian party as the 'historical embodiment and the active incarnation of class consciousness'. Not surprisingly, therefore, *History and Class Consciousness* was sharply condemned very soon after its publication by the head of the Comintern, Grigorii Zinovyev (who also fell victim later to Stalin's purges), and Lukács could not allow its reissue until as late as 1967.

In *Lenin* – written immediately after Lenin's death – Lukács put at the centre of his analysis the relationship between theory and practice. Defending Lenin against accusations that he pursued a *Realpolitik* devoid of solid theoretical foundations, Lukács insisted that Marx's final thesis on Feuerbach – 'The philosophers have only *interpreted* the world in different ways; the point, however, is to change it' – found in fact its most perfect embodiment in Lenin and his work. Among Lukács's *Political Writings, 1919–29* the most important (besides the Blum Theses) are 'Tactics and ethics', 'The role of morality in communist production', 'The question of parliamentarism', 'The moral mission of the Communist Party', 'Spontaneity of the masses, activity of the party' and 'Organization and revolutionary initiative'.

After the war Lukács frequently participated in debates about cultural policy, reviving to a significant extent the perspective expressed in his Blum Theses. As a result he was violently attacked in 1949 (the year of the establishment of one-party rule in Hungary) by party ideologues and, ominously, even the powerful Russian political/literary figure Fedeev joined in the chorus of condemnation. Lukács retreated to the domain of philosophy, writing a critique of German 'irrationalism' and its contribution to the rise of Hitler – *The Destruction of Reason* – in this period. He became politically more active again after Stalin's death, taking a leading role also in the work of the radically anti-Stalinist 'Petöfi circle' and actively supporting the revolutionary uprising in October 1956.

Together with the other members of Imre Nagy's government he was deported to Romania in November 1956. After his release in the summer of 1957 he was attacked constantly for several years. He wrote two major works of synthesis in this period – *Aesthetics* and *The Ontology of Social Being* – in which he tried to spell out his vision of an authentic Marxist theory, against the kind of orthodoxy which prevailed under Stalin. In 1968, the year of the 'Prague spring' and its military repression, he wrote an important political essay: *The Present and Future of Democratization*, which argued the need for a radical process of democratization and for a complete break with the still dominant Stalinist heritage. Publication was forbidden by the party authorities for twenty years, and it appeared long after Lukács's death, in the last days of 1988.

See also

Gramsci, Marcuse, Merleau-Ponty, Sartre, Weber.

Works

History and Class Consciousness, 1923, reprinted London, Merlin Press, 1971.
Lenin: a Study on the Unity of his Ideas, 1924, reprinted London, New Left Books, 1970.
Political Writings, 1919–29, London, New Left Books, 1972.
The Young Hegel, London, Merlin Press, 1975.
The Destruction of Reason, London, Merlin Press, 1980.
Schriften zur Ideologie und Politik, Berlin, Luchterhand, 1967.
The Present and Future of Democratization, Budapest, Magvetö, 1988.

Other works

G. H. R. Parkinson, *Georg Lukács: the Man, his Work, his Ideas*, London, Weidenfeld & Nicolson, 1970.
Istvan Meszaros, *Lukács's Concept of Dialectic*, London, Merlin Press, 1972.
Lucien Goldmann, *Lukács and Heidegger*, London, Routledge, 1977.
Theo Pinkus (ed.), *Conversations with Lukács*, London, Merlin Press, 1984.

Rosa Luxemburg
1871–1919

Rosa Luxemburg was one of the great Marxist theorists of the twentieth century; her radical conception of socialist democracy stands in opposition to both Bolshevik authoritarianism and technocratic reformism. Born in the Polish city of Zamosc, but forced to flee her homeland for political reasons, she entered the University of Zürich, where she completed a dissertation on 'The Industrial Development of Poland' (1898).

This still classic study claimed that Polish economic development was interconnected with that of the Russian empire as a whole and that a strategy based on Polish nationalism would subsequently impede modernization and prove self-defeating. Luxemburg steadfastly refused to concede that support for nationalism was anything other than a serious compromise of proletarian principle. According to her, nationalism not only perpetuates capitalism by dividing workers from one another, and serves to justify wars in which the proletariat will suffer, but is also atavistic in a period defined by global capitalism. These concerns would become evidence in her major economic work, which sought to examine the intrinsic connection between capitalism, nationalism, militarism and imperialism: *The Accumulation of Capital.*

In this work Luxemburg sought to investigate the systemic conditions which made capitalist accumulation possible in the first place. Goods obviously had to be sold, to accumulate the profit that capitalists would reinvest to perpetuate the system. But, given the claims by Marx that capitalist production necessarily outstrips demand, she noticed that no incentive existed for capitalists to reinvest. Without reinvestment the system would collapse, so that an outlet for the profitable disposition of excess goods had to exist. That outlet she saw in terms of exports to pre-capitalist territories: in short, imperialism.

Imperialism is subsequently neither a mere aberration of an otherwise healthy system, as reformers wished to believe, nor 'the highest stage of capitalism' (Lenin). Luxemburg saw it as intrinsically connected with capitalism from the beginning. And yet, since the flow of capitalist goods into pre-capitalist areas would eventually transform them into industrial ones, it was also obvious to her that capitalism must create its own historical limit beyond which looms the spectre of 'breakdown'. As for the interim, it will become marked by increasingly ferocious competition between advanced states for those steadily diminishing pre-capitalist territories. Militarism and nationalism will therefore grow in conjunction with the imperialism that capitalism engenders.

Although this provides an explanation for the First World War, Luxemburg's theory can neither explain why not every capitalist state follows an expansionist foreign policy nor envisage imperialism by a 'socialist' state. Then, too, if her theory provides no hope of reforming imperialist tendencies in the advanced capitalist states, neither does it lead to any practical revolutionary policy for the colonialized peoples. There is only the implicit need for the transnational organizations of workers to confront an ever more interdependent capitalist economy.

Throughout her career, in fact, Rosa Luxemburg involved herself with the international organization of workers – and, by 1913, she had become an important figure in the world socialist movement. Her ascent had begun with the decision to enter the powerful German Social Democratic Party (SPD) and her contribution to what became known as the 'revisionist debate'. That debate had been initiated by Eduard Bernstein, whose analysis concluded that the SPD should surrender its revolutionary political aims and concentrate on a policy of compromise with non-proletarian classes to ensure economic reforms so that socialism could gradually 'evolve' within capitalism.

In *Social Reform or Revolution* (1899) Luxemburg argued, contrary to Bernstein, that credit would not eliminate the crisis character of capitalism and that the expected concentration of capital was taking place. Fearing that an unrestricted politics of class compromise could justify any choice by the party leadership, and shift power to the trade unions, she also argued that there were limits to reform; that trade unions could never govern the actual level of wages or resolve the basic contradiction between social production and private appropriation of wealth that defines the capitalist production process. Even regulating wages and working conditions depended upon political power; without a political revolution, she argued, the reform granted under one set of conditions could be retracted under another. A simple emphasis on economic reform would thus result only in a 'labour of Sisyphus'. Indeed, without an articulated socialist 'goal', she believed, the SPD would increasingly succumb to capitalist values and so surrender its sense of political purpose.

Yet, from Luxemburg's perspective, 'revisionism' and Leninism were merely opposite sides of the same coin. Her *Organizational Questions of Social Democracy* (1904) constitutes a response to the Bolshevik leader. Though Lenin's estimation of the trade unions as purely 'defensive' organizational forms accorded with her own, which was also the case with his claim that economic reform would not automatically result in the growth of political consciousness, Luxemburg rejected his hierarchical, quasi-military conception of party organization. Though she refused to presuppose class consciousness, and recognized the need for a party to organize workers, she never believed it possible to inject consciousness into the proletariat 'from the outside' by a vanguard composed of professional revolutionary intellectuals.

Just as she rejected a revisionist vision of the party run by experts and basically concerned with incremental socio-economic issues, she opposed the idea of a revolutionary organization based on blind obedience which would erect an 'absolute dividing wall' between the leadership and the base. If socialism is to transform workers from 'dead machines' into the 'free and independent directors' of society as a whole, she argued, then they must have the chance to learn and exercise their knowledge. Indeed, this very concern led her to embrace the Russian revolution of 1905, which inspired what is arguably her finest theoretical work, *Mass Strike, the Political Party and Trade Unions.*

Luxemburg took part in the revolutionary events and experienced first-hand the innovative possibilities of the masses in democratically organizing their milieu. In fact she saw the mass strike as a way to overcome the 'artificial' bifurcation of the economic struggle of the unions from the party's commitment to a political transformation of the given order. The concept articulates her concern with furthering an organizational dialectic between party and base that would gradually build the self-administrative capacities of workers by helping them develop new democratic institutions and then, at a different stage of the struggle, even newer ones.

This radical democratic vision stayed with her throughout the years of the First World War, which she spent in a tiny prison cell. It was there that she wrote a response to the various critics of her imperialism thesis known as the *Antikritik* (1915), translated Russian authors into German, composed her

beautiful letters to friends and lovers, and – under the pseudonym Junius – produced the great anti-war pamphlet *The Crisis in German Social Democracy* (1916), which mercilessly assaulted the SPD for its willingness to support the Kaiser's war, its obsession with votes, its cowardice in the face of public opinion and its betrayal of working-class interests.

Her most prophetic work, however, was surely *The Russian Revolution.* Also written in jail, while she was in ill health and with little information other than newspapers, it exposed the compromises which would ultimately undermine the Soviet experiment. Opposed to Lenin's agrarian policy, continuing to reject the use of slogans implying the 'right of national self-determination', her analysis is best known for its demand that the 'dictatorship of the proletariat' – as the 'transitional' phase of socialist construction – should extend democracy both in terms of republican values and popular institutions that would allow for the direct participation of the working class in administering social life. And yet, she viewed these compromises and deformations as products of the regime's weakness which itself was born of underdevelopment and isolation. Indeed, Rosa Luxemburg was among the first to analyse the Russian Revolution from an internationalist perspective which stressed the unfulfilled political obligations of social democracy.

Following her release from prison in 1918, she joined the Spartacus group – which would form the nucleus of the German Communist Party (KPD) – and publicly advocated the creation of 'soviets' (or 'workers' councils'). Despite their almost legendary stature, however, the Spartacists never received the support of a proletarian majority – and Rosa Luxemburg knew it. She warned against unleashing the revolution in Germany and urged participation in the elections to a National Assembly which would constitute the Weimar Republic. But she was outvoted. The Spartacist revolt broke out in 1919 and Rosa Luxemburg, seeking to remain in contact with the masses, was brutally murdered at the hands of proto-Nazi thugs in the employ of the government.

No matter what the movement with which she was connected, Rosa Luxemburg maintained her critical perspective as well as her commitment to socialism, democracy and internationalism. Realizing that mass action necessarily incorporates an experimental dimension, she refused to admit that socialism is exhausted by the reforms and programmes of party professionals or that the interests of workers are ever directly identifiable with those of even the most dynamic party or revolutionary movement. This undogmatic commitment to an unfinished notion of freedom undercut her influence within the dominant socialist and communist organizations. At the same time it helped place her at the forefront of the most emancipatory tendencies in the socialist tradition of theory and practice – and that is precisely where she remains.

See also

Bernstein, Lenin.

Works

The Mass Strike, the Political Party, and the Trade Unions, 1906, reprinted New York, Harper & Row, 1971.
The Accumulation of Capital, 1913, reprinted New York, Monthly Review Press, 1968.
Rosa Luxemburg Speaks, ed. Mary Alice Walters, New York, Oxford University Press, 1970.
Rose Luxemburg: Selected Political Writings, ed. Robert Looker, London, Cape, 1972.
The National Question: Selected Writings of Rosa Luxemburg, ed. Horace B. Davies, New York, Monthly Review Press, 1976.

Other works

J. P. Nettl, *Rosa Luxemburg,* New York, Oxford University Press, 1966.
Paul Frohlich, *Rosa Luxemburg: her Life and Work,* New York, Monthly Review Press, 1972.
Norman Geras, *The Legacy of Rosa Luxemburg,* London, Humanities Press, 1976.
Raya Dunayevskaya, *Rosa Luxemburg, Women's Liberation, and Marx's Philosophy of Revolution,* Atlantic Highlands, N.J., Humanities Press, 1981.
Stephen Eric Bronner, *Rosa Luxemburg: A Revolutionary for our Times,* New York, Monthly Review Press, 1987.

Jean-François Lyotard   1924–

Among the many appellations one could apply to the several decades of work by Lyotard, one stands out: the requirement of witnessing which throws a whole series of traditional tropes in philosophy, ethics and politics, not to mention aesthetics, into question. The most obvious questions would be: what, precisely is being witnessed? Who is the 'I' or 'we' or 'you' or 'they' that witnesses? Finally, what makes this 'act of witnessing' a requirement, perhaps even 'the' requirement, of what Lyotard so famously named 'the postmodern "condition"'?

In his study of Barnett Newman's *Stations of the Cross,* in *The Lyotard Reader,* Lyotard argues that Jesus's age-old and utterly unanswerable question 'My God, why hast thou forsaken me?!' has only one response. The 'why path' is but an infinite and regressive journey, which only ever circles back and ends at the very place of its start, i.e., the original site of the void, whose proper name is nothing other than God. Instead, '[t]he only response to the question of the abandoned that has ever been heard', writes Lyotard, 'is not *"Know why"*, but *Be.*' This *Be* is at once both an imperative command (*Be!*) and, simultaneously, a momentary micro-slice (Lyotard calls it an 'instant') of the very 'sites of time', the erstwhile and slippery, right-now-here-right-now-abandoned 'is' or 'happening' or 'event' (*Be . . .*).

By shifting to the site of abandonment and loss, the entire problematic of the subject/object divide, which, albeit in different ways, has plagued the whole of metaphysics and a good deal of contemporary political philosophy alike (with its addenda on transcendence, existence, identity, reason, truth), is cast asunder. Something more nuanced, delicate, alive, takes its place: the virtual, plurally dimensioned, *Be.* In the instant of this instant, a prescription or task surfaces; the duty, as Lyotard calls it, of witnessing. Rather than a discovery (or analysis) of the rules of the game, it performs a kind of 'naming function', naming the very loss and abandonment of meaning. At the same time, it acts as a 'response' to the order(-cum-command) to be. It marks out 'the terror that surrounds the event, [and] the relief that *there is*'. In this way, the witnessing act becomes the ontological beginning, the 'rectilinear slash'; that is, the living, 'ineluctable' name of the 'is'. A kind of condition of the unconditional, its ontological task is, more accurately put, a chronological task, which, by the very nature of its 'instant' never remains static or complete. Indeed, it both 'links' the 'that which has been' with the 'that which will be' and exposes the 'link' itself as the very arena of the 'is'.

At the risk of straitjacketing his thinking or placing it in neatly defined categories (a move that would fly in the face of all that he has written), this 'loss-abandonment/linking/instant sites of time' remains a useful entry to the various facets of Lyotard's concerns. Because Lyotard is attempting to show us, over and again, how the witnessings, the 'patchworks', the ephemeral story-tellings, the little irritations at the sidelines of the social – like 'women who have had abortions, prisoners, conscripts, prostitutes, students and peasants ... socialist lesbians, Marx in the kitchen' – not only break up the meta-narratives of philosophy and history *per se*, but, by way of those 'little stories of life', generate political action itself. It is, as he calls it, a risk of imagination, necessary to recover from the 'sickness of knowledge and rules' inherent with absolute loss, cruelty, despair. 'You make up little stories', he remarks in his 'Lessons in paganism', 'or even segments of little stories, listen to them, transmit them and act them out when the time is right.' '"Why *little* stories?," asks a rhetorical voice. "Because they are short," answers another voice, "because they are not extracts from some great history, and because they are difficult to fit into any great history. Remember the problems the Marxist narrative, to name but one, had with the student episode. How could that be fitted into a web of relations of production and class struggle? ... That discourse of little stories is not true in the sense that a theory claims to be true, and nor is it a meta-narrative, or even a critical meta-narrative. It is a work of art in itself, a product of the pure will of the imagination.'

Many, including Lyotard himself, have claimed that despite having written well over twenty books and a myriad of articles, journalistic pieces and 'little stories', he 'only wrote four "real" books', in which the best-known of his tracts to English readers, *The Postmodern Conditon: a Report on Knowledge* (1979; translated 1984) – and, on related themes, *Postmodernism Explained to Children* (1986; translated 1992) and *Toward the Postmodern* (1993) – are not included. But it is not by accident that this, and its related work, forms a kind of parenthesis, even a kind of 'witness', to his own work not to mention to the very grist and gristle that produces/characterizes the modern world. And what is this 'modern world'? It is a world embedded in a science and technology that reaches for the grand narratives of life 'such as the dialectics of Spirit, the hermeneutics of meaning, the emancipation of the rational or working subject or the creation of wealth', while at the same time, producing, in the *telos* of that reach, its utter apotheosis: incredulity, breakage and dispersion. Modernity produces postmodernity, which, in turn, becomes the 'groundless ground' of the modern. 'Simplifying to the extreme', as Lyotard puts it, the postmodern condition is precisely the vast 'incredulity toward meta-narratives', an incredulity produced by a progress in the sciences, a progress that 'in turn, presupposes it'. The result, he writes in *The Postmodern Condition*, is that modern meta-narratives disperse into something more akin to 'the pragmatics of language particles' or 'clouds of narrative language elements – narrative, but also denotative, prescriptive, descriptive and so on. Conveyed within each cloud are pragmatic valencies specific to its kind. Each of us lives at the intersection of many of these. However, we do not necessarily establish stable language combinations, and the properties of the ones we do establish are not necessarily communicable.'

Attacking themes close to the heart of the Frankfurt School (Habermas in particular), the structuralists and orthodox Marxism, Lyotard's 'clouds', 'gaps', 'events' are teased out, and played with, in his four 'real' books, in chronological order, *Discours, figure* (1971); *Economie libidinale* (1974); *Le Différend* (1984); and *Leçons sur l'analytique du sublime* (1991). *Economie libidinale* – characterized by Lyotard as his 'dirty little book' with its denunciation of theory as terror, nod to Freud, abandonment of Lacan and re-issue of, in the words of one commentator, 'a quasi-Nietzschean monism of intensity-as-value' – generated such outrage that he was ostracized from the group Socialisme ou barbarie. Losing friends did not seem to bother Lyotard, as is evidenced in his other 'major' works, where he continues to draw upon, borrow, steal or simply re-write in his own postmodern language-games Nietzsche, Wittgenstein, Foucault, Merleau-Ponty, Proust, Lacoue-Labarthe, Nancy, Derrida and, of course, Kant. To this list could be added Lyotard himself, with his insistence on the right to change the very premises of his thematics and tools of the trade. Without a map and often circling back to earlier concerns, including the student riots of May 1968, civil disobedience, sexism, hatred, violence, loss and, indeed, love, these works weave in, around, across and through – sometimes in profoundly contradictory ways – the many problems of justice, passion, *jouissance* (pleasure) and the intricacies of the sublime. To understand and indeed 'enter' his texts/clouds, all hidden, exposed and witnessed in the instant of the 'I', 'we', 'you', 'they' layered patchworks of 'our' time(s), the reader is required at the end (or middle or beginning) of the day simply and only to: *Be*. A somewhat tall – and small – order(ing), accent on risk, imagination.

See also

Derrida, Foucault, Habermas, Merleau-Ponty.

Works

La Phénoménologie, Paris, Presses Universitaires de France, 1954, trans. Brian Beakley, *Phenomenology*, Albany, State University of New York, 1991.

Discours, figure, Paris, Klincksieck, 1971, trans. Mary Lydon, *Discourse, Figure*, Cambridge, Mass., Harvard University Press, forthcoming.

Economie libidinale, Paris, Minuit, 1974, trans. Iain Hamilton Grant, *Libidinal Economy*, London, Athlone Press, 1993. There is an excellent 'glossary of terms' in this book.

La Condition postmoderne, Paris, Minuit, 1979, trans. Geoff Bennington and Brian Massumi, *The Postmodern Condition*, Minneapolis, Minnesota University Press and Manchester, Manchester University Press, 1984.

Le Différend, Paris, Minuit, 1983, trans. George Van Den Abbeele, *The Differend: Phrases in Dispute*, Minneapolis, University of Minnesota Press, 1988.

Leçons sur l'analytique du sublime, Paris, Editions Galilée, 1991, trans. Elizabeth Rottenberg, *Lessons on the Analytic of the Sublime (Kant's 'Critique of Judgement' §§23–29)*, Stanford, Cal., Stanford University Press, 1994.

The Lyotard Reader, ed. Andrew Benjamin, Oxford and Cambridge, Mass., Basil Blackwell, 1989.

Other works

David Carroll, *Paraesthetics: Foucault, Lyotard, Derrida*, New York, Methuen, 1987.

Peter Dews, *The Logics of Disintegration: Post-Structuralist Thought and the Claims of Critical Theory*, London, Verso, 1987.

Geoffrey Bennington, *Lyotard Writing the Event*, Manchester, Manchester University Press, 1988.

Andrew Benjamin (ed.), *Judging Lyotard*, Warwick Studies in Philosophy and Literature, London and New York, Routledge, 1992.

Alasdair MacIntyre 1929–

A Scottish-born moral philosopher and one-time Marxist, MacIntyre became the best-known contemporary philosopher of communitarianism with the publication of *After Virtue*. Unlike the communitarianism of a liberal pluralist like Michael Walzer, MacIntyre's is specifically neoclassical and anti-liberal. He argues that liberals, because of their commitment to moral relativism, to detaching themselves from 'any particular standpoint' in order to practise tolerance, cannot defend any reasoned point of view about Justice or notion of virtuous practice; nor develop a unifying concept of the Good.

Societies incorporating the liberal project are thus doomed to moral incoherence and social disarray; they cannot be true communities, nor can their inhabitants, lacking commitment to any particular social roles, have real moral obligations to each other. Alternatively, philosophers should immerse themselves in the knowledge of traditions, and especially the classical ethical tradition of Aristotelianism, in order to be able to reason truly about the content of Justice, the Good and Virtue; there is no universalistic rationality outside of a specific intellectual tradition. In *Whose Justice? Which Rationality?*, MacIntyre develops his own, neo-Thomist conception of the Good, synthesizing Aristotle with the Christian tradition of Augustine and Aquinas.

The obvious difficulty with this critique of liberalism is that it fails to meet the test of being embedded (cf. Sandel) in the societies about which MacIntyre writes, most especially the United States. American culture has never been particularly neoclassical, and even less Roman Catholic. MacIntyre's Catholic conception of Justice, therefore, though it claims to be 'communal', is in its own way universalistic, detached from historical, local narratives (cf. Walzer) and lived social experience. Liberal critics also note MacIntyre's unwillingness to concede that liberal tolerance itself may be a virtuous practice in a plural society; and feminist theorists have pointed out that the moral tradition he defends and promulgates has historically been 'for men only'. Thus, more than any other theorist, MacIntyre illustrates the difficulty of arguing for communalist traditions in a world in which the defence of abstract and equal individual rights is itself a central tradition.

See also

Rawls, Sandel, Taylor, Walzer.

Works include

After Virtue, Notre Dame, Indiana, University of Notre Dame Press, 1981.

Whose Justice? Which Rationality?, Notre Dame, University of Notre Dame Press, 1988.

Catharine A. MacKinnon 1946–

Catharine A. MacKinnon is a feminist legal scholar and activist whose views received international attention in 1983, when she and the feminist writer and activist Andrea Dworkin wrote an anti-pornography ordinance that was approved by the city council of Minneapolis, Minnesota. The ordinance, vetoed by the mayor, would have allowed individuals who believed they were harmed by a particular piece of pornography to sue for sex discrimination those who produced, distributed or sold such material. A federal court later ruled that a similar ordinance confined to violent material that was passed in Indianapolis, Indiana, violated the First Amendment, although the court recognized the harm pornography does to women as real.

MacKinnon's earlier attempt to secure civil rights for women was more successful. Her book *Sexual Harassment of Working Women: a Case of Discrimination* (1979) and her work on behalf of plaintiffs were largely responsible for judges recognizing 'sexual harassment' as a form of sex discrimination for which employers could be sued.

In general MacKinnon's scholarly work advances the argument that the laws of the liberal state are predicated on male dominance and women's silence and subordination, although they maintain a pretence of neutrality and equality. 'Rape law assumes that consent to sex is as real for women as it is for men,' she writes in *Toward a Feminist Theory of the State*, just as '[p]rivacy law assumes that women in private have the same privacy men do'. But in the absence of actual social equality between men and women the same laws for unequally positioned persons merely reinforce existing forms of domination. MacKinnon argues that formal legal equality between men and women leaves men, whose values and practices define the 'normal' status of women, able to avoid state sanctions against their various abuses of women, since what looks normal is not recognized as something that deserves to be prosecuted. MacKinnon locates the root of misogynist practices in norms associated with sexuality, which make acts like rape normative rather than deviant. Such values and laws based on them, according to MacKinnon, must be changed if sex equality is to be achieved.

Works

Feminism Unmodified: Discourses on Life and Law, Cambridge, Mass., Harvard University Press, 1987.
Toward a Feminist Theory of the State, Cambridge, Mass., Harvard University Press, 1989.
Only Words, Cambridge, Mass., Harvard University Press, 1993.

Crawford Brough Macpherson
1911–1987

A democratic theorist on the left, C. B. Macpherson is best known for his critique of the dimension of modern political culture he called possessive individualism and for his efforts to retrieve aspects of liberal democracy for socialism. In *The Political Theory of Possessive Individualism* he approached seventeenth- and eighteenth-century English political theory as a reflection of the developing hegemony in Europe of a capitalist market. The work also expressed normative concerns soon to prevail in the New Left rejecting an image of people as infinite consumers whose abilities are considered by others and by themselves as saleable possessions. Macpherson regarded behaviour that conforms to this image to be rather a result of market society than its precondition in human nature, as many supporters of capitalism suppose. The contrasting culture Macpherson advocated is one where 'life is for doing rather than just getting' and where participatory democratic politics will facilitate the equal development of truly human capacities – for moral judgement, rational understanding, friendship, and so on.

Macpherson's views on liberal democracy,

given their most sophisticated defence in *Democratic Theory*, challenged those theorists, of both left and right, for whom socialism and liberal democracy are entirely incompatible, thus anticipating debates on this topic initiated by the changes in Eastern Europe shortly after his death. Liberalism, Macpherson held, was uniquely adapted to market society and antedated effective democratic constraints on it. Those constraints resulted from pressures that liberal freedoms themselves facilitated and eventually yielded an accommodation of liberalism to democracy of the sort defended by John Stuart Mill. While he thought the resulting liberal democratic values and institutions well suited to capitalism, Macpherson also argued that, properly interpreted, such things as the promotion of equal liberty and the protection of property could and should be retained in a socialist – which for him meant a non-market – environment.

Some commentators have questioned Macpherson's historical scholarship, and others have challenged what they see as an uncritical endorsement of technological progress. In addition, opinion is divided about whether Macpherson was too much a Marxist or insufficiently Marxist. No doubt some of his critics' points are appropriate, but many of them fail to identify Macpherson's orientation. Like Harold Laski, the director of his M.Sc. in economics at the London School of Economics in 1935, or Harold Innis, his senior colleague in the Department of Political Economy at the University of Toronto, where he spent almost all his academic career, Macpherson's scholarship is not easily classified by either school or discipline. Rather, using Marxist and other tools, he pursued his overriding concern to identify democratic limitations and possibilities. For example, his first major work, *Democracy in Alberta* (1953), makes use of Marxist-like class analysis to explain the atypical persistence of single-party politics in a parliamentary system of government.

Similarly, while Macpherson was a strong

advocate of direct participation in political affairs, he did not share the view of many participationists that democracy is entirely incompatible with party politics. He viewed democracy as a process, in which progress is made in ways specific to local political traditions such that direct participation can replace some aspects of existing practices and be supplemented by others. Thus in the 1965 transcribed radio lectures *The Real World of Democracy* he envisaged an expansion of democracy in the First World incorporating both strengthened individual rights and competing political parties. In the case of the Second and Third Worlds he thought democratization possible by reforming single-party state systems to ensure access to a party and democracy within it. The relative absence of class-based ruling parties in the Third World was regarded as a democratic advantage over the Second by Macpherson, while what he saw as a commitment to equality gave socialism an edge over capitalism in the competition between world systems. This competition, Macpherson opined, was shifting from economic and military terrain to moral questions about how the equal development of human capacities can best be furthered.

See also

Laski.

Works

The Political Theory of Possessive Individualism: Hobbes to Locke, London, Oxford University Press, 1962.
The Real World of Democracy, Toronto, Canadian Broadcasting Corporation, 1965.
Democratic Theory: Essays in Retrieval, London, Oxford University Press, 1973.
The Life and Times of Liberal Democracy, London, Oxford University Press, 1977.
The Rise and Fall of Economic Justice and other Papers, Oxford, Oxford University Press, 1985.

Other works

Victor Svacek, 'The elusive Marxism of C. B. Macpherson', *Canadian Journal of Political Science* 9 (1976), pp. 167–78.
Alkis Kontos (ed.), *Powers, Possessions, and Freedom:*

Essays in Honour of C. B. Macpherson, Toronto, University of Toronto Press, 1979.
William Leiss, *C. B. Macpherson: Dilemmas of Liberalism and Socialism*, Montreal, New World Perspective, 1988.
Joseph Carens, ed., *Democracy and Possessive Individualism: the Intellectual Legacy of C. B. Macpherson*, State University of New York Press, 1993.

Errico Malatesta 1853–1932

Errico Malatesta ranks with Michael Bakunin and Petr Kropotkin as one of the greatest anarchists of the nineteenth and twentieth centuries. An indomitable rebel whose sixty-year career as an activist was unrivalled among anarchists, Malatesta is remembered in the Anglo-Saxon world primarily as a revolutionary agitator. He should be recognized, however, as a man of thought as well as action. Although his stature as a theorist does not equal that of Proudhon, Bakunin or Kropotkin, Malatesta was indisputably one of anarchism's most important thinkers, his writings distinguished above all by the acute insight into human behaviour and politics, common sense, profound moral decency and love of humanity.

Born of middle-class parents in the town of Santa Maria Capua Vetere (province of Caserta, near Naples), Malatesta was inspired by the Paris Commune of 1871 to embrace socialism and join the International Working Men's Association. He soon became a fervent disciple of Bakunin and a leading figure in the Italian anarchist movement. By 1876 Malatesta had ceased to consider himself a Bakuninist, because he no longer shared all the Russian's theoretical and practical ideas. Most important, he had abandoned Bakunin's anarchist collectivism in favour of the anarchist communism later popularized by Kropotkin. After 1884, however, Malatesta's ideas began to diverge sharply from the doctrines of Bakunin and Kropotkin, rejecting above all the determinism he believed intrinsic to both their philosophies. Yet, in matters of revolutionary strategy and tactics, Bakunin's influence always remained strong. By the 1890s, when his theories took definitive shape, Malatesta's philosophy and programme ran counter in several important aspects to the Kropotkinist mainstream of the revolutionary anarchist movement in Europe. The most salient features of Malatesta's anarchism were the following: voluntarism as opposed to determinism; relativism and absence of dogma *vis-à-vis* doctrine and theory; insistence on the need for anarchists to organize themselves and go among the people as a self-conscious vanguard; emphasis on insurrection as the principal revolutionary weapon; and rejection of indiscriminate terrorism. Revolution and anarchy, Malatesta believed, were not rooted in historical or biological necessity; they were a function of human aspirations, and could be realized only through the exercise of *volontà,* free will. Refusing to subordinate anarchism to any philosophical system or scientific theory, Malatesta assumed a relativist position towards the doctrines of anarchist communism, collectivism and individualism, arguing that all such theories were hypotheses rather than dogmas. He warned his comrades that ideological exclusivism would undermine their ability to work together for common ends. Accordingly, from the 1880s to the 1920s, Malatesta was the staunchest advocate of organization among the Italian anarchists, and during periods of revolutionary activity in Italy he always attempted to form an anarchist party (by 'party' he meant an informal, non-authoritarian, non-hierarchical organization of anarchists pursuing a common programme), invariably in the face of strong opposition from the intransigent anti-organizationists. He occasionally went so far as to advocate a united front with revolutionary socialists and republicans to overthrow the monarchy. The will to act, cohesive organization and common purpose, as well as intimate contact with the people, were all vital to the anarchists' role as the revolutionary vanguard. For while only the masses could effect a revolution, Malatesta believed that a politically conscious and prepared minority was needed to profit by or to create the circumstances that would rouse the masses to attack the existing order. And the only effective means of igniting the conflagration and ultimately overthrowing the state, Malatesta believed, was an insurrectionary uprising. As a proponent of insurrectionism Malatesta sanctioned the use of force only because the existing order could never be defeated by non-violent means. He insisted, however, that institutions, not men, were to be the target of revolutionary violence, and he rejected the use of terrorism against innocent people. While polemicizing with advocates of bomb-throwing and assassination in the 1890s, Malatesta observed that terrorists and pacificists, since both were fanatics, might achieve the same end. Whereas the anarchist terrorists would destroy half of humanity in order to see their principles triumph, the pacifists would permit humanity to remain under a yoke of oppression rather than violate their principles by taking action. Malatesta, as he himself proclaimed, would have violated any principle in order to save a human being.

Too much of a legend to be killed or imprisoned by the fascists, Malatesta spent his last years in Rome under house arrest before his death on 22 July 1932. He knew he would never live to participate in the revolution and the redemption of humanity, the goals he had struggled to achieve for sixty years. Yet he never lost faith in the efficacy of the anarchist ideal, taking comfort in the conviction that, as he had once declared, what mattered most was not that the anarchists should achieve anarchism today, tomorrow or within ten centuries, but that they should march toward anarchism today, tomorrow and always.

See also

Kropotkin.

Works

Scritti, ed. Luigi Fabbri, Brussels, Risveglio, 1934.
Scritti scelti, ed. Cesare Zaccaria, Naples, RL, 1947.
Scritti scelti, ed. Gino Cerrito, Rome, Samona & Savelli, 1970.
Rivoluzione e lotta quotidiana, ed. Gino Cerrito, Turin, Antistato, 1982.

Other works

Max Nettlau, *Errico Malatesta: vita e pensieri*, New York, Il Martello, 1922.
Luigi Fabbri, *Malatesta: L'uomo e il pensiero*, Naples, RL, 1951.
Vernon Richards (ed.), *Errico Malatesta: his Life and Ideas*, London, Freedom Press, 1965.

Malcolm X   1925–1965

After the US Supreme Court's school desegregation decision in Brown *v.* Topeka Board of Education in 1954, the lives of black Americans began to change dramatically. A number of black political organizations increased the pace of their demand for civil rights, chief among them the National Association for the Advancement of Colored People, which had been established decades earlier, the Congress of Racial Equality (established in the 1940s) and the Southern Christian Leadership Conference (established by Martin Luther King, Jr, and others in 1958). Although they had political and philosophical differences, all these civil rights groups were proponents of racial integration.

During the same period, however, there was another voice, that of the Nation of Islam, also called the Black Muslims, advocating a different solution to the mistreatment of African ancestry: the total separation of blacks and whites. From Detroit the head of the Nation of Islam, the Most Honorable Elijah Muhammad (Elijah Poole), preached primarily to northern blacks, who were victims of racial oppression not by the Ku Klux Klan but by the northern white power structure. Addressing this message to an increasingly receptive audience of young black men in the northern ghettoes was his follower Malcolm X, formerly Malcolm Little, who had converted to the Nation of Islam while in prison and by the late 1950s had become the Most Honorable Elijah Muhammad's most prominent advocate.

The rise of Malcolm X paralleled that of Martin Luther King, Jr. Malcolm preached in the north, east and west to black urban America. King and other civil rights leaders tended to preach in the south. The Nation of Islam, and Malcolm, called for the total separation of blacks and whites, called for a 'black revolution', rejected the term 'Negro', considered Islam the religion of Africans, and aligned themselves with people of colour throughout the world. Though it was more militant, there was a good deal of similarity between many of the tenets of the Nation of Islam and those of its predecessor, the Universal Negro Improvement Association of Marcus Garvey; both Elijah Muhammad and Malcolm X's father had been members of the UNIA.

The philosophical foundations of Malcolm's ideas were formed when he was a member of the Nation of Islam and a follower of Elijah Muhammad. However, by late 1963 Malcolm had been forced out of the Nation of Islam for challenging Elijah Muhammad's dictatorial power, and he subsequently began to rethink the Nation of Islam's version of Black Nationalism. In moulding his new ideas about Islam, Black Nationalism and the fight for justice and equality for blacks in the United States and elsewhere, Malcolm travelled to Africa, Mecca and Europe. From Cairo, on 29 August 1964, he wrote a letter directed both at his supporters and at his enemies, to clarify some of the differences between himself and the Nation of Islam. In it he said, 'Let me restate my own position: I believe in human rights for *everyone* [emphasis added], and that none of us is qualified to judge each other, and that none of us should therefore have that authority.'

Malcolm returned to the United States a radically changed man. He still fought for equality and justice for blacks, but now he was eager to fight alongside other civil rights organizations and leaders, including even King, whom he had previously scorned. Additionally, Malcolm now rejected the racist component of the teaching of the Nation of Islam, namely that only blacks could be Muslims; his trip to Mecca had proved to him that Islam was not the religion of black people exclusively. He also joined the American left in opposition to the Vietnam War, an opposition which grew out of the view that American blacks should be at one with other peoples of colour. In a series of speeches and interviews in 1964 and 1965 he continued to argue for a militant position, asserting that 'you have had a generation of Africans who actually believed that you could negotiate, and eventually get some kind of independence ... But you're getting a new generation that has been growing right now, and they're beginning to think with their own minds and see that you can't negotiate up on freedom nowadays ... If something is yours by right then fight for it or shut up.' At the same time, however, he now said that 'Afro-Americans are not yet filled with hate or the desire for vengeance as the propaganda of the segregationists would have you believe ... Most intelligent whites will admit without hesitation that they are already being punished for the evil deeds committed against the Afro-Americans by their fathers. Thus it is not necessary for the victim – the Afro-American – to be vengeful.'

Thus Malcolm would have said that he did not preach violence, but rather collective self-defence; even when he was still a member of the Nation of Islam he considered himself not anti-white but pro-black; and he considered himself not anti-Christian but pro-Muslim. Up to the moment of his assassination at the hands of followers of Elijah Muhammad he continued to believe strongly in Black Nationalism; but he left behind him the complex legacy of a man firmly rooted in both his African and his American heritage; committed to his religion; and committed to bringing equality and justice to all people of whatever race or religion.

See also

Garvey, King.

Works

The Autobiography of Malcolm X, New York, Grove Press, 1965

Malcolm X Speaks: Selected Speeches and Statements, ed. George Breitmann, New York, Merit, 1965.
By any Means Necessary: Speeches, Interviews and a Letter by Malcolm X, ed. George Breitman, New York, Merit, 1970.

Other works

C. Eric Lincoln, *The Black Muslims in America*, Boston, Mass., Beacon Press, 1961.
Elijah Muhammad, *Message to the Blackman in America*, Chicago, Muhammad's Temple No. 2, 1965.
John Henrik Clark (ed.), *Malcolm X: the Man and his Time*, New York, Macmillan, 1969.
George Breitman (ed.), *The Last Year of Malcolm X: Evolution of a Revolutionary*, New York, Merit, 1970.
Lenwood G. Davis, *Malcolm X: a Selected Bibliography*, Westport, Conn., Greenwood Press, 1983.
James H. Cone, *Martin and Malcolm and America: a Dream or a Nightmare?*, New York, Orbis, 1990.
Bruce Perry, *Malcolm: the Life of a Man who Changed Black America*, Barrytown, N.Y., Station Hill Press, 1991.

Karl Mannheim   1893–1947

Karl Mannheim was a social theorist active in Hungary, Germany and England between 1917 and 1947. His most influential works turn on two distinct conceptions, the 'sociology of knowledge' and 'planning for freedom'. They bear clearly on central issues of political theory, but they defy unambiguous political classification.

Mannheim developed his sociology of knowledge in writings that culminated in *Ideology and Utopia*, a volume of connected essays first published in Germany in 1929 and revised for English publication in 1936. Through his sociology of knowledge Mannheim proposes a social-scientific way of encountering and partially transcending the irrational elements present in all thinking, as evidenced by the disorienting effectiveness of political strategies attacking all aspects of opponents' world views as nothing but ideologies or utopias. While this destructive insight was first loosed upon the political world by Marxism, it soon became common property among all parties in Weimar Germany, generating a crisis of mutual distrust and poisoning political processes dependent on self-confident reflection, enquiry, debate and justification. If sociology of knowledge can disinterestedly and irresistibly show how contrasting styles of knowing are grounded in diverse social locations, the common consciousness among politically active strata concerning this piece of social knowledge – itself based on a commitment to synthesis sociologically imputable to the intelligentsia as stratum – can gradually expand to grasp the wider structural social diagnosis that it implies. Awareness of ideology and utopia would undergo a decisive change in function, from paralysing political poison to organon for a knowledge-oriented but not conflict-free politics.

With the destruction of these hopes in 1933, Mannheim turns to 'planning for freedom' as the motif of his writings in exile, beginning with a German-language essay collection published in 1935 and much enlarged in English in 1940. He argues that the National Socialist dictatorship exploits a socially unconscious mass response to a worldwide crisis in the self-reproductive institutions of liberal civilization, involving the absolescence of its regulative social technologies – from markets to parliaments to selective humanistic education. Mannheim pleads for a pre-emptive move to a planned social order, strategically utilizing the emerging social technologies that undermine the spontaneous self-ordering of the previous epoch. By relying greatly on induced self-regulation and other unbureaucratic means of co-ordinating activities that proceed best when experienced as uncontrolled, a differentiated, consensual reconstruction could make maximal provision for the invaluable human qualities and diversities earlier privileged by liberalism, unlike the violent homogenization imposed by communist or national socialist control through command. Awareness of the impending crisis among leaderships whose positions have been as yet sheltered from the full force of the decisive structural changes, notably the English elite of gentlemanly professionals, can tame the processes that would otherwise simply destroy the old liberal civil-

ization and prepare mass populations for usurped tyrannical direction. Planning for freedom presupposes a reorientation among traditionally legitimated elites, their acceptance of a sociological diagnosis of the times and their mastery of prophylactic and therapeutic techniques. But such planning also counts on deep continuity at pre-rational levels of substantive personalistic commitment, as well as its reproduction in subsequent generations.

The outcome of the crisis that Mannheim addressed with muted optimism in 1929 forced him into a situation where he had to recognize that his earlier claims concerning the political mission of disinterested sociology of knowledge lacked relevance. Instead of a crisis where all political actors were equally demoralized by discrediting exposures of irrational blood lines in their reasoning, he found in the England of 1936 bland self-assurance about the sufficiency of vested prejudices among all whose judgement bore decisively on politics. The sociology of knowledge had to unsettle this self-confidence, to foster a sense of crisis that could lead this comparatively intact elite to look to an outsider's sociology for diagnostic and therapeutic help. This shift, amounting almost to a reversal in emphasis, leaves confusing tracks in the English version of *Ideology and Utopia*.

The prime victims of the confusion were American sociologists, because they comprised the least resistant English-speaking audience for Mannheim's sociology of knowledge. Since they resonated to neither of the rhetorical sonorities now discordantly compounded in *Ideology and Utopia*, they typically abstracted elements from the overall texture of the work and moulded them to fit their own quite different intellectual strategies, dismissing the remainder as historically conditioned pretension. Mannheim's *Man and Society in an Age of Reconstruction* was largely received by a different sub-group among American social scientists, who treated his sociology of knowledge as irrelevant, except for its most commonplace cautions against the pervasiveness of misleading ideologies, and who sifted out accessible generalizations about social technologies for problem-oriented planners and educators. In that way the two works soon dwindled to the status of minor classics, superseded scientifically but useful for pedagogical exercises in academic curricula.

The original political vision of *Ideology and Utopia*, however, corresponds to concrete strategies promoted by distinguished groups among intellectuals loyal to Weimar, including innovative economists of industrial renewal, jurists dedicated to the democratic reconstitution of civil society and unorthodox Christian socialists; these groups recognized their aspirations in Mannheim's intelligentsia. The seemingly abrupt shift to instrumental rationality in his English work fits into two unrelated contexts: Mannheim's didactic relationship with conservative but socially-minded Christian thinkers, and his hope that the more developed forms of American pragmatism, by no means reducible to Weber's category of means–end rationality, would inform the reception of his work in the United States.

Theoretical reflection suggests new reasons for an encounter with Mannheim's overall design, especially since the main theoretical approaches that had so confidently declared his work anachronistic and hopelessly eclectic have themselves fallen upon hard times. The self-aware and self-critical rhetorical constituents in his thinking, his sensitivity to cultural contexts, his informed scepticism about Marxist historical ontologies, his recognition of multiple modes of knowing, and other features of his prematurely disrupted thinking, repay critical attention today.

Works

Ideology and Utopia, London, Routledge, 1936.
Man and Society in an Age of Reconstruction, London, Routledge, 1940.
Diagnosis of our Time, London, Routledge, 1943.
Essays on the Sociology of Knowledge, London, Routledge, 1952.
Structures of Thinking, London, Routledge, 1982.
Conservatism, London, Routledge, 1986.

Other works

Kurt H. Wolff (ed.), *From Karl Mannheim*, New York, Oxford University Press, 1971.
A. P. Simonds, *Karl Mannheim's Sociology of Knowledge*, Oxford, Clarendon Press, 1978.
David Kettler, *Karl Mannheim*, Chichester, Ellis Horwood, 1984.
Colin Loader, *The Intellectual Development of Karl Mannheim*, Cambridge, Cambridge University Press, 1985.
Volker Meja and Nico Stehr, *The Sociology of Knowledge Dispute*, London, Routledge, 1990.

Mao Zedong 1893–1976

Meo Zedong started his political activities when China, oppressed by imperialist powers and devastated by continuous civil wars fought by warlords' armies, fell into deep national crisis. As the revolution of 1911 did not bring the expected results, and the October revolution of 1917 in Russia inspired progressive Chinese intellectuals and stimulated their interest in Marxism–Leninism, Mao was convinced that this new theoretical weapon was the means to save China.

Central to Mao Zedong's political thought was the application of Marxism–Leninism to the situation of Chinese society. The revolution in China should be accomplished in two stages: the democratic stage aiming at smashing the old state machine and replacing it by the proletarian dictatorship; and the socialist stage, aiming at building the socialist society to ensure its transition to communism through the dictatorship of the proletariat. But, within this framework of Marxist–Leninist revolutionary development, Mao's contributions in the Chinese context (mostly in the first stage) had their own specific content which, by 1943, had come to be called Mao Zedong thought.

In the stage of democratic revolution, Mao's political thinking and practice were mainly concerned with the seizure of state power. Five main features can be discerned, as follows: (1) on the basis of a class analysis of Chinese society, sorting out the enemies to strike and isolate and friends to unite in different periods of the revolution; (2) developing armed struggle, which relied mainly on the peasantry through the setting up of revolutionary bases in the countryside which would encircle the urban centres; (3) upholding the absolute leadership of the Communist Party in all spheres, giving attention to policy tactics, political propaganda and organizational work; (4) relying on the masses, to win over their wholehearted support; and (5) always being confident of winning the class struggle by looking down on the enemy as a paper tiger in the long term while treating him as a dangerous opponent during the actual course of the struggle.

In the late 1920s and early 1930s Mao's revolutionary base area strategy had been carried out with relative success but was interrupted by the interference of the Comintern, whose agents adopted a line of leftist adventurism that contributed to the complete failure of the early revolutionary bases in the southern provinces. When the Red Army was forced to embark on the Long March in late 1934 the situation within the Chinese Communist Party leadership began to change. During the course of the Long March Mao's leadership was affirmed at the Zunyi conference in 1935 and further consolidated ideologically in the early 1940s through a rectification campaign. Guided by Mao Zedong Thought, the revolutionary base areas expanded remarkably during the Anti-Japanese War, and, in the civil war which followed, the People's Liberation Army occupied nearly the whole mainland of China by 1 October 1949, when the People's Republic of China was founded. The blueprint of the new system had been drawn up by Mao a few months earlier in *On the People's Democratic Dictatorship* (1949), in which such a dictatorship is defined as 'democracy for the people and dictatorship over the reactionaries'. As the founder of the new republic, Mao's prestige was so high that his leadership was absolutely unchallengeable.

If in the stage of democratic revolution Mao emphasized how to seize power, then in the stage of socialist revolution his main emphasis was on how to safeguard state power and advance his own understanding of socialism. He paid considerable attention to economic development and produced a number of works dedicated to socialist construction in the early and mid-1950s, for example *On the Ten Major Relationships* (1956), *On the Correct Handling of Contradictions among People* (1957), and significant achievements were made in this period. Yet, given his inclination to class struggle, and shocked by Khrushchev's de-stalinization, Mao soon adopted a radical line in both political life and economic development which resulted in a series of setbacks. Soon after the excessive Anti-rightist movement in 1957, the Great Leap Forward was launched. This was, at least in part, to compete with Khrushchev's brand of communism by mobilizing mass movements, which had worked so well in the civil war, for economic development. When initial problems with the Great Leap became clear, the campaign against rightist opportunism was carried out to silence those Communist Party members who dared to raise doubts and criticisms.

From the early 1960s onward Mao focused his energy on continuing class struggle under the proletarian dictatorship and pronounced revisionism as the main danger. This time he identified alleged 'capitalist roaders' within the Communist Party as the main target. In his view, class struggle under the proletarian dictatorship was a long-term task and, as the revisionists within the party had allegedly been trying to restore capitalism, it became necessary to carry out class struggle against them and practise all-round proletarian dictatorship in all fields of the superstructure.

Following this line, Mao launched the disastrous Cultural Revolution. Although he advocated that revolution could promote production, in fact all political campaigns carried out since the 1950s produced a contrary result. But the personal cult of Mao was so deeply rooted in the feudal remnants of Chinese society that once the decision had been made by him it could not be changed.

In the international sphere, mainly from the 1960s onward, Mao also advocated class struggles against imperialism, revisionism and reactionaries, and the ideological disputes with the Soviet Union broke into armed conflict in the late 1960s. But surprisingly the reconciliation with the United States, which was largely designed to counter the Soviet threat, came about through President Richard Nixon's visit in 1972. Mao did seek to exert his influence on the outside world, especially the Third World, but with limited success.

Mao's merits have been reassessed since the Third Plenum of the eleventh Congress of the CPC (1978), mostly in *The Resolution of Certain Questions in the History of our Party* (1981), where his faults were dealt with in some detail but greater attention was paid to his merits. Since then Mao's theory of class struggle as the key link, which he hoped would be maintained for hundreds of years after his death, has been disowned and the Communist Party has placed greatest emphasis on economic development. Moreover Mao Zedong thought has been interpreted as a collective creation rather than Mao's personal achievement. Yet his legacy, good or ill, is so far-reaching that it will take generations to evaluate.

Works

Selected Works of Mao Tse-tung, five volumes, Peking, Foreign Languages Press, 1967–77.

Other works

Stuart Schram, *Mao Tse-tung*, Harmondsworth, Penguin, 1967.

Frederic Wakeman, *History and Will: Philosophical Perspectives of Mao Tse-tung's Thought*, Berkeley, Cal., University of California Press, 1973.

D. Wilson (ed.), *Mao Tse-tung in the Scales of History: a Preliminary Assessment*, Cambridge, Cambridge University Press, 1977.

Frederic C. Teiwes, *Politics and Purges in China: Rectification and the Decline of Party Norms, 1950–65*, White Plains, N.Y., Sharp, 1979.

Resolution on CPC History (1949–81), Beijing, Foreign Languages Press, 1981.

Brantly Womack, *The Foundations of Mao Zedong's Political Thought, 1917–35*, Honolulu, Hi, University Press of Hawaii, 1982.

Roderic McFarquhar, *The Origins of the Cultural Revolution*, two volumes, New York, Columbia University Press, 1974, 1983.

Stuart Schram, *The Thought of Mao Zedong*, Cambridge, Cambridge University Press, 1989.

Frederic C. Teiwes, *Politics at Mao's Court: Gao Gang and Party Factionalism in the early 1950s*, Armonx, N.Y., Sharpe, 1990.

Herbert Marcuse   1898–1979

Herbert Marcuse was associated with the Frankfurt school and participated in its attempt to update Marxian theory in response to changing historical conditions from the 1920s to the 1970s. Marcuse gained notoriety as 'father of the New Left'; in the 1960s he was perceived as both an influence on and a defender of the so-called 'New Left' in the United States and Europe. His theory of 'one-dimensional' society provided critical perspectives on contemporary capitalist and state communist societies and his notion of the 'great refusal' won him renown as a theorist of revolutionary change and 'liberation from the affluent society'.

Marcuse's first published article in 1928 attempted a synthesis of phenomenology, existentialism and Marxism, which decades later would be carried out again by various 'existential' and 'phenomenological' Marxists. Marcuse argued that much Marxist thought had degenerated into rigid orthodoxy and thus needed immersion in concrete 'phenomenological' experience to revivify the theory; at the same time, he believed that Marxism neglected the problem of the individual, and throughout his life he was concerned with individual liberation and well-being, in addition to social transformation and the possibility of a transition from capitalism to socialism. Thus his was the first major review in 1933 of Marx's newly published *Economic and Philosophical Manuscripts of 1844*; the review anticipated the tendency to revise interpretations of Marxism from the standpoint of the more humanistic works of the early Marx. Similarly, his study of Hegel's *Ontology and Theory of Historicity*

(1932) contributed to the Hegel renaissance that was taking place in Europe.

In 1933 Marcuse joined the Institute for Social Research in Frankfurt and soon became deeply involved in its interdisciplinary projects, which included working out a model of radical social theory, developing a theory of the new stage of state and monopoly capitalism, and providing a systematic analysis and critique of German fascism. Marcuse identified deeply with the critical theory of the institute and throughout his life was close to Max Horkheimer, Theodor Adorno and others in the institute's inner circle.

In 1934 he fled from Nazism and emigrated to the United States, where he lived for the rest of his life. His first major work in English, *Reason and Revolution*, traced the genesis of the ideas of Hegel, Marx and modern social theory. A defence of Hegel against the current notion that he was a forerunner of fascism, it demonstrated the similarities between Hegel and Marx, and introduced many English-speaking readers to the Hegelian–Marxism tradition of dialectical thinking.

After service in the US government (the wartime Office of Strategic Services and the post-war State Department) from 1941 to the early 1950s, which Marcuse always claimed was motivated by a desire to fight fascism, he returned to intellectual work and in 1955 published *Eros and Civilization*, in which he attempted an audacious synthesis of Marx and Freud and sketched the outline of a non-repressive society. While Freud argued in *Civilization and its Discontents* that civilization inevitably involved repression and suffering, Marcuse argued that other elements in Freud's theory suggested that the unconscious contained evidence of an instinctual drive towards happiness and freedom. This evidence is articulated, Marcuse suggests, in daydreams, works of art, philosophy and other cultural products. Based on this reading of Freud, and study of an emancipatory tradition of philosophy and culture, Marcuse sketched the outlines of a non-repressive civilization which would involve libidinal and

non-alienated labour, play and open sexuality, resulting in a society and culture which would further freedom and happiness. His vision of liberation anticipated many of the values of the 1960s counter-culture and helped Marcuse to become a major influence on the New Left in that decade.

Marcuse argued that the current organization of society produced 'surplus repression' by imposing socially unnecessary labour, unnecessary restrictions on sexuality and a social system organized around profit and exploitation. In light of the diminution of scarcity and the prospect of increased abundance, Marcuse called for the end of repression and the creation of a new society. His radical critique of existing society and its values and his call for a non-repressive civilization led to a dispute with his former colleague Erich Fromm, who accused him of 'nihilism' (towards existing values) and irresponsible hedonism. Marcuse had earlier attacked Fromm for excessive 'conformity' and 'idealism' and repeated the charges in the polemic over *Eros and Civilization* and Marcuse's use of Freud.

During his period of government work Marcuse had been a specialist in fascism and communism, and he published a critical study of the Soviet Union in 1958 (*Soviet Marxism*) which broke the taboo in his circle against speaking critically of the USSR. While attempting to develop a many-sided analysis of the USSR, Marcuse focused his critique on Soviet bureaucracy, culture, values and the differences between Marxian theory and the Soviet version of Marxism. Distancing himself from those who interpreted Soviet communism as a bureaucratic system incapable of reform and democratization, Marcuse pointed to the 'liberalizing trends' which ran counter to Stalinist bureaucracy, and which indeed eventually materialized in the 1980s under Mikhail Gorbachev.

Next Marcuse published a wide-ranging critique of both advanced capitalist and communist societies in *One-Dimensional Man*. This book theorized the decline of revolutionary potential in capitalist societies and the development of new forms of social control. Marcuse argued that 'advanced industrial society' created false needs which integrated individuals into the system of production and consumption. Mass media and culture, advertising, industrial management and contemporary modes of thought all reproduced the existing system and attempted to eliminate negativity, criticism and opposition. The result was a 'one-dimensional' universe of thought and behaviour in which the very aptitude and capacity for critical thinking and oppositional behaviour were withering away.

Not only had capitalism integrated the working class, the source of potential revolutionary opposition, but it had developed new techniques of stabilization through state policies and the development of new forms of social control. Thus Marcuse questioned two of the fundamental postulates of orthodox Marxism: the revolutionism of the proletariat and the inevitability of capitalist crisis. In contrast with the more extravagant demands of orthodox Marxism, Marcuse championed non-integrated forces such as minorities, outsiders and the radical intelligentsia, and attempted to nourish oppositional thought and behaviour.

One-Dimensional Man was severely criticized by orthodox Marxists and theorists of various political and theoretical commitments. Despite its pessimism, though, it influenced many in the New Left, as it articulated their growing dissatisfaction with capitalist and Soviet communist societies alike. Moreover, Marcuse continued to call for revolutionary change and defend the newly emerging forces of radical opposition, thus winning the hatred of the establishment and the respect of the new radicals.

One-Dimensional Man was followed by a series of books and articles which articulated New Left politics and critiques of capitalist societies in 'Repressive tolerance' (1965), *An Essay on Liberation* (1969) and *Counterrevolution and Revolt* (1972). 'Repressive tolerance' attacked liberalism and those who refused to take a stand during the controversies of the 1960s. It won Marcuse the reputation of being an intransigent radical and ideologue of the left. *An Essay on Liberation* celebrated all the existing liberation movements from the Viet Cong to the hippies and exhilarated many radicals while further alienating establishment academics and those who opposed the movements of the 1960s. *Counterrevolution and Revolt*, by contrast, articulates the new realism that was setting in during the early 1970s, when it was becoming clear that the most extravagant hopes of the 1960s were being dashed by a turn to the right and 'counter-revolution' against the 1960s.

During this period of his greatest influence Marcuse also published many articles and gave lectures and advice to student radicals all over the world. Never surrendering his revolutionary vision and commitment, he continued to defend Marxian theory and libertarian socialism until his death.

Marcuse also dedicated much of his work to aesthetics, and his final book, *The Aesthetic Dimension*, briefly summarizes his defence of the emancipatory potential of aesthetic form in so-called 'high culture'. Marcuse thought that the best of the bourgeois tradition of art contained powerful indictments of bourgeois society and emancipatory visions of a better society. Thus he attempted to defend the importance of great art for the projection of emancipation and argued that cultural revolution was an indispensable part of revolutionary politics.

His work in philosophy and social theory generated fierce controversy, and most studies of his work are tendentious, frequently sectarian. Although much of the controversy involved his criticism of contemporary capitalist societies and defence of radical social change, Marcuse left behind a complex and many-sided body of work comparable to the legacies of Ernst Bloch, Georg Lukács and Theodor Adorno.

In retrospect, his vision of liberation – of the full development of the individual in a non-repressive society – distinguished his work, along with a sharp attack on existing forms of domination and oppression. Primarily a philosopher, Marcuse's work lacked the sustained empirical analysis in some versions of Marxist theory and the detailed conceptual analysis in some versions of political theory. Yet he constantly showed how science, technology and theory itself had a political dimension, and he produced a solid body of ideological and political analysis of many of the dominant forms of society, culture and thought during the turbulent era in which he lived and struggled for a better world.

See also

Adorno, Bloch, Freud, Fromm, Horkheimer, Lukács.

Works

Reason and Revolution, New York, Oxford University Press, 1941.
Eros and Civilization, Boston, Mass., Beacon Press, 1955.
Soviet Marxism, New York, Columbia University Press, 1958.
One-Dimensional Man, Boston, Mass., Beacon Press, 1964.
A Critique of Pure Tolerance, Boston, Mass., Beacon Press, 1965.
An Essay on Liberation, Boston, Mass., Beacon Press, 1969.
Five Lectures, Boston, Mass., Beacon Press, 1970.
Counterrevolution and Revolt, Boston, Mass., Beacon Press, 1972.
Studies in Critical Philosophy, Boston, Mass., Beacon Press, 1972.
The Aesthetic Dimension, Boston, Mass., Beacon Press, 1978.
Negations, Boston, Mass., Beacon Press, 1989.

Other works

Stefan Breuer, *Die Krisis der Revolutionstheorie*, Frankfurt, Syndikat, 1977.
Douglas Kellner, *Herbert Marcuse and the Crisis of Marxism*, London, Macmillan, 1984.
Robert Pippin *et al.* (eds.), *Marcuse: Critical Theory and the Promise of Utopia*, South Hadley, Mass., Bergin & Garvey, 1988.

José Carlos Mariátegui
1894–1930

The most innovative of the early Marxist thinkers in Latin America, Mariátegui was born into the lower classes in the southern Peruvian town of Moquegua. Crippled and largely self-educated, he began to work as a copy boy for a large Lima daily when he was fourteen. He soon rose to prominence as a journalist and editor. Forced into exile in 1919 by the repressive Leguía regime, he spent three years in Europe, where he strengthened his understanding of Marx and was introduced to innovative thinkers like V. I. Lenin, Antonio Gramsci, Leon Trotsky and George Sorel and to the creativity of the Russian revolution.

Upon his return to Peru in 1923 he began to fashion a Peruvian and Latin American Marxism that was based on local conditions and was very much adapted to the Third World reality. Thus the Inca empire was reclaimed as part of the tradition of Third World collectivism and the mostly Indian peasants were cast as a revolutionary class that could, along with the workers, miners and conscious members of the intelligentsia, engage in revolutionary praxis and thus build socialism in Peru and Latin America. The mechanisms he chose for political education included his lectures to the People's University, his famous magazine, *Amauta*, his prolific output of articles and his short-lived working-class newspaper, *Labor*. After the loss of his stronger leg in 1924, Mariátegui was confined to a wheelchair. None the less, he continued to write and speak publicly. By 1928 and 1929 he was engaged more heavily in political organization, founding the Peruvian Socialist Party in 1928 and the General Confederation of Peruvian Workers in 1929. He also began to send trained Quechua-speakers into the highlands to begin the arduous task of organizing the Peruvian Indians.

Far from being a dogmatist, the Peruvian thinker displayed a kaleidoscopic understanding of world events and the importance of Third World identity. His diverse writings were informed by readings of Marx, Engels, Lenin and Bukharin, as well as by the ideas of Rosa Luxemburg and Antonio Gramsci. He continually championed the importance of indigenism in the development of Peruvian Marxism and wrote one of the most sagacious studies of the Peruvian and Latin American reality to date. *Seven Essays in Interpretation of Peruvian Reality* (1928) is a comprehensive study of Peru that draws on insights gained from Marxist theory to explain multiple aspects of the nation. It employs general concepts such as exploitation, economic imperialism, racism and classism to elucidate Peruvian history, social structure and culture, and draws heavily on statistical data and a new generation of radical pro-Indian writers and artists in Peru and Mexico. Mariátegui was also one of the first Latin Americans to employ the concept of dependent development and anticipated the empirically based radical analysis that has distinguished Latin American social science in recent years.

His *Defensa del marxismo* and *Ideologia y politica*, both written in instalments in the late 1920s and published posthumously, are the best examples of his adaptation of Marxism to native conditions. Not closely tied to turgid interpretations of classical texts, he was also influenced by Freud, Spengler and Benedetto Croce. Although he considered himself an international Marxist, he never depreciated the importance of national conditions, original formulations or interpretations based on specific local conditions. As the stalinization of the Communist International began to mitigate against such interpretations, the Peruvian's relations with the Moscow-based organization were often strained, as when he resisted the directive to change the name of the Peruvian Socialist Party to Communist, or to move from a (directed) mass to a cadre party structure. It was only after his death in 1930 that the name and organization of the party were changed.

Arguing that Latin American Marxists had to develop their own Indo-American socialism that was not a 'copy or imitation of any other', he was very much part of a generalized movement among Latin American intellectuals to break with rigid European forms and traditions when they stultified local understanding and initiative. Like his contemporary, Víctor Raul Haya de la Torre, he believed that it was necessary to adapt the best ideas from Europe and Latin America to local conditions. Unlike Haya de la Torre, he believed Marxism provided the best method of doing so. Thus many of Mariátegui's approaches were similar to those of more contemporary Third World thinkers like Mao (in regard to the role of the peasants in revolution) and Amícar Cabral (fitting Marxism to specific conditions). He was clearly a great innovator and is usually referred to in Marxist circles as the *Amauta*, the Quechua word for the wise ones who taught and advised the Inca.

He is now revered as Latin America's greatest early Marxist thinker and father of the Peruvian left. The *Seven Essays* have been translated into seven languages, including Russian and Japanese, and have seen more than thirty editions in Spanish. Even the ultra-radical Shining Path guerrillas adopted his name (Sendero Luminoso José Carlos Mariátegui). The *Amauta* clearly continues to represent the best of the autonomous, dynamic tradition in Latin American Marxist thought, and will continue to be essential reading in the post-*perestroika* era.

See also

Bukharin, Cabral, Croce, Freud, Gramsci, Lenin, Luxemburg, Mao, Sorel, Trotsky.

Works

Obras completas de José Carlos Mariátegui, twenty volumes, Lima, Amauta, 1959–72.
Defensa del marxismo: polémica revolucionaria, Lima, Amauta, 1967.
Ideologia y politica, Lima, Amauta, 1972.
Seven Interpretative Essays on Peruvian Reality, Austin, Tex., University of Texas Press, 1972.

Other works

Harry E. Vanden, 'The peasants as a revolutionary class – an early view from Peru', *Journal of InterAmerican Studies and World Affairs* 20, 2 (May 1978).
Jesús Chavarría, *José Carlos Mariátegui and the Rise*

of Modern Peru, 1890–1930, Albuquerque, N.M., University of New Mexico Press, 1979.

Harry E. Vanden, 'Marxismo, comunismo and other bibliographic notes', Latin American Research Review 14, 3 (Fall 1979).

Harry E. Vanden, National Marxism in Latin America: José Carlos Mariátegui's Thought and Politics, Boulder, Colo., Lynne Rienner, 1986.

Jacques Maritain
1882–1979

French Roman Catholic theologian, best known for developing a human rights argument from a traditional Catholic natural law perspective. A major influence on the many late twentieth-century Catholic theologians who have developed an interventionist position towards politics and the state based on the natural law framework.

See also

Niebuhr.

Works

Christianity and Democracy, trans. Doris C. Anson, New York, Scribner, 1945.
Man and the State, Chicago, University of Chicago Press, 1951.
Scholasticism and Politics, Garden City, N.Y., Image, 1960.
Reflections on America, New York, Image, 1964.
The Social and Political Philosophy of Jacques Maritain, selected readings, ed. Joseph W. Evans and Leo R. Ward, Garden City, N.Y., Doubleday, 1965.

Mihailo Markovic   1923–

The monolithic power of communist party control effectively stifled critical political thought in Eastern and Central Europe for much of the post-war period. Even in Yugoslavia, which had broken away from Stalin's domination in 1948, the radical criticisms of existing power structures made by Milovan Djilas met with imprisonment. However, the relative success of the Yugoslav system of workers' self-management in the 1950s and early 1960s generated a body of radical democratic political thought organized around the Praxis group of social philosophers. The group, which started in 1964 and disbanded in 1975 under pressure from the Yugoslav authorities, engaged in theoretical reinterpretations of Marx's thought and investigated contemporary problems concerning human freedom, equality and the effects of technology and bureaucracy. A series of summer schools were held on the island of Korcula which attracted leading theorists from around the world, such as Marcuse, Habermas, Fromm and Lucien Goldmann. Some of the members of the Praxis group launched a journal, Praxis International, in 1980.

The most prominent political theorist associated with the Praxis group is Mihailo Markovic. His early work, translated into English as The Contemporary Marx and From Affluence to Praxis, concentrated on reinterpreting Marx's work to emphasize the centrality of the humanist philosophy found in the early writings, and to emphasize the dialectic of theory and practice symbolized in the word 'praxis'. For Markovic the conception of humanity found in Marx meant that Marx's analyses of capitalism and the politics of his day were imbued with a sense of what ought to be, and this method could be applied to the practical problems of overcoming alienation in contemporary society. The themes of combating compulsion and striving for genuine democratic control are found in an outstanding collection of essays, Democratic Socialism. Markovic's political philosophy was supplemented by the political economy of Branco Horvat and the political sociology of Rudi Supek and Svetozar Stojanovic.

In Eastern Europe the state has generally been intolerant of original political thought, but an exception occurred briefly in Hungary in the late 1960s, when the government allowed considerable freedom of discussion to accompany a radical reform of the economic structure. The work of a group of social scientists known as the Budapest school was brought to the attention of the West by its mentor, Georg Lukács, in 1971. An anthology of their early work has been translated as The

Humanisation of Socialism, by Andras Hegedus, Agnes Heller, Maria Markus and Mihaly Vajda. Here the attempt was to politicize the unstated power structures of everyday life, in the home, the community and the workplace, in order to widen the demands for social transformation. Andras Hegedus, who had briefly been Prime Minister in 1956, published an important work (*On Bureaucracy*) which criticized the inflexibility of existing methods of administration and their harmful social consequences, although for the most part the approach constructively advocates a mixture of organizational options. Agnes Heller developed a theory of human needs in contemporary industrial society from her reading of Marx in *The Theory of Need in Marx* (1976) and emphasized the fertility of the idea of the 'realm of freedom'.

When the most radical aspects of the economic reform were reversed in 1972 and 1973 critical political theory ceased to be acceptable to the Hungarian government, and the writers of the Budapest school were dismissed from their academic posts. In 1983 Ferenc Feher, Agnes Heller and Georgy Markus, who were all by then in teaching posts in Australia, published *Dictatorship over Needs*, one of the most important analyses of the structural crisis of East European states and a challenge to Western socialists who still harboured hopes that those regimes could reform themselves. The total rejection of any claims these societies made to be progressive reflected the writers' fierce commitment to civil liberties and social responsibility, which has been reiterated recently in Feher and Heller's *The Postmodern Political Condition* (1989) and Heller's *Beyond Justice* (1989).

See also

Djilas, Fromm, Habermas, Hegedus, Heller, Horvat, Lukács, Marcuse.

Works

From Affluence to Praxis: Philosophy and Social Criticism, Ann Arbor, Mich., University of Michigan Press, 1974.

The Contemporary Marx: Essays on Humanist Communism, Nottingham, Spokesman, 1974.
Praxis: Yugoslav Essays in the Philosophy and Methodology of the Social Sciences (with G. Petrovic), Dordrecht, Reidel, 1979.
Democratic Socialism: Theory and Practice, Brighton, Harvester, 1982.

Other works

Oskar Gruenwald, *The Yugoslav Search for Man: Marxist Humanism in Contemporary Yugoslavia*, South Hadley, Mass., Bergin, 1983.

Charles Maurras   1868–1952

Theoretician of French 'integral nationalism', Charles Maurras led the most influential and the longest-lived of the right-wing radical nationalist leagues that emerged in the wake of the Dreyfus affair – the neo-royalist Action Française. Born in a small fishing village near Marseilles into a petty-bourgeois family of mixed royalist and liberal traditions, Maurras attended *collège* in Aix-en-Provence. Prevented by deafness from a traditional family career in the navy, he moved to Paris to take up a literary career as a poet, critic and journalist.

The Dreyfus affair provided the initial setting of Maurras's rise to prominence as a radical nationalist. All Dreyfusards were traitors in Maurras's eyes, but he reserved his most vituperative attacks for the 'rootless' ones whom he charged with plotting to open France to external enemies by destroying its classical heritage and vigour with their foreign ideas and values. Maurras's list of antinational conspirators was long – immigrants, Jews, Protestants, Freemasons, socialists and, after 1920, communists. However, at the head of his list of enemies were the Jews, and Action Française became noted for its virulent antisemitic diatribes, particularly during the Popular Front period.

What may have begun as an aesthetic reaction to a feeling of cultural decline became a new mode of nationalist agitation that mixed appeals to the intellectual elite with riots and political intimidation. Ideologically there was a fundamental difference between Maurras's movement and traditional royalism in that his was always more nationalist than royalist: its base was a selective analysis of French history rather than the usual dynastic loyalty. Maurras's oft-repeated deductive formula was that, because France's problems came from being 'divided and headless', only monarchy, which by his definition stood above parties and partisan interests, could place the national interest first. Hence the Maurrasian phrase 'integral nationalism' represented monarchy as constituting the sole basis for restoring 'religious, civic and military' order in society.

Maurras advertised Action Française as an 'open conspiracy' against the republic, emphasizing the necessity of violent action – a *coup de force* – to overthrow 'the democratic and republican regime'. In addition to its major arm, a daily newspaper, Action Française spawned several activities designed to develop a 'royalist spirit'. Among them were a party 'college', a publishing house, student organizations and perhaps the first of the organized party militias – the Camelots du Roi – whose violence, particularly during the riots of 6 February 1934, seemed to lend credence to Maurras's threatening rhetoric of radical change.

For more than three decades Maurras led the attack on the republic and its political establishment through the columns of Action Française's daily newspaper. Paradoxically, although his movement always recruited heavily from traditional royalist and Catholic circles, he was ultimately rejected by the pretender to the French throne and by the Papacy. When Vichy replaced the republic he joyously welcomed the advent of Pétain and gave unswerving support to a regime which seemed to represent the triumph of so many of his political and social ideas. Hostile to the Resistance, supporter of Vichy's antisemitic and anti-foreign legislation, Maurras was arrested, tried and sentenced to life imprisonment for collaboration by a liberated France. His bitter words on hearing his sentence were 'It is the revenge of Dreyfus.'

Works

La République ou le Roi: Correspondance inédite, 1888–1923, (with Maurice Barrès), Paris, Plon, 1970.
Enquête sur la monarchie, Paris, Nouvelle Librairie Nationale, 1924.
Au Signe de Flore: Souvenirs de vie politique, Paris, Oeuvres représentatives, 1931.
Pour un jeune français: mémorial en résponse à un questionnaire, Paris, Amiot-Dumont, 1949.
Kiel et Tanger: *La République Française devant l'Europe*, Paris, Nouvelle Librairie Nationale, 1913.

Other works

William Curt Buthman, *The Rise of Integral Nationalism in France*, New York, Columbia University Press, 1939.
Michael Curtis, *Three against the Third Republic: Sorel, Barrès, and Maurras*, Princeton, N.J., Princeton University Press, 1959.

Maurice Merleau-Ponty 1908–1961

Merleau-Ponty was among a generation of radical intellectuals who strove to revitalize political thought and policy in post-war France. Although primarily an academic, he also produced numerous pieces of political journalism. He began with a rejection of both pre-war Kantian liberalism, whose philosophy of clean hands had rendered it inert in the face of fascism, and the post-war Marxism of the French Communist Party (PCF), which he condemned as rigid and simplistic. Accusing both of a rationalism which failed to situate actors within a contingent history, he sought an approach that would combine commitment to progressive politics with a non-dogmatic interpretation of everyday experience. He found it in existentialist phenomenology, which he initially declared compatible, indeed almost synonymous, with humanist Marxism.

This approach was reflected in *Les Temps Modernes*, which Merleau-Ponty founded with Sartre in 1945. By the mid-1950s, however, he had pronounced Marxism fatally flawed by its equation of historical truth with proletarian victory. Concluding that its dialectic, like his own early phenomenology, remained contaminated by Cartesianism, he turned to the linguistic theory of Saussure in order to reconceive the process by which reason appears in history.

In challenging Cartesian rationalism Merleau-Ponty had argued from the beginning that meaning originates in our perceptual encounters with the world rather than being imposed upon it by disembodied minds. The symbolic order we subsequently evolve can never free itself from the ambiguity and contingency of these perceptual foundations; the attempt engenders sterility and violence. The emphasis on language facilitated similar conclusions but offered new ways of understanding how subjects can be both constrained and free. For the relationship between creative speech and linguistic structure suggested a way in which political actors, too, might find themselves both constrained by history yet enjoying a limited freedom to lead events in a chosen direction, provided they engaged creatively with those limitations rather than trying to ignore or suppress them (as he believed liberals and Stalinists did). In striving to articulate this intertwining of mind and body, speaker and language, subject and history, in a more radically non-Cartesian way, Merleau-Ponty was driven towards the end of his life to rethink his whole ontology. Although his interests were by then focused more on language and aesthetics, he nevertheless saw these later works developing the ontological underpinning necessary to a genuinely non-dogmatic politics. He provisionally associated this with a form of Weberian neo-liberalism, which allowed him to support a non-communist left.

Although Merleau-Ponty's work subsequently suffered from the accusations of idealism that structuralists levelled against existentialism, phenomenology and humanist Marxism, there is already within it an anticipation of structuralist and post-structuralist themes that would excite French intellectuals during the following decades. Yet in his continuing concern with political engagement and with the freedom and morality of subjects situated within historical structures, we may perhaps discern suggestions for avoiding political and theoretical impasses in which his successors would find themselves.

See also

Sartre, Weber.

Works

Phenomenology of Perception, 1945, trans. C. Smith, London, Routledge, 1962.
Humanism and Terror, 1947, trans. J. O'Neill, Boston, Mass., Beacon Press, 1969.
The Primacy of Perception, 1947, trans. J. Edie, Evanston, Ill., Northwestern University Press, 1964.
Sense and Non-sense, 1948, trans. H. L. Dreyfus and P. A. Dreyfus, Evanston, Ill., Northwestern University Press, 1964.
Adventures of the Dialectic, 1955, trans. J. Bien, London, Heinemann, 1974.
Signs, 1960, trans. R. McCleary, Evanston, Ill., Northwestern University Press, 1964.
The Visible and the Invisible, 1964, trans. A. Lingis, Evanston, Ill., Northwestern University Press, 1969.

Other works

J. O'Neill, *Perception, Expression and History: the Social Phenomenology of Maurice Merleau-Ponty*, Evanston, Ill., Northwestern University Press, 1970.
S. Kruks, *The Political Philosophy of Merleau-Ponty*, Brighton, Harvester, 1981.
J. Schmidt, *Maurice Merleau-Ponty: between Phenomenology and Structuralism*, London, Macmillan, 1985.
K. Whiteside, *Merleau-Ponty and the Foundation of an Existential Politics*, Princeton, N.J., Princeton University Press, 1988.

Robert Michels 1876–1936

Robert Michels was born in Cologne to a Catholic manufacturing family of German–Italian–French heritage. Quitting the Prussian army in 1904, he moved to Marburg and started his academic career. Between 1903 and 1907 he was an active member of the German Social Democratic Party (SPD) while maintaining close contact with French syndicalists like Sorel and Lagardelle. Michels criticized the SPD for its moderation despite its revolutionary rhetoric and advanced a syndicalist alternative, favouring class struggle through extra-parliamentary working-class organizations, utilizing agitation and strikes.

Unable to obtain a university post in Germany owing to his socialist views, Michels moved in 1907 to the University of Turin, having been recommended by Max Weber, with whom he had formed a close and important intellectual friendship several years earlier. At Turin Michels met Gaetano Mosca and Vilfredo Pareto and was converted to elite theory, finding an explanation for the failure of the SPD's radicalism. Later that year he resigned from the German and Italian socialist parties.

With the publication of *Political Parties* in 1911 Michels established himself as a major elite theorist, going beyond Mosca and Pareto to explain why elite domination is inevitable. Drawing on his detailed knowledge of the SPD, Michels argues that elites are more capable, that the multitude are psychologically submissive and that organization itself fosters oligarchy. Just as Marx argues that capitalist domination depends on the separation of the worker from control of the means of production, Michels contends that oligarchy derives from the way organization separates the member from the means of collective power. The division of labour makes leaders functionally indispensable, elevates their social position above the proletariat and thereby transforms their class interests, leading them to forsake radical goals in favour of organizational preservation. Simultaneously, organization denies members opportunities to participate, educates them to be subservient and prevents them from controlling decision-making. Struggles between elites occur, but concessions and co-operation ensure their continuity. Revolts from below challenge the leaders' ability to set the issue agenda, but their control of administration guarantees elite domination. As Michels summarizes the 'iron law of oligarchy', 'Who says organization says oligarchy'.

The moralism evident in his early commitment to socialism is also manifest in other phases of Michels's life. His unwillingness to support the war in 1914 led him to end his friendship with Weber and resign from an editorial post with which Weber had favoured him. His disillusionment with democracy and the masses led him in the 1920s and 1930s to support Italian nationalism and Mussolini's fascism, arguing in his *First Lectures* that only charismatic leadership could transcend organizational conservatism and engender mass support for great tasks. And in 1928 he accepted Mussolini's offer of a Chair in the openly fascist Faculty of Political Science at the University of Perugia.

Michels's elite theory provides the main argument against the possibility of participatory democracy and socialism. No matter how committed the participants, or how extensive the formal procedures of democracy, a few at the top inevitably dominate. With the prospect of direct democracy dashed, democracy became identified with the competition between elites for the votes of a passive electorate. Most students of political parties and voluntary groups, particularly trade unions, draw on Michels' insights. Organization theory is indebted to his analysis of deviation from professed norms, while his analysis of organizational autonomy has found new currency in recent neo-corporatist and state-centred theories.

See also

Mosca, Mussolini, Pareto, Sorel, Weber.

Works

Political Parties: Sociological Study of the Oligarchical Tendencies of Modern Democracy, New York, Free Press, 1962.
First Lectures in Political Sociology, Minneapolis, Minn., University of Minnesota Press, 1949.

Other works

P. Cook, 'Robert Michels's political parties in perspective', Journal of Politics 33 (1971), pp. 773–96.
D. Beetham, 'From socialism to fascism', *Political Studies* 25 (1977), pp. 3–24, 161–81.
L. Scaff, 'Max Weber and Robert Michels', *American Journal of Sociology* 86 (1981), p. 1269–86.

Kate Millett   1934–

Born in St Paul, Minnesota, Kate Millett is best known as the author of *Sexual Politics*. On its appearance in 1971 the book had an enormous influence on the developing Women's Liberation movement, providing much of the theoretical background. It continues to be read as a basic text of modern feminism.

After graduating from the University of Minnesota in 1956 she went on to take a first class degree at St Hilda's College, Oxford, then worked as a teacher and a sculptor, living in Japan and New York city before pursuing her Ph.D. at Columbia. It was while a member of the English Department at Barnard College, and active in the civil rights movement, that she wrote 'Sexual politics: a manifesto for revolution' in connection with the organization of the first Women's Liberation group at Columbia University in 1968. This brief paper, banned by the official campus media, encapsulated the argument of the later book to justify feminism as a political movement by defining the relationship between the sexes as based on power and sustained by an ideology, hence political.

Relationships between classes and races had already been recognized as political in the sense used by Max Weber and other sociologists; Millett was the first to extend such recognition to the apparently 'natural' relationship between the sexes. The nearly universal male control of women was not a biological given but the result of the social structure called patriarchy.

Patriarchy, she argued, was so deeply entrenched that it could scarcely be perceived as a political system; it perpetuated itself as a way of life and in the formation of character structure. In 'free' contemporary societies women continued to be excluded from the sources of power not so much by force or coercion as by social conditioning. From infancy women were trained to accept as natural and desirable a world in which power in the public sphere was reserved for men. This early socialization, reinforced by the lessons of formal education, popular culture, religion, art and psychoanalysis (she singled out Freud as a particular villain, seeing his theories of femininity as prescriptive rather than descriptive) ensured that women would keep themselves subordinate through ignorance and the fear of being 'unnatural'.

Sexual Politics was radical in concept and continues to be controversial; in content it is a hybrid of literary and cultural criticism, a major part of it being devoted to an analysis of four male (and presumably representative) writers. Her study of D. H. Lawrence, Norman Mailer, Henry Miller and Jean Genet revealed that power, not eroticism or sexual passion, was their real subject, and the urge to dominate was at issue in their every written sexual encounter.

Millett went on to write two autobiographical works exploring her own sexuality, *Flying* (1974) and *Sita* (1977), as well as *The Prostitution Papers* (1976), *The Basement: Meditation on a Human Sacrifice* (1979) and *Going to Iran* (1981). At the invitation of some Iranian women she went to Iran in 1979 to help in the struggle for women's rights but was expelled by Khomeini's government. Less politically active in the 1980s, she has continued to work as a sculptor.

See also

Khomeini, Weber.

Works

'Sexual politics: a Manifesto for revolution', in *Notes from the Second Year*, New York, Radical Feminism, 1970.
Sexual Politics, New York, Avon, 1971.

Other works

Juliet Mitchell, 'Kate Millett: Freud, facts and fantasies', *Psychoanalysis and Feminism*, London, Penguin, 1982.
Hester Eisenstein, *Contemporary Feminist Thought*, London, Unwin Hyman, 1984.
Cora Kaplan, 'Radical feminism and literature: rethinking Millett's *Sexual Politics*', in *Sea Changes: Culture and Feminism*, London, Verso, 1986.

C. Wright Mills   1916–1962

Charles Wright Mills, American radical theorist, was born in Waco, Texas. Graduating from the University of Texas at Austin in 1939 with both a B.A. and an M.A. in philosophy, he did his doctoral work in sociology at the University of Wisconsin, where he came into contact, most notably, with a young, German-born sociologist, Hans H. Gerth, who had been forced to flee his homeland in 1938. A former student of Karl Mannheim, Gerth encouraged Mills's interest in the sociology of knowledge and helped to push him towards a fuller and more intense engagement with such European thinkers as Marx, Weber and others, including emerging theorists of the Frankfurt school. Over the next decade, in the course of a sometimes difficult collaboration, Mills and Gerth produced several important works. A co-authored 1942 article, 'Marx for the managers', rejected James Burnham's theory of the 'managerial revolution' for a class analysis of power; *From Max Weber*, a co-edited volume that appeared in 1946, was the first major collection of Weber's writings in English; their ambitious 1953 synthesis, *Character and Social Structure*, attempted to supplement (Mills would have preferred to replace) Freudian or biological interpretation with a historical and sociological account of character development.

Yet Mills, while drawn to European theory, remained pugnaciously 'American' in his basic way of thinking. He felt a strong affinity with home-grown pragmatism, the subject of his 1942 Ph.D. thesis, and always viewed himself, intellectually and politically, as, in his own words, 'more a "wobbly" than a "socialist"'. This became especially apparent when Mills took his first full-time job at the University of Maryland in late 1941. There he befriended several younger American historians, who exposed him to a body of historical scholarship still dominated by the 'Progressive' vision of such native sons as Charles Beard. Mills swiftly settled on an insurgent, neo-Beardian analysis of the American past that stressed economic inequality, the virtues of the underdog and the progressive function of conflict between 'the people' and 'the interests'. By the early 1940s, consequently, Mills's thought already showed a characteristic and persistent tension: the Progressive strained against the Marxist, the wobbly against the socialist, the angry rebel against the fearful sceptic.

At virtually the same time Mills's furious opposition to the Second World War – the traumatizing event, he said, that 'made' him a radical – forced him to reconsider theoretical assumptions then common on the left. Mills moved against the tide of pro-war opinion, becoming more rather than less critical as time passed, and eventually allied himself with the independent, anti-war radicalism of Dwight Macdonald's *Politics* magazine, established, with Mills's strong support, in 1944. Increasingly dissatisfied with the 'conflict' perspective of prevailing theory, he began to show the obsession with consensus and domination that was to characterize his mature work. A seminal essay in the second issue of *Politics*, 'The powerless people: the role of the intellectual', already hinted at his defining nightmare vision of a new, bureaucratic and oppressive age in which war, or preparation for war, was to be a permanent reality.

Nevertheless, Mills's confidence in one tenet of 'old left' thinking revived briefly after 1945, when he moved to New York city to join Paul Lazarsfeld's Bureau of Applied Social Research (where, never fitting in, he was to stay only a few years) and, in due course, the Department of Sociology at Columbia. In New York, Mills fell under the influence of the veteran labour journalist J. B. S. Hardman, contributed regularly to Hardman's journal *Labor and Nation*, did his best to concentrate on labour research at the BASR and, in his writing, optimistically linked the fate of radicalism to a re-emergent union movement. By the time Mills published *The New Men of Power*, however, his pro-union enthusiasm was clearly on the wane. In that, his first major book, Mills showed strong elitist tendencies by placing what little faith he still had in union leaders rather than in the rank and file. He concluded, even then, that a radical union movement was unlikely to materialize. Never again would 'the labor metaphysic' (Mills's own derogatory phrase) prove central to his work.

Mills next proceeded in two great works of the 1950s, *White Collar* and *The Power Elite*, to explore a grim, monolithic American reality – the post-Progressive and post-Marxist future he had glimpsed in the 1940s – that confounded older forms of political analysis. His basic argument in *White Collar* was that oppressed but status-driven members of the 'new' middle classes, 'sweating it out in the middle of the twentieth century', would neither sustain a healthy democratic politics, as liberals predicted, nor ally themselves, as Marxists and other radicals had hoped, with workers in resistance to the *status quo*. Rather, the 'cheerful robots' and 'idiots' in the white-collar ranks would remain passive, or even, Mills suggested, become the 'shock troops' of a reactionary if not fascist establishment. In *The Power Elite* he produced an equally harsh, revisionist analysis of how and why, in the United States, the few had come to dominate the many. Taking issue with 'liberal' or 'pluralist' theories of balance and containment, he argued that power was in fact concentrated, largely unrestrained and dangerous; also rejecting 'ruling class' analysis, Mills instead identified a 'power elite' made up of individuals drawn from military and political as well as business higher circles. Mills made it clear that the policies of 'the high and the mighty', reflecting both elite interests and the irrationalities of a 'military metaphysic', undermined democracy and pointed inexorably towards war.

Yet neither *White Collar* nor *The Power Elite*, while they unquestionably said 'no' more loudly than they said 'yes', were fatalistic books. In both, Mills repeatedly emphasized that he was describing trends and not inevitabilities: for him, history was still open to human intervention, elites vulnerable to

opposition, 'drift' susceptible to 'mastery'. At the heart of his distinctive brand of radical analysis lay an animating confidence – sometimes muted, but always present – that engaged intellectuals, practising a 'politics of truth', could bring about 'the presumptuous control by reason of man's fate'. This militant intellectualism grew stronger during the late 1950s, when Mills met and drew inspiration from dissident thinkers throughout the world – British new leftists, Eastern Bloc and Russian revisionists, Latin American radicals and even, in 1960, the successful Cuban revolutionary, Fidel Castro.

Mills's growing sense of urgency showed up in two polemical tracts for the times, *The Causes of World War Three*, which assailed American foreign policy and demanded change, and *Listen, Yankee*, which defended Castro's Cuban revolution against Kennedy administration attacks. In *The Causes of World War Three* Mills also boldly asserted that intellectuals had, in effect, themselves become agencies of change. This same rationalistic assumption likewise informed his last two scholarly books, *The Sociological Imagination* and *The Marxists*, as well as sections of an unfinished but important theoretical work on intellectuals entitled 'The cultural apparatus'.

Mills sounded what amounted to a final call to arms in his 'Letter to the New Left', which first appeared in the British *New Left Review* in 1960 and the next year, with revisions, in the American *Studies on the Left*. He denounced the 'end of ideology', thinking of the Cold War years, proclaimed both liberal and Marxist orthodoxies dead, and aggressively endorsed a new radicalism based upon the promise – and potential power – of a 'young intelligentsia'. Mills concluded with a prescient celebration of recent student/ university activism as presaging the emergence of a 'new left' in the 1960s. This fiery manifesto had, in fact, a special impact on the already well read Millsian youths of Students for a Democratic Society, accounting for some of the ideas and much of the passion in SDS's own celebrated 'Port Huron Statement' of 1962.

In December 1960 Mills suffered a severe heart attack while preparing for a national television debate on Cuba, and died of heart failure fifteen months later at the age of forty-five.

See also

Castro, Mannheim, Weber.

Works

The New Men of Power: America's Labor Leaders, New York, Harcourt Brace, 1948.
White Collar: the American Middle Class, New York, Oxford University Press, 1951.
The Power Elite, New York, Oxford University Press, 1956.
The Causes of World War Three, New York, Simon & Schuster, 1958.
The Sociological Imagination, New York, Oxford University Press, 1959.
Listen, Yankee: the Revolution in Cuba, New York, McGraw-Hill, 1960.
The Marxists, New York, Dell, 1962.

Other works

Irving Louis Horowitz (ed.), Politics, Power and People, New York, Ballantine Books, 1963.
Peter Clekac, 'C. Wright Mills: the lone rebel', Radical Paradoxes: Dilemmas of the American Left, 1945–70, New York, Harper & Row, 1973.
Richard Gillman, 'C. Wright Mills and the politics of truth: The Power Elite revisited', American Quarterly, October 1975, pp. 461–79.
Richard Gillman, 'White Collar from start to finish: C. Wright Mills in transition', Theory and Society, Winter 1981, pp. 1–30.
Rick Tilman, C. Wright Mills: a Native Radical and his American Intellectual Roots, Philadelphia, Pa, Pennsylvania State University Press, 1984.
James Miller, 'C. Wright Mills reconsidered', Salmagundi, 70–1 (Spring/Summer 1986), pp. 82–101.

Juliet Mitchell 1940–

Juliet Mitchell has been an influential contributor to the development of feminist theory. She has entered into and affected some of the most important intellectual and political debates stimulated by the re-emergence of women's movements in the late 1960s. Her special interest has been in the realm of 'ideology', which means to her the ways men and women live the material conditions of their lives. Mitchell's pursuit of a better understanding of this realm has lead her to rethink and write upon literature, Marxism, psychoanalysis and feminist theories.

She was born in New Zealand. In 1944 she moved to England. She took a degree in English at St Anne's College, Oxford, and did postgraduate work there. From 1962 to 1970 Mitchell taught English literature at Leeds and Reading Universities. During the 1960s she was active in left-wing politics. She was an editor of the New Left Review, an influential British journal in which many debates about Marxist theory and practice were generated and discussed. Mitchell was also involved in the women's movement as it re-emerged in Britain in the late 1960s.

One of the most important questions for feminists during this period was the utility of Marxist theories and practices to the analysis and overcoming of women's oppression. Debate about this question was especially vigorous in Western Europe, where there are strong labour parties and a history of Marxist politics. Mitchell's article 'Women: the longest revolution', in the New Left Review in 1966 was one of the first to address this question. Her argument was elaborated in her first book, Women's Estate. Mitchell adopts Louis Althusser's concept of an ideological sphere which can be relatively autonomous from the economic base. She distinguishes women's oppression from their exploitation. Oppression is rooted in the ideological realm, which includes the reproduction of children, sexuality and socialization. In capitalist societies these three functions are primarily or first carried out by the family. Hence the family plays a key role in the oppression of women. Women are exploited as workers in production. These four elements of material life interact with each other, so that women cannot be emancipated unless revolutionary changes occur in all of them. Marxists are mistaken in believing that socialism can solve the 'woman question'. The roots of women's oppression will not automatically wither away under socialism. Women must organize autonomous feminist movements to fight against oppression, since historically (as also in the 1960s) left-wing organizations have been insensitive or actively hostile to women's concerns.

Mitchell's interest in the ideological realm, especially the family, led her to the study of a second controversial topic: psychoanalysis. Many feminist theorists such as Betty Friedan and Kate Millet dismissed Freud's ideas (and hence all psychoanalysis) as exemplars of patriarchal thought. In 1974 Mitchell published *Psychoanalysis and Feminism*, in which she argued for the utility of psychoanalysis, especially the work of Freud and Jacques Lacan, to the feminist project of understanding women's oppression. In this book and in essays later published in *Feminine Sexuality* and *Women: the Longest Revolution* Mitchell argues that the psychoanalytic concepts of the unconscious and sexual difference are essential to an understanding of how women are made. She argues that Freud provides a description of the process by which men and women are engendered; his theory is not normative, nor does he believe that gender is innate or a natural consequence of anatomical differences. Psychoanalysis is necessary to an understanding of how and why sexual difference becomes a constituting force in human subjectivity. Only if we understand how this occurs can we hope to overcome women's oppression.

After the publication of *Psychoanalysis and Feminism* Mitchell was trained at the Institute of Psychoanalysis and is now a practising analyst in London. She continues to write and lecture on feminism, literature and psychoanalysis. Few feminists today would disagree with her criticism of the inadequacies of Marxist theories and practices, although some have gone further to analyse the gender biases in fundamental Marxist concepts such as production, labour and class. Mitchell's arguments about the utility of psychoanalysis

to an understanding of gender were very influential in the subsequent development of feminist thought. While her claims are still strongly contested, many writers are developing or utilizing feminist psychoanalytic theories. However, her support of Lacanian psychoanalysis is questioned by many, especially in the United States, where object relations psychoanalysis has also been influential. Mitchell's influence on political thought has been affected by the segregation in contemporary intellectual life in which feminist theory as a whole tends to be ignored by non-feminists.

See also

Althusser, Freud, Millett.

Works

Women's Estate, New York, Pantheon, 1971.
Psychoanalysis and Feminism: Freud, Laing, and Women, New York, Pantheon, 1974.
Women: the Longest Revolution, London, Virago, 1984.
Feminine Sexuality, New York, Norton, 1985.

Other works

Rosemarie Tong, *Feminist Thought*, Boulder, Colo., Westview Press, 1984.
Teresa Brennan (ed.), *Between Feminism and Psychoanalysis*, London, Routledge, 1989.

Hans Joachim Morgenthau
1904–1980

The most influential American scholar and theorist in the field of international politics in the quarter-century following the Second World War, Morgenthau situated himself firmly in the 'realist' tradition that traced back to Thucydides, Machiavelli and Hobbes and was joined in modern times by such diverse figures as E. H. Carr, Raymond Aron, Nicholas Spykman, Reinhold Niebuhr, Arnold Wolfers, George Kennan, John Herz and Kenneth Waltz.

He was born in Coburg, Germany. Following a classically German education in history, law, economics and philosophy at the Universities of Berlin, Frankfurt and Munich, and practising and teaching law, he wrote a dissertation entitled 'The International Judicial Function: its Nature and its Limits'. It was to set the theme of his powerful later works: 'What really mattered in relations among nations was not international law, but international politics.' Law divorced from power was useless. Drawing heavily upon history, but – like Carr – particularly influenced by the 1930s and the collapse of the League of Nations (which he watched from the vantage point of Geneva, where he taught in the early 1930s, before emigrating to America), as well as by the American effort to revive the League in the form of the United Nations, he expanded the theme in *In Defense of the National Interest*.

In it he inveighed against the dangerous delusions of 'utopianism, sentimentalism and neo-isolationism', and argued for diplomacy that recognized the interests and power of all states in the system. The struggle for power was universal: like Niebuhr, he located it in the nature of mankind. In periods of history such as the nineteenth century the struggle for power among major states could be contained through balance-of-power policies because states shared a common heritage; the Great War of 1914–18 marked a watershed, however, giving rise to a period when doctrines claiming universalistic application made traditional diplomatic compromise far more difficult. Yet world politics remained essentially the struggle of states for power in which diplomacy and the possible use of force must always be joined. The national interest – defined essentially as survival in a largely Hobbesian world – could be sought only through prudent statecraft that included power considerations. Periods of empire, the current structure of bipolarity, universalist conceptions could appear – and appear for a while to be dominant – but balance-of-power considerations reflecting the pluralist nature of the political world would always reappear,

and statecraft, whether by leaders of large or small states, consisted in being able to grasp this. The study of international politics must be based upon it, too, and Morgenthau firmly rejected what he saw as the triviality of behavioural approaches. Ethical theory and morality were as central to his thought as they were to that of Hobbes. It was moralizing that he rejected.

The themes reappeared in dozens of less theoretical and more directly practical essays. If, all along, he opposed American participation in the Vietnam War it was, as in the case of George Kennan, from the base of prudential statecraft, not from notions that the war was fundamentally wrong. (If India aligned itself with the Soviet Union and Pakistan with communist China, and communist China aligned itself with Nixon's United States and against a Vietnam aligned with the Soviet Union, it all came as no surprise to Morgenthau.) In the end, the limitations of his simplified realist theory became more evident in the face of growing interdependence and more subtle theorizing. Yet as late as the 1980s revised editions of his textbook *Politics among Nations*, first published in 1948, remained the most widely used text in undergraduate international relations courses, and in a very real sense it set the bounds for most subsequent debate in the field.

See also

Aron, Niebuhr.

Works

Scientific Man vs Power Politics, Chicago, University of Chicago Press, 1946.
Politics among Nations, 1948, sixth edition, New York, Knopf, 1985.
In Defense of the National Interest, New York, Knopf, 1951.
The Purpose of American Politics, New York, Knopf, 1960.

Gaetano Mosca   1858–1941

Mosca's political theory reflected the cynical and conservative liberalism of the professional classes of southern Italy to which he, born in Palermo, belonged. A politician as well as an academic, he combined the teaching of constitutional law at the universities in Palermo, Turin, Milan and Rome with a political career as a member of the Chamber of Deputies from 1908 to 1918 and subsequently as a senator.

His theory combined the insights of the professional politician with those of the constitutional philosopher. Mosca argued that all societies contained a relatively small class that rules and a much larger class containing the majority of the population that is ruled. He maintained that the ruling class owed its position to the organizational advantages of a small group over a large group, and to the superior talents of its members. The composition of the ruling class might change with time, for as societies became increasingly complex and technologically sophisticated new skills were required of its leaders. As a result, what Mosca called the 'political formula' or ideological mechanisms which they employed to legitimize their power would also alter. But no change in the form of government could alter the basically elitist nature of all political systems. Democracy did not introduce majority rule, therefore; it merely made the manipulation of the ruled by their rulers more subtle. In a brilliant critique of the modern party system, Mosca showed how deputies employed all sorts of methods from false promises to outright bribery to get themselves elected. That they were freely chosen by the electorate was a myth. Although he engaged in a futile quarrel with Pareto over who had originated this sociological law, Mosca's conception of the ruling class differed greatly from his compatriot's notion of the elite. Unlike Pareto's theory, Mosca's elitism was prescriptive rather than descriptive in intent, being an attempt to justify and secure the rule of the bourgeois liberal class to which he belonged.

Mosca was something of a monomaniac, essentially writing three versions of the same book and elaborating increasingly sophisticated versions of his thesis. The first version, the *Teorica dei governi e governo parliamentare* of 1884, laid down the bare outlines of his doctrine. The second version, the *Elementi di scienza politica* of 1896, refined his theory in two ways. First, he distinguished between the actual holders of governmental power, or 'political class', and other elements of the elite, such as industrialists, members of the professions, etc. He now recognized that the ruling class comprised these groups as well as politicians. Second, he argued that more complex societies evolved moral and legal mechanisms of restraint and mutual control in order to regulate social interaction and modify egoistic behaviour. These phenomena formed what he called a society's 'juridical defence'. The final version of his theory, the second edition of the *Elementi* of 1923, to which he added a whole new volume, produced the most dramatic alteration of his views. Until then Mosca had regarded democracy as a very mixed blessing and had opposed all attempts to extend it. Socially a conservative, he resented the opportunities it offered for the rise of populist elites. However, unlike his follower Michels and his rival Pareto, he did not turn to fascism. Instead the socialist and fascist agitation of the post-war years led him to advocate the need to strengthen the constitutional framework within which the competition between rival parties took place – a position which resulted in his producing an early version of the pluralist democratic theories associated with thinkers such as Schumpeter and Dahl. He remained an outspoken opponent of Mussolini until his death in 1941.

See also

Dahl, Michels, Mussolini, Pareto, Schumpeter.

Works

The Ruling Class, New York, McGraw-Hill, 1939.

Other works

John H. Meisel, *The Myth of the Ruling Class: Gaetano Mosca and the Elite*, Ann Arbor, Mich., University of Michigan Press, 1962.
Norberto Bobbio, *On Mosca and Pareto*, Geneva, Droz, 1972.
Ettore Albertoni, *Mosca and the Theory of Elitism*, Oxford, Blackwell, 1987.
Richard P. Bellamy, *Modern Italian Social Theory: Ideology and Politics from Pareto to the Present*, Cambridge, Polity, 1987.

Benito Mussolini   1883–1945

Benito Mussolini was the founder of Italian fascism and the fascist dictator of Italy from 1925 to 1943. He began as a socialist in Switzerland, where he resided from 1902 to his expulsion in 1904. By 1912 he was editor of the Italian Socialist Party's official newspaper, *Avanti*. His shift from non-intervention to interventionism in the First World War led to his resignation from *Avanti* and expulsion from the party. Returning from the war an ardent nationalist, Mussolini founded the Union of Combat (Fascio di Combattamento) in 1919 and the Fascist Party in 1921. He headed a coalition government in 1922 but it was at the beginning of 1925 that he announced the formation of a fascist state, which was established by 1927. Following the allied invasion of Sicily, a group of fascist leaders removed Mussolini from power in 1943 in order to initiate moves for peace. Mussolini was captured and shot by partisans in 1945.

The systematic expression of Mussolini's ideas and of Italian fascist ideology was not set out until 1932, when *The Doctrine of Fascism* was published in volume XIV of the *Enciclopedia Italiana*. Its late appearance was explained by Mussolini as being due to fascism's birth out of political activity and action rather than its being predetermined by intellectual endeavour. However, whereas it is possible to argue that the state can be seized without an ideology, its transformation and elevation require one. The article is divided into two parts, 'Fundamental ideas', which is generally acknowledged to have been written by Giovanni Gentile, and 'Political and social doctrine'. Although both parts appear under Mussolini's name and were meant and need to be considered as one, Gentile's contribution is the more profound.

Central to fascist doctrine was the subordination of the individual to the state and the totality of that state. This idea was developed as follows. First, socialism, liberalism and democracy were rejected as unsuitable to the changing conditions of the twentieth century: 'If the nineteenth century was the century of the individual (liberalism signifies individualism) one may think that this will be the century of "collectivism", the century of the State.' Second, there was a symbiotic relationship between the individual and the state. Life was conceived as a struggle, and it was the duty of the individual and the nation, humanity, to conquer that life. This could only be fulfilled through the state, for the state is the expression of the individual. Third, it follows that the state must be supreme, and, fourth, for the fascist the state was total, with no limits to its authority.

The Doctrine of Fascism was more than a theory of dictatorship; it was a theory of totalitarianism. Other themes, such as corporatism, and the justification of violence as a 'new style of Italian life' and imperialism, as a manifestation of national vitality, were included. It served as the *raison d'être* of the fascist regime in Italy. As a system of ideas it does not rank in the first or even second order but concepts such as corporatism and totalitarianism have greatly influenced our understanding and misunderstanding of the twentieth century.

See also

Gentile.

Works

'The Doctrine of Fascism', [1932] in *Readings on Fascism and National Socialism*, selected by Members of the Department of Philosophy, University of Colorado, Denver, Colo., Alan Swallow, n.d.
My Autobiography, New York, Scribner, 1928.

Other works

Frederico Chadbod, *A History of Italian Fascism*, London, Weidenfeld & Nicholson, 1963.
A. James Gregor, *The Ideology of Fascism: the Rationale of Totalitarianism*, New York, Free Press, 1969.
Richard P. Bellamy, *Modern Italian Social Theory: Ideology and Politics from Pareto to the Present*, Cambridge, Polity Press, 1987.
Walter Laqueur (ed.), *Fascism: a Reader's Guide*, London, Wildwood House, 1988.
Stanley C. Payne, *A History of Fascism, 1914–1945*, Madison, University of Wisconsin Press, 1996.

Jayaprakash Narayan
1902–1979

J.P., as he is popularly known, was born into a middle-class Kayastha family in Bihar, India. He participated in the struggle for independence and went to jail in 1932, 1940 and 1942. Increasingly convinced that violence was the only way to dislodge British rule, he escaped from prison in 1942 and set up a training camp for a guerilla army. Arrested ten months later, he was tortured and sentenced to solitary confinement. When India gained independence in 1947, J.P. was one of its most popular leaders.

During most of this period J.P. was a socialist with strong Marxist sympathies. He was one of the founding fathers of the Congress Socialist Party, set up in 1934, and provided a theoretical statement of its philosophy in *Why Socialism?* Though more sympathetic than M. N. Roy and other socialists to Gandhi's ideas on decentralization, rural-based models of economic development and non-violence, he was critical of his 'timid economic analysis and ineffective moralizing'. After the Soviet purges and the Comintern's somersault on the Second World War, J.P. became critical of communism but remained sympathetic to Marxism and called himself a 'democratic socialist'.

Increasingly he became dissatisfied with Marxism and criticized its materialism, collectivism, historicism, amoralism, quasi-utilitarian and manipulative view of man and, above all, its insensitivity to human freedom and individuality. He thought that Gandhi was strong where Marx was weak and sought to integrate the two. Soon Gandhi gained the upper hand, and his doctrine of *Sarvodaya* (uplift of all, based on belief in universal harmony of interests) claimed J.P.'s undivided allegiance. J.P. now pleaded for a 'moral' and later for a 'total' revolution. It encompassed not merely the economic and political but all areas of life, aimed at changing not just institutions but also values and sensibilities, and was to be brought about by moral suasion backed up by non-violent resistance. He spelled out his new position in several articles and speeches and especially in *A Plea for the Reconstruction of Indian Polity* (1959) and *Swaraj for the People* (1961). He pleaded for a federally constituted and 'partyless' polity based on self-governing villages, and paralleled by a co-operative, decentralized and labour-intensive economy based on agro-industrial units. In his view such a 'communitarian' democracy would avoid the interrelated evils of atomization and centralization and strengthen both the individual and the community. J.P.'s polity was very like M. N. Roy's 'organic' democracy and Gandhi's *Swaraj*, and like them claimed to offer an alternative to the modern state.

Convinced that the state and the state-oriented political parties could not by definition bring about a total and non-statist revolution, J.P. began to turn away from the politics of the state (*rajniti*) and towards the politics of the people (*lokniti*). He joined Vinoba Bhave's *bhoodan* (land gift) movement in 1953, in 1954 dedicated the remaining years of his life to the 'cause of the country' in a public ceremony of *jeevandan* (gift of life), resigned his membership of the Socialist Party in 1957, and saw himself as the impartial custodian and conscience of the country. Disturbed at the 'precipitous fall in the moral standards' of public life during the late 1960s and early 1970s, J.P. increasingly began to campaign for 'natural regeneration' and pinned his hopes on youth, especially the students. Like Herbert Marcuse, but unlike Gandhi, he thought their idealism and energy made them ideal agents of moral revolution. He set up Chhatra-Yuva Sangharsha Vahini, a student and youth-based movement, which under his leadership mounted a vigorous and at times highly coercive campaign against Indira Gandhi's government. In panic she declared a national emergency in 1975 and locked up J.P. and his allies. When she declared elections two years later he played a leading role in defeating her and putting into power a hastily cobbled together Janata, or people's government. It was gerontocratic, had little use for the idealism and energy of the youth, lacked the discipline required for the coherent exercise of power, ignored J.P. and his ideas and was ousted two years later by Mrs Gandhi. J.P. died three months later, a bitterly disappointed man. His transition from Marxism to democratic socialism, Gandhian socialism, Gandhism and eventually to the non-Gandhian form of activism was propelled by an endearing but also maddening combination of great intellectual vitality, moral integrity and political naivety.

See also

Gandhi, Marcuse, Roy.

Works

Why Socialism? Benares, All India Congress Socialist Party, 1936.
From Socialism to Sarvodaya, Wardha, Akhil Bharat Serva Sava Sangh, 1959.
Total Revolution, Varanasi, Serva Seva Sangh Prakashan, 1975.
Prison Diary, Pune, Abhay Prakashan, 1977.

Other works

Ajit Bhattacharya, *J.P.:a Political Biography*, Delhi, Vikas, 1975.
Ram Chandra Gupta, *J.P.: from Marxism to total Revolution*, Delhi, Sterling, 1981.
Bimal Prasad, *Gandhi, Nehru and J.P.: Studies in Leadership*, Delhi, Chanakya, 1985.

D. Selbourne, *In Theory and in Practice: Essays on the Politics of Jayaprakash Narayan*, Delhi, Oxford University Press, 1985.

Reinhold Niebuhr
1892–1971

Reinhold Niebuhr was a German-American Protestant pastor and seminary professor of social ethics who became the pre-eminent spokesman of the 'realist' school in American political philosophy. The ironic tone of Niebuhr's work is best captured in his most famous aphorism: 'Man's capacity for justice makes democracy possible; man's capacity for injustice makes democracy necessary.'

Born in Wright City, Missouri, Niebuhr was the son of German immigrants. His father was a theologically sophisticated pastor of the German Evangelical Synod. Gustav Niebuhr was the role model for Reinhold and his brother, H. Richard, himself a major twentieth-century theologian.

Reinhold Niebuhr received his early education at Elmhurst College, a denominational boarding school in Chicago, and he entered Yale Divinity School in 1913. He took his first and only pastorate, Bethel Evangelical Church, in Detroit. He sprang to the defence of the allied cause in the First World War, eager to prove his American loyalties in a German immigrant community that had genuinely mixed emotions about the conflict.

From 1915 to 1928 Niebuhr immersed himself in the daily concerns of his parish and the larger concerns of an emerging industrial city, the city built by Henry Ford. Niebuhr cut his political teeth as a critic of Ford. He became an eloquent opponent of what he considered the unchecked power of the owners of capital. He committed himself to work for a socialist redistribution of economic and political power. His *Moral Man and Immoral Society* reflects his Marxist inclinations during this period.

By the time he left Detroit to become a professor of Christian ethics at Union Theological Seminary in New York, Niebuhr had begun to develop his mature political philosophy. Though he considered himself a liberal, he was nearly as critical of liberalism as of conservatism. In the 1920s and 1930s he plunged into various left-wing causes. As a pacifist and socialist he criticized Franklin D. Roosevelt's New Deal as a ruse designed to save capitalism from its inevitable downfall. But, even as head of the Fellowship of Socialist Christians, Niebuhr frequently criticized not only Marxist tactics but socialist policies as well. His study of democracy, *The Children of Light and the Children of Darkness*, illustrates his evolving estrangement from Marxism.

Niebuhr's encounter with Marxism proved to be a turning point in his political odyssey. In a 1959 retrospective essay, 'Biblical faith and socialism', he wrote about his changing view of capitalism and socialism. 'The "capitalistic" culture which was also a democratic one had more moral and political resources to avoid catastrophe than either the Marxists or their Christian fellow-travelers believed. . . . We Christian "prophetic" sympathizers with Marxism were as much in error in understanding the positive program of socialism as we were in sharing its catastrophism.'

Niebuhr came to believe that 'the vast system of mutual services which constitute the life of economic society . . . [can] best be maintained by relying on the "self-interest" of men rather than their "benevolence" or moral suasion, and by freeing economic activities from irrelevant and frequently undue restrictive political controls' (*Faith and Politics*).

As his economic views were changing, so also were his views of international conflict. After the First World War Niebuhr and many other Protestant churchmen excoriated themselves for so blithely endorsing the allied cause. Thus Niebuhr became a strong and credible advocate of pacifism in the 1930s. But as the threat posed by Hitler in particular, and by totalitarianism in general, loomed, Niebuhr concluded that violence in a just cause was morally preferable to the isolationism and self-righteousness he saw in his fellow pacifists. He became one of the most important proponents of America's entry into the Second World War.

In the post-war period Niebuhr refined his idea of the free society and his support for democratic capitalism and human rights. He praised the great experiments in democracy, especially Britain and the United States. He contrasted the free society and its pragmatic use of checks and balances with the totalitarian alternative. But now he spoke of the totalitarianism of Stalin, not of Hitler. He wrote, 'Utopianism is the basis of the evil in communism as well as of its greater danger. It provides a moral facade for the most unscrupulous political policy, giving the communist oligarch the moral warrant to suppress and sacrifice immediate values in the historical process for the sake of reaching so ideal a goal' (*Christian Realism and Political Problems*). Niebuhr's compatriots in the 'realist' school of foreign policy, including George Kennan, Hans Morgenthau and Kenneth Thompson, argued that communism must be contained by American power and that such power owed as much to national interest as to moral ideals.

To the end of his life Niebuhr remained a tireless critic of the irresponsible use of power. Though in his later years he criticized American involvement in the Vietnam War and advocated the withdrawal of US forces, he continued to insist that the United States had a duty to defend freedom in the face of communist aggression.

What is his political legacy? It is the fundamental idea of freedom, properly understood. Niebuhr elaborated a twentieth-century defence of democratic capitalism and he built that defence on a theological foundation, a theology of man and of history.

As a major Protestant theologian of the twentieth century, Niebuhr's role paralleled that of the Roman Catholic theologian and political theorist Jacques Maritain. Like Niebuhr, Maritain began his scholarly career as a socialist and eventually became a defender of democratic capitalism. While Niebuhr showed how a Protestant paradoxic view of the relation of religion and culture led to a qualified defence of American democracy, Maritain constructed a Catholic analogic view of the religion-and-culture equation that likewise led to a defence of the American system. Neither theologian argued that democratic capitalism is the Christian form of social organization, but both argued that it is the system that is most compatible with the Christian ideal.

See also

Maritain, Morgenthau.

Works

Moral Man and Immoral Society, New York, Scribner, 1932.
Christianity and Power Politics, New York, Scribner, 1940.
The Children of Light and the Children of Darkness, New York, Scribner, 1944.
Christian Realism and Political Problems, New York, Scribner, 1953.
The Structure of Nations and Empires, New York, Scribner, 1959.
'Biblical faith and socialism: a critical appraisal', in *Religion and Culture: Essays in Honor of Paul Tillich*, ed. Walter Leibrecht, New York, Harper, 1959.
Faith and Politics, New York, Braziller, 1968.

Other works

Jacques Maritain, *Man and the State*, Chicago, University of Chicago Press, 1951.
John A. Hutchinson (ed.), *Christian Faith and Social Action*, New York, Scribner, 1953.
Ronald H. Stone, *Reinhold Niebuhr: Prophet to Politicians*, Nashville, Tenn., Abingdon, 1972.
John W. Cooper, *The Theology of Freedom: the Legacy of Reinhold Niebuhr and Jacques Maritain*, Macon, Ga, Mercer University Press, 1985.
Richard Fox, *Reinhold Niebuhr: a Biography*, New York, Pantheon, 1985.

Robert Nozick   1938–

Robert Nozick is an American academic philosopher and libertarian political thinker. His *Anarchy, State and Utopia* made him the best-known contemporary critic of liberal egalitarianism, especially of the work of John Rawls. Nozick's is an 'invisible hand' theory justifying the minimal state, and nothing more than the minimal (non-redistributive, non-welfarist) state. According to the invisible-hand conceptualization of the origins of the state, the self-interested and rational actions of individuals in a state of nature lead them to hire agencies to protect their property; interaction among these agencies will eventually lead to one of them becoming the dominant protective agency within a given territory: a minimal state. If original acquisition in the state of nature has been just – that is, non-violent – and successive acquisitions of property have occurred according to the principle of just – that is, voluntary – transfer, then any property holdings within that sequence are themselves just, and the state may not interfere with them for reasons of social utility or Rawlsian reasons of fairness. Nozick calls this the entitlement theory of distributive justice, as opposed to an end-state of patterned principle such as Rawls's; following Friedrich Hayek, he argues that all end-state principles of (re)distribution necessarily entail the violation, by the state, of the rights of property-holders who have acquired their property through 'capitalist acts among consenting adults'. Although Nozick's theory is powerful within its limits, his notion of 'rights' is ungrounded; that is, he fails to explain as opposed to simply asserting why property rights should not be overridden by considerations of social utility or Rawlsian equality on certain occasions. In addition, the notions of 'voluntary transfer' and 'consent' are empirically and historically empty, in that Nozick neither explores nor refutes the standard psychological or sociological (Marxian) accounts of the ways in which 'consent' is constrained rather than freely given. Moreover, the theory is anachronistically gender-biased, in that the acquisitive state of nature is clearly for childless men only. However, the deductive theory remains valuable as a rigorous demonstration of just what and how much has to be assumed in order to legitimize the minimal capitalist state.

See also

Rawls, Hayek.

Works

Anarchy, State, and Utopia, New York, Basic Books, 1974.
Philosophical Explanations, Cambridge, Massachusetts, Harvard University Press, 1981.
The Examined Life: Philosophical Meditations, New York, Touchstone Books, 1989.

Other works

Tibor R. Machan (ed.), *The Libertarian Reader*, Totowa, N.J., Rowan and Littlefield, 1982.
Tom Campbell, *Justice*, Atlantic Highlands, N.J., Humanities Press, 1988.

Julius Kambarage Nyerere 1922–

The concept of freedom and its attainment are central to the thought and political career of Julius Kambarage Nyerere of Tanzania. For Nyerere freedom is not merely an achievement to be celebrated annually. It is a historical process. Nyerere identified four aspects of freedom with respect to Africa and Africans: freedom from foreign and racist minority rule; from external economic domination; from poverty, injustice and oppression of Africans by Africans themselves; and from mental subjugation to the ideas of others. His views on democracy, equality and socialism may be said to spring from these understandings of freedom which he sought to bring to bear on both Tanzanian and continental African politics during his long political leadership from 1943 to 1985.

The son of the chief of the minor Zanaki tribe, Nyerere was born in Butiama, north-western Tanganyika. Of unusual intellectual ability, he went to mission schools and was one of the first Africans under the League of Nations' trusteeship of Tanganyika to attend university – Makerere and Edinburgh. He was one of the founding members of the Tanganyika African National Union (1953), first Prime Minister of independent Tanganyika

(1961), first President of the United Republic of Tanzania (from Tanganyika and Zanzibar after the revolution in the island state in 1964) and one of the first African leaders to retire, voluntarily, from the presidency of his country. The most respected and consistent of post-independence leaders on the continent, Nyerere has refused to accept any of the grandiose titles common among Africa's post-colonial leaders, apart from that earned as a schoolteacher at Pugu, outside Dar es Salaam, namely Mwalimu, teacher. Nyerere, and the late Kwame Nkrumah of Ghana, were the only two African leaders to carry out the OAU's resolution and take their country out of the Commonwealth over the Rhodesian Prime Minister Ian Smith's Unilateral Declaration of Independence in 1965, thereby losing much needed assistance from Britain. He condemned the apartheid regime in South Africa as well as African racists such as Idi Amin.

From early on, Nyerere recognized that the most pressing and important freedom for Africa was freedom from alien rule. He argued that it is better for a people to endure oppressive self-rule than to enjoy the fruits of a benevolent but alien authority. Nkrumah had encouraged his followers to seek first the political kingdom and all things would be given unto them; Nyerere's philosophy was more subtle. In order to secure true political freedom it was necessary to prosecute the struggle for economic independence and to establish a social system which would abolish poverty, injustice and oppression.

Thus Nyerere proceeded in February 1967 to fashion what was to become an immediate inspiration for African, and indeed Third World, radicals. This was the Arusha Declaration – *Ujamaa na Kujitegemea*, translated as Socialism and Self-reliance. It called for large-scale nationalization of the country's economic assets, and at a time when most planners placed their trust in industrial development Nyerere emphasized agriculture as the way forward. With his guidance, subsequent declarations developed and clarified specific aspects of this momentous departure: *Education for Self-reliance* (March 1967), *Socialism and Rural Development* (September 1967), *Mwongozo* I (party guidelines, 1971), *Decentralization* (1971), the Musoma Declaration (1974), the Lindi Resolution (1976) and *Mwongozo* II (1981), four years before doing *kung'atuka* (retiring) from the presidency for a younger man, Ali Hassan Mwinyi. Taken together, these measures stressed the importance of the new nation depending on its people rather than on foreign aid and investment for development. Nyerere's hand or influence was also evident in less well-known or less commented-upon measures, such as electoral and language policies, which sought to minimize tribal and racial, linguistic, regional (etc.) differences and emphasize the factors which unite Tanzanians of all backgrounds, including former settlers.

These steps towards the attainment of freedom were guided by three elements in Nyerere's social and political thought. For Nyerere unity is essential to the African's project of achieving freedom and respect, and this informed his approach to the question of regional unity, particularly the union between Tanganyika and Zanzibar. Central to Nyerere's concept of unity, however, is a profound mistrust of political pluralism. Thus in 1964 he formalized what had been a natural process whereby TANU (from 1977, Chama Cha Mapinduzi, the Party of the Revolution) dominated political life. The single-party system, complete control of trade unions by the state, the rubber-stamping role of the legislature, the highly centralized executive with power to intervene in diverse areas of social and political life, established a frighteningly unified order in the country. The only mitigating factors are the relative inefficiency of institutions and the first and second Presidents' moderation in the use of power.

The second idea which has informed much of Nyerere's political action is the notion of equality. For him the good social order strives to ensure that individuals realize equality within the great collectivity. All Tanzanians are workers, irrespective of their structural location within the social order. The worker is not to be contrasted merely with the employer or the owner of capital; rather, the worker is to be seen in contrast to the 'loiterer' and the 'lazy' person. In his world, Nyerere's individuals, consistent with his sense of unity, may be differently located but are all contributing in their different ways to a common enterprise – the good of all. Not only are all persons engaged in a common effort to attain the good of all, but the good itself is necessarily the good of the community as a whole. The 'exploiter' is therefore the loiterer, the lazy man who contributes nothing to the body social – *man* because Nyerere is full of praise for Tanzanian women, whom he perceives as hard-working contributors to the whole.

The third aspect of Nyerere's thought which underscores his political career has been his consistent attempt to situate his thinking in the African past rather than to seek inspiration from ideological systems from non-African sources. Whilst free of the angst of identity and personality several other African leaders/thinkers experienced, Nyerere, like Amilcar Cabral and others, rejected important elements of both the liberal moral and political philosophy of the West and the Marxism–Leninism of the East. What he calls 'doctrinaire socialism' posits a situation of 'class war', and, whilst he is much admired by liberals, Nyerere harbours a deep distrust of their conviction that individuals are best able to determine the social good. For Nyerere African socialism or *Ujamaa* (familyhood/brotherhood) is rooted, or must find its bearings, within African pre-colonial practices rather than in Marxism–Leninism or liberalism. These ideologies, based on non-African experience, are respectively divisive and inequitable. His prescription, therefore, is that Africans must look to their own past and accept the inspiration found there. For example, democracy is not to be defined by the adversarial institutions of the West such as prosecution and defence in the courtroom, government and opposition in the legislature or capital and labour in the market place; rather, democracy is for him a condition in which opposing views contend within a unitary whole/forum (the party) but people must be allowed to 'argue until they agree', as their forefathers did 'beneath a tree'.

This stress on the African past is not unique to Nyerere, nor is the emphasis he places on African unity and the resultant unitary political system. Most African leaders have articulated much the same views on these matters. None, however, has given such careful thought to them and, perhaps with the exception of Robert Mugabe of Zimbabwe, none has taken more care to effect a socio-political system for a post-colonial Africa. In doing so Nyerere sometimes succeeded in moderating his potentially oppressive, closed and monolithic political system by a touch of both the rationalism of the enlightened ruler and the humanity of the historicist romantics. At the same time, if what we see here is a Rousseau-like naivety mixed with a profound Catholic faith, leading to a simplistic sociology, then we must also hear an echo of early Jeffersonianism's confidence in the possibility of a new nation building its future on an idyllic, undifferentiated and unified agricultural democracy. As with Jefferson, however, it is difficult to see how men and women of lesser vision – perhaps the real litmus test of any new system – will be able to work humanely with what he has bequeathed.

See also

Cabral.

Works

Ujamaa: Essays on Socialism, London, Oxford University Press, 1968.

Freedom and Unity/Uhuru na Umoja, London, University Press, 1974.

Freedom and Development/Uhuru na Ujamaa, London, Oxford University Press, 1976.

Our Leadership and the Destiny of Tanzania, Harare, African Publishing Group, 1995.

Other works

Lionel Cliffe, *One-party Democracy*, Nairobi, East African Publishing House, 1967.

William R. Duggan and J. R. Viville, *Tanzania and Nyerere: a Study of Ujamaa and Nationalism*, New York, Orbis, 1976.

Cransford Pratt and Bismarck Mwansasu (eds.), *Towards Socialism in Tanzania*, Toronto, University of Toronto Press, 1979.

D. Milazi, 'African school of thought: sociological analysis and synthesis', *African Review* (Tanzania) 12 (1985).

Harry Goldbourne, *Popular Struggles for Democracy in Africa*, London, Zed, 1987.

——*Post-Arusha Tanzania*, Dar es Salaam, Tanzania Publishing House, forthcoming.

Michael Joseph Oakeshott 1901–1990

Oakeshott was arguably the most important English political thinker of the century. He developed a concept of civil society of great dialectical subtlety and explored the postulates on which such a theory is necessarily based. He examined some of the major questions raised by the development of the modern state. He also greatly influenced the way in which the history of political thought is studied and taught. And, although some of his more recent work was often dauntingly complex, most of what he wrote on these matters displays a notable elegance of style. It also reveals his character as a nonconformist in the sense that he denied many of the orthodoxies of the age, an array of dissent which, despite a self-acclaimed conservatism, made him something of a radical. At a time when philosophy was coming under the sway of various forms of logical or linguistic analysis he found inspiration in the generally discarded idealism of Hegel and Bradley. In an epoch dominated by science, he refused to accept it as master of the intellectual field. He asserted the autonomy of history against the ever more pressing claims of naturalistic interpretation and didactic purpose. And, while learning and its institutions increasingly became the plaything of progressive theory or some pragmatic purpose, he insisted on rigorously conceived academic values pursued for their intrinsic worth.

As for political issues, he was always deeply sceptical about the virtues claimed for the major tendency of modern times – the growth of the purposive state and all it involves – and, in the name of freedom and individuality, was profoundly critical of the arguments by which the trend might be defended. Moreover, if it was urged that political philosophy was dead, he sustained his point of view through a corpus of theoretical work which finds its rationale and unity alike in a particular concept of philosophical inquiry.

Some philosophers undertake the construction of a complete system of ideas of which politics is a part. Others, more sceptical, or diffident perhaps, have no such archetectonic in mind but rather explore the potential of a way of thinking through its application to different fields of thought and activity of which politics may be one. Oakeshott falls into the second of these two categories. So it is not by chance that a good part of his *oeuvre* takes the form of essays on particular subjects. The range of interests they reflect is considerable: religion and theology, historical explanation, education, the moral life, aesthetics, ideologies, jurisprudence and much else, from the thought of Hobbes to political economy. Nor is it surprising that Oakeshott offered no single, collected account of his ideas about civil society. *On Human Conduct* does indeed provide a systematic (and intricate) examination of the central themes. But the fullest exposition of several of his characteristic opinions about politics still has to be sought elsewhere. Further, what might be called the dispersed nature of his thought is accentuated by the changes which occurred over the years in focus, emphasis and idiom, innovations in the last being particularly marked.

The concept of philosophy from which Oakeshott's civil theory emerges is most fully explored in *Experience and its Modes*, where the philosophical engagement is seen as the attempt to understand human experience as a whole and for its own sake. Certain aspects of the flow of 'goings-on' stand out, are recognized by their characteristics, and given an identity. In this way certain modes of experience are differentiated, specifically those worlds of ideas called 'practice', 'history' and 'science'. It is the philosopher's business critically to examine the assumptions in terms of which such an identity is constructed and maintained so as to expose any deficiency in these postulates and if possible to establish a more coherent view. Yet whatever is thus achieved is always conditional, and further scrutiny is likely yet again to reveal inadequacy. Oakeshott's own work exemplifies this, for he explained, in his essay on 'poetry', how he had previously failed to see aesthetic imagination as constituting a distinct mode of experience in its own right. Equally he was late in presenting a theoretization of the character of civil society.

It follows that to philosophize about politics must be to show how specifically political experience may be recognized, identified and theorized in terms of the postulates involved. And because politics is a form of human conduct this must be similarly examined.

Such conduct is constituted by intelligent agents responding to contingent situations in pursuit of their wished-for outcomes and doing so in the context of a multiplicity of 'practices'. These are of two kinds. They may be 'prudential', prescribing behaviour designed to achieve a given purpose, like the routine of an office. Or they may be 'moral', rules which are not thus instrumental and which do not specify action: a principle that men should act honestly does not direct what should be said or done in a particular situation. This distinction is reflected in the two categorically discrete modes of human association which Oakeshott discerned and which he called *universitas* and *societas*. The former is people united in the pursuit of a common objective. Its practices are thus 'prudential' in nature, designed to realize that end (whatever it is). In contrast *societas* is a 'moral' relationship between free agents who severally acknowledge only the authority of certain conditions which are necessary to association and action but which otherwise leave those involved free to pursue their own goals.

These two concepts, together with their associated vocabularies, are, Oakeshott believed, the poles around which European reflection about the modern state has turned. For political society itself may be seen in the mirror these images provide. It may be regarded as a 'teleocracy', a joint endeavour to seek the satisfaction of a collective substantive want, in which case the office of government is to manage the purposive concern. Or its practices may be a 'nomocratic' framework of conduct which does not specify any such goal and which offers simply a 'negative gift': the removal of some of the circumstances that might otherwise frustrate the achievement of whatever individuals seek. 'Civil association', a society conceived in this latter way, offers no salvation (as through the promised securing of a common end) but simply the organization of human affairs such that no one who is able is prevented from seeking felicity after his own fashion. Any modern European state is likely to manifest an unresolved tension between these irreconcilable dispositions. However, Oakeshott's view of the antithesis is expressed in varying mood. He wavers with some ambiguity between the acknowledgement of both tendencies and the deploration, through a subtle mixture of argument and reproof, of the (to him less acceptable) claims of the state seen as *universitas*. He certainly devoted much attention to exploding the fallacies by which a false view of the state has often been sustained. For instance, 'rationalism' is repudiated as a mistaken understanding of political knowledge which leads to an unfortunate reliance on ideology as a guide to action. Similarly he was critical of 'naturalism', the idea that it is possible to establish a mistake-proof science of human conduct in general or of politics in particular. He was scathing, too, about the nature of the 'mass man' and 'his' role as a factor in the development of the modern state. Indeed, he was at pains to explore at some length the way in which this state had emerged in Europe, and

in terms which invariably leave no doubt about his judgement of the process. In this fashion he diagnosed the predicament and folly of contemporary beings as the hopeless attempt to build a stairway to heaven, a tendency he parodied in a retelling of the old story about 'The Tower of Babel'.

He once wrote that political philosophers are prone to take a sombre view of the human situation. Whether the diagnosis he presents is accurate or not is matter for discussion. What is not is the profound care and insight with which he explored the dilemma and the fundamental nature of the terms in which he pointed out a possible way to liberate people from intellectual sophistry and the distraction of political illusion.

Works

Experience and its Modes, Cambridge, Cambridge University Press, 1933.
Rationalism in Politics and other Essays, London, Methuen, 1962.
On Human Conduct, Oxford, Clarendon Press, 1975.
On History and other Essays, Oxford, Blackwell, 1983.

Other works

W. H. Greenleaf, Oakeshott's Philosophical Politics, London, Longman, 1966.
J. L. Auspitz, et al., 'A Symposium on Michael Oakeshott', Political Theory 4 (1976), pp. 261–367.
Bhikhu C. Parekh, 'The Political Philosophy of Michael Oakeshott', British Journal of Political Science 9 (1979), pp. 481–506.
P. Franco, The Political Philosophy of Michael Oakeshott, New Haven, Conn., Yale University Press, 1990.

José Ortega y Gasset
1883–1955

José Ortega y Gasset was born in Madrid. In 1898 he left behind the Jesuit-inspired education of his early years by enrolling at the Central University of Madrid, and from then on committed himself to reforming elements in a burgeoning Spanish middle class. Like many Spaniards of the period eager to seek an alternative to what they conceived to be the dead-end of pre-modern parochialism,

Ortega went to Germany (in 1905, 1906 and 1911) and returned confirmed in the belief that economic, political and cultural modernization was the key to Spanish regeneration. In 1921 he wrote *España invertebrada* (*Invertebrate Spain*), in which he analysed the history of Spain's continuing decline in terms of the lack of a responsible and able national elite; he then accepted General Miguel Primo de Rivera's *pronunciamiento* in 1923 for the 'short, sharp shock' it would give the body politic in restoring order and putting an end to political corruption. In 1929 his sociology and politics of elitism reached their most sophisticated level with the publication of the internationally famous *La rebelión de las masas* (*The Revolt of the Masses*). Ortega argued that the distinction between mass and elite was a matter of social fact in any walk of life, that it was the duty of the mass to follow the guidance of the elite and that a properly constituted mass and elite were the key to any nation's well-being. This approach places him firmly in the tradition of other elite theorists such as Vilfredo Pareto, Gaetano Mosca and Robert Michels. Such ideas, together with Ortega's stress on the importance of the nation and his corporatist notions of political leadership, strongly influenced José Antonio Primo de Rivera, the founder of the Falange. Ortega never publicly favoured this Spanish version of fascism, however, and it was his enduring sense of the value of the individual that led him to oppose both fascism and bolshevism. As leader of his own party of intellectuals, Ortega was elected to the Cortes of the Second Republic (1931– 6) and served as deputy for León and Jaén before increasing disillusionment with the republic led him to resign in August 1932. Civil war broke out in 1936 and Ortega travelled to Paris, where he began a self-imposed exile which was to last for the rest of his life. He maintained a public silence on political matters until his death, but private papers suggest that he favoured a Nationalist victory during the war, although he rapidly lost confidence in Franco after it, believing him to be pursuing policies which would guarantee the isolation of Spain from the international community. The rest of Ortega's life was spent pursuing his philosophical interests and speaking at international conferences in favour of an ill defined but politically significant universalist liberal humanism. He died in Madrid of stomach cancer.

See also

Michels, Mosca, Pareto.

Works

Invertebrate Spain, New York, Norton, 1957.
The Revolt of the Masses, South Bend, Ind., University of Notre Dame Press, 1985.

Other works

R. McClintock, *Man and his Circumstances: Ortega as Educator*, New York, Teachers' College Press, 1971.
Antonio Elorza, *La razón y la sombra*, Barcelona, Anagrama, 1984.
Andrew Dobson, *An Introduction to the Politics and Philosophy of José Ortega y Gasset*, Cambridge, Cambridge University Press, 1989.
R. Gray, *The Imperative of Modernity: an Intellectual Biography of José Ortega y Gasset*, Berkeley, Cal., California University Press, 1989.

George Orwell
1903–1950

Eric Blair was born in India, the son of an official in the Opium Department. His mother brought him to England at the age of three, where he went to preparatory school and then, on a part-scholarship, to Eton. Most of his contemporaries went on to university but he, while reading widely in private, refused to work for public exams. He joined the Burma Police but resigned in 1927, disgusted with the snobbery and insensitivity of his fellows.

His first novel, *Burmese Days* (1934), was strongly anti-imperialist but not necessarily socialist. At that time, indeed, he called himself, if with some irony, 'a Tory anarchist'. He was aware of socialist doctrines but did not declare himself until 1935. On his return from Burma he had set out to be a writer, without much clear idea of what to write; so, being at first a failure, and thus poor, he became interested in poverty and began spasmodic bouts of living with tramps. Afterwards he said that he wrote *Down and Out in Paris and London* (1933) to see whether we treated our poor as badly as we treated the Burmese. On the whole he thought we did. These experiences enriched his future writing: unlike the academic social theorists, he knew what harsh survival meant.

This led to the publisher Victor Gollancz commissioning him to describe the life of the unemployed. The first part of *The Road to Wigan Pier* is an almost ethnographic study of unemployment, but the second is a semi-autobiographical statement of what was needed to win the lower middle class over to socialism. He announced his conversion as part of a polemic against intellectual 'fellow-travellers' who ignored justice and liberty and worshipped, he said, the machine-age image of Soviet power. In his own characteristic way Orwell clearly recycled beliefs of the early socialists and Victorian radicals about the primacy of the ethical and the libertarian, and about the dangers as well as the emancipatory potential of urban industrial civilization.

Concern with egalitarianism and participatory democracy became central in *Homage to Catalonia*, in which he tried to substitute a scathingly common-sense description of what actually happened for the ideological distortions and plain lies of communist propaganda on Spain. The book was fiercely criticized by communists and other left-wing reviewers, and sold badly, but it was defended by anarchists, Trotskyites, the Independent Labour Party and the Partido Obrerode Unificatión Marxista, as well being praised for its pure writing by some dissident communist critics.

Until the very day war broke out Orwell took the Trotskyite and ILP line that the coming conflict was simply a capitalist war for the control of colonies, as in his essay 'Not count-

ing the niggers'. This is also shown in his novel *Coming up for Air* (1939), which prophesied, with relish, a bloody and sudden end to the old order. The book is sometimes called 'nostalgic', but the nostalgic hero, George Bowling, is not Orwell, and his 'rural nostalgia' is sardonically introduced as the fatal flaw of the English common man. And Orwell attacked communism equally. His English socialism was by then firmly rooted, and he never changed his mind that liberty must be the means as well as part of the end. The end was a society both egalitarian and free which would have eradicated the economic exploitation that was largely a product of excessive centralization, whether in private or in public hands. The seeds of the political doctrines of *Animal Farm* were planted early. But Orwell did not naively advocate return to William Morris's pastoralism; instead he sought a creative balance between town and country, urban development and rural preservation. And several of his essays were pioneering studies of popular culture. The humanitarian face of socialism was more important to him than the collectivist face. 'A writer cannot be a *loyal* member of a political party.'

On the outbreak of war his anti-militarism (never pacificism; he had fought in Spain) turned into a democratic patriotism. He said that he preferred the imperfect democracy of even Neville Chamberlain's England to Nazi domination, but claimed in *The Lion and the Unicorn* that a political and social revolution was necessary to win the war. War itself, he saw, could be an agent of social change and it could lead, in Britain, to the vindication of those democratic socialist values of liberty, equality and fraternity suppressed by the individualistic success ethic of capitalism. Again he argued that the leadership which could unlock the energy, as well as the essential decency, of the common people must come from the ranks of the lower middle class.

From the events and thoughts of war emerged *Animal Farm*. Because part of it was an attack on Stalin, 'our wartime ally', he had difficulty publishing it, and communist sympathizers were to brand it as simply a super-weapon in the ideological Cold War. But that misses its broader context. It can be read as one of the classic statements of old 'democratic Socialist' (Orwell's preferred capitalization) doctrine: an exaltation of the need to abolish economic exploitation, a paean of praise for liberty and equality but also (the forgotten value) for fraternity, together with a lament for the revolution that betrayed and a grim satire on the corrupting effect of centralized, bureaucratic power.

After the war he did not change his values but came to see that 'the revolution' in Britain, especially under Attlee's well-meaning but pedestrian government, could not be an event like 1917 or 1789, only at best a long revolution, a process through time. His concern about the corrupting effects of absolute power, especially when fortified by the mental images as well as the killing potential of atomic power, were expressed finally in *Nineteen Eighty-four.* This again was represented as simply anti-Soviet, which misses completely at least three other satiric thrusts: the arrogant division of the world between great powers; the general tendency for truth and linguistic clarity alike to be debased by rigid political ideologies; and the debasement and enfeeblement of the 'proles' by a trivialized and semi-pornographic popular press. He knew full well that the Soviets attempted to mobilize popular power by propaganda, so this struck home-truths at the British popular press – his rage that the opportunities of mass literacy were squandered in the interests of capitalist consumerism.

He was not a systematic thinker or theorist. But there are few who expressed the values and doctrines of English socialism so clearly and imaginatively, or who criticized the failings of his own camp more honestly. Amid the decay, dilution or transformation of Marxist theory he will come to be taken more seriously as a thinker, though he chose the novel, the satire and, above all, the speculative essay as his media, not the so often internal-ized learned monograph or article. His reputation as a political thinker has always been higher among dissident intellectuals in the former Communist Bloc than in his own country.

Works

The Road to Wigan Pier, London, Gollancz, 1937.
Homage to Catalonia, London, Secker & Warburg, 1938.
The Lion and the Unicorn, London, Secker & Warburg, 1941.
Animal Farm, London, Secker & Warburg, 1945.
Nineteen Eighty-four, London, Secker & Warburg, 1949.
The Collected Essays, Journals and Letters, London, Secker & Warburg, 1968.

Other works

George Woodcock, The Crystal Spirit: a Study of George Orwell, Boston, Mass., Little Brown, 1968.
William Steinhoff, George Orwell and the Origins of 'Nineteen Eighty-four', Ann Arbor, Mich., University of Michigan Press, 1975.
Bernard Crick, George Orwell: a Life, London, Penguin, 1980.
P. Buitenhaus and I. B. Nadel (eds.), George Orwell: a Reassessment, London, Macmillan, 1988.
Bernard Crick, Essays on Politics and Literature, Edinburgh, Edinburgh University Press, 1989.

Ōtsuka Hisao   1907–1996

Born in Kyoto, Ōtsuka Hisao was the founder of the Ōtsuka school of Japanese economic history. Influenced by both Marxism and the sociology of Max Weber, the focal point of Ōtsuka's work was the analysis of the formation of modern capitalism, or the transition from feudalism to capitalism. Throughout his career, this emphasis was linked with his efforts to provide a theoretical basis for an understanding of the nature of Japan's own political development, specifically the rise of militarism and authoritarianism in the pre-war period. The young Ōtsuka attended the Third Higher School and then Tokyo Imperial University, where he concentrated on economics. At university he fell under the Christian influence of Uchimura Kanzō; his conversion to Christianity provided a certain spiritual basis for Ōtsuka's scholarship. After graduating in 1930, he became an assistant and then full professor at Hōsei University in Tokyo; in 1939 he was appointed assistant Professor of Economics at Tokyo Imperial University, where he became a full professor in 1947. After retiring from Tokyo University in 1968 he became a professor at International Christian University.

Ōtsuka's work progressed through five stages. In the first, as a young scholar in pre-war Japan, Ōtsuka focused on the transformation of the earliest forms of capital, mercantile and usury capital to industrial captial as they lost their 'irrationalism'. The results of this early work were published in *On the Category of So-called Early Capital*. In the second period he sought in English economic history the internal basis of the establishment of modern industrial capitalism. In *Preface to the Economic History of Europe* (1938) Ōtsuka began to focus on the contradiction between weaving or textile manufacture in villages and in towns. The results of his own research into this question led Ōtsuka to critique the classic interpretations of Evgenii Kosminsky and Michael Postan on agricultural theory and the manorial system. More important, at this point he began to fall under the influence of Max Weber's *The Protestant Ethic and the Spirit of Capitalism*. Thus in the third period Ōtsuka developed themes he had encountered in Weber, and after the publication of *The Position of Commerce in the History of the Development of Capitalism* his subsequent *Introduction to the Economic History of Modern Europe*, which won the first Mainichi Cultural Award after the war, *The Ancestry of Modern Capitalism* and *Religious Reform and Modern Society* presented his own theoretical understanding of modernity on the basis of a combination of Marxian materialism and Weberian sociology. The apparent economic emphasis of the works written before and during the war actually offered him a vehicle for a critical examination of the existing Japanese state. At a time when Marxists who had more directly attacked the character of the Japanese were being brutally repressed, Ōtsuka's scholarship drew broad support among leftist and other scholars as a basis for resistance to the increasingly authoritarian and militaristic order.

Ōtsuka moved into the fourth period of his work when earlier writings came under criticism in the newly liberalized post-war atmosphere. Turning now to concentrate more heavily on the economic aspects of his work, Ōtsuka published his *Basic Theory of the Kyōdōtai (Community)* (1955). Influenced by Karl Marx's *Precapitalist Economic Formations*, he saw the basic process of the establishment of modern society in the development of a division of labour and then classes within the primitive community, leading to the establishment of local marketing areas. Here Ōtsuka was developing further the position of the pre-war Japanese Communist Party loyalist faction, the Kōzaha. This faction had stressed the development of the *kyōdōtai* in Japan and the notion of the Asiatic mode of production in seeking to account for what they saw as Japan's backwardness, evidenced in its increasing authoritarianism and militarism.

The 1960s marked yet another stage in the development of Ōtsuka's work. Now, involved in the movement protesting against the security treaty of 1960, in this new phase, there was once again an intimate relationship between Ōtsuka's theoretical work and his political activity. In his *Religious Reform and Modern Society*, published in a revised edition in 1961, Ōtsuka argued that modern society tended to produce an ossified bureaucracy. This observation led him to focus more closely on Marx's concept of alienation and Weber's 'sociology of domination' in seeking to understand that phenomenon. These efforts produced a rethinking of *The Method of Social Science* (1966), to be applied to the study of development processes in the Third World.

See also

Weber.

Works

Kindai Ōshu keizai shi josetsu (Introduction to the Economic History of Modern Europe), 1944.

Kindai shihon-shugi hattatsu shi ni okeru shōgyō no chi'i (The Position of Commerce in the History of the Development of Capitalism), 1941.

Kindai shihon-shugi no keifu (The Ancestry of Modern Capitalism), 1946.

Ōtsuka Hisao chosakushū (Collected Writings of Ōtsuka Hisao), ten volumes, Tokyo, Iwanami Shoten, n.d.

Shūkyō kaikaku to kindai shakai (Religious Reform and Modern Society), 1948, revised edition 1961.

The Spirit of Capitalism: the Max Weber Thesis in an Economic Historical Perspective, Tokyo, Iwanami, 1982.

Other works

Fukui Norihiko, 'Sur l'oeuvre de Hisao Ōtsuka' (on the work of Ōtsuka Hisao), *Actuel Marx* (Marxism Today) (Paris) 2, *Le Marxisme au Japon* (Marxism in Japan), pp. 85–8.

Vilfredo Pareto   1848–1923

Born in the year of liberal revolutions, and dying only one year after the fascist seizure of power, Pareto mirrored in his evolution as a thinker the changing fortunes of Italian liberalism during this period. He came to prominence as a propagandist of libertarian economic and political ideas. A disciple of John Stuart Mill and Herbert Spencer, he championed both parliamentary reform and a free-market economy on the grounds that they fostered individual liberty and led to the moral and material progress of society. Originally a supporter of the socialists in their struggle against the oppressive policies of the Italian state, he remained strongly opposed to socialist economic theories. If he castigated the Italian bourgeoisie for using the state to promote what he called 'bourgeois socialism' through customs duties, monopolies and military expenditure designed to enhance the position of certain industrialists and landowners, he thought a 'popular socialism' which employed the state to redistribute wealth to the workers would be even worse, as the number of expropriators would be greater than the number of wealth creators. At first he hoped that a more democratic system would produce a situation in which neither class could take hold of the state for its own advantage. However, he regarded the social reforms introduced by liberal politicians at the turn of the century as a successful attempt to incorporate the socialist leaders into their patronage network. By 1905 he had become thoroughly cynical about democratic politics and predicted that the Italian bourgeoisie would ultimately concede so much that they would lose their dominant position only to be replaced by a more corrupt group of socialist politicians. He now thought majority rule a sham, since all parties were employed by economic and political elites who sought to manipulate the state to their own advantage.

Pareto's political sociology was born of this disillusionment. During the 1880s he gained a formidable reputation as an economist, developing econometric techniques which he applied to the new equilibrium theory of Léon Walras. He maintained that a free-market system had to be allowed to reach its natural point of equilibrium, where it would achieve optimum want satisfaction. The task he set himself in his *The Mind and Society Treatise on General Sociology* (1917–18) was an investigation of the psychological mechanisms which inhibited individuals from following the rational utility-maximizing strategy assumed by classical economic theory. He argued that most human reasoning was nonlogical, because it adopted irrational premises which were not susceptible to empirical testing. These premises were manifestations of various psychic states, which Pareto proceeded to classify. He termed these states 'residues' because they reflected the residuum found at the bottom of a spurious theory or 'derivation'. Of the fifty-two derivations he claimed to have identified, two were especially important. Class I, which he called the 'instinct of combination', was found among liberal politicians and entrepreneurs who employed cunning and strategic concessions to win people to their cause. Class II was a conservative tendency, the 'persistence of aggregates', typical of *rentiers* and politicians keen on law and order and willing to use force. Pareto argued that social development exhibited a cyclical pattern, reflecting a regular fluctuation in the preponderance of the different psychic states corresponding to these two residues within people. The composition of the ruling elite mirrored this cycle, a phenomenon Pareto termed the 'circulation of elites'. When Class I residues were in the ascendant, the economy was dominated by entrepreneurial speculators and the political system by fox-like intriguers. Whilst this phase was initially characterized by an economic boom and liberal attitudes, over-consumption and the need for the politicians to make more concessions to maintain themselves in office gave rise to feelings associated with Class II residues and led to calls for the re-establishment of political and economic controls. Power now passed to the political 'lions', who reasserted the authority of the state. The economy became dominated by *rentiers* and a period of capital accumulation. When people grew tired of these restrictions a new cycle was initiated. Pareto believed Mussolini's victory confirmed his thesis that Italy had reached the end of a cycle in which the policies associated with Class I residues had become inoperable. There can be little doubt that had he lived longer he would have come to regard the fascist regime as exemplifying the parallel dangers of a system built on a preponderance of Class II residues.

Works

The Mind and Society, 4 vols, London, Cape, 1935.
Sociological Writings, Oxford, Blackwell, 1966.
The Other Pareto, London, Scolar Press, 1980.

Other works

S. G. Finer, 'Pareto and pluto-democracy: the retreat to Galapagos', *American Political Science Review* 57 (1968), pp. 440–50.

Norberto Bobbio, *On Mosca and Pareto*, Geneva, Droz, 1972.
Richard P. Bellamy, *Modern Italian Social Theory: Ideology and Politics from Pareto to the Present*, Cambridge, Polity Press, 1987.

Evgenii Pashukanis 1891–1937

Evgenii Pashukanis was a Russian legal theorist, active in the 1920s and the first half of the 1930s, who made an important attempt to collate and develop Marx's critique of law. His major work, *Law and Marxism*, was published in 1924 as a contribution to the rich theoretical discussions on law and the state held in the early years of the bolshevik revolution.

The strength of Pashukanis's work is that he sought to derive a Marxist theory of law not from Marx's occasional comments on the law but systematically from the method which Marx developed in his critique of political economy. Just as Marx analysed money and capital as the historical expression of definite social relations of production, Pashukanis argued that law is a historical form of regulation expressing the emergence of definite social relations between individuals and not a generic category valid for all societies. He criticized the tendency in legal theory to universalize law, either by idealizing it as the essential requisite of social order or by technicizing it as a mere instrument of domination. In both cases he saw an instance of a bourgeois ideology which naturalizes the conditions of bourgeois life.

The political significance of Pashukanis's theory lay in his rejection of economism, in the sense that he conceived of the transition from capitalism to communism as a transformation not only of economic relations but also of relations of authority/power/control/ domination. His radical claim was that legal forms of domination have definite characteristics which render them unsuitable for communist society and that new forms of domination, which he called 'technical regulation', should and would replace the law. He therefore rejected the concept of 'proletarian law' as a self-contradiction.

Pashukanis saw law as a fetishistic form of domination which abstracted individuals, as legal subjects, from their real social existence. The law, he argued, reproduced inequality and dependence under the umbrella of merely formal freedom and equality before the law. It elevated the rights of subjects at the expense of indifference towards the needs of the exploited and the sins of the exploiters. It reflected the conflict of private interests, mutual indifference and all-round competition characteristic of capitalist society rather than the co-operation, comradeship and collectivity which were the hallmark of communist relations. It developed into a seemingly transcendent force, mystifying the domination of one class by another in the form of mutual subordination to an impersonal authority. Finally, it legitimized state power, whose real nature lay in the exercise of brute force on behalf of the economically dominant class.

Pashukanis saw the foundation of law as lying in the exchange of commodities. He argued that, just as value (the fundamental category of economics) is the fetishistic expression of the products of human labour when they are taken to market as commodities, so too the legal subject (the fundamental category of law) is the fetishistic form of the guardians or owners of commodities as they exchange their goods in the market place and then contract one with the other.

In the context of the Soviet Union in the 1920s Pashukanis promoted a gradual 'withering away of law' as commodity exchange was replaced by state ownership of production and state planning of distribution. As an important legal official in the latter half of the 1920s he did his best to encourage the 'dejuridification' of legal education, personnel and procedure.

Pashukanis analysed the 'technical form of regulation', which he saw as replacing law under communism, as having roots in capitalist society – in the relations between doctor and patient, in the internal organization of the workplace, in the co-ordination of trains and perhaps in the administration of the state. He defined technical regulation as a form of regulation appropriate to a situation in which all parties are seeking the same goals in a non-antagonistic and co-operative fashion.

Pashukanis seems to have believed that this form of regulation was becoming stronger in the Soviet Union in the 1920s with the growth of the state sector and the state bureaucracy. In 1929 he accepted Stalin's pronouncement that communism was being achieved with the introduction of the first Five Year Plan and then with the assault on the peasantry. Pashukanis drew the naive conclusion that 'the role of the pure juridical superstructure, the role of law, is now diminishing, and from this one can infer the general rule that technical regulation becomes more effective as the role of law becomes weaker and less significant'. In the 1930s, however, the tide turned against Pashukanis as the consolidated Stalinist regime turned to the celebration of what it called 'socialist legality'. Pashukanis was viciously attacked by leading Stalinist officials, notably Vishinsky, for his doctrine of the 'withering away of law'. Finally, in 1937, it seems that Pashukanis was murdered by the Stalinists without even the legal formality of a show trial.

Pashukanis's theory suffered from a superficial and one-sided critique of the fetishism of law. Tracing the roots of law to exchange rather than production, he saw only the negative side of exchange (private interest, indifference, competition) and ignored its positive side (independence, freedom, equality, etc.). He ignored the different production relations which underlie exchange and the different form and content assumed by the law as production relations change. In his critique of legal formalism he saw nothing of the democratic advance represented by the historical development of law in bourgeois society or of the democratic functions of law in socialism. In his celebration of technical regulation he substituted one fetish for another, technicism for law, thereby legitimating the subsumption of law to the bureaucratic arm of the state. By positing the withering away of law before the withering away of the state he opened up a Pandora's box of authoritarian statism.

In short, in spite of his brilliant and lasting theroetical insights into the social character of law, Pashukanis combined an over-critical theory of law with an uncritical theory of bureaucracy, a truly unfortunate mixture in the context of the transition from revolutionary bolshevism to Stalinism.

There was a considerable revival of interest in the writings of Pashukanis in the late 1970s and the early 1980s. To many contemporary Marxists his re-publication represented the recovery of an authentic Marxist tradition of juridical critique. This revival was in turn criticized by legal theorists and historians such as Robert Sharlet who, following Hans Kelsen, argued that the rule of law and the defence of rights, though perhaps born under capitalism, are necessary conditions of any democratic society. Finally, there have been attempts to develop – in more dialectical fashion than Pashukanis – the rational kernel of Marxist critiques of law.

Works

Law and Marxism, London, Ink Links, 1978.
Pashukanis: Selected Writings on Marxism and Law, ed. Piers Beirne and Robert Sharlet, New York, Academic Press, 1980.

Other works

Hans Kelsen, *The Communist Theory of Law*, New York, Praeger, 1955.
Sheila Fitzpatrick (ed.), *Cultural Revolution in Russia, 1928–31*, Bloomington, Ind., Indiana University Press, 1974.
John Holloway and Sol Picciotto (eds.), *State and Capital: a Marxist Debate*, Austin, Tex., University of Texas Press, 1978.
Alan Norrie, 'Pashukanis and commodity form theory', *International Journal of the Sociology of Law* 10 (November 1982).
Robert Fine, *Democracy and the Rule of the Law: Liberal Ideals and Marxist Critiques*, London, Pluto Press, 1984.

Carole Pateman   1940–

Carole Pateman has written numerous books and essays which are known throughout Europe, Australasia and North America. Her reputation lies in the originality of her synthesis of conceptual problems in liberal democratic theory with the theory of the patriarchal basis of sexual politics. This combination is no accident, for it is through her exploration of components of contractarian and liberal theories, such as participation, obligation and consent, that she has developed the thesis that contradictions in these concepts (and between them and political practice) can be explained only by recognizing that the social contract presupposes a sexual 'contract'.

In *Participation and Democratic Theory* the connections between the two elements are not yet made. Here she deals with participation in classical and revisionist theories of democracy: for one, the *sine qua non*; for the other, something to be minimized. Rousseau, particularly but not exclusively, inspires her view that the inconsistency between universal formal rights and class inequality in participation can be resolved only through structures that encourage self-management. Self-management and self-assumed obligation are also dealt with in *The Problem of Political Obligation*. Here she shows that liberal democratic theory cannot explain why individuals consent to be governed without defectively employing voluntaristic concepts normally associated with social or civil relations or without describing obligation as something like obedience, the very feature of patriarchal rule said to have been overthrown by the triumph of contractarianism. She illuminates the paradoxes of liberal thinking by reference to how contractarians have thought about women; these themes are elaborated in *The Sexual Contract*. In both these books she points out that, with few exceptions, all contractarians deem women as incapable of moving from natural to civil society except as the subordinates of men. The claim that contractarianism defeated patriarchy, then, is only half true. Sons defeated the father-right of rule but the new 'free and equal' individuals were, literally, a fraternity. The dominion of fathers over women was also broken but re-established as the dominion of all men over all women. In maintaining, contrarily, that relations between the sexes are private, liberal theorists remove the subject from political enquiry. But, without acknowledgement that women are incorporated into civil society differently from men, theoretical and practical enterprises designed to promote a social contract in which participation at work or in politics is not class-based will do little to alter the status of women. Without acknowledging that women in liberal society are not 'individuals' in the same way as men, reforms designed to make their contractual opportunities more similar to those of men cannot alter fundamentally the sexual basis of the social contract. Pateman has thus contributed to the reconstruction of a social contract that might be truly classless. But she herself points out (1988, 1989) that identifying the sources of women's subordination is only the beginning of reconstructing politics and institutions free from sex inequality. In addressing societies where contractarianism and liberalism are deeply embedded, and where many people believe that women can be 'written in', her ideas naturally arouse controversy. The most significant commentary, which also criticizes contractarian feminism but in a different way, is that of Diana Coole.

Works

Participation and the Democratic Theory, Cambridge, Cambridge University Press, 1970.
The Problem of Political Obligation: a Critical Analysis of Liberal Theory, Cambridge, Polity Press, 1985.
The Sexual Contract, Cambridge, Polity Press, 1988.
The Disorder of Women, Cambridge, Polity Press, 1989.

Other works

Diana Coole, 'Carole Pateman, *The Sexual Contract*', and reply by C. Pateman, *Politics* 10 (1990).

Georgii Valentinovich Plekhanov 1856–1918

Born in Tambov Province, Plekhanov was to become 'the father of Russian Marxism'. He became politically active in 1876 when the movement of the intelligentsia 'to the people' was under way. As a leader of the populist organization Land and Liberty Plekhanov opposed the increasing use of terror; arrested twice, he fled abroad in 1880. In his populist phase Plekhanov argued that history is not unilinear, that capitalism is the necessary predecessor of socialism only in the West, and that in Russia the existing form of communal land ownership by the peasants might serve as the starting point for a transition to socialism.

However, during 1880–2 Plekhanov completely converted to Marxism. With other exiles he founded the Emancipation of Labour group in 1883. That the revolutionary movement became influenced by Marxism was due to the diffusion of Plekhanov's works – especially *Socialism and Political Struggle* (1883) and *Our Differences* (1885). In 1882 Plekhanov had published his translation of *The Communist Manifesto* with a new preface by Marx that did not altogether reject the idea of avoiding a capitalist stage. Now Plekhanov proved more Marxist than Marx, answering the question 'Will Russia go through the school of capitalism?' with the reply 'Why should she not finish the school she has already begun?' After showing that Russia was developing in a capitalist direction and that the village community was internally differentiating and disintegrating he said to the populists, 'While the development of present economic relations is carrying you increasingly further away from your community ideals, our communist ideals are coming closer and closer to us through that same development.' In *Our Differences* he stated bluntly that ten years of bitter disappointment has shown the organization of a revolutionary movement among the peasantry to be impossible. It was necessary to concentrate on the strike-prone industrial centres rather than the countryside.

The difficulty that the inevitability of a capitalist stage posed for practical socialist activity Plekhanov solved by arguing that it was in the interests of the proletariat to combine with the bourgeoisie in a political revolution against absolutism in order to secure space for its own development as a class. Given its own independent organization and programme, instead of being the mere tool of the bourgeoisie, the proletariat would achieve 'hegemony' in the alliance with it and prevent any backsliding by the liberals. Such a complex perspective for working-class activity meant that a high degree of class consciousness was necessary on the part of the proletariat. Plekhanov averred that 'without revolutionary theory there is no revolutionary movement'. He gave an important role to the socialist intelligentsia in this respect: to explain to the working class its political and economic interests. But he disbelieved in the early possibility of a socialist government in Russia. A circle of conspirators could not substitute itself for the wheel of history in this matter. In sum, the impending revolution would be bourgeois-democratic in character, but the proletariat would play a leading role.

In the 1890s Plekhanov intervened vigorously in the intellectual life of Russia and the International. In his 1891 article on Hegel's anniversary he coined the term 'dialectical materialism'. He published an influential work on historical materialism, *Development of the Monist View of History* (1895). He came out against Bernstein's 'revisionism' immediately. He savagely attacked the 'economist' trend in Russian socialism.

Lenin's generation found all this congenial, and in 1900 Lenin and Plekhanov united their forces abroad in order to publish *Iskra* and to make preparations for an all-Russian Social Democratic Party. There was one significant question on which they were always to disagree: Lenin wanted an alliance with the peasantry; Plekhanov, with the bourgeois liberals. When the party split in 1903 Plekhanov

initially sided with Lenin's organizational proposals, seeing in them a barrier against opportunism, on the basis that 'the welfare of the revolution is the highest law'. But shortly he joined in assailing Lenin's 'dictatorship'.

In later years Plekhanov became absorbed in applying the materialist method in various fields of knowledge. After the February revolution of 1917 he returned to Petrograd from thirty-seven years' exile. He died on 30 May 1918, denouncing the October revolution as 'a violation of all the laws of history'. Notwithstanding that, on Lenin's recommendation his more philosophical works were kept in print. Thus Plekhanov's belief that Marxism provided an all-encompassing world view, and his elaboration of historical materialism, made a continuing contribution to shaping twentieth-century Marxist orthodoxy. In spite of his professed admiration for Hegel his theoretical work is paradigmatic of the scientistic positivism characteristic of much Second International Marxism.

See also

Bernstein.

Works

The Role of the Individual in History, London, Lawrence & Wishart, 1940.
Selected Philosophical Works I, London, Lawrence & Wishart, 1961.
Fundamental Problems of Marxism, New York, International, 1969.

Other works

Leopold H. Haimson, *The Russian Marxists and the Origins of Bolshevism*, Cambridge, Mass., Harvard University Press, 1955.
Samuel Haskell Baron, 'Between Marx and Lenin: Georg Plekhanov', in L. Labedz (ed.), *Revisionism*, London, Allen & Unwin, 1962.
Samuel Haskell Baron, *Plekhanov: the Father of Russian Marxism*, London, Routledge, 1963.
Leszek Kolakowski, *Main Currents of Marxism* II, *The Golden Age*, Oxford, Clarendon Press, 1978.

Karl Pølanyi 1886–1964

Born in Budapest. An economic historian, author of the most important twentieth-century critique of free-market capitalism, *The Great Transformation*. In it he argued that, by the extreme consequences of its own logic, the rise of a fully developed market economy necessarily engendered a self-protective reaction that eventuated in the welfare state.

See also

Frank.

Works include

The Great Transformation, Boston, Mass., Beacon Press, 1944.

Karl Raimund Popper 1902–1994

Popper was born in Vienna and lived there until 1937. Poverty, nationalism, economic depression, world war, the rise of communism and the onslaught of fascism influenced him greatly during these formative years. So also did the hope of social democracy and the humanitarian promises of Marxism (which he later rejected as a pseudo-science). In 1928 Popper received his doctorate in the methodology and psychology of thinking; and in 1934 he published his path-breaking *Logik der Forschung*, which, in explicit criticism of the positivism of the Vienna Circle, rejected induction and the psychology of sense data, substituted falsifiability for verifiability as the demarcation criterion for scientific propositions, and insisted on the potential fertility of metaphysics as a source of scientific imagination. In 1937, as war and the horrors of Hitler's programme drew near, Popper emigrated to New Zealand, where he wrote his principal political works. From 1946, through his knighthood in 1965 until his retirement in 1969, he taught logic and scientific method at the London School of Economics. During and after this period he published several influential works and collections, including *The Logic of Scientific Discovery* (1959), *Conjectures and Refutations* (1963), *Objective Knowledge: an Evolutionary Approach* (1972) and (with Sir John Eccles) *The Self and its Brain* (1977). The three-volume *Postscript* to *The Logic of Scientific Discovery* was published, after considerable delay, in 1982.

As a political thinker Popper is best known for *The Open Society and its Enemies* (1945) and *The Poverty of Historicism* (1944–5 in *Economica*, 1957 as a book). Indeed, these were not only Popper's first major works published in English but also his own 'war effort', as he later put it. The works range over an enormous terrain of problems in the 'philosophy of politics' and may be understood as the political complement to his theory of scientific knowledge, best described as 'critical rationalism'. They figure in the liberal tradition of Immanuel Kant or of John Stuart Mill (in whose 'school' or 'radical liberalism' Popper counted his father). Popper's political writings express, as he put it, 'the belief of a liberal – the belief in the possibility of a rule of law, of equal justice, of fundamental rights, and a free society'. He did not derive these liberal beliefs from first principles or build them upon foundations, in the manner of, say, John Rawls. Rather, he defended them in expressly dialectical fashion as a result of criticizing previous political thinkers.

Plato, Hegel and Marx are the principal (but by no means the only) targets of Popper's criticism. In Plato he found the philosophical roots or justification of propaganda and totalitarian justice; in Hegel, of nationalism and the worship of the state; in Marx, of class war and violent revolution. In all these 'false prophets' he found advocates of a closed society that suppresses free speech, equal rights and critical deliberation. We need to remember the political uses to which these thinkers were put, before and during the Second World War, since Popper's admittedly 'emotional and harsh' criticism of them subsequently proved to be highly controversial as interpretations of the relevant texts. This politicized context is made clear in the dedication to *The Poverty of Historicism*: 'In memory of the countless men and women of all creeds or nations or races who fell victims to the fascist and communist belief in Inexorable Laws of Historical Destiny', the deterministic belief which forms the theoretical core of historicism. Historicism, however, could not be rationally vindicated because the historical process was singular and unique and influenced by the unpredictable growth of human knowledge. Thus the future could not be predicted in accordance with rational scientific methods. Popper was no less critical of utopianism, centralized planning and 'holistic social engineering' because they also fell foul of the limits of human problem solving. So too, it turned out, did other somewhat less nefarious forms of political theory and practice, such as the classical utilitarian search for the greatest happiness of the greatest number.

In defending the open society Popper articulated several distinctive political beliefs, over and above those shared by the liberal tradition. As something of a sceptical gradualist he argued for incremental social reform and 'piecemeal social engineering'. He also championed a 'negative' utilitarianism, one which sought to eliminate unhappiness rather than maximize happiness. His praise of democracy, toleration and freedom was always mitigated by his belief that, when pursued in absolute terms, they were paradoxical and unrealizable. Absolute toleration, for example, paradoxically undermines itself when it counsels toleration of the actions of those who are intolerant. Popper, furthermore, did not praise democracy – which he calls 'government by discussion' – as a solution to the ancient problem of 'who rules best'. Rather, it provided the best available means for the non-violent popular control of political leaders, as well as 'the institutional framework for the reform of political institutions'. These cautious and complex political judgements fit with Popper's conception of the limits of human reason because they best accommodate learning from our mistakes. The deeply moral character of his liberalism also deserves to be underscored. Individual responsibility – entailed by our freedom and our decisions – animates the whole of his political theory. Even 'adopting critical rationalism' is a 'moral decision'.

Popper clearly found much of the justification for liberalism in the fallibilistic concept of science which he championed and popularized. Yet his critique of certain features of the theory and practice of science – the 'aping of the physical sciences', the alleged 'authority of the specialist' and so-called 'normal science' in Kuhn's sense – revealed the political implications of his thought for science and its philosophy as well. Popper's liberalism, then, might best be viewed as a scientific philosophy of politics and a political philosophy of science.

See also

Rawls.

Works

The Open Society and its Enemies, 1945, reprinted London, Routledge, 1966.
The Poverty of Historicism, 1957, reprinted London, Routledge, 1961.
The Logic of Scientific Discovery, 1959, reprinted London, Hutchinson, 1972.
Unended Quest: an Intellectual Autobiography, La Salle, Ill., Open Court, 1976.

Other works

Bryan Magee, *Popper*, London, Fontana, 1973.
Paul Arthur Schilpp (ed.), *The Philosophy of Karl Popper*, La Salle, Ill., Open Court, 1974.
Anthony Quinton, 'Karl Popper: politics without essences', in *Contemporary Political Philosophers*, New York, Dodd & Mead, 1975.
Hans Albert, *Treatise on Critical Reason*, Princeton, N.J., Princeton University Press, 1985.

Nicos Poulantzas   1936–1979

Nicos Poulantzas was born in Athens, Greece, but in many ways he has become identified as one of the French Marxist intellectuals who dominated academic debates during the 1960s and 1970s. During his brief academic career Poulantzas became one of the best-known and most controversial theorists of contemporary Marxism. Through a series of studies published during the 1960s and 1970s he made his mark originally as one of the group of Marxist intellectuals influenced by the work of Louis Althusser. Towards the end of his short life, however, he had emerged as a key political thinker among Marxist intellectuals who were attempting to fashion a vision of democratic socialism in opposition to the authoritarian statism of Stalinist regimes.

Poulantzas's early intellectual development was a product of the political climate created in Greece in the aftermath of the civil war. His experiences during this period aroused his interest in Marxist theory and left politics, and developed his lifelong interest in the study of the various forms of fascism and the exceptional state. His subsequent intellectual journey was, however, to be fashioned by the Marxist theorists he encountered after he had left Greece and settled in France. It was in France that he developed his understanding of the work of Sartre, Gramsci, Althusser and other Western Marxist theorists who were to influence his own work throughout his career.

Poulantzas's first major book, *Political Power and Social Classes*, began to establish his reputation as an original Marxist political theorist. First published in French in 1968, it rapidly became the focus of widespread debate when it was published in English in 1973, and his attempt to develop a Marxist theory of the state gave rise to much controversy and debate. In his study Poulantzas attempted to use the insights of Althusser and Gramsci to develop a Marxist conception of the capitalist state, a project which he saw as filling a major gap in existing Marxist theories of politics. His central concern, which he was to return to in other works, was to develop a theory of the relationship between politics, classes and state power. His key argument was that previous Marxist theories of the capitalist state as the 'instrument' of the capitalist class were inadequate in that they did not capture the complex relationship between the political and other spheres of capitalist societies. From his perspective, although the state was the product of class struggle in the political sphere, it was also 'relatively autonomous' from any particular capitalist fraction and from the economic sphere generally. It was therefore important to develop a specific theory of the state, and of its relation to the process of accumulation and class struggle.

Political Power and Social Classes led to a wide-ranging debate, and also influenced a number of historical and empirical studies of state power. Many of its key arguments, e.g. about the 'relative autonomy' of the state, were subjected to criticism from a variety of perspectives. This debate helped to establish Poulantzas's reputation as one of the most original, and controversial, Marxist theorists of his generation.

Poulantzas's interest in the analysis of fascism is reflected in two of his other major books. *Fascism and Dictatorship* attempted to analyse the development of Italian and German fascism as a particular political phenomenon, and to explain the state institutions to which fascism gave rise. His subsequent *The Crisis of the Dictatorships* looked specifically at the decline of the 'exceptional' political regimes of Portugal, Spain and Greece during the mid-1970s. Both these studies were at the forefront of attempts to analyse the political institutions associated with fascist regimes, and helped to shape subsequent discussion.

Another of Poulantzas's key interests was in theorization of the changing nature of class relationships and political power in advanced capitalist societies. This interest led to *Classes in Contemporary Capitalism*, an ambitious attempt to analyse the changes in class relations that had taken place in advanced capitalist societies. In particular he attempted to analyse the changing nature of the new middle classes, the role of class alliances in political struggle and the internationalization of class relationships.

Perhaps the most important, and lasting, impact of Poulantzas's work is to be found in the arguments he sought to develop in his last book, namely *State, Power, Socialism.* Although the book did not abandon his earlier concerns, it focused more centrally on the need to develop a democratic conception of socialism, on the role of new social movements, and on the dangers of authoritarianism. Many of the ideas in this volume signalled new concerns in Poulantzas's work, but he was prevented from developing them further by his untimely death.

Throughout his career Poulantzas's work met with a mixed response. His works were popularly regarded as difficult to read and jargon-ridden. Yet others saw him as one of the major Marxist political theorists of our time. During his brief career he was at the forefront of many of the debates that shaped the development of a Marxist political sociology. Since his death he and his work have fallen into relative obscurity. There are already clear signs, however, that key aspects of his work are being re-evaluated and are helping to inspire researchers in a variety of disciplines and theoretical approaches. His works do not fit in well with many of the current fashions of political and social theory. Many of his key concepts, such as 'relative autonomy', have been shown to be inadequate tools of theoretical and historical analysis. His work, however, forms a key part of the intellectual history of contemporary Marxism and raises important questions for those who are interested in rethinking the nature of political power, social classes and socialism. Perhaps his lasting contribution will be seen in terms of the questions he raised rather than in the answers he provided.

See also

Althusser, Gramsci, Sartre.

Works

Political Power and Social Classes, trans. T. O'Hagan, London, New Left Books, 1973.
Fascism and Dictatorship: the Third International and the Problem of Fascism, trans. J. White, London, New Left Books, 1974.
Classes in Contemporary Capitalism, trans. D. Fernbach, London, New Left Books, 1975.
Crisis of the Dictatorships: Portugal, Greece, Spain, trans. D. Fernbach, London, New Left Books, 1976.
State, Power, Socialism, trans. P. Camiller, London, New Left Books, 1978.

Other works

Bob Jessop, *Nicos Poulantzas*, Basingstoke, Macmillan 1985.

Raul Prebisch   1901–1986

Born in Tucuman, Argentina; Argentinian Finance Minister. One of the drafters of the International Monetary Charter in 1946, he was Secretary General of UNCTAD in 1964. He was one of the founders of the dependence school and a leading proponent of the view of development as a problem between (dominant) North and (dependent) South.

See also

Frank.

Works include

The Economic Development of Latin America and its Principal Problems, New York, United Nations, 1950.

Ayn Rand   1905–1982

Ayn Rand, born into a Jewish family in St Petersburg, Russia, is famous for novels and essays that unabashedly endorse selfishness and condemn altruism. Rand moved to the United States when she was twenty-one, and, fascinated by the United States as it was depicted in the silent Hollywood films, settled in Los Angeles. Weeks later, in 1926, she turned a chance meeting with Cecil B. De Mille into a job writing screenplays – her primary source of income for almost a decade. She married Frank O'Connor, an actor, in 1929.

Throughout her life and work Rand extolled the 'virtue of selfishness' (the title of a collection of her non-fiction essays), and stated that her intellectual mission was to provide a moral defence of free enterprise, which she believed was the only economic system that was based on objective reason. Thus she distanced herself from economists who supported unregulated markets on purely utilitarian grounds. A self-proclaimed 'radical for capitalism', she disparaged state as well as private efforts to redistribute wealth.

Rand's fiction and non-fiction celebrate individuals who single-mindedly pursue their self-interest in the face of adversaries who advocate socialism. Her first major critical and popular success was *The Fountainhead*, which was made into a movie in 1949. The protagonist, Howard Roark, is an architect who feels betrayed when government bureaucrats adhere to most of his blueprint for the construction of a public housing project but add a different facade. Rand glorifies Roark's decision to destroy the buildings. *Atlas Shrugged*, her next novel, describes a society in which the 'men of the mind' go on strike. Like other Rand novels, the narrative is marked by characters who Rand herself acknowledged were no more than mouthpieces for philosophical abstractions. The chaos that she depicts as a consequence of the refusal of capitalists and intellectuals to work serves her thesis that most people are parasites who survive only because of the productivity of economic elites. The novel attracted tremendous critical attention (most of it negative) and was a best-seller.

Rand's ideas were brought into the mainstream of American political culture in the 1960s, largely through the efforts of her disciple Nathaniel Branden. In 1958, under the auspices of the Nathaniel Branden Institute, Branden offered a series of lectures on Rand's philosophy, which Rand and Branden decided to name 'objectivism'. Rand's defence of egocentrism was particularly popular among college students, and by 1968 Branden's institute had branches in over eighty cities in the United States. Rand and Branden also coedited *The Objectivist Newsletter* (later *The Objectivist*), which contained essays that criticized the civil rights movement, supported United States actions in Vietnam and advocated what was later dubbed 'supply-side economics' – a policy that gave preferential tax breaks to capitalists at the expense of consumers. 'Objectivist' study groups continue to appear sporadically on college campuses. Rand also exerted influence over the direction of the Libertarian Party, which was guided, in the early 1970s, by Rand devotees.

In 1968 the Objectivist movement splintered after Rand and a core group of her followers had denounced Branden because he had begun an extra-marital relation with one of his students. At the time Branden was also romantically involved with Rand (who was still married to O'Connor). Although the Objectivist movement as such never fully recovered after the rupture, Rand's desire to decrease the involvement of the government in markets was further institutionalized when a Rand protégé, Alan Greenspan, was selected by President Ronald Reagan to chair the board of the United States Federal Reserve in 1987.

Works

The Fountainhead, New York, Bobbs-Merrill, 1943.
Atlas Shrugged, New York, Random House, 1957.
The Virtue of Selfishness, New York, New American Library, 1964.

Other works

Douglas Den Uyl and Douglas Rasmussen (eds.), *The Philosophical Thought of Ayn Rand*, Chicago, University of Illinois Press, 1984.

Mimi Reisel Gladstein, *The Ayn Rand Companion*, West-
port, Conn., and London, Greenwood Press, 1984.
James T. Baker, *Ayn Rand*, Boston, Mass., Twayne, 1987.
Nathaniel Branden, *Judgment Day: my Years with Ayn
Rand*, Boston, Mass., Houghton Mifflin, 1989.

John Rawls   1921–

No single philosophical work of the twentieth
century has had as great an influence on
Anglo-American political philosophy as John
Rawls's *A Theory of Justice*. Rawls was born
in Baltimore, Maryland. After receiving his
Ph.D. in philosophy from Princeton University he taught at Princeton, Cornell and
Harvard Universities. Since 1976 he has held
the John Cowles professorship at Harvard.

When Rawls began writing *A Theory of
Justice* in the 1950s philosophers were busy
lamenting the death of political philosophy.
Other than the emotivist view that morality is
just a matter of opinion, if any systematic political philosophy could claim adherents in the
academy it was utilitarianism, which asserted
the seemingly simple principle 'maximize
social welfare'. Utilitarianism was also
extremely influential outside the academy. It
seemed to provide a straightforward and rigorous method by which public officials could
solve hard political problems: for every policy
alternative, add up the social benefits, subtract
the social costs, and implement the alternative
that maximizes net benefits.

The common intuition that the rights of
individuals should not be sacrificed for the
sake of social welfare somehow persisted
alongside the academic ascendancy of utilitarianism. But believers in rights lacked systematic philosophical arguments against the
opposing Benthamite intuition that rights are
nothing more than 'nonsense on stilts'. Rights
advocates also lacked a convincing response
to the enduring Marxist critique of rights as
not nonsense but the common sense of capitalists, confusing the class interests of the
bourgeoisie with the universal interests of
humanity.

Political thinking in the academy has
changed since the 1950s and early 1960s in at
least three significant ways. First, most rights
advocates now embrace part of the Marxist
critique, and defend not only the traditional
list of civil and political liberties but also a
more equal distribution of income, wealth,
education, job opportunities, health care and
other goods essential to secure the welfare and
dignity of the disadvantaged. Second, most
prominent advocates of systematic political
theory are now rights theorists. Utilitarianism
is everywhere on the defensive. Third, grand
political theory is once again alive in the
academy. All three of these changes are
attributable to the influence of *A Theory of
Justice*.

To appreciate the political substance of
Rawls's theory, it is best to begin with the first
and most specific change that Rawls has
wrought: the integration of socialist criticism
into liberal theory. The first principle of Rawlsian justice – the equal liberty principle – gives
priority to securing basic liberal freedoms:
freedom of thought, conscience, speech,
assembly, universal suffrage, freedom from
arbitrary arrest and seizure, the right to hold
public office and personal property. Con-
spicuously absent among the basic liberties
are capitalist market freedoms: to own commercial property, to appropriate what one has
produced, to inherit or to pass on one's possessions. The absence of these freedoms from
the list of basic liberties is no oversight or
inconsistency on Rawls's part. Unlike the parties to Locke's social contract, Rawlsian 'con-
tractors' must choose distributive principles
without knowing their relative wealth or their
social class. Unaware of whether they are capitalists or workers, they will care more about
securing a decent life for themselves and their
children than about protecting the profits of
property owners.

The second principle of Rawlsian justice
has two parts. The first (and most famous)
part – the 'difference principle' – justifies only
those social and economic inequalities that
maximize benefits to the least advantaged citizens. The second part requires 'fair equality

of opportunity' for all, equalizing not only job opportunities but life chances. People with 'similar abilities and skills should have similar life chances ... irrespective of the income class into which they are born'.

Rawlsian justice is a liberalism for the least advantaged, a liberalism that pays a moral tribute to the socialist critique. The difference principle prevents the poor from falling (even into a safety net) so long as it is possible to raise their life prospects higher. Nothing short of securing their highest practicable life prospects will satisfy Rawlsian demands. Similarly, fair equality of opportunities goes far beyond the classical liberal idea of careers open to talents. It also requires compensatory education and limits on economic inequalities so that 'in all sectors of society there should be roughly equal prospects of culture and achievement for everyone similarly motivated and endowed'.

The first principle is the liberal core of Rawls's theory, rejecting equalization at the expense of the basic liberties of any citizen. The second principle is the socialist core of Rawlsian justice, rendering liberal freedoms far more than mere formalities for the disadvantaged. Rawls is, of course, not the first philosopher to suggest a way of narrowing the gap between classical liberalism and socialism. He follows a long line of liberal philosophers – Mill, Sidgwick, Green, Hobhouse, Tawney and Dewey, among others – who defend a politics more explicitly egalitarian than Lockeanism and explicitly more libertarian than Marxism. But Rawls's conception of justice is the most systematic and coherent integration of liberal and socialist ideals.

This integration of liberal and socialist principles explains both the appeal of Rawlsian principles to the left liberals and the criticisms levelled at the theory by more traditional liberals and socialists. Liberals such as Robert Nozick who believe in distribution according to market or individual desert (or both) have criticized Rawls for not counting the freedom to appropriate the fruits of one's own labour as among basic liberties. Socialists who believe capitalist ownership of large-scale enterprises to be a post-feudal form of private government have criticized Rawls for leaving the choice between private and collective ownership of large-scale industry open to empirical argument rather than settling the choice on moral grounds. On the other hand, some so-called 'analytic' or 'rational choice' Marxists have argued that under certain contingencies the abolition of private property in the means of production can be justified from a Rawlsian perspective.

Rawls has also been criticized by 'communitarians' for what they consider his abstract universalism. Thus Michael Walzer argues that 'justice' can be only local, parochial, dependent on the shared conceptions of an historical community. Other communitarian critics of Rawls, such as Michael Sandel, focus not on the explicit politics of *A Theory of Justice* but on its implicit metaphysics. They argue that Rawls's theory rests upon a mistaken and incoherent conception of people as unencumbered by shared, socially given ('constitutive') ends. In his Dewey Lectures and more recent essays Rawls denies that his theory presupposes any distinctive metaphysical conception of the person. As a political, not a metaphysical, theory *A Theory of Justice* aims to achieve an overlapping consensus among citizens of a pluralistic democracy who will inevitably differ in their religious commitments and metaphysical conceptions (unless a repressive state forces them to conform).

The communitarian critics point to the Rawlsian idea of the 'original position' as evidence of his metaphysical conception of the person. The 'original position' is a hypothetical situation in which a 'veil of ignorance' deprives us of knowledge of our natural talents, moral views and place in the social order so that we can rationally choose principles of justice that are not biased in our own favour. Not knowing your own religion, you will choose a principle of religious toleration to govern society. Not knowing your social class, you will choose principles that guarantee fair equality of opportunity and maximize your life prospects if you turn out to be among the least advantaged citizens. And so will every other rational person choose these principles, because there is nothing to distinguish us from each other in the original position. There we are all rational choosers. Here (in everyday social life) we are all 'free and equal moral persons', led by our sense of 'justice as fairness' to accept the 'original position' as the fairest way to agree about political principles, to forge a new social contract.

Rawls's revival (and revision) of social contract theory gave rise to the second significant change in political thinking in the academy: the ascendancy of rights theory over utility. Ronald Dworkin, Thomas Nagel, T. M. Scanlon and Bernard Williams, along with other contemporary philosophers, have elaborated the challenge. Although utilitarians and social contract theorists are both committed to equality, their commitments differ dramatically. For utilitarians, treating people as equals means counting each person's interests equally in calculations of social welfare. For social contract theorists, it means securing each person's basic interests against routine calculations of welfare. Philosophers still contend over which understanding is morally correct, but utilitarianism is now on the defensive against Rawls's argument that social contract theory is a better public philosophy for a democratic society governed by a Bill of Rights.

A Theory of Justice offers principles derived from a hypothetical social contract to govern an ideal society. The theory says little about the obligations of citizens or public officials in existing non-ideal societies. But the goal of Rawls's theory 'to guide the course of social reform' has stimulated scholars in many disciplines – law, philosophy, political science, economics, education and medicine, among others – to delve into issues of practical ethics in non-ideal societies. These scholars have broadly influenced public debate on a wide variety of controversial issues, among them affirmative action for minorities and women, the legalization of abortion, the distribution of health care and education, the prevention of international famines, conscientious objection, civil disobedience, nuclear deterrence and foreign aid.

All this being said, it has become clear that the original project of A Theory of Justice was beset by philosophical and political problems. Philosophically, the Kantian conception of moral personality informing the parties in the original position may be seen as challenging Rawls's claim that his theory was independent of metaphysical doctrines. The most crucial political problem is whether expectation of an overall agreement on the two principles of justice is really feasible. In his later work, Rawls has addressed both problems.

In responding to the philosophical issue, Rawls redefined his arguments as political views derived from the political culture of a democratic society. This political culture already possesses a fund of shared beliefs and intuitive ideas which can be articulated into a coherent conception of justice. Rawls now sees the idea of the person as a moral agent, and the idea of society as a public system of fair co-operation, as the two intuitive ideas that serve as foundations of his contract. This political grounding, as Rawls has rightly argued, was present in A Theory of Justice, but was not explicit. By placing his theory squarely within the political culture of the United States, Rawls has brought those grounds to the surface and sought to distance justice as fairness somewhat from the more metaphysical (in 'Justice as fairness: political not metaphysical') Kantian tradition.

In Political Liberalism (1993), Rawls addresses the political issue. There he puts forward the idea of an overlapping consensus as another expression of the political character of his project, and as proof that it is feasible. Rawls argues that the intuitive ideas underlying his principles of justice are strictly political, which means that they are independent of comprehensive philosophical or religious doctrines. By locating themselves on political grounds, Rawls suggests that exponents of all reasonable comprehensive doctrines in a democratic society would be able to agree on a political conception of justice, a goal that would not be possible if each were to insist on using its metaphysical grounds as the foundations of a public agreement on justice. As Rawls sees it, a public endorsement of metaphysical grounds is not possible, given the fact of pluralism and the presence of incommensurable visions of the human good in modern liberal societies. This means that comprehensive doctrines should be excluded from public deliberations on justice. Rawls has gone further and claimed that those doctrines are central in the private identity of citizens, but not in the public sphere which is the arena where political goals are articulated.

In *Political Liberalism*, Rawls has modified some of his previous arguments, but he believes that the core of his conception of justice remains intact. Actually, Rawlsian political liberalism can now be seen as a theoretical enterprise that seeks to offer a smooth transition from the original position to the concrete context of democratic politics. This transition has shifted the attention of his philosophy from the principles of justice to reasons that citizens might have to support them.

Rawlsian liberalism has thus proven to be a resilient theoretical paradigm. Yet, there is a problem that Rawls might have to address in any future redefinition of his arguments. In the original version, Rawls suggested that, once the principle of equal liberties was in operation, the standard of legitimacy for a well-ordered society was the maximization of the long-term expectations of the most disadvantaged. However, in *Political Liberalism*, Rawls seems to have dropped this standard in favour of what he calls a social minimum. This is an important modification, for a social minimum presumably would not be able to maximize the long-term expectations of the least advantaged members of society and, accordingly, it would not comply with Rawls's

own standard of legitimacy. This is a political problem that introduces an important element of uncertainty into his otherwise compelling defence of justice as fairness.

Still, *A Theory of Justice* is a triumph within the tradition of grand political theory, which it helped revitalize within the academy. The triumph rests on more than the philosophical richness, originality and wisdom that Rawls's work manifests to a degree not seen since John Stuart Mill. It rests on more than its influence in renewing philosophical defences of human rights. Rawls's most distinctive contribution to the tradition of grand theory is his defence of a method of justification which he calls 'reflective equilibrium'.

Grand theorists as different as Plato, Hobbes and John Stuart Mill wrote as if their conceptions of justice were justified for all people at all times. They searched for a set of eternal forms, a self-evident truth or a very simple first principle from which to derive all practical moral imperatives. In defending the method of 'reflective equilibrium', Rawls is the most modest – and in this respect wisest – of the grand philosophers. He argues that we have no better way of justifying principles that meet the minimum standards of moral reason (logical consistency, generality and so on) than by translating the principles into social practices and judging whether the practices are consistent with our moral convictions. If a practice derived from the principles conflicts with a conviction, then we must either reformulate the principle or change our conviction. To decide which course to take, we must use our practical judgement to weigh a variety of considerations (the firmness and consistency of our convictions, the certainty of the principles and evidence underlying the practice, and so on). When philosophers sidestep this process of approaching reflective equilibrium they act on faith rather than reason.

Most philosophers today accept some version of Rawls's method of 'reflective equilibrium'. The method challenges every critic of Rawls to offer constructive revisions of justice as fairness, to defend another systematic political theory whose premises and conclusions are intuitively more compelling, or to justify something other than a systematic political theory (such as a plurality of principles refined and balanced by our practical judgement of particular cases). This is a formidable but fair challenge. An extraordinary number of philosophers, political scientists, economists and constitutional lawyers have accepted it and together with Rawls have influenced the political thinking of our time.

See also

Dewey, Hobhouse, MacIntyre, Nozick, Sandel, Tawney, Taylor, Walzer.

Works

A Theory of Justice, Cambridge, Mass., Harvard University Press, 1971.
'Kantian Constructivism in moral theory: the Dewey Lectures, 1980', *Journal of Philosophy* 77 (September 1980), pp. 515–72.
'Justice as fairness: political not metaphysical', *Philosophy and Public Affairs* 14 (Summer 1985), pp. 223–51.
Political Liberalism, New York, Columbia University Press, 1993.

Other works

Norman Daniels (ed.), *Reading Rawls: Critical Studies of a Theory of Justice*, New York, Basic Books, 1975.
Amy Gutmann, *Liberal Equality*, New York, Cambridge University Press, 1980.
Michael Sandel, *Liberalism and the Limits of Justice*, New York, Cambridge University Press, 1982.
Armartya Sen and Bernard Williams, *Utilitarianism and Beyond*, Cambridge, Cambridge University Press, 1982.

Wilhelm Reich   1897–1957

Wilhelm Reich's doomed and spectacular career is unique in the annals of the twentieth century. Psychoanalyst, communist, exile, founder of an *outré* therapeutic movement based on a kind of bio-cosmology, and finally victim of state repression during the Eisenhower administration – the one certainty about Reich is his utter originality, indeed, uniqueness. This is not the place to pass judgement on the bio-cosmological orgone theory for which he is best known and too facilely dismissed. The political content of his life and work bears examination on its own.

Reich's hectic life may be understood as the unfolding of an uncompromising radicalism of messianic proportions. As a youth he was drawn into radical left politics, which he first pursued in the heated atmosphere of post-First World War Germany and Austria. Turning to the study of medicine, he soon encountered psychoanalysis, embraced it, and moved rapidly up the psychoanalytic hierarchy. He achieved an early reputation for important studies in character formation and analytical technique. In those years Freud's discoveries had not yet become a psychology of adjustment, and Reich was able to seize upon certain emancipatory potentials in psychoanalysis and drive them to their extreme.

At issue was the role of sexuality in the neuroses. Freud had always held it to be central, yet a crucial distinction remained to be drawn between actual sexual gratification on the one hand and, on the other, the role of sexual fantasy. Freud and the main body of the psychoanalytic movement argued for a major causative influence of fantasy as such. Reich rejected this from the start: fantasy was only epiphenomenal, and real sexual gratification, embodied in complete orgastic release, was the key to the neuroses, both for understanding and for cure. Indeed, there is no exaggeration in the claim that orgasm became a kind of *summun bonum* for Reich.

From this position there is a more or less straight line to the later orgone theories. But there was also an influential and remarkably consistent set of political interventions. Since real gratification was crucial, real conditions had to be provided for gratification. This led Reich to develop, more or less singlehanded, a politics of sexual liberation and, upon its basis, a politics of the family and of everyday life consistent with sexual liberation. It also gave his interpretation of psychoanalysis a thoroughly materialistic character which became suitable for a synthesis with Marxism.

Reich pursued these goals as a member of the German Communist Party. He travelled to the Soviet Union, developed a series of 'Sex–Pol' clinics wherein working-class youth could find counselling for their sexual needs and produced the first synthesis of Marx with Freud. In his Marx–Freud project Reich emphasized the importance of material yet non-economic conditions for social transformation. His studies of sexuality, character formation and the family culminated in a critique of economism and, especially in *The Mass Psychology of Fascism*, the warning that the irrational and mystical appeal of Hitler would win the repressed German masses over.

The radicalism of Reich's views led to the remarkable distinction of expulsion, in 1934, from both the Communist Party and the International Psychoanalytic Association. This set in motion the chain of events leading to his establishment of the orgone therapy movement in the United States – and in his eventual persecution, which culminated in imprisonment and the burning of his books.

In these later years Reich became mentally disturbed (with grandiose delusions and identification with Jesus Christ), and right-wing (for example, he admired Eisenhower, whom he considered a 'genital character'). Yet in certain respects the influence of his final phase has been greater than that of all the others. Especially since his death in prison, he has been appropriated by anarcho-libertarians as a martyr of the radical spirit. He has also remained influential as a philosopher of nature. Despite his delusions, and though manifestly apolitical, Reich continued with a powerful critique of domination and the state. He also emphasized collective and decentralized production – what he termed 'work-democracy' – as well as a thorough transformation of everyday life and child-rearing to create healthy characters for a future revolutionary society. Finally, Reich anticipated many of the 'holistic' and ecological tendencies which have come to the fore in recent years in the context of the environmental crisis. Ultimately his life's work focused on an increasingly unmediated relationship with nature – so much so that, for all his identification with the spirit of science, he would have to be finally grouped (in so far as such a character could be grouped at all) among religious and utopian thinkers.

See also

Freud.

Works

The Mass Psychology of Fascism, New York, Simon & Schuster, 1970.
Lee Baxandall (ed.), *Sex-Pol Essays; 1929–34*, New York, Random House, 1972.

Other works

Myron Sharaf, *Fury on Earth*, New York, St Martin's Press, 1983.
Joel Kovel, 'Why Freud or Reich?', in *The Radical Spirit*, London, Free Association Books, 1988.

Karl Renner   1870–1950

Born in Unter-Tannowitz, Austria, he was an Austro-Marxist, responsible for the pioneering Marxist study of law. He was Bauer's opponent in the Social Democratic Party as a leader of the more right-wing reformists. He was the first Chancellor of the Austrian Republic in 1918 and again of the Second Republic in 1945. His theory of the state remains important, since he was one of the first to emphasize the need for Marxist theory to deal with the reality of state intervention in the economy and to raise the question of the role of the new middle class.

See also

Hilferding.

Works include

Der Kampf der Österreichischen Nationen um der Staat, Vienna, Deuticke, 1902.

The Institutions of Social Law and their Social Functions,
London, Routledge, 1949.

John E. Roemer   1945–

Roemer is the leading theorist of the late twentieth-century revisionist school of 'analytical Marxism'. Taking off from the rational-choice methodology of Rawls, he argues that the working class can be considered exploited in capitalist society if, and only if, within existing resource constraints, its members would be contingently better-off under a feasible alternative (e.g. socialist) organization of the means of production. Concomitantly, most of the specifically political analyses of analytical Marxists have to do with explicating the short-run (or even medium-run) rationality that has led organized workers in capitalist societies to eschew revolutionary goals.

See also

Rawls.

Works include

Analytical Foundations of Marxian Economic Theory, New York, Cambridge University Press, 1981.
A General Theory of Exploitation and Class, Cambridge, Mass., Harvard University Press, 1982.
(ed.) *Analytical Marxism*, Cambridge, Cambridge University Press, 1986.

Richard Rorty   1931–

Richard Rorty's reputation initially was not as a political thinker. It was established by the book *Philosophy and the Mirror of Nature* (1980), a work whose major concern was with themes in Anglo-American analytical philosophy, especially philosophy of language and philosophy of mind. Offering a subtle and wide-ranging critique of these that chimed in with the growing fashion now generally known as postmodernism, Rorty went on in subsequent writings to deploy some of the central elements of that critique in support of a distinctive liberalism: at once flexible and open, rich in its literary sources, and genial in tone.

Rorty's attachment is to a liberalism which he characterizes as 'bourgeois', and used to describe, before 1989, as 'cold war'. However, his outlook is more radical than this might suggest. He is indeed sceptical that there could now be any future for Marxism as a political project, and by his own admission he has given up on socialism. The nature and the fate of the regimes presided over by what he has called Marxist 'thugs' have settled that question for him. At the same time, Rorty acknowledges the values held in common between his own brand of pragmatist liberalism – or, as he sometimes refers to it also, social democracy – and more authentic traditions of Marxist radicalism. He sees these two engagements as part of a shared, humanist and pro-Enlightenment, conversation, a conversation he urges his readers not to give up on. (In this and one or two other respects he also has reservations, therefore, about some of the leanings of postmodernist thinkers.) If Rorty expresses himself more warmly towards what America represents than is standard amongst leftists and radicals, still, so does he speak severely about the rapaciousness of the wealthy and the governments tending their interests, in the light cast upon them by Third-World, and for that matter First-World, poverty and loss of hope.

In *Philosophy and the Mirror of Nature* and *Consequences of Pragmatism*, Rorty challenged the model of truth and belief as a relation between humans and objects: a relation of correspondence or mirroring in which the subject aims for an accurate picture of reality, the thing just as it is, objectively, 'out there'. Opposing a long epistemological tradition, he suggested we should think instead of truth and belief as a matter of agreement within communities, of conversation with one's peers – of a pragmatic concern with what works for us, enabling us to cope within our sets of social and material practices. A certain paradox emerges from these themes when they are extended to moral and political deliberation. For, on the one hand, they would appear to license inferences of a plainly anti-democratic sort, as Rorty for his part pointed out. Which people are entitled to moral consideration, to having their suffering cared about, to the very status of personhood itself, can now be seen as a question of who counts as being a member of our community, 'one of us'. On the other hand, Rorty was happy to trade on the circumstance that, for the particular 'us' to which he belongs, this issue has come, by historical accident, to be settled in a more or less humanist way, egalitarian and cosmopolitan in tendency. There is no more justification of our moral beliefs and practices than that. No non-circular defence of them is available. Human solidarity is good, according to Rorty, and bourgeois liberalism the best version of it to date, but this is not because it accords with anything beyond itself, with God or truth or human nature; it is only by virtue of beliefs and practices internal to the liberal tradition itself.

In *Contingency, Irony, and Solidarity* (1989) and two collections of essays published shortly after it, in his Amnesty lecture on human rights, and in sundry other pieces since, Rorty has gone on to reaffirm and enlarge upon this viewpoint, always in engaging and provocative style; proffering fresh material for reflection, chiding, humouring, surprising – be this with the imagination and skill of a persuasive connection or with the deft footwork of an intellectual evasion.

Liberalism for him has come to centre on the thought that cruelty is the worst thing we do; to privilege sensitivity to the pains of others, the specifically human sort of pain which is humiliation amongst them; to emphasize the search for happiness, comfort and tolerance, but as a piecemeal, reformist project, not some grand scheme of human 'emancipation'. This project is, again, grounded on nothing but the beliefs and sentiments nurtured by the tradition Rorty favours. It does not correspond to our human

nature, for we have none: we are what we are made by our culture and society, or what we make of ourselves within and against them. Democracy is about a plurality of discourses attempting in their own ways to cope, and with room both for public ones about justice and for private ones about self-creation. It is about discursive freedom. Human rights and solidarity are about extending outwards the sense of sympathy and community, the scope of the notion of 'one of us'. Progress, likewise, is about education of the sentiments in this direction, an education in which, precisely, sentimental discourses – the story, the novel – are as important as any more narrowly logical. The search for a deeper or more permanent, a rational, foundation from which to press for these values is misplaced.

Rorty's work is rich not only in the irony he actively commends but also in paradoxes and contradictions by which he seems not to be embarrassed. In one passage after another he denies there is any common human nature; and in one passage after another he relies on there being exactly that, appealing as he does over and again to characteristically and generically human traits, whether ways of suffering, or language, or the poetic imagination. Relativism is renounced by Rorty in one voice when he tells us that not all beliefs are equally good, since *our* beliefs (those of liberals, in a broad sense) are better. Relativism is restored by him in another voice when he tells us that there are no non-circular justifications for thinking this, and that *anything* may be made to look good by being redescribed. He urges that pragmatist, anti-foundationalist views are especially apt to supporting liberalism; and also that pragmatist, anti-foundationalist views could equally support any political standpoint whatsoever.

Rorty's work is good to think about. Good to argue with. Good to read.

See also

Rawls, Sandel.

Works

Philosophy and the Mirror of Nature, Oxford, Basil Blackwell, 1980.
Consequences of Pragmatism, New York and London, Harvester Wheatsheaf, 1982.
Contingency, Irony, and Solidarity, Cambridge, Cambridge University Press, 1989.
Essays on Heidegger and others, Cambridge, Cambridge University Press, 1991.
Objectivity, Relativism, and Truth, Cambridge, Cambridge University Press, 1991.
'Thugs and theorists', *Political Theory* 15 (1987), pp. 564–80.
'Human rights, rationality, and sentimentality', in *On Human Rights: the Oxford Amnesty Lectures 1993*, ed. Stephen Shute and Susan Hurley, New York, Harper-Collins 1993, pp. 111–34.

Other works

Terry Eagleton, 'Defending the free world', in *Socialist Register 1990*, ed. Ralph Miliband and Leo Panitch, London, Merlin Press, 1990, pp. 85–94.
Alan Malachowski (ed.), *Reading Rorty*, Oxford, Basil Blackwell, 1990.
Richard J. Bernstein, *The New Constellation*, Cambridge, Mass., MIT Press, 1992, chapters 8 and 9.
David L. Hall, *Richard Rorty: Prophet and Poet of the New Pragmatism*, Albany, SUNY Press, 1994.
Norman Geras, *Solidarity in the Conversation of Humankind: the Ungroundable Liberalism of Richard Rorty*, London, Verso, 1995.
Norman Geras, 'Progress without foundations?', *Res Publica* 2 (1996), pp. 115–28.

Sheila Rowbotham   1943–

Sheila Rowbotham is a feminist, socialist and historian whose writings represent an important strand in British radical politics. Part of the generation whose political ideas were formed by the New Left, she studied history at St Hilda's, Oxford, and subsequently became involved in left-wing politics in London: she joined the Labour Party Young Socialists and, for a brief period, International Socialism (now the Socialist Workers' Party), and she was on the editorial board of *Black Dwarf*. She has been active in the women's movement since its origins in the 1960s, and has drawn on her experiences to advocate a participatory, decentralized approach to social change that links the needs and struggles of all oppressed groups. A pro-

lific freelance writer, she has also taught in a wide variety of institutions, and in the 1980s she worked for the Popular Planning Unit of the Greater London Council until it was abolished by the Conservative government in 1986.

Her best-known historical writings, *Women, Resistance and Revolution* and *Hidden from History* were pioneering works that sought to rediscover women's history and have since generated whole new fields of study. Her interest was inspired by her own involvement with the contemporary women's movement, and her aim was to reclaim the past for women as a source of knowledge and strength that could contribute to the present struggle. This theme was continued in *The Past is before Us*, which charts the multifarious strands of the women's movement and suggests that our understanding of the past can point the way to the future. As a Marxist, she sees the struggle for women's liberation as essentially bound up with the struggle against capitalism; her histories document the complex relationships between class exploitation and women's oppression, and argue that movements to end them can succeed only when the struggles are combined.

In *Women's Consciousness, Man's World* she drew on personal experience as well as more formal academic studies to examine the situation of modern women and the possibilities of change. This kind of method was then unusual but has since been widely emulated; it embodies a central tenet of modern feminism by integrating personal and at first sight trivial concerns with wider political and theoretical issues. The writings collected in *Dreams and Dilemmas* continue this approach.

Beyond the Fragments (with Lynne Segal and Hilary Wainwright) excited much discussion in left-wing circles by challenging the organizational assumptions of Leninism. It used the experiences of the women's movement and other radical groupings to attack hierarchy and authoritarianism and to argue in favour of an open, democratic and libertarian socialist movement and a wider conception of political struggle.

All Rowbotham's writings are infused with a sense of deep commitment to the twin goals of socialism and feminism. As teacher, chronicler, participant and theorist of left-wing politics her ideas have had a significant impact both on academic study and on radical political movements.

Works

Women, Resistance and Revolution, Harmondsworth, Penguin, 1972.
Women's Consciousness, Man's World, Harmondsworth, Penguin, 1973.
Hidden from History, London, Pluto Press, 1973.
Beyond the Fragments (with Lynne Segal and Hilary Wainwright), London, Merlin Press, 1979.
Dreams and Dilemmas, London, Virago, 1983.
The Past is before Us: Feminism in Action since the 1960s, London, Pandora, 1989.
A Century of Women, London, Penguin, 1997.

Manabendra Nath Roy
1887–1954

Born into a priestly family in Bengal, M. N. Roy, whose real name was Narendra Nath Bhattacharya, became a militant nationalist at an early age. He was arrested in 1907, 1909 and 1910 for terrorism but released on each occasion for lack of evidence. In 1915 he left for Japan and China in search of arms and support and, travelling under various names and disguises, reached Mexico, where he founded the Communist Party. At Lenin's invitation he left for Moscow, stopping on the way in Berlin, where he had long discussions with Bernstein, Kautsky and Hilferding. In the Soviet Union Roy emerged as a major Marxist theorist on Asia and helped Lenin formulate a clear policy on the colonial question. He rapidly rose to the highest positions in the Comintern, but his views on China and post-Lenin developments in the Soviet Union angered Stalin. Fearing for his life, he quietly flew out to India with Bukharin's help, only to find himself arrested and imprisoned for six long years.

During his incarceration he reflected deeply on the reasons why Marxism had degenerated into Stalinism. He blamed Marx's historicism and collectivism, and traced them to his mechanistic and somewhat crude theory of historical materialism. Roy produced over 3,000 pages of still not fully published 'Prison manuscripts'. Selected poems were later published in such works as Fascism (1938), The Historical Role of Islam (1939), Materialism (1940) and Science and Philosophy (1947).

Roy's search for a 'new political theory' combining the central insights of liberalism and Marxism and, at a different level, of idealism and materialism led him further and further away from Marxism and towards what he called 'radical humanism'. In Beyond Communism to Humanism (1946) and Reason, Romanticism and Revolution (1952) Marxism was reduced to little more than a passionate concern for social justice and recognition of the limiting but not causally determining role of economic forces. Like J. P. Narayan he attacked both the atomic individualism and the centralized state characteristic of modern liberal democracy, advocating 'organized', 'radical' or 'co-operative' democracy. Radical democracy, a logical entailment of radical humanism, implied a loosely structured polity of self-governing local units, enjoying the power to recall their representatives and to initiate and comment on legislation at the regional and national levels. It was paralleled by a co-operative economy that was neither capitalist nor state-owned and permitted different forms of joint ownership.

Roy was convinced that such a society could not be brought about and sustained without cultural revolution involving the development of such basic human capacities as rationality, love of freedom, equality and co-operation among the masses. He did not think much of the centralized and state-oriented political parties, and stressed the catalytic role of a small band of nationally spread out 'radical democrats' uninterested in political power and acting as 'guides, friends and philosophers of the people'.

217

Following his own advice, Roy disbanded in 1948 the Radical Democratic Party he had set up in 1941, concentrating all his energies on the newly established Indian Renaissance Institute. It became an intellectual think-tank, held summer schools, produced critical philosophical literature and trained talented men from different walks of life who went on to set up Renaissance clubs in several parts of the country. Lacking a clear programme of action, and being heavily dependent on individuals, the clubs achieved little and Roy's own institute decayed after his death. In moving successively from militant nationalism to Marxism, qualified Marxism and eventually to Enlightenment liberalism Roy summed up the intellectual journey of many an Indian Marxist intellectual.

See also

Bernstein, Bukharin, Hilferding, Kautsky, Lenin, Narayan, Stalin.

Works

Materialism, Calcutta, Renaissance, 1951.
Reason, Romanticism, and Revolution, Calcutta, Renaissance, 1952.
Politics, Power, and Parties, Calcutta, Renaissance, 1960.
New Humanism, Calcutta, Renaissance, 1961.

Other works

S. Ray (ed.), *M. N. Roy: a Symposium*, Calcutta, Renaissance, 1959.
Gouriswar P. Bhattacharya, *Evolution of the Political Philosophy of M. N. Roy*, Calcutta, Minerva, 1971.
D. C. Glover, *M. N. Roy: a Study of Revolution in Indian Politics*, Calcutta, Minerva, 1973.

Bertrand Russell   1872–1970

Bertrand Russell insisted that he was not a political philosopher. Responding to his critics at the end of *The Philosophy of Bertrand Russell*, he said that he had written on ethics, politics and religion not 'as a philosopher' but as a human being appalled by the misery and pain of his fellow human beings. There was an element of exaggeration in this, but it is true that he was not a systematic political theorist in the fashion of Hobbes or of his godfather, John Stuart Mill. After an early flirtation with the idealist philosophy of McTaggart, and the ethical intuitionism of G. E. Moore's *Principia Ethica*, Russell adopted what he described as a 'subjectivist' view of ethics and politics, according to which ethical and political judgements express and influence emotional attitudes but cannot be appraised for truth and falsity. Since philosophy was, for him, a matter above all else of assessing our beliefs for their truth, it followed that, once philosophy had given an account of the logic of moral and political judgement, there was no further relationship between philosophy and morals or philosophy and politics.

Russell was politically active at many times in his life. He was roused to speak against Joseph Chamberlain's imperialism and on behalf of free trade in 1904; he stood for Parliament in 1907 as a suffragist Liberal, and again as a Labour candidate in 1923 and 1924 – though always in seats he could not win. He was one of the leaders of the No Conscription Fellowship during the First World War, and president of the Campaign for Nuclear Disarmament in the 1950s. He was jailed in 1918 and 1961, the first time for 'insulting an ally' when he remarked that an American army in Europe would doubtless be used for putting down strikes as it had been at home, the second time for inciting civil disobedience in protest against British atomic weapon tests. When he died in 1970 he was still battling against the American war in Vietnam, and protesting against all forms of colonialism, whether exhibited in Vietnam by the United States or in Czechoslovakia by the Soviet Union. It is this angry old man that most people think of when they think of Russell.

None the less, Russell had a systematic vision of the nature of politics, and the role of politics in securing the good life for as many people as possible. It is spelled out in *The Principles of Social Reconstruction*, a book of lectures he delivered during the First World War, at a time when he was fiercely opposed to the war itself, to the foreign policy that had produced it, and to the measures of conscription to which it had led. There Russell founds politics on two opposing forms of human impulse, the possessive and the creative; possessive impulses are those desires whose satisfaction excludes others – success in competition, the glory of coming first, ownership of individual property, for instance – while creative impulses are those which can be satisfied for one person without loss to anyone else – such as writing a poem, or discovering a mathematical theorem.

Russell thought that societies which fostered possessiveness were evil in themselves and doomed to fight one another; 'social reconstruction' would promote creativeness and diminish possessiveness. In practice, this meant a commitment to a form of guild socialism, an emphasis on progressive education, and something close to pacifism. Though Russell often seemed to lose interest in politics, his underlying convictions did not alter. *The Practice and Theory of Bolshevism* was perhaps the first expression of a Western radical's disillusionment with the Soviet Union; the authoritarianism and brutality of Lenin and Trotsky's rule, and the dictatorial regime they had established, were a bad joke against the sort of socialism he had envisaged. When it was reprinted in 1947 he was happy to say that his views had never changed, and that he detested Stalin as much as he had loathed Hitler.

Russell's picture of social improvement concentrated on private social relations as much as on large issues of war and peace. *Marriage and Morals* won him the Nobel Prize for literature; it caused tremendous offence when it appeared in 1929 but now seems a very moderate defence of extramarital sex and companionate marriage. *On Education* still seems utopian in its hopes of what education might achieve but mild in its proposals for reform – more good nursery schools, secondary schooling for all,

independent of family income or wealth, unfussed sex education and no political censorship of syllabuses. What lifts these works out of the rut of everyday commentary is less their philosophical distinction than Russell's passion and his extraordinary literary skill.

He will be remembered longest for the way he linked the pursuit of world peace with this search for private happiness. The essays of the 1950s and 1960s on the nuclear threat reiterate the simple message that humanity must throw off religious and ideological blinkers to see that nothing is worth the destruction of human life. People with a proper concern for their own happiness would not allow themselves to be dragged down the path of mutual destruction, and the search for peace is one with the search for an unsuperstitious concern for individual happiness. Russell often said that he was a child of the eighteenth century rather than the twentieth, and at least in this Voltairean view of the sheer pointlessness of great-power politics he was.

Works

Principles of Social Reconstruction, London, Allen & Unwin, 1916.
The Practice and Theory of Bolshevism, New York, Harcourt Brace, 1920.
Marriage and Morals, New York, Liverwright, 1929.
On Education, London, Allen & Unwin, 1932.
Autobiography, Boston, Mass., Little Brown, 1967.

Other works

A. Schlipp, The Philosophy of Bertrand Russell, New York, Harper & Row, 1963.
Ronald W. Clark, The Life of Bertrand Russell, New York, Knopf, 1976.
Alan Ryan, Bertrand Russell: a Political Life, New York, Hill & Wang, 1988.

Michael Sandel   1953–

American political theorist, author of *Liberalism and the Limits of Justice*. A leading communitarian critic of liberalism, he argues that liberal political philosophy justifies an individualism radically unembedded in concrete social institutions, and wrongly gives priority to the pursuit of abstract equal justice over a communal, moral good. In *Democracy's Discontent* he extends this argument to claim that the alleged desuetude of democratic politics in the late-twentieth-century United States is due to this misguided ordering of priorities. Commentators have pointed out that this communitarian argument tends to confuse a supposed lack of embeddedness and, concomitantly, social morality with the American actuality of liberal pluralism. The latter, they note, neither posits nor is built around 'unembedded' persons but instead recognizes multiple and often conflicting versions of social embeddedness in each person; rather than being amoral, it calls for equal, mutual tolerance as the moral glue binding the social order. Whether such a democracy can 'long endure' is perhaps the real question that Sandel raises.

See also

MacIntyre, Rawls, Taylor, Walzer.

Works include

Liberalism and the Limits of Justice, Cambridge, Cambridge University Press, 1982.
Democracy's Discontent: America in Search of a Public Philosophy, Cambridge, Mass., Harvard University Press, 1996.

Jean-Paul Sartre   1905–1980

Born into a prominent Parisian bourgeois family, Sartre became at an early age a strong critic of his class. Throughout his life he supported many causes on the left, and as a consciously committed intellectual he exercised an enormous impact on public events, often to the extreme dislike of the establishment. Voicing the interests of the latter, *Paris-Match* once carried an editorial with the title 'Sartre, civil war machine'. In a similar vein in 1964, on the occasion when Sartre was awarded the Nobel Prize, even the Christian existentialist Gabriel Marcel denounced him as the 'grave-digger of the West', in tune with the Vatican's special decree which a few years earlier had placed the whole of Sartre's work on the Index.

A graduate of the pinnacle of French Academic institutions, the Ecole Normale Supérieure, Sartre taught philosophy in the 1930s. The first of his works to receive great critical acclaim was the philosophical novel *Nausea* (1938). In it Sartre painted with resignation and 'Melancholia' (the original title) the dilemmas of individual existence and the triumph of reification and alienation, paying very little attention to the social and political dimension of the problems identified. All his early philosophical writings – from *The Transcendence of the Ego* (1936) and *Sketch for a Theory of the Emotions* (1939) to *The Imaginary* (1940), constituting a major but never completed project on philosophical psychology – were in the same mould.

The war brought a significant change in this respect, in that Sartre became the champion of a politically activist version of existentialism. He advocated a 'philosophy of freedom', in order to be able to insist on every individual's 'total responsibility'. The inescapability of freedom, depicted as arising from the 'ontological structure' of existence, was the main theme of his monumental philosophical work, *Being and Nothingness* (1943), complemented by the investigation of the countless ways in which (through 'bad faith', etc.) people tried to escape in the historically given world from their freedom, because of the heavy burden of responsibility which it imposed upon them. This concern with freedom and its dilemmas remained Sartre's central preoccupation to the end of his life, even if his terms of reference changed significantly as time went by. Thus, whereas his early formulations tended to be rather abstract, later he directly related his fundamental concern to tangible social and political demands and constraints, insisting that 'no one is free unless everybody is free; freedom is conditioned –

not metaphysically but practically – by protein'.

The Sartrean conception of freedom and 'authenticity' predicated the necessity for the individual to remain free from institutional determinations and compromises, even in the midst of the most intense social and political commitment, which Sartre advocated. For this reason, in order to avoid his own institutionalization, Sartre rejected all official honours, from membership of the Académie Française and the Collège de France to the Légion d'Honneur and even the Nobel Prize. Nevertheless, he could command the attention and the respect even of President de Gaulle.

Sartre's ideal of political organization was the RDR (Rassemblement Démocratique Révolutionnaire), a short-lived grouping with which he was associated for a while after the war. The RDR tried to appeal directly to the consciousness of individuals, cutting across all their other allegiances. When in 1968 Sartre assumed an active role in one of the Maoist groups he tried to define its political organization in the same spirit, arguing that 'the militants of La Cause du Peuple do not constitute a party. It is a political group [rassemblement] which can always be dissolved. This procedure allows a way out of the rigidity in which the Communist Party has imprisoned itself.'

At the outbreak of the Cold War Sartre's political activity greatly intensified. He voiced his fear of total nuclear annihilation in the most dramatic terms, arguing that 'In order to prevent the world from following its own course, they threaten the suppression of history through the liquidation of the historical agent' ('La bombe H'). He became a prominent figure in the world peace movement, writing articles and making numerous speeches on the subject of world peace. At the same time he advocated the establishment of a new Popular Front as the guarantor of peace on the plane of internal politics.

For the same reason he looked for a good working relationship with the French Communist Party, convinced that its members were the most committed to the defence of peace. Two of his books – The Communists and Peace (1952) and L'Affaire Henri Martin (1953) – bear witness to this. He remained close to the French Communist Party for many years (though never a member), trying to influence its policies. They quarrelled over the Russian repression of the Hungarian uprising in October 1956 (we find a record of this in Sartre's Fantôme de Stalin, 1956–7) and even more over the French Communist Party's role in the Algerian war. However, the complete break came only after May 1968, when he condemned the way in which the party helped to restabilize the established order which was experiencing an extreme crisis.

After May 1968 Sartre supported the beleaguered left groupuscules, taking on the editorship of the Maoist journal La Cause du Peuple, in open defiance of the government, which outlawed it. François Mauriac accused him of a 'thirst for martyrdom' through arrest, which Sartre rebutted by saying that, on the contrary, he wanted to stay out of jail, in order to demonstrate that in the bourgeois order there is a double standard. In the end he proved his point: he was never arrested for defying and breaking the law.

The most prominent feature of Sartre's work from the war years to the end was intense moral and political commitment. He expressed it graphically when he wrote that 'The most beautiful book in the world will not save a child from pain: one does not redeem evil, one fights it. The most beautiful book in the world redeems itself; it also redeems the artist. But not the man. Any more than the man redeems the artist. We want the man and the artist to work out their salvation together, we want the work to be at the same time an act; we want it to be explicitly conceived as a weapon in the struggle that men wage against evil.' (What is Literature?, 1947). The efforts of the literary imagination had to conform to the same demand as the theoretical and directly political works. Thus Sartre's plays – among them the most powerful: In Camera

221

(*Huis clos*, 1943), *The Respectful Prostitute* (1946), *Dirty Hands* (1948), *Lucifer and the Lord* (1951) and *Altona* (1960) – were written in the service of this ideal, as was his novel cycle, *Roads to Freedom* (1945–9). The latter was abandoned, after three volumes, when Sartre became convinced that the complexities and 'ambiguities' of fighting evil in the post-war world could not be expressed adequately within the framework of an enterprise depicting the 'black or white' war experience.

Sartre never thought that combining politics with morality could be an easy matter. He summed up his views on it in an extremely paradoxical form: 'There is a morality of politics – a difficult subject, and never clearly treated – and when politics must betray its morality, to choose morality is to betray politics. Now find your way out of that one! Particularly when the politics has taken as its goal bringing about the reign of the human' ('Merleau-Ponty', 1961). In his attempt to sort out these problems he tried to combine his own brand of activist existentialism with Marxism. Some of the most representative essays belonging to this phase of development were included in *Between Existentialism and Marxism*. And the most important theoretical writing of the same period, the *Critique of Dialectical Reason* (1957–9), attempted to explain the historical process, with all its contradictions and morally and politically frustrating perversions, as ultimately a rational project. The line pursued in this work was to 'make intelligible the singular universal' – through the analysis of the 'formal structures of history' – as the framework in which the 'totalization of individual experience' becomes possible.

Sartre coined the much quoted phrase 'Hell is the other' in his early play, *Huis clos*. It was echoed many years later in his *Critique of Dialectical Reason* when he asserted that 'hell is the practico-inert': that is, the oppressive inertial force of accumulated social practice. However, he could never complete the second volume of the *Critique*, in which he tried to address the paralysing impact of the 'practico-inert' – and the feasibility of a successful struggle against its 'infernal power' – in terms of 'real history', in contrast to theorizing the abstract 'possibilities of combination of the formal structures' the way we find it in the first volume.

Works

In Camera (*Huis clos*), London, Hamish Hamilton, 1946.
The Respectful Prostitute, London, Hamish Hamilton, 1949.
Dirty Hands, London, Hamish Hamilton, 1949.
What is Literature? London, Methuen, 1950.
Lucifer and the Lord, London, Hamish Hamilton, 1952.
'La bombe H, une arme contre l'histoire', *Défense de la Paix* (July 1954).
Being and Nothingness, London, Methuen, 1958.
Altona, London, Hamish Hamilton, 1960.
'Merleau-Ponty', in *Situations*, New York, Braziller, 1965.
The Communists and Peace, London, Hamish Hamilton, 1969.
Between Existentialism and Marxism, London, New Left Books, 1972.
Critique of Dialectical Reason, London, New Left Books, 1976.
Life/Situations Essays Written and Spoken, New York, Pantheon, 1977.
Sartre in the Seventies: Interviews and Political Essays, London, Deutsch, 1978.

Other works

Maurice Merleau-Ponty, 'Sartre and ultrabolshevism', in *Adventures of the Dialectic*, London, Heinemann, 1973.
Raymond Aron, *History and the Dialectic of Violence*, Oxford, Blackwell, 1975.
Pietro Chiodi, *Sartre and Marxism*, Hassocks, Harvester, 1976.
István Mészáros, *The Work of Sartre: Search for Freedom*, Brighton, Harvester, 1979.
Ronald Aronson, *Jean-Paul Sartre: Philosophy in the World*, London, New Left Books, 1980.
Simone de Beauvoir, *Adieux: a Farewell to Sartre*, London, Deutsch and Weidenfeld & Nicolson, 1984.

Carl Schmitt 1888–1985

Among the most brilliant, prolific and influential German political and legal theorists of this century, Schmitt remains the most controversial. Born into a devout Catholic family in Plettenberg, he received his law degree from the University of Strasbourg in 1910, and held professorships of law at Bonn and Berlin. Through thirty books and countless articles over a sixty-year period he addressed the problems of four distinct political systems, from the monarchy to the Federal Republic. While his Catholic heritage and neo-Kantian idealism greatly affected his early writings, the horrors of the First World War and instability of post-war Germany led him to adopt Hobbes's political realism. Among the most widely read and respected Weimar thinkers, he provided original, incisive works on constitutional theory, romanticism, liberalism, sovereignty, dictatorship, the crisis of parliamentary government and on presidential emergency powers under article 48 of the Weimar constitution.

Schmitt's theory of Decisionism emphasized the sovereign state, executive power and *Ausnahmezustand* (exceptional case), and the need to govern and interpret law in the light of political and social realities. He thus challenged the value-neutral and purely legalistic approach of Hans Kelsen's normativist school and Harold Laski's liberal pluralism. His Hobbesian political theory also contested liberal optimism about political and social progress. Man remained a dangerous, dynamic being and the basic characteristic of political life was the distinction between friend and enemy, with political conflict an immutable reality. The state was the decisive institution, because only it could protect its citizens from foreign enemies and maintain domestic order, peace and stability. Liberalism's attempt to separate politics and society was unrealistic, since no sphere was immune from potential political conflict and in a crisis the state must intervene to counteract an enemy or it will abrogate its sovereignty. But he never advocated totalitarian control, for in normal times a plurality of social and political entities could exist within the state.

To Schmitt, liberalism's inability to adjust to mass democracy, illustrated by fratricidal party politics, necessitated a strong executive to compensate for the failures of a paralysed Weimar parliament and to preclude leftist or rightist revolutions. Despite his sharp criticism, Schmitt was not anti-republican. He argued consistently that the constitution was 'inviolable' and his *Legality* and *Legitimacy* (1932) warned against allowing anti-constitutional parties the 'equal chance' to acquire power legally. He designated the President as the 'defender of the constitution' who, in extreme crises, must exercise broad emergency powers to restore stability and preserve the state and constitution. These theories became particularly relevant during the 1930s when the depression, parliamentary paralysis and political radicalization threatened Weimar with demise. As the constitutional adviser to the presidential system (1930–3) that governed Germany through emergency decrees under article 48, he urged the constitutional suppression of the Nazi and communist parties.

After Hitler's seizure of power, Schmitt collaborated to protect himself against his anti-Nazi past and to try to direct the new regime in a more traditional conservative direction. Though acquiring the reputation of 'Crown Jurist' of the Third Reich, he remained merely a figurehead, with no influence on Nazi theory or politics. When attacked by party ideologues as an opportunist whose political theory neglected Nazi racial ideology, Schmitt unsuccessfully attempted to defend himself by making reprehensible compromises with Nazi racism and anti-semitism in contradiction of his theories as well as his past close relationships with Jews. Although he withdrew from Nazi associations in 1936, and joined the 'inner emigration', he had tainted his reputation for ever. After the war he lived in internal exile but remained intellectually active for the next forty years, publishing extensively on political and constitutional theory, with works ranging from partisan warfare to a classic study of the rise and fall of the European state system.

Critics have long argued that his ideas undermined Weimar democracy and paved the way for Hitler's dictatorship, while more recent scholarship demonstrates that he sought to stabilize the Weimar system and offered fairly accurate, authoritative analyses of crucial political and legal questions. New research continues to establish and illuminate his intellectual legacy. During Weimar his ideas were used by the intellectual proponents of the 'conservative revolution' as well as by Walter Benjamin, Otto Kirchheimer and Franz Neumann of the leftist Frankfurt school. Political philosophers such as Carl J. Friedrich, Hans Morgenthau and Leo Strauss owe a similar intellectual debt to him. Though condemnation persists, the enduring relevance of his political thought is evidenced by the recent international renaissance in Schmitt studies prompted by an incessant flow of publications by conservatives, liberals and leftists.

See also

Laski, Morgenthau, Strauss.

Works

The Concept of the Political, trans. George Schwab, New Brunswick, N.J., Rutgers University Press, 1976.
Political Theology: Four Chapters on the Concept of Sovereignty, trans. George Schwab, Cambridge, Mass., MIT Press, 1985.
The Crisis of Parliamentary Democracy, trans. Ellen Kennedy, Cambridge, Mass., MIT Press, 1986.
Political Romanticism, trans. Guy Oakes, Cambridge, Mass., MIT Press, 1986.

Other works

George Schwab, The Challenge of the Exception: an Introduction to the Political Ideas of Carl Schmitt between 1921 and 1936, Berlin, Duncker & Humblot, 1970.
Joseph W. Bendersky, Carl Schmitt: Theorist for the Reich, Princeton, N.J., Princeton University Press, 1983.

Olive Schreiner   1855–1920

Until the 1980s Olive Schreiner's reputation among scholars rested primarily on *The Story of an African Farm*, an evocative and trailblazing novel of religious doubt and feminist advocacy. Neither this work nor her much touted set of finely crafted allegories, *Dreams* (1890), was esteemed for its political content,

despite the fact that prominent early twentieth-century British suffragettes credited one of these allegories, 'Three dreams in a desert', with emboldening their staunch resistance to forced feeding when they were imprisoned for acts of civil disobedience. Even Schreiner's widely published feminist treatise, *Woman and Labour*, which Vera Brittain, a leading figure in inter-war feminist and pacifist movements, hailed as the Bible of the women's movement, was largely forgotten after Schreiner's death. Far less well known both in her lifetime and afterwards, Schreiner's political writings on anti-imperialism, anti-racism, socialism and pacifism have only just begun to garner their deserved scholarly attention.

Olive Emilie Albertina Schreiner emerged in the 1890s as the foremost South African critic of British imperialism, ethnocentrism and racism. Her decision to assume the role of South African reformer arose upon her return to her native land in 1889 after eight years in England. Born of missionary parents in Wittebergen, on the border of Basutoland, she sought during adolescence to leave South Africa and settle in England, where she would eventually earn a living as a doctor and writer. For various reasons, not only did her medical career plans unravel but homesickness, especially for the South African landscape, propelled her back to her homeland. Through political tracts, public addresses in England and South Africa and works of fiction (most notably, her novella, *Trooper Peter Halket of Mashonaland* (1897)) replete with trenchant arguments and fiery warnings, she laboured valiantly but in vain to alter British and white South African imperial and racist attitudes and policies and to transform South Africa into a culturally plural, democratic nation. Schreiner's political agitation for South African social democracy culminated with her published proposals for a federal constitution, *Closer Union*. Characteristic of the praise she received from eminent radical political thinkers of her time, J. A. Hobson identified her as the only one he knew in South Africa who fully grasped the interplay of racism, imperialism and capitalism in fomenting the Anglo-Boer War (1899–1902).

Throughout her adult years Schreiner argued against capitalism and, unlike her close friend Eleanor Marx, professed an ethical socialism that would obviate the need for violent class struggle. Her socialist ideas, however, are scattered, embedded in passages in her fiction as well as in her non-fictional analyses of dominant Victorian and turn-of-the-century views of class, race and gender. Arguably, her most focused socialist statement was her brief address in 1905 in support of striking female shop assistants in Johannesburg.

Schreiner's thoughtful and cogent analysis of the roots of war and the case for pacifism appear in her unpublished manuscript, 'The dawn of civilization', a small excerpt from which was published after her death. In this work, unlike her discussion of war and peace in *Woman and Labour*, she views women as well as men as irrationally attracted to warfare. Schreiner's pacifism, as indeed her political outlook as a whole, owed much to the writings of John Stuart Mill, Goethe, Ruskin, Heine, Spinoza, Carlyle, Engels, Bebel and translations of Buddhist texts.

The combination of her feminist, pacifist, socialist, anti-imperialist and anti-racist writings establishes Schreiner as one of the turn-of-the-century's most original, wide-ranging and acute minds. The shortcomings in her political thought reflect her lack of formal education and her relative inexperience of political processes. Although unifying themes can be discerned in her writings, e.g. her attempt to dissolve the dualistic and hierarchical institutional and intellectual frameworks of her era, she did not propose a systematic, coherent political theory. Further, her idealism occasionally led her to underestimate the depth and tenacity of social and political conflicts, e.g. her belief that a small band of dedicated South Africans could move their nation in the direction of racial democracy. Her intellect is most piercing and perceptive when she dissects the destructive consequences of dominant gender, race and class assumptions and practices, and demolishes the logic of Social Darwinism (as especially in the reflective chapters in her unfinished and posthumously published novel *From Man to Man*).

See also

Hobson.

Works

The Story of an African Farm, London, Chapman & Hall, 1883.
An English South African's View of the Situation: Words in Season, London, Hodder & Stoughton, 1899.
Closer Union, London, Fifield, 1909.
Woman and Labour, London, Unwin, 1911.
From Man to Man, or, Perhaps only. . ., London, Unwin, 1926.

Other works

Ruth First and Ann Scott, *Olive Schreiner*, London, Deutsch, 1980.
Cherry Clayton (ed.), *Olive Schreiner*, Johannesburg, McGraw-Hill, 1983.
Joyce A. Berkman, *The Healing Imagination of Olive Schreiner: beyond South African Colonialism*, Amherst, Mass., University of Massachusetts Press, 1989.

Ernst Friedrich Schumacher 1911–1977

Ernst Friedrich Schumacher was an academically trained economist who grew to distrust all economists and most academics, a civil servant in a massive government enterprise who came to champion the small and the decentralized, and a reclusive Anglo-German scholar whose first book, at the age of sixty-two, was a worldwide best seller. In the age of giantism and global overdevelopment he stood for community and the human scale; in an era of technological complexity and super-science he advocated 'appropriate' economics and small-scale technology; yet he became a prophet and mentor for millions, especially in the industrialized world, and the phrase he coined, 'Small is beautiful,' became the motto of social critics and activists everywhere.

Schumacher was born in Bonn, Germany, his father a professor of economics, his mother a proper *Hausfrau*. After *Gymnasium* in Berlin he attended Bonn University for a year (1929), then tried the London School of Economics, was invited to a seminar by John Maynard Keynes at Cambridge, went back to England on a Rhodes Scholarship for two years at Oxford (1930–2) and extended it to cover an additional year at the School of Banking at Columbia University in New York. After all that, he never did earn a formal degree, and tried his hand instead at international trading in Berlin (1935–6) and investment counselling in London (1937–9), all the while reading omnivorously and writing articles and papers.

Schumacher was not a scholar in the formal sense, nor a theorist of any identifiable discipline, but he spent a lifetime generating ideas and proposals that proved to be among the most important of his time.

In England in the early 1940s, working on a Northampton farm (as a wartime 'enemy alien'), he produced a paper on international monetary payments that Keynes incorporated into his own 1943 Bretton Woods proposal. Shortly after, by then transferred to the Oxford Institute of Statistics, he developed a visionary plan for post-war full employment that became the cornerstone of Beveridge's never-enacted report to the government in 1944.

Taking a position in 1949 with the National Coal Board, Schumacher as principle economic adviser spent the next twenty years offering advice on humanizing the workplace, decentralizing authority, rationalizing production and improving safety techniques. Early on, he realized the crucial role of energy as the most important element in a national economy, and was among the first to raise the alarm about the dangers of being tied to Middle Eastern oil (the area too volatile, the supply too risky) or nuclear power (the cost too high, the dangers too great).

During the early 1950s, in what he was later to call 'the turning point of the rest of my life', Schumacher became an avid organic gardener and an ardent member (later president) of the Soil Association, warning against the chemicalization of British agriculture; he studied Indian and Chinese philosophy, read deeply in Gandhi, and became a pupil of a local Buddhist mystic and philosopher, Edward Conze; he championed the idea of household and community self-sufficiency, started baking bread at home for his family and experimented in do-it-yourself industry (though without much success).

In 1955, serving as a UN-sponsored economic adviser to the Burmese government – ostensibly to advise it on its path towards industrialization and development – Schumacher realized that the people of Burma were relatively contented and peaceful, having little but wanting little, living ordered, purposeful lives, and he concluded that what they needed was not more development but freedom from it, not more Western capitalism but less of it. Thus evolved the concept of 'Buddhist economics' that was to guide him for the rest of his life: first, that all economies should be based on renewable rather than finite resources, using nature's 'interest', as it were, rather than its 'capital', and those resources should be developed conservatively; second, that 'poorer' countries should develop only to the point of economic sufficiency, based on their own resources and traditional knowledge.

In 1962, after being invited to India, again to advise on economic 'development', Schumacher evolved the concept of 'intermediate technology' – a technology more productive than traditional tools but using local materials and labour, and not as complex and capital-intensive as Western high technology – as the key to achieving Buddhist economies in the Third World. Three years later he helped establish the Intermediate Technology Development Group in London to promote the concept around the world, under the slogan 'Find out what people are doing and help them do it better.'

Finally, retiring from the Coal Board in 1970, Schumacher decided to put his amalgam of heretical ideas into a book, which appeared as *Small is Beautiful*. It was a forthright attack not only on conventional economic thinking (in which, for example, an increase in GNP is regarded as beneficial, no matter what it is that is being produced) but on the value system behind it (in which, for example, economics is divorced from the natural world and depletion, pollution and despoliation are treated as 'externalities'). It presented the old Schumacherian themes in a new light, as well as some new thoughts on peace, soil, property, socialism, ownership, statistics, forecasting and religion, all put convincingly, in strong and sometimes even poetic prose, from beginning – 'one of the most fateful errors of our age is the belief that the problem of production has been solved' – to end: 'the guidance we need for [our] work cannot be found in science or technology, the value of which utterly depends on the ends they serve; but it can still be found in the traditional wisdom of mankind'.

The book was an immediate success. It appealed to conventional economists, at a time of stagflation and escalating energy prices; to small businessmen becoming aware that the crucial modern problems were those of scale (especially size of workplace and distribution range), and to multinational executives wrestling with the problems of overdependence on Middle Eastern oil. And it appealed to members of the 'counterculture', proponents of alternative technologies and self-sufficiency, progressive activists, theorists of all stripes and youth searching for a critique of industrial society. Before the decade was out, *Small is Beautiful* had been translated into fifteen languages and had sold more than half a million copies; E. F. Schumacher was a worldwide celebrity, the recipient of a multiplicity of honours and awards, including honorary degrees from four universities.

Schumacher entered upon a whirlwind series of lectures and appearances in the following years, while managing to write a number of articles and a further book, *A Guide for the Perplexed*. That work, a distillation of his progress from atheism to Buddhism to Eastern mysticism to Catholicism, was designed to provide a religio-spiritual underpinning for those who, moved by *Small is Beautiful* themes, actually wanted to save the Western world before it was too late. He gave an extended series of lectures in the United States in 1976, an exhausting tour in which he spoke to an estimated 60,000 people and which ended with an audience with President Jimmy Carter, and this formed the substance of his final book, *Good Work*. On one of his lecture jaunts to Europe he died in Switzerland.

Once, when accused, with all his odd views, of being a 'crank', Schumacher is said to have replied that, yes, perhaps he was a crank, but a crank was an appropriate tool, simple, strong and useful. And, he said, very good for making revolutions.

See also

Gandhi, Keynes.

Works

Asia: a Handbook, London, Blond & Briggs, 1967.
Small is Beautiful, London, Blond & Briggs, 1973.
A Guide for the Perplexed, London, Cape, 1977.
Good Work, London, Cape, 1979.

Other works

Barbara Wood, *Alias Papa: a Life of Fritz Schumacher*, New York, Harper & Row, 1984.

Joseph Alois Schumpeter 1883–1950

In the tradition of his great predecessors, Marx and Weber, Schumpeter was an economist who profoundly affected political theory. Born in Austria, he established his reputation as an economist with the publication of *The Theory of Economic Development* in 1911 and served briefly as Austrian Finance Minister. Thereafter he contributed to a wide variety of periodicals on economic affairs, taught at several German universities and lectured widely. In 1932 he took up an appointment as a professor at Harvard University, where he remained until his death. There he completed *Business Cycles* (1939) and engaged in the research that resulted in the posthumously published *History of Economic Analysis* (1954).

Schumpeter's influence as a political thinker rests on his contribution to a fertile debate over the character of socialism that erupted in the early 1940s and included such works as Pølanyi's *The Great Transformation*, Hayek's *The Road to Serfdom* and Burnham's *The Managerial Revolution*. In *Capitalism, Socialism and Democracy* Schumpeter, like Hayek and Burnham, argued that capitalism was evolving into a bureaucratic form marked by monopoly and similar in many respects to socialism. But Schumpeter went beyond the other interpretations of the period to offer a revised theory of democracy that complemented his economic and historical analysis of capitalism. He argued that democracy is valued to the extent that it achieves ends that we find agreeable rather than as an end in itself. In contradistinction to what Schumpeter termed the 'classical doctrine' of democracy, in which democracy is viewed as dependent upon a shared notion of the common good, he refashioned the concept to signify an 'institutional arrangement for arriving at political decisions in which individuals acquire the power to decide by means of a competitive struggle for the people's vote'. Political democracy is thus understood as analogous to the competitive, interest-based competition of economic markets. The purposive pursuit of a common good would degenerate into disagreement and threaten the social and material progress that has been the unplanned legacy of free-market capitalism, he claimed, while the shortsighted pursuit of political interests unintentionally safeguards that legacy by leaving policy decisions in the hands of autonomous elites. Understood in this limited sense, democracy was thus seen to be compatible with bureaucratic political and economic institutions.

Schumpeter's theory of democracy as a process of elite selection was taken up by empirical political and social scientists in the United States in the 1950s, such as Robert Dahl and Anthony Downs, as well as later by theorists of political culture – most famously Gabriel Almond and Sidney Verba in *Civic Culture* (1963) – who developed the idea that democracy requires limited citizen participation. This last idea, together with Schumpeter's criticism of intellectuals as capitalism's potential gravediggers, later formed the core of the so-called neo-conservative political thought associated with such authors as Samuel Huntington and Irving Kristol.

See also

Burnham, Dahl, Hayek, Pølyani, Weber.

Works

Capitalism, Socialism and Democracy, 1942, third edition, New York, Harper Torchbooks, 1975.

Other works

Peter Bachrach, *The Theory of Democratic Elitism: a Critique*, Boston, Mass., Little Brown, 1967, chapter 2.
David Miller, 'The competitive model of democracy', in *Democratic Theory and Practice*, ed. Graeme Duncan, Cambridge, Cambridge University Press, 1983.
Richard D. Coe and Charles K. Wilber (eds.), *Capitalism and Democracy: Schumpeter Revisited*, Notre Dame, Ind., University of Notre Dame Press, 1985.

Ali Shari'ati   1933–1977

Ali Shari'ati's father was a religious scholar with active political sympathies on the nationalist left, for which he and his son spent time in Shah Pahlavi jails. After a literary university education at Meshed, Ali Shari'ati won a government scholarship (in 1959) to study at the Sorbonne. It was the time of the Algerian revolution, of the Congo crisis and general ferment over Third World liberation. He read Sartre and Fanon (and translated the latter into Persian) and attended courses by many of the leading academics at the time, notably the orientalist Massignon (Islamic mysticism) and the sociologist Gurvitch. He completed his doctorate (in philology) and returned to Iran in 1965, to be arrested and kept in jail for six months. On his release he taught at a provincial secondary school, then a college. In 1969 he moved to Tehran to take up an appointment as lecturer at the Husaynieh-e Ershad, a charitable Islamic foundation. It was these lectures which established his fame and following among the young intelligentsia. They were circulated on audio cassettes and printed as books. Best known among them were *Islamshenasi* (Islamology) and *ummat va imamat* (community and leadership). In 1972 the Husaynieh was closed down, and soon after Shari'ati was arrested for propagating 'Islamic Marxism', to spend eighteen months in jail, then released, reportedly upon the petitioning of the Shah by members of the Algerian government who knew him in Paris. In 1977 Shari'ati was able to obtain a passport to travel to England, where he died (apparently of a heart attack) soon after.

Shari'ati's thought combined radical liberationist ideas (many of Marxist derivation) with strands of Islamic (primarily Shi'i) doctrine, myth and symbol. It was a formula that appealed greatly to a modern intelligentsia committed to progressive politics but at the same time wishing to retain its national cultural roots and, above all, contact with the masses. By its nature it was highly eclectic, not always consistent and far removed from religious orthodoxy.

Shari'ati asserted the unity of God, nature and man. Among the attributes of man made by God is a structured society and a historical process with its own laws of evolution. The historical process governs the rise, decadence and decline of civilizations (though Islamic Shi'i civilization seems to be exempt). The main mechanisms of historical evolution pos-

tulated by Shari'ati are social contradictions and class struggles, much like the Marxist version, except for his insistence that class consciousness and action are not economically determined but follow from cultural and religious commitments and leadership. He also postulated historical stages, closely following the Marxist theory of 'modes of production'. Shari'ati argued that accounts and explanations of these historical and social processes are contained in the Qu'ran and the traditions of the Prophet and the (Shi'i) Imams, hence 'Islamic sociology'.

For Shari'ati, Islam occupies a special place in the historical scheme. The religion revealed by God to the Prophet was a charter of liberation, for the end of private property, exploitation and oppression, and for the establishment of a true community of brotherhood and equality. However, this religion was subverted after the Prophet's death by some of his companions for their own gain. Subsequently, Shi'i Islam represented a continuing assertion of the original values of justice and equality, only to be subverted, in turn, by impious rulers and their clerical servants. Historically, there developed two ongoing strands of Shi'ism: the red Shi'ism of the people and the liberators, and the black Shi'ism of the traditional clergy and their political masters. This latter strand has concentrated on the interpretations and elaborations of minute rituals and observances, to the neglect of the essential spiritual and liberationist content of their religion, which they, naturally, have combated as heresy.

As against the traditional clergy, Shari'ati designated the enlightened intelligentsia, *raushanfekr* (which may include individual clerics), as the vanguard of liberation, whose task it is to enlighten the masses with the teachings and symbols of the true Shi'ism. In the absence of the Imam of the Age (whose return as the delivering Messiah is awaited by all Shi'a), it is the people, guided by the intelligentsia, who must liberate themselves and establish the true and the just community. This ideal of liberation was addressed to the whole of humankind, and in particular to the oppressed masses of the Third World. It is not clear, however, how non-Muslim and non-Shi'i masses would benefit from this liberating potential.

Shari'ati's ideas were part of the general contemporary current of Third World liberationism. The anti-imperialist struggle was not merely economic and political but essentially cultural. Iranian Marxists, he charged, followed Marx's materialist and atheist philosophy, which was antithetical to the basic heritage of the masses, when they should have favoured his economics and sociology.

Shari'ati's Islamic liberationism played an important part in the Islamic revolution in Iran. The political clergy who took over the revolutionary government allowed his canonization and some even claimed him as their own. His anticlerical strictures are tacitly omitted, and political opposition coinciding with his ideas, such as that of the People's Mojahidin, is violently suppressed.

See also

Fanon, Sartre.

Works

On the Sociology of Islam, trans. Hamid Algar, Berkeley, Cal., Mizan Press, 1979.

Other works

Nikki Keddie, Roots of Revolution, New Haven, Conn., and London, Yale University Press, 1981.
Ervand Abrahamian, Radical Islam: the Iranian Mojahedin, London, Tauris, 1989.
Sami Zubaida, Islam, the People and the State, London, Routledge, 1989.

George Bernard Shaw
1856–1950

Bernard Shaw was born in Dublin in 1856 and died in Hertfordshire ninety-four years later. His writing career spanned almost seventy years and he was prolific, especially in the middle of his life. As a young man Shaw left his native city to join the rest of the family, who had moved to London, and he quickly sought to establish himself among the intelligentsia of the metropolis. Originally a failed novelist, he became a playwright of the first order. The critic and writer William Archer convinced Shaw that dramatic dialogue was his *forte* and introduced him to the work of Ibsen. Around the same time Shaw was also introduced to Marxist thought by H. M. Hyndman, and this, as Shaw later said, gave him a purpose in life and made a man of him. So Shaw became a socialist. His socialism not only suffused his drama but motivated him to become one of the best platform orators of his day, a founder member of the Fabian Society and a vestryman (councillor).

Shaw's socialism was paternalistic. He believed that society was best run by some Platonic ruling group, not so much of philosophers as of political scientists, and it is not surprising that he collaborated with his friends the Webbs in establishing the London School of Economics and Political Science precisely to train the new guardians. He rejected participative democratic socialism from the beginning, arguing that, if asked why the people should not make their own laws, he would reply by asking why they should not write their own plays. He still called himself a democrat but defined democracy as a social order aimed at the greatest available welfare of the whole population. In fact he called himself a totalitarian democrat, because he believed that a government should be judged only by its capacity to get things done. Of course, Shaw was well aware that a number of socialists would have had good grounds for wishing to eject him from the socialist camp, but the only criterion of judgement concerning socialism that he himself would accept was the alleviation of poverty.

The young Shaw believed passionately in equality of income – the only thing about human beings that could be equalized – and even if he drifted away from the idea later he never entirely abandoned it. Equality of income, though, was to be enforced by the guardian class, with the rest of society regimented and indoctrinated in order to secure the utmost freedom. (Indeed, Shaw announced, in the pages of the *Tribune* much later, that the Russians were the freest people in the civilized world.) Because the rule of the guardians would be wise, revolt was unthinkable. When a railway porter directs us to platform 10, he suggested, we do not strike him to the earth with a cry of 'Down with tyranny!' and rush to platform 1. Shaw clearly believed that the indoctrinated masses would concede to their guardians an expertise in government similar to that accorded to railway porters in respect of arrivals and departures. Parliamentary democracy, on the other hand, was a sham as far as Shaw was concerned: a balloon filled with hot air, sent up so that we are kept looking at the sky while others pick our pockets.

Shaw's socialism, then, was unambiguously combative. He hated poverty with passion but for him the natural consequence of that hatred was distrust of the political capacities of the poor. These are the themes of his early plays, most important among which are *Widowers' Houses*, *Mrs Warren's Profession* and *Major Barbara*.

But Shaw underwent a second conversion just as important as his discovery of socialism, and, whilst he saw no compatibility between his new and his old faiths, others have been less confident. Towards the end of the century Shaw came increasingly under the influence of the philosopher Bergson's concept of creative evolution through the life force. Shaw strove to adapt his own ideas of progress through the guardian class to the evolutionary ideas of Bergson and those of Schopenhauer, Blake and Butler. The Shavian synthesis was an evolutionary theory which, one critic said, gave Shaw both a fresh sense of individual significance and cosmic sanction for his socialism.

According to Shaw it is the life force within us which obliges us to aspire to forms of social organization that will encourage all people truly to fulfil themselves. What Shaw proposed was nothing less than the taking in hand of evolution to achieve 'socialist' goals. Thus for him the only true socialism became the socialization of the selective breeding of man; in other words, of human evolution. John Tanner in *Man and Superman* may be assumed to represent Shaw's socialist superman who has a capacity for radical political leadership and an awareness of his biological function: to advance the race.

Thus the central themes of Shavian socialism became an ever continuing striving for higher forms of social structure, allowing for the development of higher forms of human existence, until finally the pleasures of contemplation, according to Shaw, would intensify to a chronic ecstasy surpassing that now induced momentarily by the sexual orgasm. As G. K. Chesterton argued, Shaw recognized that man was incapable of socialism, but instead of abandoning socialism he abandoned man. He set in train the quest for a new man – socialist man – as different from bourgeois man as is bourgeois man from Neanderthal man.

Shaw's influence on political life and thought in Britain declined as he concentrated on the evolutionary aspects of his thought but his lucid prose style and his great fame continued to give him a ready audience for his views. Though his faith in great men and women and eugenics led him originally to praise the aims of Mussolini and Hitler, he was never to lose his passionate hatred of poverty and inequality, nor his biting criticism of the inhumanity and incompetence of capitalism.

See also

Hitler, Mussolini.

Works

Widowers' Houses and *Mrs Warren's Profession*, in *Plays Unpleasant*, London, Grant Richards, 1900.
Man and Superman, London, Constable, 1903.

St Joan, London, Constable, 1924.
Major Barbara, London, Constable, 1926.
The Intelligent Woman's Guide to Socialism and Capitalism, London, Constable, 1929.

Other works

G. K. Chesterton, *George Bernard Shaw*, London, Lane, 1910.
Hesketh Pearson, *Bernard Shaw: his Life and Personality*, London, Collins. 1942.
J. P. Smith, *Unrepentant Pilgrim*, London, Gollancz, 1966.
Leon Hugo, *Bernard Shaw, Playwright and Preacher*, London, Methuen, 1971.
A. Turco, *Shaw's Moral Vision*, London, Cornell University Press, 1976.
R. F. Whitman, *Shaw and the Play of Ideas*, London, Cornell University Press, 1977.
Michael Holroyd, *Bernard Shaw I, The Search for Love*, London, Chatto & Windus, 1988.
Michael Holroyd, *Bernard Shaw II, The Pursuit of Power*, London, Chatto & Windus, 1989.

B. F. Skinner   1904–1990

Burrhus Frederic Skinner was one of the many mid-twentieth-century thinkers who have attempted to make the social sciences more scientific. Skinner was central to the development within psychology of behaviourism, and he argued that the knowledge gained in the analysis of behaviour could be used to the benefit of society. Skinner presented his case fictionally in *Walden Two*, argued for it in *Beyond Freedom and Dignity*, and defended it in *About Behaviorism* and numerous essays, the most important being 'Freedom and the control of men'.

Skinner's thesis is that behaviour is orderly, lawfully determined and, therefore, appropriately the subject matter of the natural sciences. Skinner's enterprise, therefore, is to understand the determinants of behaviour. He argued in *Beyond Freedom and Dignity* that 'Behavior is shaped and maintained by its consequences,' that most such control is aversive and that, using positive reinforcements, it is possible to reshape an individual's behaviour. 'The problem is to induce people not to be good but to behave well.' Changing the behaviour of a group of people requires changing the culture ('contingencies of reinforcement') within which the individual members of the group reside so that adaptive behaviour is reinforced. Skinner contends that the illusory concepts of human freedom and human dignity stand in the way of radically improving behaviour. 'The problem is to free men, not from control, but from certain kinds of control, and it can be solved only if our analysis takes all consequences into account.'

Skinner's work laid the foundation for the field of applied behaviour analysis, which involves the development of technology for improving socially important behaviour. Probably the best-known application is so-called teaching machines. These were once controversial but, with computer technology, are now widely accepted.

In addition, a number of communal societies have been established to try to put Skinner's ideas into practice. The two best known – Twin Oaks in Virginia and East Wind in Missouri – are fairly successful communities but have largely abandoned the *Walden Two* model. The smallest community – Los Horcones in Mexico – is still wedded to the model and so far is quite successful.

There have been many critics of Skinner. Some simply rejected his whole approach, arguing that psychology cannot be treated as if it were a science like biology or physics. Other criticisms were directed at the content of Skinner's utopia, as described in *Walden Two*, finding it dull and lifeless. Skinner rejects the criticisms as misreadings of the evidence, or he asserts that, while the evidence is not conclusive, it will be in the future. Yet other critics argued that Skinner reduces values to behavioural phenomena. Skinner rejects this argument as misconstruing the nature of values; for him values are reinforcers or consequences of behaviour. What someone 'values' is what is reinforcing to that person.

A few critics have argued that Skinner fails to make his case even if his assumptions are accepted. The best of these critics contend that his social and political ideas are radically incoherent and contradict his own assumptions. Even if the behaviour of groups can be shaped over long periods of time, we are left with fundamental problems of social and political theory with which we have been wrestling since Plato. 'Who controls the controllers? Who chooses the behaviour to be shaped? Who do we allow for and encourage social change? Is there a right to be wrong?'

Skinner argues that such questions stand in the way of the creating of a more adaptive society. He argues that communities should be willing to experiment with their cultural practices and take the responsibility of doing so. On the one hand, the state of contemporary society strongly reinforces Skinner's position. On the other, much social thought, from Dostoyevsky on, has suggested that such a society may not be worth the price.

Works

Walden Two, New York, Macmillan, 1948.
'Freedom and the control of men', American Scholar 25 (Winter 1955–6), pp. 47–65.
Beyond Freedom and Dignity, New York, Knopf, 1971.
About Behaviorism, New York, Knopf, 1974.

Other works

Philip H. Scribner, 'Escape from freedom and dignity', Ethics 83 (October 1972), pp. 13–36.
Finley Carpenter, The Skinner Primer: Behind Freedom and Dignity, New York, Free Press, 1974.
Peter G. Stillman, 'The limits of behaviorism: a review essay on B. F. Skinner's social and political thought', American Political Science Review 69 (1975), pp. 202–13.

Georges Sorel   1847–1922

Born in Cherbourg, Georges Sorel studied engineering at the Ecole Polytechnique in Paris. He worked for the state bureau of roads and bridges after earning his diploma, but retired in 1892 upon receiving a small inheritance. Turning his full attention to social questions, from 1892 to his death in Paris in 1922 Sorel applied the principles of historical materialism to problems of philosophy and social evolution. More of an intellectual publicist than a political activist, he contributed to the most important French periodicals of Marxist inspiration of his time, but he never joined a political group or party. This politically committed but independent activity coincided with a formative period in modern French history. The Third Republic, based upon universal suffrage, was constituted in 1871; trade unions were given legal status in 1884; the Second Socialist International was founded in 1889; the first important socialist electoral gains were scored in 1892; the General Confederation of Labour (CGT) was created in 1895.

Sorel sought to clarify the relation between socialist theory and practice at a time when socialism was strongly marked by utopian thought. He argued in his first published articles that perceptions of reality were necessarily deformed, and that the presence of such 'illusions' must always be assumed. Accordingly, he focused much of his attention on the deformations of social perception that ideology both reflected and perpetuated.

Such considerations underlay his critique of the new discipline of sociology. He was the first French socialist to discuss the importance of the new sociological thought in France, that of Gabriel Tarde, Gustave Le Bon and Emile Durkheim. In 1895, in his journal, Le Devenir Social, he analysed Durkheim's Rules of Sociological Method (1895), professing admiration for the author but warning that the sociologist was, for socialism, 'an adversary of the first order'. Sorel's capacity to appreciate the scientific qualities of theoretical or analytical work, while admitting concomitant political dangers, can also be seen in his consideration of the Marxist revisionism contained in Eduard Bernstein's Evolutionary Socialism (1899). Sorel agreed with Bernstein that the capitalist system was nowhere near collapse and that the socialist movement must adapt to new circumstances, but he rejected Bernstein's reformist strategy. Much of the confusion concerning Sorel's position is related to his refusal to choose between the rigidified dogma of the orthodox Marxists and the opportunism of the revisionists.

Sorel has often been accused of changing his intellectual and political orientation, but lying behind shifts of interest and emphasis is his consistent opposition to electoralism as a means of solving social problems. A characteristic of the revolutionary syndicalist movement, this 'anti-political' bias gained ground towards the end of the century. Rejecting electoral politics, whether of the revolutionary sort proclaimed by Jules Guesde or of the reformists led by Jean Jaurès, the revolutionary syndicalists attempted to synthesize Marxism and the tactics of 'direct action' championed by the anarchists. Between 1898 and 1908 Sorel published a number of articles defending this position in both practical and theoretical terms. His most famous book, *Reflections on Violence* (1908), was a collection of them.

The success of *Reflections on Violence* was undoubtedly due primarily to the Socialist International's rejection of revisionism, and to a wave of sometimes violent strikes during the years 1904–7. Nevertheless, Sorel's advocacy of the revolutionary general strike and his affirmation of the positive effects of direct action on working-class consciousness established his reputation as a leading revolutionary theorist. It was in this book that Sorel developed his idea of the role of 'myths' in the mobilization of mass movements. Drawing upon the 'new psychology' of Le Bon, Bergson and others, Sorel explained that myths were the dynamic elements of political ideologies. The myth of the general strike, for example, involves 'a complex of images capable of naturally evoking all the feelings which are raised in the struggle of the socialist movement against the existing society'.

Such concerns explain Sorel's preoccupation with the ideas of social class and class struggle. At a time when Marxian conceptions were just beginning to influence the political consciousness of French workers, Sorel was one of the few revolutionaries to recognize that. The relatively liberal social policies of the governments elected in 1899 and 1902, and the new disciplines of sociology, obscured class divisions and called into question the idea of an inevitable struggle between socio-economic classes with irreconcilable interests. Sorel maintained that this new dimension of ideological struggle was all the more urgent given the phenomenon of 'embourgeoisement', the assimilation by working-class people of bourgeois values and social perceptions. He was, therefore, one of the earliest critics of what can be called the ideology of 'consensus'. His willingness to admit the failings of Marxism and the contradictions of the socialist movement, and his analysis of new trends within democratic polities, have made Sorel a controversial figure.

See also

Bernstein, Durkheim.

Works

Reflections on Violence, New York, Collier, 1961.
The Decomposition of Marxism, London, Routledge, 1961.
The Illusions of Progress, Berkeley, Cal., University of California Press, 1969.
From Georges Sorel: Essays in Socialism and Philosophy, New York, Oxford University Press, 1976.

Other works

R. Vernon, *Commitment and Change: George Sorel and the Idea of Revolution*, Toronto, University of Toronto Press, 1978.
Larry Portis, *Georges Sorel*, London, Pluto Press, 1980.
J. J. Roth, *The Cult of Violence: Sorel and the Sorelians*, Berkeley, Cal., University of California Press, 1980.
John L. Stanley, *The Sociology of Virtue: the Social and Political Theories of Georges Sorel*, Berkeley, Cal., University of California Press, 1981.
Jeremy Jennings, *Georges Sorel: the Character and Development of his Thought*, London, Macmillan, 1985.

Josef Vissarionovich Stalin 1879–1953

Born Josef Vissarionovich Dzhugashvili, at Gori in Georgia, 'Stalin' was the last of several revolutionary aliases he adopted. After education at a church elementary school and at a seminary, he joined the Tiflis organization of the embryonic Russian Social Democratic Party (Marxist) in 1898, and took the Bolshevik side in the internal schism which divided the RSDP at its Brussels conference in 1903. He first met Lenin at the Tammerfors party conference in 1905. Co-opted on to the party Central Committee in 1912, he helped to organize and produce *Pravda*.

This period marks Stalin's first significant theoretical composition, *Marxism and the National Question*, a work which earned Lenin's strong approval. In this essay Stalin seeks to draw a middle course between those Marxists who regarded any kind of nationalism as incompatible with international socialism and those who regarded nationalism as an essential element within it, the latter being exemplified by the Austrian school.

The February revolution of 1917 released Stalin from the sixth of the spells of imprisonment or internal exile that he experienced under tsarist rule. Following the October revolution, in which he did not play a prominent part, he was appointed People's Commissioner for Nationalities. In 1919 he became a foundation member of the new Politbureau, a member of the commissariat of the Workers' and Peasants' Inspection (Rabkrin). When the functions of the last of these were assumed by the new control commission of the party Stalin's membership was transferred to the new body. In April 1922 Stalin achieved what events would prove to be his most important post when he was appointed General Secretary of the party. For this post would give him powers of organization and patronage which, combined with his native cunning, would prove invaluable in the Kremlin power struggles which were to follow (and indeed precede) the death of Lenin in 1924.

These rivalries would occasion Stalin's most distinctive contribution to theory. In 1922 when he had published *Foundations of Leninism* he had taken an orthodox view of the imminent necessity of proletarian revolution in the West. Two years later, however, in *Questions of Leninism* he distanced himself from this position by propounding the theory of 'socialism in one country'.

Stalin's triumphant emergence by the late 1920s from the aforementioned power struggles gave him the opportunity to put his theory into effect. Agriculture was collectivized and the 'command economy', based upon detailed centralized planning, introduced. All this was enforced by a heightening of political repression, which in the 1930s, in the form of terror and the political purge, would be applied to the party itself.

The conflicts of these years gave rise to Stalin's next significant modification of traditional Marxist thought, this time pertaining to the theory of the state. According to Stalin, as the class conflicts generated by the struggle for socialism intensified, and the strategems of the enemies of socialism grew ever more desperate, so it would prove necessary to enhance and expand the power of the state. There could be no question of that power simply 'withering away'. Indeed, the nearer the triumph of socialism the greater the need for the intensification of state power.

The year 1938 saw the publication of *The History of the Communist Party of the Soviet Union (Bolshevik): Short Course*. This study is of obvious interest in historiographical terms, as history was fabricated to exaggerate and varnish Stalin's role, and to minimize and blacken the parts played by his erstwhile rivals, in the history of the CPSU. In terms of political theory, however, the work's significance lies in its form more than in its content. It represents an attempt by Stalin to reduce Marxism-Leninism to a highly simplified and numbered catechism of questions and answers for rote learning.

In May 1941 Stalin became chairman of the Council of People's Commissars. Following the German invasion of 22 June 1941 he assumed the office of Commissar for Defence. Thereafter he would become commander-in-chief of the Soviet armies and accept in time the titles of marshal and generalissimo.

After the war Stalin would occasionally make minor contributions to the realm of ideas, usually in predictable fields like economics, but occasionally in unlikely areas like linguistics.

His contribution to socialist thought is far too slight and superficial to place him among the great figures of that tradition. His importance lies much more in his general role, for good or ill, as one of the commanding presences of modern history. His interest in ideas was always severely practical and instrumental, as he used them to advance his personal ambitions or policies. This interest was combined with a dogmatic cast of mind and a pronounced tendency to coarsen and oversimplify complex arguments.

See also

Lenin.

Works

Works (thirteen volumes), London, Lawrence & Wishart, 1955.

Other works

Bruce Franklin, *The Essential Stalin: Major Theoretical Writings, 1905–52*, London, Croom Helm, 1973.
Robert C. Tucker, *Stalin as Revolutionary*, London, Chatto & Windus, 1974.
Adam B. Ulam, *Stalin*, London, Allen Lane, 1974.
Robert C. Tucker (ed.), *Stalinism: Essays in Historical Interpretation*, New York, Norton, 1977.
G. R. Urban (ed.), *Stalinism: its Impact upon Russia and the World*, London, Temple Smith, 1982.

John Strachey   1901–1963

Born near Guildford in England. Best known as a highly successful popularizer of Marxism through such books as *The Coming Struggle for Power* and *The Theory and Practice of Socialism*. He was a founder member in the 1930s of the influential Left Book Club. Later he sought theoretical justification for democratic socialism in *Contemporary Capitalism*.

Works include

The Coming Struggle for Power, London, Gollancz, 1932.
The Theory and Practice of Socialism, London, Gollancz, 1936.

Contemporary Capitalism, London, Gollancz, 1956.

Other works

Michael Newman, *John Strachey*, Manchester, Manchester University Press, 1989.

Leo Strauss   1899–1973

A Plato whose Socrates envisages a city in *The Republic* not as a utopia to be striven for but as a warning about the limits of politics; a Xenophon who, contrary to the common opinion affirming his mediocrity, gives us profound insights into Socratic philosophy; a Thucydides for whom piety has a place in the relations between states; a Locke who builds on Hobbes rather than Hooker – these are some of the characters who inhabit Leo Strauss's world. It is a world that radically revises the accepted readings of the political philosophers of the past under the guidance of an interpretative mode that aims to understand the thinkers of the past exactly as they understood themselves, rather than to begin from the standpoint of the superiority of one's own approach or of one's time. The re-readings, though, are not undertaken in the service of historical accuracy; they come rather from denial of the Enlightenment belief in progress and concern about the power of science. Rejecting the optimism of his mentor, the German neo-Kantian Hermann Cohen, Strauss claimed that the worst things that Cohen experienced were the Dreyfus scandal and the pogroms in tsarist Russia. Cohen did not experience communist Russia or Hitler's Germany. Those calamities arose in a world enamoured of the idea of progress, an idea bound up with the human conquest of nature through science. In such a context philosophy is no longer disinterested contemplation of the eternal but the relief of human discomfort. The ancients, properly understood, can revive the activity of true philosophy.

Conventional histories of political philosophy study the thinkers of the past to learn about them, not from them. Such studies, according to Strauss, turn philosophers into epiphenomena of the societies from which they come and of the lives which they lived. Dismissing these historical readings, Strauss insists that we return to the philosophers of the past as one turns to tradition, in order to learn from it the truths that the modern world in its exaltation of the power of the human will has too cavalierly dismissed. Histories treat the thought of the past as not necessarily binding on the present generation; Strauss, in contrast, envisages a great gigantomachy between the ancient (and medieval) authors and the moderns. The moderns are winning, but their victory might be forestalled by a liberal education that returns us to the study of the ancient authors and their commitment to pursue the truth.

Strauss's criticisms of the theoretical underpinnings of the modern world are many. Tracing modernity back to Machiavelli, who he declares in *Thoughts on Machiavelli* to be a teacher of evil, Strauss laments in *What is Political Philosophy?* the modern rejection of questions that motivated the ancient authors, questions about the good life, the good regime and the harmony between the excellence of an individual and the excellence of the citizen, between wisdom and law-abidingness. Unwilling to ask about the good society, modernity has been unable to deal with the horrors of Nazism or Stalinism. Replacing a concern with the good life, the object of ancient philosophy, is modern science, which avoids questions of value or, as he puts it in *Liberalism Ancient and Modern*, 'no longer has any essential connection with wisdom'. Science as method does not distinguish between good and bad, nor does it justify the ends to which it seeks the means. It thus becomes the servant of its customers, i.e. the masses.

The attack on a science divorced from wisdom led Strauss and several of his associates to attack social science in particular in a volume of essays called *The Scientific Study of Politics* (1962). In 'An epilogue' Strauss accused behavioural political science of removing itself from politics by rejecting the language of politics in favour of a precision inappropriate to the complexities of political life. Further, by reducing politics to the 'sub-political', it denied the possibility of a common good and assumed a value-free stance that refuses to distinguish between good and bad. By putting a premium on the observation of data, i.e. the behaviour of citizens, social science cannot assess what it observes. It is not only inadequate as a tool for studying political life, it encourages the most dangerous proclivities of democracy, teaching the equality of all desires. Earlier, in his *Natural Right and History*, Strauss had analysed the work of Max Weber ('the greatest social scientist of our century') to present the consequences of value-free social science, or, as he called it in that book, historicism. Weber, propounding an ethically free social science, separating the Is and the Ought, according to Strauss, thrust us into a relativistic world. Weber rejected the possibility of any scientific knowledge of what is true. Strauss does not reject such a possibility and in turn rejects the sciences that begin from this premise.

Though Strauss insists on the possibility of such knowledge, he does not claim to have discovered 'the truth'. Political philosophy is not the possession but the pursuit of truth. We can pursue the truth by carrying on a discourse with the ancient authors, but to do so we must understand the pre-modern practice of esoteric writing. In *Persecution and the Art of Writing* Strauss begins with the assumption that philosophy is held suspect by most. Those who were genuine philosophers could not openly express their philosophical views without being subject to some form of persecution. Their works were therefore written on two levels: the exoteric teaching which remains on the surface and is intended to edify the 'non-philosophic' majority and the esoteric teaching which must be gleaned from hints such as silences and obvious mistakes and is directed to the philosophical few who search for a truth inaccessible to the many. Strauss's readings of the ancient philosophers depend on this methodology to reveal the 'inner beauty' of those texts which 'disclose themselves only after very long, never easy, but always pleasant work'. With detailed analyses attending to title, silences, structure, analogies, blunders and dramatic content, Strauss slowly leads his reader through the texts of the ancient and early modern authors. Conclusions, often briefly cryptic, never summarize. Instead, they send the reader back to the beginning of the article or book and especially back to the text.

Though the numerous articles and books analysing often ignored texts of the ancient authors (e.g. Xenophon's *Oikonomicus* and *Reminiscences* and Plato's perhaps spurious *Minos*) never explicitly state the 'truth' for which Strauss claims we must plumb these works, underlying the analyses always is the pursuit of natural right, that which is best by nature and not by convention, a nature that can be discovered only by philosophy. Yet, running through Strauss's work, from its earliest expression in his first book, on Spinoza, to his posthumously published *Studies in Platonic Political Philosophy*, is the confrontation, as he puts it, between Athens and Jerusalem, reason and faith. Both philosophy and revelation claim wisdom, but, Strauss claims in the lecture 'Progress or return', one cannot accept the wisdom of one without denying the wisdom of the other. No one can be both a philosopher and a theologian, but every one of us can and ought to be either. Strauss's work demonstrates the irreconcilable devotion to both and his opposition to a modern world that has denied the possibility and the relevance of both.

Seldom have philosophers who have stayed so far away from direct political activity, within the confines of academe, sparked such a vitriolic response to their work. Strauss's attack on the behavioural sciences drew forth its defenders from the fledgling discipline. His insistence on the capacity to evaluate the good and the bad, the high and the low, was perceived as anti-democratic, despite his claim that 'we are not permitted to be flatterers of democracy precisely because we are friends and allies of democracy'. His curt dismissal of the history of political thought as conforming to the most dangerous forms of historicism evoked the response that Strauss himself had constructed a tradition that never existed and that the esoteric exegesis itself is an undisciplined methodology. Whether it was the power of his personality or of his writings, Strauss spawned a school of colleagues and students educated primarily at the University of Chicago known as Straussians. Though the subject matter studied by Straussians ranges widely, Straussian work is marked by careful textual analysis of the major philosophers of the past, often with attention to the esoteric meanings, the sharp distinction between the ancient and modern worlds and the denial that modern science can help us answer the most important questions about the meaning and practice of virtue and of natural right.

See also

Weber.

Works

Persecution and the Art of Writing, Glencoe, Ill., Free Press, 1952.
Natural Right and History, Chicago, University of Chicago Press, 1953.
Thoughts on Machiavelli, Glencoe, Ill., Free Press, 1958.
What is Political Philosophy? and other Studies. Glencoe, Ill., Free Press, 1959.
'An epilogue', in *Essays on the Scientific Study of Politics*, ed. Herbert Storing, New York, Holt Rinehart & Winston, 1962.
Liberalism Ancient and Modern, New York, Basic, 1968.
Studies in Platonic Political Philosophy, Chicago, University of Chicago Press, 1983.

Other works

Victor Gourevitch, 'Philosophy and Politics' I and II, *Review of Metaphysics* 22, 1 (1968), pp. 58–84, and 2, pp. 281–328.
Allan Bloom, 'Leo Strauss, September 20, 1899–October 18, 1973', *Political Theory* 2, 4 (1974), pp. 372–92.
John Gunnell, 'Political theory and politics: the case of Leo Strauss', *Political Theory* 13, 3 (1985), pp. 339–61.

Shadia B. Drury, *The Political Ideas of Leo Strauss*, Basingstoke, Macmillan, 1988.

Sun Yat-sen   1866–1925

As a democratic revolutionary and political thinker Sun Yat-sen played a crucial historical role in the progress of Chinese society. Being the leader of the revolutionary party, Tong Meng Hui (United League), Sun led the revolution of 1911 which overthrew the Qing dynasty and founded the Republic of China. He was fully aware that the revolution had not yet succeeded and continued to struggle against the war lords and imperialist powers until the end of his life.

Sun Yat-sen's doctrine for the remoulding of Chinese society was known as *The Three Principles of the People* (1924), ie. nationalism, democracy and people's livelihood, a doctrine which encompassed his political and economic thinking. He wished to achieve his goals through a gradual process consisting of various stages. In his major works, *National Reconstruction* and *The Fundamentals of National Reconstruction* (1924), he outlined his proposals for Chinese reconstruction in his time.

Being a patriot and a highly public-minded person, Sun Yat-sen fought selflessly for the Chinese revolution. Broad-minded as he was, for a long time he neglected the importance of controlling the armed forces, which led to numerous setbacks in his career. In spite of that, he was confident and firm in achieving his aims. He understood the disunity of the Chinese people, whom he once described as 'a sheet of loose sand', and sought to awaken them and promote national unity. As a result of his revolutionary experience he was convinced that it was extremely important to secure the support of nations who would treat China on the basis of equality. He reorganized the Chinese Revolutionary Party into the Kuomintang in 1919. In his later years he adopted a policy of alliance with Soviet Russia, co-operation with the Communist Party of China, supporting the interests of China's workers and peasants.

Among the important contemporary politicians of China, Sun Yat-sen is unique in being accepted on both sides of the Taiwan Straits as a national hero, although usually the nationalists and communists emphasize different aspects of his career. As a result, Sun's legacy still is regarded with great reverence throughout China.

Works

The Three Principles of the People (ed. F. W. Vrio), Taipei, China Publishing House, 1981.

Other works

Leng Shao-Chuan and N. Palmer, *Sun Yat-sen and Communism*, London, Thames & Hudson, 1961.

H. Schiffrin, *Sun Yat-sen and the Origins of the Chinese Revolution*, Berkeley, Cal., University of California Press, 1968.

P. Linebarger, *Sun Yat-sen and the Chinese Republic*, New York, AMS Press, 1969.

L. Sharman, *Sun Yat-sen: his Life and its Meaning*, Stanford, Cal., Stanford University Press, 1984.

Cheng Chu-Yuan, *Sun Yat-sen's Doctrine in the Modern World*, Boulder, Colo., and London, Westview Press, 1989.

Richard Henry Tawney 1880–1962

R. H. Tawney was perhaps the most important socialist thinker in Britain in the twentieth century. On the occasion of his eightieth birthday, *The Times* claimed in an editorial that 'No man alive has put more people into his spiritual and intellectual depth than has Richard Henry Tawney.' He was born in Calcutta and educated at Rugby and Balliol College, Oxford. He subsequently worked at Toynbee Hall, a university settlement in the East End of London; as an economics lecturer at Glasgow University; as a member of the executive and lecturer for the Workers' Educational Association; as an occasional journalist on the *Manchester Guardian*. He became Reader in Economic History at the London School of Economics in 1920 and subsequently held a Chair in the school until his retirement.

Tawney's social and political thought revolved around a number of related ideas – equality, social function, the common good and service – all of them underpinned by his Christian socialist perspective. As a young man at Balliol he had been influenced by the writings of T. H. Green and other British Idealists such as Edward Caird, along with William Temple, subsequently Archbishop of Canterbury. While Tawney did not write books on metaphysics and philosophical theology, as many of these thinkers did, his basic ideas did rest on a Christian basis.

Tawney took the view that the claim of equality rested upon a sense of common humanity between human beings and an idea of the equal worth of each person. The idea of common humanity did not imply equal capacities or equal potential but rather that all persons had a fundamental moral equality which was based upon the fact that under God all human beings have common limitations. Even the greatest do not transcend the moral capacities of the generality of persons; equally, none are so irredeemable that other people cannot see in them the basic attributes which make human life valuable. In Tawney's view from the standpoint of faith even the most superior persons 'judged by their place in any universal scheme . . . are all infinitely great or infinitely small'. The same considerations apply to the idea of mutual obligation and duty, which has links with his idea of freedom. In Tawney's view freedom lies not, as the classical liberal believes, in the absence of intentional coercion, but rather in self-fulfilment (here the influence of the Idealists can be seen) but self-fulfilment is seen not just as gratification, but also as involving duty, service and obligation. It also involves the idea of fellowship, because in Tawney's view individualism and atomism were not ingrained or sustainable features of human life. This sense of self-fulfilment in service is also permeated by his Christian beliefs. Without what he called some supernatural reference point the idea of mutual obligation would be difficult if not impossible to justify.

In Tawney's view equality did not mean strict arithmetical equality of income. However, inequalities had to be related to social function. This has two senses. First, that rewards should be commensurate with social function or service to the community. Second, that persons should have what they need to serve the community (and thus fulfil themselves).

This idea of function also underpins Tawney's attitude to rights. He argues that rights derive from a sense of social function and social service. Rights are therefore not categorical entities which are ascribed to individuals outside a particular social framework but arise out of, are recognized and claimed in terms of particular societies with a democratically arrived-at idea of the common good.

Tawney links the idea of service with industry and commerce. The real goal or purpose of commercial activity, he argues in *The Acquisitive Society*, is not individual enrichment or profit but service to society. It was a distortion of human nature and of the circumstances of human life for production and accumulation to become ends in themselves. In contrast to the acquisitive society Tawney posited the functional society, in which industry served social purposes. Social purpose, social function, the public interest or the common good were not Platonic abstractions but would emerge from the debates of a democratic society.

In order to achieve some sense of the common good and the social purpose of industry Tawney argued for a radical democratization of society and for the dispersal of power. He rejected the centralizing tendencies of the thought of the Webbs and recoiled from the idea of socialism being imposed by a managerial/political elite. Tawney argued that power should be dispersed as widely as possible, and greater social and economic equality was a means to this. However, where power had to be concentrated it had not to be arbitrary, it had to be capable of being revoked, and it had to be based on the achievement of a social purpose which was democratically approved. If power was thus linked with the idea of a democratically articulated social purpose it would in fact become authority rather than power, having democratic legitimacy and recognition which flowed from the values of the community. Democratic citizenship was thus a central aspect both of the critique of capitalism, which gave power to those who owned resources without necessarily performing a concomitant social function, and of centralized and managerial forms of socialism favoured by the Webbs. The idea of democratic citizenship informed Tawney's work for the WEA, as he saw education as a necessary condition of greater democratic participation.

Tawney did not believe equality and the democratization of society had any value as ends in themselves. Rather, his basic value, it could be argued, is that of fellowship and a sense of community. It is important to recognize that Tawney did not advocate fellowship as a political value in terms of a great sense of fellow feeling or the psychological aspects of community. That would hardly be appropriate in the modern world. Fellowship as he understood it was to be seen far more in terms of right and principled relations between citizens, based upon equality and service, and these relationships could be given an institutional embodiment. Tawney was convinced that no society could exist without a sense of fellowship, which as he understood it was essential to the maintenance of any society. Without fellowship the other socialist values such as liberty and equality might be seen merely as a radical way of trying to empower individuals, which is good in its way, but he was convinced that the communitarian aspect of socialism was indispensable to the cohesion of a democratic socialist society.

See also

Sidney and Beatrice Webb.

Works

The Acquisitive Society, London, Bell, 1920.
Religion and the Rise of Capitalism, London, Murray, 1926.
Equality, London, Allen & Unwin, 1931; revised edition 1952.
Land and Labour in China, London, Allen & Unwin, 1931.
The Radical Tradition, ed. Rita Hindon, London, Allen & Unwin, 1964.

Other works

R. Terrill, *R. H. Tawney and his Times*, London, Deutsch; 1974.
D. Reisman, *State and Welfare*, London, Macmillan, 1982.
A. Wright, *R. H. Tawney*, Manchester, Manchester University Press, 1987.

Charles Taylor   1931–

Throughout his career as a professor of philosophy and political science at McGill University in Montreal, Charles Taylor has sought to revise the ontology of self that informs modern political theory and analytic philosophy. His collected philosophical papers, published in 1985, questioned the premise of atomistic individualism dominant in modern political theory. That premise has been attractive, Taylor argued, because it promises disengagement and thus freedom for human actors, but ultimately fails to account for the fact that human beings constantly interpret their lives in order to confer meaning. Without an understanding of that interpretative process, he asserted, human agency cannot be adequately comprehended. In these early writings, Taylor argued that human agency, rights and freedom exist only in a social context, and that modern political theory does not adequately account for the reciprocity of relations among individuals and between individuals and society. This stance placed him among a diverse group of scholars loosely affiliated as communitarian critics of liberalism.

In *Sources of the Self*, published in 1989, Taylor extended his argument that human agency may be understood only from the premise that persons exist as 'embodied individuals' engaged both in self-interpretation and in constant interaction with others. Individuals, he argued, engage in 'strong evaluation' throughout the course of their moral lives; they criticize and transform themselves through the interpretation and reinterpretations of their rights and obligations. They do not, however, do so in a vacuum, responding only to the contingencies of a particular time and place. Individuals appeal to moral sources – secular, religious, literary and philosophical – to impart meaning to their actions; they inevitably act with an implicit concept of the good life.

Understanding the modern self, then, requires a sense of history; the social and linguistic context within which human action occurs is of critical importance. For Taylor, moral action is internally motivated, albeit played out against an historical context, which distinguishes Taylor from communitarians who locate moral imperatives primarily outside of the individual in shared social norms. Thus, Taylor is more optimistic than many communitarians about the possibilities for dialogue and strong evaluation among citizens about the nature and content of the good life; he likewise disdains postmodern accounts of political action. A committed Roman Catholic, Taylor has been criticized as espousing a theistic account of the good life and failing to articulate adequate standards for determining which sources of moral authority should take precedence.

In recent years, Taylor has also addressed the philosophical issues associated with cultural membership. This work has grown in part out of his concerns for understanding the self in a social context, and in part out of his political commitment to the struggles of the Quebecois in Canada as an active member of the New Democratic Party. In 'Recognition and Cultural Membership', Taylor advances an argument for supporting minority cultures. He argues that recognition of minority cultures is important as a means of according respect to both groups and individuals within those groups. According such respect, he argues, is essential if dominant and minority groups can hope to engage in a sustained dialogue about the nature and content of a shared understanding of the good life.

See also

MacIntyre, Rawls, Sandel, Taylor, Walzer.

Works

Philosophical Papers, two vols, Cambridge, Cambridge University Press, 1985.
Sources of the Self, Cambridge, Cambridge University Press, 1989.
'Recognition and cultural membership', *Multiculturalism: Examining the Politics of Recognition*, Princeton, N.J., Princeton University Press, 1992.
Philosophical Arguments, Cambridge, Mass., Harvard University Press, 1995.

Leon Trotsky   1879–1940

Leon Trotsky was born on 7 November, by coincidence the very day on which, thirty-eight years later, he would organize the insurrection that brought the Bolsheviks to power. His real name was Lev Davidovich Bronstein. The son of a Jewish farmer in the southern Ukraine, he was an academically bright and confident youth. His involvement in revolutionary politics from early adulthood was to lead to two periods of imprisonment and Siberian exile, both terminated by successful escapes, and followed by longer periods in Europe within the well populated Russian revolutionary emigration, where he became a prominent political activist. Trotsky was an outstanding orator, and a writer and polemicist of great acumen and power.

He took issue with Lenin, after a brief collaboration with him on the journal *Iskra*, criticizing his ideas on party organization as domineering and narrow – in the name of a broader, self-reliant workers' democracy. A year later, during the first Russian revolution of 1905, he played a leading part in the St Petersburg workers' soviet, which he saw as the most promising instance of just such a vigorous proletarian democracy. In the light of the experience of 1905, Trotsky first formulated the theory of permanent revolution. It further distanced him from Lenin and the Bolsheviks, with their different strategic perspective for the Russian revolution. In 1917, however, during the course of which Trotsky became one of that revolution's principal leaders, he at last joined forces with Lenin, putting aside as mistaken his misgivings about the latter's organizational views, at the same time as Lenin for his part implicitly came over to the notion of permanent revolution.

Trotsky was a key figure in the Bolsheviks' early years in power: negotiating the Treaty of Brest-Litovsk with Germany; building and guiding the Red Army through civil war; participating in all major debates on international, domestic and cultural policy; writing, always writing. After Lenin's death in 1924 he was the chief critic and opponent of Stalin's growing power and of the constricting bureaucratization of Soviet political life. Defeated by Stalin, driven from all seats of power, then into exile and from one temporary refuge to another, he continued to wield his critical pen, elaborating further the theory of permanent revolution, formulating an original analysis of the nature of Soviet society and polity under Stalin's baleful regime, composing a towering history of the Russian revolution, writing presciently on the rise of Nazism in Germany and on the affairs of many other countries. In 1938 he founded the Fourth International. He died on 21 August 1940, murdered by one of Stalin's agents.

It was the theory of permanent revolution, first broached in *Results and Prospects* (1906), that formed the main unifying thread of Trotsky's political thought over more than three decades. He was the first within the Russian socialist movement to anticipate that the series of proletarian revolutions foretold by the classical Marxist tradition might begin to unfold not from the Western centres of advanced capitalism, as was the orthodox expectation, but rather in Russia, economically still backward and with a vast peasant majority. Trotsky's analysis began from what he would later call, in his *History of the Russian Revolution* (1931), the 'law of combined and uneven development'. The uneven development of capitalism in different countries and regions, he argued, led to the interpenetration of different modes of production, an intermingling of more and less advanced technologies and social forms, as the latest methods and techniques were exported from more to less developed economies. In Russia, that kind of evolution, encouraged by the state and pressed forward by foreign capital in its own interests, had produced a small but comparatively modern industrial sector, with a highly concentrated proletariat, within the more antiquated social and political structures of the tsarist order.

The political dynamics to which this combination of social forms gave rise were uncongenial, Trotsky held, to the prospects of achieving any stable bourgeois democracy. The indigenous bourgeoisie was small and weak, pre-empted by the speed and the external provenance of capitalist development. And it was politically timid, caught between a militant proletariat on the one hand and a vast, repressive state apparatus on the other. It would seek a compromise with the tsarist state, a constitutional monarchy, perhaps, and modest social reforms. It was the proletariat, therefore, which would have to make itself the agent of radical bourgeois revolution, fighting for political democracy and thoroughgoing agrarian reform – the proletariat, supported by the land-hungry peasants. Thus far Trotsky's perspective was similar to Lenin's, opposing them both to the Mensheviks, who looked to bourgeois-liberal forces for leadership of the bourgeois revolution.

Trotsky, however, did not believe, as Lenin did, that the workers would be able to confine themselves within the limits of a purely bourgeois democratic-revolution. The same dynamics that pushed this class into the leading revolutionary role would compel it to go beyond those limits and begin the construction of socialism. Otherwise, conservative opposition from bourgeois and pro-tsarist forces would prevent it even from obtaining its minimum demands. To win the eight-hour day, for example, the working class would have to break the resistance of factory owners, who in response resorted to dismissal and lock-out; have to take over the factories themselves and put them into public ownership. If the political representatives of the proletariat once came to power, they could draw no hard-and-fast line between the minimum and maximum programmes, the bourgeois-democratic and socialist revolutions.

This running together of two types of revolutionary transformation is what was signified by 'permanent' revolution: a combined, continuous social transition. At the same time Trotsky was too much a classical Marxist to believe that socialism could be fully achieved in a country as economically backward as Russia was, alone. The Russian revolution had to, and would, be the first of a series of European proletarian revolutions. Its own ultimate success depended on theirs. Should they fail, then the young workers' state in Russia was doomed.

That prognosis formed the point of departure later – when revolutions to the West *had* failed and the hopes of 1917 had been stifled by the consolidation and terrible repressions of Stalin's rule – for Trotsky's analysis of the nature of the Soviet regime. His expectation that, isolated, the new workers' state would soon fall had, he conceded, been wrong; the state had instead undergone a severe degeneration. At the deepest level this was, again, a reflection of the law of combined development. For, having to move forward on its own, its low level of economic development aggravated by the destruction and disruption of world war, civil war and foreign intervention, Russia became the site of what Trotsky would describe, in *The Revolution Betrayed* (1936), as 'the application of socialist methods for the solution of pre-socialist problems'.

Not Marx's realm of freedom, growing out of technical productivity and relative plenty, but a realm of acute economic scarcity and social and cultural underdevelopment – this was the reality of post-revolutionary Russia. It was the basis on which a parasitical bureaucratic caste had usurped the political power of the working class. Trotsky declined to characterize the Soviet bureaucracy as fully a class in the Marxist sense; nor would he accept, as some were already then suggesting, that the Soviet Union represented a new type of (state or bureaucratic) capitalist formation. For him the chief gain of the Bolshevik revolution, the abolition of private property in the means of production, was still intact and Russia still a transitional, albeit deformed, society, between capitalism and socialism. All the same, he had come to believe that a new, political revolution would be necessary to remove the bureaucracy from power and allow a resumption of the best traditions of 1917 – the tradition, in particular, of socialist democracy. The prospects of such a healthy outcome he continued to regard as bound up with the prospects of socialist revolution in the West.

The theory of permanent revolution was a remarkable anticipation, more than a decade before the event, of the actual course of the Russian revolution. On the other hand, consistently with the entire classical Marxist tradition, it overestimated the ease and speed with which revolutions might carry from one country to another, vaulting across national frontiers. Then again, recent developments in Russia and Eastern Europe are set to finish by belatedly confirming the theory's more negative prognostications as to the dependence of the future of socialism on the destiny of the most advanced capitalist societies.

Trotsky's reputation as a thinker has benefited neither from the decades of vilification by Stalin's supporters, sympathizers and apologists – and the reminder is perhaps necessary today that that is no small number of people – nor from the beliefs and practices, sometimes weird and sometimes worse than weird, of dogmatic and sectarian currents within Trotskyism itself. He was one of the very greatest of Marxist thinkers to date, a fact which is obvious but still widely overlooked: in the breadth of his knowledge, the range and depth of his analyses, the volume and power of his writing; in the creative application, these taken all together now, of the concepts of historical materialism to an understanding of the politics of the first half of the twentieth century.

There was too in Trotsky's thought and activities – not unflawed, nor absolutely continuously, but deeply and persistently, for all that – a commitment to and grasp of the democratic content of Marxism's revolutionary goals, in a coupling – of revolution and democracy – that has been too often sundered in the history of socialism.

See also

Lenin, Stalin.

Works

The History of the Russian Revolution, Ann Arbor, Mich., University of Michigan Press, n.d.
The Permanent Revolution and Results and Prospects, London, New Park, 1962.
The Revolution Betrayed, New York, Merit, 1965.
My Life, New York, Grosset & Dunlap, 1960.

Other works

I. Deutscher, *The Prophet Armed*, London, Oxford University Press, 1954.
I. Deutscher, *The Prophet Unarmed*, London, Oxford University Press, 1959.
I. Deutscher, *The Prophet Outcast*, London, Oxford University Press, 1963.
B. Knei-Paz, *The Social and Political Thought of Leon Trotsky*, Oxford, Oxford University Press, 1978.
M. Lowy, *The Politics of Combined and Uneven Development*, London, Verso, 1981.
N. Geras, *Literature of Revolution*, London, Verso, 1986.

Uno Kōzō   1899–1977

Founder of the most influential school of Marxian economics in post-war Japan, Uno Kōzō was born into a merchant family. He took a degree in economics at Tokyo Imperial University in 1921 and joined the Ōhara Institute for the Study of Social Problems (Ōhara Shakai Mondai Kenkyūjo). From 1922 to 1924 he studied in Europe, primarily Berlin, and on returning to Japan joined the faculty of Tōhoku University. There Uno taught economic policy and began to study the major theme of his life's work. Drawing a careful distinction between theory and practical policy, he studied Marx's *Capital*, German capitalism and the history of world capitalist development, seeking to systematize a theory of economic policy. In 1936 he published the first volume of *The Theory of Economic Policy (Keizai seisakuron)*, which established the basis of his theory of three stages of world capitalist development. In February 1938 Uno was arrested in the Professors' Group Incident along with others associated with the dissident Marxist Rōnō-ha school (which had broken away from the Japanese Communist Party in 1927) but was acquitted on appeal. In 1941 he resigned his post at Tōhoku University and joined the Japan Trade Institute of the Japanese Association for the Promotion of Trade. In 1944 he moved to the Mitsubishi Institute of Economics, and after the war edited the institute's journal, *Economic Affairs (Keizai Jōsei)*.

In the post-war era Uno wrote journalistically on inflation and other economic issues, criticizing the views of the revived pre-war Marxist factions, the Rōnō-ha and the Japanese Communist Party loyalist Kōza-ha. He maintained his standing in the academic world, however, becoming professor of the University of Tokyo's Institute of Social Science. As head of the institute from 1949, he organized collaborative studies of forestry (1954) and the land tax reforms (1957–8). As for his own research, Uno returned to the study of basic Marxian economics, seeking to systematize what he called a pure theory of capitalism (*gen riron*). The results appeared in *The Theory of Value, Studies in the Theory of Value*, and his rewriting of the three volumes of *Das Kapital* as the two-volume *Principles of Political Economy*. Uno retired from the University of Tokyo in 1958, to become Professor of Sociology at Hōsei University.

Uno students, such as Ōuchi Tsutomu and Hiroshi Iwata, have made substantial theoretical contributions to Marxist economic theory by drawing on his work. Uno's influence gained ascendancy among Marxist economists in the aftermath of the criticism of Stalin in 1956. In subsequent years Uno completed his *Methodology of Economics* (*Keizaigaku hōhōron*). In addition, many associated with his school helped to articulate the Japanese Socialist Party's new platform in the 1980s.

During the debate on Japanese capitalism from 1927 to 1937 Uno remained unallied, officially, with either the Rōnō-ha (Labour–Farmer faction) or the Kōza-ha (the faction loyal to the Comintern-guided Japanese Communist Party). He was, however, much more critical of what he saw as the Kōza-ha's mechanistic application of Marx's abstractions from the Western European experience to the analysis of Japan's development. To Uno it was understandable that the Kōza-ha should be so disappointed with Japan's 'semi-feudal' characteristics, given the group's simplistic interpretation and application of Marxist theory. This view became the basis of Uno's post-war innovations in Marxist economic theory. As presented in the completion of his *Theory of Economic Policy* published in 1954, Uno argued that Marxist economic research must proceed on three levels: (1) the study of the basic pure principles of capitalism, particularly as they were manifested in the development of nineteenth-century Britain; (2) the analysis of the three stages of world capitalist development, viz. mercantilism, dominated by British mercantile capital; liberalism, dominated by British industrial capital, especially in textiles; and imperialism, led by British, American and German finance capital and described by Lenin as the highest and final stage of capitalist development; (3) empirical analysis of specific current economic problems. The second level of research embraced the analysis of the development of the world capitalist economy up to the First World War and would lay the groundwork for the analysis of world capitalism after the First World War, which would occur only at the third level. Uno's three-step *(san-dankai)* approach would avoid the Kōza-ha's tendency to compare abstract theory with concrete reality and the Rōnō-ha's insistence on seeing Japan in terms of development towards a pure, idealized capitalism, to the neglect of the peculiar aspects of Japan's capitalist development. In addition to his *san dankai* theory, Uno's work is respected for its contribution to the Marxist theory of value.

See also

Lenin.

Works

Keizai seisakuron (The Theory of Economic Policy), Tokyo, Kōbundō Shobō, 1936, third edition, 1948, enlarged and revised edition, 1971.
Kachi ron (The Theory of Value), Tokyo, Kawade Shobō, 1947.
Keizai genron (Principles of Political Economy), two volumes, Tokyo, Iwanami Shoten, 1950–2.
Kachi ron no kenkyū (Studies in the Theory of Value), Tokyo, Tōkyō Daigaku Shuppankai, 1952.
Keizaigaku hōhōron (The Methodology of Economics), Tokyo, Tōkyō Daigaku Shuppankai, 1962.
Shihon-ron gojūnen (Fifty Years of Capital), two volumes, Tokyo, Hōsei Daigaku Shuppankyoku, 1970–3.
Uno Kōzō chosakushū (Collected Works of Uno Kōzō), ten volumes and supplement, Tokyo, Iwanami Shoten, 1973–4
Principles of Political Economy: Theory of a Purely Capitalist Society, trans. Thomas T. Sekine, Brighton, Harvester Press and Atlantic Highlands, N.J., Humanities Press, 1977.

Other works

Ōuchi Shūmei, *Uno keizaigaku no kihon mondai* (Basic issues of Uno Economics), Tokyo, Iwanami Shoten, 1971.
Furihata Setsuo, *Uno riron no kaimei* (An Exposition of Uno's Theory), Tokyo, San'ichi Shobō, 1973.
T. Sekine, 'Uno-riron: a Japanese contribution to Marxian political economy', *Journal of Economic Literature* 13, 3 (1975).
Ōuchi Hideaki, Kamakura Takao, Hayashi Takehisa and Saeki Naomi, *Uno Kōzō chosaku to shisō* (Uno Kōzō: his Writings and his Thought), Tokyo, Yūhikaku Shinsho, 1979.
Sakurai Tsuyoshi, *Uno riron to shihonron* (Uno's Theory and Capital), Tokyo, Yūhikaku, 1979.

Shōken Mawatari, 'The Uno school: a Marxian approach in Japan', *History of Political Economy* 17, 3 (1985).

Thorstein Veblen   1857–1929

Thorstein Veblen was reared in Scandinavian Lutheran communities in the upper Midwest. He was the fourth son of Norwegian immigrant farmers who sent their children to Carleton College in Minnesota. There he received training in economics under the tutelage of John Bates Clark, who later became a prominent neoclassical economist. After receiving his bachelor's degree at Carleton, Veblen taught for a year and then enrolled at Johns Hopkins for graduate study, where he was a student of C. S. Peirce and Richard Ely. After a short stay he moved to Yale, where he obtained his Ph.D. in philosophy and economics in 1884, while studying under such noted academicians as Noah Porter and William Graham Sumner. He was then idle for seven years, much of which was spent living with relatives or in-laws in the Midwest. Veblen's agnosticism made him unemployable in schools with religious affiliations and he had not yet established a reputation in economics.

Finally, in 1890, he obtained a graduate position at Cornell University, where he once again became a Ph.D. candidate, this time in economics. The eminent economist J. Laurence Laughlin was impressed by him, and in 1892, when Laughlin moved to the University of Chicago, he took Veblen with him. Veblen soon became managing editor of the *Journal of Political Economy* and began publishing in the field of economics. In 1899 his most famous book, *The Theory of the Leisure Class*, appeared and achieved a notoriety all its own. But Veblen's personal idiosyncrasies, his radicalism and his failure to 'advertise' the university properly, offended the administration at Chicago and he was forced to move. His next job was at Stanford, where, in a few short years, he encountered similar difficulties, exacerbated by his 'womanizing'. He was compelled to move again, this time to the

University of Missouri. The First World War found Veblen briefly in Washington as an employee of the Food Administration. After the war he served for a short time as one of the editors of the *Dial*, a journal of literary and political opinion, and as a member of the faculty of the New School for Social Research in New York city. By then, even though his reputation as a scholar and publicist was at its peak, his academic career was at an end. Veblen retired and moved to California, where he died shortly before the onset of the Depression.

For many Veblen is a prophet with an ethical and an aesthetic message, while others view him simply as an insightful social scientist. Although his significance is still widely disputed, his ideas of conspicuous consumption, display and emulation have been shown to have significance in explaining not only ruling-class hegemony but also consumer behaviour, corporate predation, international politics, militarism, sport and fashion changes. Veblen is also credited with demonstrating the link between ostentatious display and the oppression of women.

Political sociologists and students of modernization respond sympathetically to such Veblenian concepts as 'the penalty for taking the lead' in industrialization, the notion of 'trained incapacity' and the idea of 'conscious withdrawal of efficiency'. Veblen is also recognized for his contributions to the theory of latent and manifest functions so popular in sociology. He is praised for his ideas regarding social stratification and the sociology of knowledge. Finally, radical political theorists often refer to his critique of social institutions and their links with corporate power centres.

Veblen's interpreters have focused on themes of contemporary significance in his work. In the 1920s their attention was riveted on what appeared to be the prime deficiencies of the American capitalist order: its waste of resources on luxury goods and its indulgence in emulatory consumption. Also, his satirical wit and irony were appreciated as part of an *exposé* of conformist leisure-class morals and foibles. In the 1930s, however, the focus shifted to Veblen's study of business cycles and the roots of economic instability, exploitation of the working class and the responsibility of corporations for the Depression debacle.

By the late 1930s, with the rise of fascism, Veblen's predictions regarding a resurgence of authoritarianism in Germany and Japan attracted attention for their obvious relevance to understanding those two political systems. In the 1940s and 1950s the focus was on Veblen's work on the linkage between imperialism, colonialism and war. Still, only a few years later the New Left paid him little attention, although institutional economists continued to stress the explanatory power of his social theory and the appeal of his values.

Political activists often criticized Veblen for offering no plausible solutions to social ills and having little to say on current political issues. They believed he was unfortunately silent regarding the role of unskilled workers and the general population in the new social order that seemed to be emerging. Also, Veblen's Darwinian, evolutionary view of the future was typically vague, cynical or pessimistic. Activists claimed that he rejected not only business civilization but also the socialist alternative and had no viable third way. His espousal of the empirical study of institutions provided the inspiration and set the stage for the important school of institutionalism, yet his avowed followers, the institutionalists, having shed his radicalism, were often bound to him only by their devotion to factual study and quantitative methods.

Interpreters of Veblen often suggest there were two Veblens. One was the detached intellectual, reluctant to take sides, while the other, the revolutionary Veblen, emerged more clearly during and after the First World War. In this view, his later writings take the form of concrete application and propaganda, moving away from the abstraction, aloofness and greater objectivity of his earlier work.

Nevertheless, five ideas are found in Veblen that are representative of his thinking and are of enduring significance. The first is his emphasis on the emancipatory potential of the machine process, provided it can be harnessed to the idea of community serviceability. The second is the antithesis between business and industry with its stress on the difference between making money and making socially useful goods. He emphasized the anti-social tendency of business enterprise on account of its emphasis on profit instead of community serviceability. A third is Veblen's view of legal and political institutions as the vesting of economic interests or, in contemporary jargon, a 'zero-sum' game in which the wealthy and powerful 'win' and the underlying population 'lose'. Also, Veblen's emphasis on the compulsive force of idea patterns and the inability of the common man to overcome their hold on him is exemplified in his theory of emulatory consumption. Finally, Veblen's belief in the bankruptcy of commercial values and a business culture dominated by them is ultimately rooted in his conviction that they thwart realization of the generic ends of life, which are critical intelligence (idle curiosity), altruism (parental bent) and proficiency of craftsmanship (instinct of workmanship).

Characteristically, Veblen did not distinguish between economics and politics. For him, business interests dominated both industry and politics, and that domination resulted in economic stagnation and waste. Reformers often criticized him for not realizing that social legislation and government control of business would serve to stabilize the system indefinitely. Thus Veblen's emphasis on upper-class hegemony in modern society led him to discount the likelihood of social reform.

Veblen ignited controversy not only in economics, his primary interest, but in sociology and political science as well. The number and quality of the responses to his work provide evidence of the novelty and explanatory power of his ideas.

Works

The Theory of the Leisure Class, New York, Macmillan, 1899.

The Theory of Business Enterprise, New York, Scribner, 1904.

The Instinct of Workmanship, New York, Macmillan, 1914.

Imperial Germany and the Industrial Revolution, New York, Macmillan, 1915.

The Higher Learning in America, New York, Huebsch, 1918.

The Place of Science in Modern Civilization, New York, Huebsch, 1919.

The Engineers and the Price System, New York, Huebsch, 1921.

Absentee Ownership and Business Enterprise in Recent Times, New York, Huebsch, 1923.

Other works

J. Dorfman, *Thorstein Veblen and his America*, New York, Viking Press, 1934.

M. Lerner, 'What is usable in Veblen', *New Republic* 83 (May 1935), pp. 7–10.

C. W. Mills, introduction to *The Theory of the Leisure Class*, New York, Mentor, 1953.

R. Tilman, 'Veblen's ideal political economy and its critics', *American Journal of Economics and Sociology* 31 (July 1972), pp. 307–17.

J. P. Diggins, *The Bard of Savagery: Thorstein Veblen and Modern Social Theory*, New York, Seabury Press, 1978.

Eric Voegelin   1901–1985

Born in Cologne, Germany, Voegelin came to the United States in 1938. He spent most of his academic career at Louisiana State University. In his later years he was affiliated with the Hoover Institution in Stanford, California.

Voegelin abandoned his original field of enquiry, the history of political ideas, in 1943, and turned to a theory of history as consciousness and consciousness as history. He sought an account of 'the process of reality in which man participates with his conscious existence'. Articulation of this reality led Voegelin to develop a theory of symbolic forms and an analysis of their transformation (and deformation) through human history. Central to his analysis was the notion that a political order is a complex symbolic system

by which 'societies interpret themselves as representatives of a transcendent truth'. Ideas, institutions, laws and other representations are all elements of symbolic structuring.

In his major work, *Order and History*, Voegelin set out to explore these symbolic structurings historically, beginning with the ancient Near East (volume 1), proceeding to the world of the polis (volume 2), Plato and Aristotle (volume 3), ending with the 'ecumenic age', the era of the modern nation state (volume 4). Underlying *Order and History* is the ontological thesis that human participation in reality must be understood in terms of the 'leaps in being' that distinguish the search for truth. Thus 'the order of history emerges from the history of order'. But *Order and History* is also a sequential narrative that presents the history of philosophy (and politics) as a climactic journey to the heights of Christian–Hellenic thought, where Western civilization's consciousness of truth reached its apex. Subsequently, the narrative continues, the search for truth experienced 'derailment' and degeneration into what Voegelin called 'gnosticism' in modernity.

The distinguishing characteristic of modernity – its gnosticism – Voegelin argued, is found in the abandonment of the Christian realm of transcendent values and in the displacement of the Platonic 'metaxy'. The 'metaxy', a symbolic construct central to Voegelin's theory, captures the noetic consciousness of human existence as 'in between' the poles of life and death, time and timelessness, and 'the Beyond and the Beginning'. In place of this noetic consciousness has arisen the consciousness of 'man as the measure' of human existence. In modernity, man is led to believe 'he himself is God, when as a consequence man is transfigured into superman'.

Parts of Voegelin's analysis of modernity, especially his critique of scientism, historicism and relativism, resemble that of Leo Strauss and other German *émigrés* of the post-war period. But the magnitude of Voegelin's symbolic reconstruction of historical processes gives his theory a unique (and problematic) sweep that eschews context and particularity in favour of world historical generalizations. The *dénouement* of *Order and History*, for example, is Voegelin's attack upon a wide variety of modern political and intellectual movements, all of which he perceived as manifestations of 'gnosticism'. Thus liberalism, constitutionalism, fascism, communism, racism, Marxism, Hegelianism and psychoanalysis are alike in their elimination of the experience of transcendence prized by Greek philosophers and Christian revelation. In *The New Science of Politics* Voegelin held that political science (or 'the philosophy of order') must not only expose the derailment of the modern age but also illuminate the truth of human existence itself.

See also

Strauss.

Works

The New Science of Politics, Chicago, University of Chicago Press, 1952.
Order and History, four volumes, Baton Rouge, La, Louisiana University Press, 1956, 1957, 1957, 1974.
Science, Politics, and Gnosticism, Chicago, Regnery, 1968.
Anamnesis, ed. and trans. G. Niemeyer, Notre Dame, Ind., University of Notre Dame Press, 1978.

Michael Walzer   1935–

American political theorist; co-editor of *Dissent*, the leading organ of American democratic socialism; and, since 1980, Professor of Social Science at the Institute for Advanced Study in Princeton, New Jersey. A prolific writer and critic, his most important work is *Spheres of Justice: A Defence of Pluralism and Equality* (1983), a sophisticated argument for a communalist and pluralistic liberalism. Walzer argues for what he calls 'complex' as opposed to 'simple' equality; that is, a notion of distributive justice based on different rules of distribution for different social goods, rather than one Procrustean rule requiring equal holdings of everything for everyone. Politics, the economy, the family, the workplace, the military etc. are each different spheres having different principles of distribution. The requirement of justice is that the integrity of each sphere should be maintained against encroachment from the others: for example, and most obviously, that the polity or the family should not be corrupted by the dominance of money, which rightly rules only in its own sphere of the market for goods.

In an implicit critique of the neo-Kantianism of John Rawls, however, Walzer asserts that the various principles of justice in each sphere are local rather than universal: they can be based only on the communal understandings of a particular population with an historical identity. Walzer extends this argument in *The Company of Critics* (1988), in which he extols those social critics (e.g., Camus) who remain in some degree tied to rather than alienated from their communal roots. It is also prefigured in *Just and Unjust Wars* (1977), which makes the boundaries of the nation-state central to such issues as the permissible limits to external intervention in civil wars.

Because of his attachment to local rather than general principles of justice, and his arguments about the moral legitimacy of the nation-state and the need for critical intellectuals to be socially rooted, Walzer is often taken to be a major (perhaps *the* major) voice of the 'communitarian' turn in late-twentieth-century American political thought, along with Michael Sandel (*Liberalism and the Limits of Justice*), and Alasdair MacIntyre (*After Virtue*). Against what most communitarians take to be the overly abstract individualism of liberalism, communitarian political theory argues, methodologically, for the inevitable embeddedness of individuals in a concrete social order. Politically, communitarians tend to emphasize the importance of particularistic moral traditions; and to express a preference for the collective pursuit of virtue rather than the defence of individual rights, as a principle of social order.

Seen in this light, Walzer is only questionably a 'communitarian' himself. Politically quite distinct from Sandel and especially MacIntyre, he is much less interested in moral traditions and collective virtues than in issues of political organization, public policy and political economy. He insists (in an essay titled 'The Communitarian Critique of Liberalism') that the American people are basically liberal and pluralist in their traditions and preferences, and thus even on local principles can't sensibly be expected to be otherwise. *Interpretation and Social Criticism* makes clear that his method for identifying 'local' principles of justice (including the somewhat abstract-seeming principle of the 'integrity of spheres' itself) is interpretative rather than simply descriptive. *Spheres of Justice* strikingly concludes with a plea for what looks suspiciously like a (liberal) version of democratic socialism: a political stance that does not appear to be strongly embedded in the notoriously unsocialist American polity.

See also

Camus, MacIntyre, Rawls, Sandel, Taylor.

Works

The Revolution of the Saints, New York, Atheneum Press, 1968.
Obligations, Cambridge, Mass., Harvard University Press, 1970.
Just and Unjust Wars, New York, Basic Books, 1977.
Radical Principles, New York, Basic Books, 1980.
Spheres of Justice, New York, Basic Books, 1983.
Interpretation and Social Criticism, Cambridge, Mass., Harvard University Press, 1987.
The Company of Critics, New York, Basic Books, 1988.
'The Communitarian Critique of Liberalism', in Amitai Etzioni (ed.) *New Communitarian Thinking*, Charlottesville, University of Virginia Press, 1995.

Booker T. Washington
1856–1915

From the days of Reconstruction in the aftermath of the Civil War to the eve of the First World War, the ideas of Booker Taliaferro Washington had the greatest currency among most African-Americans. Booker T. Washington was a man of his era – slavery, reconstruction and the segregation era. He was also a southerner and, of course, a black man. Washington accepted the demographic and political realities of the 1880s, namely that 90 per cent of the black population lived in the rural south, were poor, generally uneducated and had no political power.

By 1895, when he gave his now famous 'Atlanta compromise' speech, all hope of equality was dead: Union troops had withdrawn from the south, segregation constitutions had been established throughout the Old Confederacy, and Democrats had replaced Republicans in state and local elections. Washington argued that blacks and whites in the south had together created southern society. Given this historical relationship, again, as in the past, blacks and whites must work together to create a 'new south'. Therefore it was important for whites not to fear blacks. Moreover, it was important for blacks to work with and for whites, because whites were better educated and therefore better able to assist blacks in their attempts to help themselves.

Additionally, by 1895, it was evident to almost the entire black population in and outside the south that neither the federal government nor the Republican Party of Abraham Lincoln considered blacks as equal citizens. Reconstruction had failed to redistribute power in any meaningful way. The passage of the Thirteenth, Fourteenth and Fifteenth Amendments had not materially changed the life of most blacks, especially in the south. Nor could blacks rely on the federal courts for enforcement of the 'equal protection clause' of the Fourteenth Amendment, as the Slaughter House case of 1873 had demonstrated.

Blacks, according to Booker T. Washington, must reconstruct their own lives themselves: '*Cast down your bucket where you are* . . . to those of my race who depend upon bettering their condition in a foreign land, or who underestimate the importance of cultivating friendly relations with the Southern white man who is their next-door neighbor, I would say: *Cast down your bucket where you are* – cast it down in making friends, in every manly way, of the people of all races of whom we are surrounded.' Booker T. Washington's philosophy is embodied in his autobiography, *Up from Slavery*; published in 1901, it remains in print today. Washington narrates how he changed his life, which began as a Virginia mulatto slave who attended Hampton Institute, where he learned the value of education and self-discipline. When he established his own institution, Tuskegee Normal and Agricultural Institute on 4 July 1881, industrial education remained the foundation of his educational philosophy. His organizational skills in establishing Tuskegee notwithstanding, it was the 'Atlanta compromise' that catapulted the black educator into national and later international prominence.

Washington's self-help ideas received an enthusiastic reception throughout the south among educators white and black, but especially white. Tuskegee's curriculum emphasized industrial education, not political rights. Social interaction between the races was also discouraged by Washington and his supporters. Social and political equality could come, Washington argued, only after blacks had become economic co-equals to whites. Moreover, whites should not be forced to accept blacks. Racial segregation, Washington argued, could be a positive phase in the educational development of blacks, permitting blacks the necessary time to catch up with their white neighbours.

By the time of his sudden death in 1915 Washington and his 'Tuskegee machine', as it was called by some, dominated educational and intellectual life among blacks, especially in the view of whites. Supported by southern politicians and northern philanthropists, Washington became the advocate of the Negro from 1895 to his death. He met the northerners who helped reshape black education throughout the south. In the north he opposed blacks who sought political freedom

at that time; he opposed unions, especially black membership of unions. For Washington, labour should be a 'friend' of factory owners, not their adversary. Not surprisingly, most industrialists of the day, including the Peabodys, Slaters, Vanderbilts, Morgans and even President Theodore Roosevelt viewed Washington as a friend.

An 'accommodationist' is what many of Booker T. Washington's critics called him. His strongest critics were William Monroe Trotter and W. E. B. Du Bois. Washington, they argued, did not defend the political rights of blacks but, rather, sought 'accommodation' with white racists in the north and in the south. Additionally, Washington's critics noted that any 'self-help' programme had to be based on the fact that blacks were citizens with certain political rights, a fact Washington was generally not willing to press. One outgrowth of the opposition to him was the formation of the Niagara Movement in 1905, which failed, and the National Association of Colored People in 1909, which succeeded.

See also

Du Bois.

Works

The Future of the American Negro, Boston, Mass., Small Maynard, 1899.
The Story of my Life and Work, Naperville, Ill., Hertel Jenkins, 1900.
Up from Slavery, 1901, reprinted, New York, Penguin, 1986.

Other works

Samuel R. Spencer, Jr, *Booker T. Washington and the Negro's Place in American Life*, Boston, Mass., Little Brown, 1955.
Hugh Hawkins (ed.), *Booker T. Washington and his Critics: the Problem of Negro Leadership*, Lexington, Mass., Heath, 1962.
August Meier, *Negro Thought in America, 1880–1915*, Ann Arbor, Mich., University of Michigan Press, 1963.
Howard Brotz, *Negro Social and Political Thought, 1850–1920*, New York, Basic Books, 1966.

Louis R. Harlan, *Booker T. Washington*, two volumes, New York, Oxford University Press, 1972.

Louis R. Harlan *et al.* (eds.), *The Papers of Booker T. Washington*, Urbana, Ill., University of Illinois, 1972.

James D. Anderson, *The Education of Blacks in the South, 1860–1935*, Chapel Hill, N.C., University of North Carolina Press, 1988.

Sidney Webb   1859–1947
Beatrice Webb   1858–1943

Sidney James Webb was the son of shopkeepers who brought him up to be a commercial clerk, but he turned his great talents to academic competition and in 1883 won a senior post in the Colonial Office. He was already dabbling in radical politics and journalism when his friend and ally George Bernard Shaw recruited him to the newly founded Fabian Society in May 1884, and he soon became its chief ideologist.

Webb came from a utilitarian background and was much influenced by Comte, Spencer and the neo-Hegelians. A fluent reader of German, he carefully studied *Das Kapital* before rejecting the doctrine of surplus value in favour of the marginal utility theories of W. S. Jevons and P. H. Wicksteed. Where such sectarian socialists as H. M. Hyndman and William Morris argued for conversion and class struggle, Webb stood for education and steady evolution towards the collectivist state – a process he later characterized as the inevitability of gradualness.

The Fabian tactic of permeation followed from these assumptions. Webb saw the central problem of politics as the combination of popular control with administrative efficiency, and Fabian policies were to be non-partisan and intrinsically useful means to that end, offered to sympathetic politicians and applied by competent public servants. It was an ingenious tactic at a time when party loyalties were notably in flux, but it isolated Webb from the emerging Independent Labour Party and made him look like a broker as he hawked his wares impartially to his old radical friends, to the Liberal imperialists and even the Conservatives. This reputation for inconsistency

and manipulation was intensified when he married Beatrice Potter in 1892 and began their celebrated fifty-year working partnership.

Martha Beatrice Potter was the daughter of a liberal-minded railway director. She made up for the lack of a formal education by formidable intelligence and a thirst for knowledge that was shaped by Herbert Spencer, a close family friend. Spurred by a sense of guilt at her privileged position, her search for a creed led her from Spencer's individualism through the religion of science to Comte's religion of humanity, a pilgrimage she described as a shift of the evangelical impulse from the service of God to the service of man. Bred a member of the governing class, a gifted and handsome woman denied a direct role in public life, Beatrice matched her skills in salon politics to Sidney's civil service training to make them notorious wirepullers in Edwardian politics, though their true vocation lay in research.

Beatrice had served her apprenticeship as a social investigator on Charles Booth's survey of the London poor, and written a book on consumer co-operation. On their marriage Sidney resigned from the Colonial Office, Beatrice's private income and his journalism permitting them to work first on the working-class response to industrialization. (*The History of Trade Unionism, Industrial Democracy*) and then to begin the monumental series of volumes in *The History of English Local Government* which appeared between 1907 and 1929.

Sidney was also much involved in Fabian affairs and, as a progressive member, in the recently established London County Council, to which he was elected in 1892. Believing that education was the key to both moral and social reconstruction, as positivists and Fabians alike believed, Sidney seized his chance as chairman of the Technical Education Board to create a school system in London which became the national model until 1944, helped to design a comprehensive University of London and – with Beatrice – founded the

London School of Economics and Political Science in 1895. Like the *New Statesman*, their other joint foundation in 1913, they intended it to diffuse soundly based ideas about economics and politics instead of the collectivist shibboleths so current in the socialist movement.

The Webbs were reformers, innovators, but they made only one significant foray into public agitation. Destitution had been the main target of the Victorian philanthropic tradition in which Beatrice grew up, but the combination of charity and an increasingly ramshackle Poor Law system proved unable to cope with unemployment, sickness and old age. Beatrice's membership of the Royal Commission on the Poor Law (1906–8) was the platform from which the Webbs launched their contentious minority report, an elaborate scheme for bringing all kinds of social casualty up to a national minimum which anticipated much of the post-1945 welfare state. But Lloyd George, the Cabinet Minister responsible, preferred the simpler and politically more viable idea of National Insurance, and despite a whirlwind campaign the Webbs were pushed back into a political *impasse* from which they did not emerge until 1916.

Sidney had always opposed the idea of a Labour Party formed by a coalition of socialists and trade unionists, but it was now becoming a serious alternative to the divided Liberal Party and the last political resort for him. As Fabian nominee on Labour's national executive he drafted both the new constitution and the manifesto (*Labour and the New Social Order*) which led to the party's post-war successes. Elected as MP for Seaham Harbour in 1922, Sidney served as President of the Board of Trade in the minority Labour government of 1924 and as Colonial Secretary in its successor in 1929. Becoming Lord Passfield, he found that Beatrice's increasing radicalism made her refuse ever to use the title.

She had shared with Sidney the production of *A Constitution for the Socialist Common-wealth of Great Britain* (1920) and *The Decay of Capitalist Civilisation* (1923), which reflected a dull concern with the machinery rather than the substance of politics, but she mostly left Sidney to his own parliamentary interests while she worked at an autobiography based on the celebrated diary she kept from childhood until her death. *My Apprenticeship* (1926) was the only volume published in her lifetime, but the whole manuscript is now seen as a major commentary on her life and times.

In particular it reveals how the Webbs drifted towards the bureaucratic centralism and zealotry of Soviet communism. For Beatrice the new faith concluded her lifelong search for a creed; for Sidney the Soviet regime was proof that collectivism could lift a backward country into the modern age. After a brief conducted tour of Russia in 1934, and on the basis of massive documentation supplied by Soviet officials, the credulous Webbs published *Soviet Communism: a new Civilisation?* in 1935, just as the collectivization famine and the onset of the great purges made their constitution-mongering look turgid and sadly irrelevant. Their endorsement of Stalinism shadowed the last active phase of their lives, for Sidney soon after suffered a stroke and lived in seclusion until his death.

The Webbs, laid to rest in Westminster Abbey, also found a place in the pantheon of the Labour Party they so long opposed. They had made a general contribution to its rise to power, for their pragmatic collectivism had fused with ethical socialism, trade unionism and consumer co-operation to form its eclectic alternative to Marxism. But, in particular, they had laid the foundations of Labour policy in health, education and welfare, and brought scholarship and politics together in a partnership distinctively their own.

See also

Shaw.

Works

The History of Trade Unionism, 1894, reprinted New York, AMS Press, 1975.
Industrial Democracy, 1897, reprinted New York, Kelley, 1965.
Labour and the New Social Order, 1918, reprinted London, Victoria House, 1950.
Soviet Communism: a New Civilisation?, New York, Longman, 1935.

Other works

Margaret Cole, *The Webbs and their Work*, London, Muller, 1949.
Peter Clarke, *Liberals and Social Democrats*, New York, Cambridge University Press, 1962.
Alice M. McBriar, *Fabian Socialism and English Politics*, Cambridge, Cambridge University Press, 1962.
Willard Wolfe, *From Radicalism to Socialism*, New Haven, Conn., Yale University Press, 1975.
Norman and Jeanne Mackenzie, *The First Fabians*, New York, Simon & Schuster, 1977.
Norman Mackenzie (ed.), *The Letters of Sidney and Beatrice Webb*, Cambridge, Cambridge University Press, 1978.
Stanley Pierson, *British Socialists: the Journey From Fantasy to Politics*, Cambridge, Mass., Harvard University Press, 1979.
Norman and Jeanne Mackenzie, *The Diary of Beatrice Webb*, Cambridge, Mass., Belknap Press, 1982.

Max Weber   1864–1920

The political thought of Max Weber has had an enduring impact throughout the twentieth century. This stems not only from Weber's political prescience and theoretical sophistication but also from his powerful exploration of ethical dilemmas, characteristic of contemporary political action. Weber is also a paradoxical and complex figure.

Born into a wealthy family of liberal Protestant industrialists and politicians, he upheld liberal values such as personal moral responsibility and individual freedom. His father was a lawyer and member of the National Liberal Party in the Reichstag, while his mother was a well-read and devoted Protestant. The milieu of the household in which Weber grew up involved constant engagement with politicians and intellectuals. This environment focused on the politics of the German nation-state, as understood by liberal nationalist nation-builders.

Weber's liberalism was, however, very far from being self-congratulatory, or optimistic about the future. Rather it was informed by a critical engagement with the challenges posed by Marxism, German idealism and Friedrich Nietzsche. Such influences inflected his liberalism with an awareness of structural obstacles to individual freedom associated with capitalism, and a realization that the search for meaning in social life drew on romantic as well as materialist impulses. Furthermore the Nietzschean announcement of the death of God raised the problem of how personal ethics and political authority were to be grounded in a post-religious epoch characterized by value-pluralism rather than a set of legitimate core values.

Weber's liberalism was therefore haunted by a sense of fate. The most powerful image of that fate is the 'iron cage', that is a world in which personal freedom and moral responsibility have become displaced by concern for the most efficient ways of realizing given and taken-for-granted ends. In the iron cage, notions like moral duty and explicit conflict between values become incoherent, as the logic of rationalization takes over. By rationalization Weber refers to a fateful process in which social action becomes intellectualized, subjected to calculability and sanctioned by impersonal norms. This process promises great advances in technologies of control over nature, and domination over people. This leads to what Weber called 'the disenchantment' of the world, whereby religious faith, romantic impulse and moral passion are driven out by cost–benefit analysis, bureaucracy and routinization.

The master-process of rationalization and the spectre of the iron cage represent the culmination of Weber's social and political thought. The route by which he arrived at this general argument involved an extensive intellectual apprenticeship in law, history, economics and philosophy. A student at Heidelberg, Berlin, Strasbourg and Göttingen, Weber's research in the late 1880s and 1890s included a doctorate on medieval trading companies

(1889), and a further thesis on Roman agrarian history and law (1891). Emergent themes in this early work included the historical institutionalization of modern rational capitalism, through the joint-stock company and double-entry book-keeping, and analysis of the relationship between political structures and economic institutions. Such concerns were taken up in political commentaries on contemporary matters, notably the importation of Polish labour by East Elbian landowners replacing German peasants. Weber's evaluative yardstick was that of the German national interest, seen as overriding economic self-interest. This passionate nationalism is reflected in his 1895 inaugural address on appointment to a chair at the University of Freiburg.

After a personal breakdown in the late 1890s following an unresolved quarrel with his father, and his father's subsequent death, Weber resumed active intellectual work in the early 1900s, developing an approach which was more explicitly sociological. He became co-editor of the influential *Archiv für Sozialwissenschaft und Sozialpolitik* in 1904, and co-founder of the German Sociological Society in 1912. The period 1900–20 saw a vastly expanded cross-civilizational elaboration of his analysis of rationalization, together with important statements on the methodology of the social sciences and on science and politics as vocations.

Weber saw rationalization as multi-faceted rather than a simple product of the capitalist economy. We may speak of rationalization of government, thought, music and architecture, as much as the economic rationalization of accounting, business organization and the deployment of labour. The causal explanation of the rise of rationalization is therefore complex rather than reducible to a simple formula or evolutionary law.

The issue underlying the often misunderstood Protestant ethic thesis, published in 1904–5, was not how to explain economic acquisitiveness but rather how to explain the rational social psychology of modern capital-

ism. How was it that economic traditionalism with its restrictions on market freedom gave way to the relentless pursuit of profit, through rational technique and organization, as a way of life, pushing aside community controls? For Weber part of the answer lay in the affinity between religious types of 'this-worldly asceticism' characteristic of certain Protestant sects, and the worldly asceticism of the emergent capitalist entrepreneur. A sense of religious vocation demanding self-discipline and strict accountability for one's actions was translated into a sense of economic vocation motivated by a similarly relentless inner drive for worldly achievement.

This argument was subsequently extended between 1911 and 1914 from an argument about Protestantism in Western Europe into a general sociology of world religion. Weber argued that the absence of this-worldly asceticism in most of the other world religions of Asia and the Middle East helps explain why it was only in the West that rationalization developed.

The politics of rationalization are equally important for Weber. He argued that political order may arise not only through coercion but also through compliance. Coercion in the form of power (*Macht*) could arise from multiple sources, such as material inequalities in the ownership of capital or marketable skill (class), conflicts over honour or prestige associated with the ascribed characteristics of groups (status), or power for its own sake (party), evident in the oligarchical leadership of political parties. Yet coercion represents a potentially unstable basis for order, without some element of legitimate authority (*herrschaft*). In the unfinished project published retrospectively as *Economy and Society*, Weber identified three bases for legitimacy, namely tradition, charisma and rational-legal authority. The latter was seen as characteristic of the West. Rational-legal authority deriving from enacted law, embodied in impersonal rules of procedure and staffed by a bureaucracy devoted to impersonal routine created a climate of predictability and tools of instrumental efficiency conducive to rational capitalist development and administration. The spectre of the iron cage would none the less beset any large-scale rationalized organization whether governmental or corporate capitalist.

How then could the iron cage be overcome? In a number of lectures and comments made in the aftermath of the 1917 Russian Revolution, and during his renewed academic career in Vienna (1918) and Munich (1919–20), Weber made it very clear that he regarded proletarian revolution as no answer. Attempts to redistribute power and authority rationally to the people would strike up against the need for impersonal administration and rationalized modes of authority, which would only magnify the problem of bureaucracy and frustrate democracy. Weber looked instead to charisma as the only effective counter-weight to the iron cage. Charisma meant strong personalized leadership able to stand above both sectional conflicts and bureaucratic attempts to monopolize administration. In 1919, he pursued these ideas as unofficial adviser in discussions over the shape of the future republican constitution for Germany. His advice was to strengthen personal presidential powers with respect to the legislature, creating space for a strong charismatic leader.

What is lacking here is any confidence in democracy and citizenship rights as an alternative political strategy. Weber's pessimistic political legacy subsequently became an important component of critical theory as developed by the Frankfurt School during the 1930s and 1940s in the even less auspicious epoch of fascist and Stalinist authoritarianism.

The fatefulness of Weber's political prognoses were further compounded by his emphasis on the unintended consequences of action, derived in part from contact with Austrian neoclassical economists. The difficulty here was that well-intentioned political action even when rationally planned often led to outcomes quite the reverse of those intended. Weber saw in this a conflict and dilemma between the ethics of ultimate ends which justified action in terms of moral imperatives, and the ethics of responsibility, whereby action was evaluated in the light of actual consequences.

And what of intellectuals? In his important lecture 'Science as a vocation' (1918) Weber insisted on a sharp separation between intellectual matters relating to the pursuit of truth, and political partisanship. His immediate target was those, including many professorial social reformers, who would use the lectern as a political soap-box. Yet he saw the vocation of scientist as very far from being contemplative or quietist. This was because all science is value-relevant in the sense that the objects of scientific enquiry derive from the interests and concerns of scientists as social and political actors. Belief in the importance of scientific truth is itself a value, for Weber, in the sense that the fruits of scientific enquiry are not intrinsically worth knowing. Rather scientists must believe in the value of this kind of knowledge for it to be accepted and used. The appropriate role of the scientist within public policy was therefore to explain to the politician what it was possible to do in the light of scientific enquiry, and sometimes to assist policy-makers in clarifying what they wished to do. The vocations of science and politics should remain distinct.

Weber's political thought is comforting neither to those committed to political revolution or democratic reform nor to those who believe in the virtues of public planning. Yet he was not an apologist for market capitalism, and clearly opposed what is today called economic rationalism. The play of paradox in his work suggests there are no certain political answers just as the Calvinists before him believed there was no certainty of salvation. Weber's ultimate political position is one of stoic fortitude.

See also

Mills, Strauss.

Works include

The Protestant Ethic and the Spirit of Capitalism, 1903, reprinted London, Allen & Unwin, 1976.

From Max Weber: Essays in Sociology, ed. Hans H. Gerth and C. Wright Mills, New York, Oxford University Press, 1946.

Wirtschaft und Gesellschaft, trans. Ephraim Fischoff *et al.* as *Economy and Society: an Outline of Interpretive Sociology*, ed. Guenther Roth and Claus Wittich, New York, Bedminster Press, 1968.

Other works

Wolfgang Schluchter, *The Rise of Western Rationalism: Max Weber's Developmental History*, Berkeley, Cal., University of California Press, 1981.

Wolfgang Mommsen, *Max Weber and German Politics, 1890–1920*, Chicago, Ill., University of Chicago Press, 1984.

Dirk Kasler, *Max Weber: an Introduction to his Life and Work*, Oxford, Polity Press, 1988.

Robert Holton and Bryan Turner, *Max Weber on Economy and Society*, London, Routledge, 1989.

Simone Weil   1909–1943

Few twentieth-century thinkers are more perplexing and unnerving than Simone Weil, the French political theorist and mystic whom de Gaulle called mad and Camus deemed 'the only great spirit of our time'. Weil was born in Paris and studied with the philosopher Alain (Amile Auguste Chartier) before entering the Ecole Normale Supérieure in 1928. She graduated with a degree in philosophy and taught intermittently, from 1931 to 1937, in various girls' *lycées*. She is perhaps best known for her political activism on behalf of the poor and the working class, her idiosyncratic mysticism and her untimely death, at the age of thirty-four, in a sanitarium outside London. Her death resulted not only from her identification with those in hunger under wartime rationing but from the physical complications of a lifetime of demanding personal asceticism and self-evisceration.

Yet, as her biographer, Simone Pétrement, has noted, to write of Weil's life means to deal with her work, for the bond between the two was exceedingly close. Only recently, however, has the actual substance of her political and social thinking, in addition to her spiritual reflections, been accorded more than summary treatment. Coming to terms with the diverse, almost bewildering, body of her writings – some fifteen volumes are now available in English – is not an easy task. Most of the published volumes are actually compilations of essays, letters, notes and *pensées*. Therein Weil draws variously, and often simultaneously, upon Marxist materialism, radical syndicalism, Kantian moral philosophy, eighteenth-century French romanticism, Pascalian aphorism, Hindu mysticism, the pre-Socratics, Plato and the New Testament. The enormous range of her writings and their resistance to systematic categorization have led some interpreters to split her work into 'rational' and 'spiritual' phases, but this division fails to capture the interweaving of the material, mystical, contemplative, analytical, religious and political elements that is perhaps the most distinctive feature of Weil's thinking.

'Reflections on the causes of liberty and social oppression' (1934), which Weil called her *magnum opus*, analyses the dehumanization of degrading factory labour and argues that equivalent harm is being inflicted upon contemporary society as a whole. The so-called advance of modern technology and science, along with the numbing conformity of the social realm, have bred thoughtlessness, disequilibrium and despair. Weil argued that the only prospect of recovering liberty lies in the revitalization of 'methodical thinking', the decentralization of the state and the reconciliation of manual and intellectual labour, wherein human beings recognize their limitations and their collective dependence upon one another.

The Iliad, or, The Poem of Force (1940) presents Homer's epic as an indictment of war and the dehumanizing power of force to turn people into 'things'. Weil found universal value in the poet's sense of balance, and his great impartiality. In *The Iliad*, she wrote, 'victors and vanquished are brought equally near us; under the same head, both are seen as counterparts of the poet and the listener as well.' This human capacity to grasp the equal humanity of all living beings, reject the will to force and face affliction Weil called *attention*. She explored attention in mystical as well as moral terms, nowhere perhaps more movingly than in her essays 'On the love of God and affliction' and 'Human personality'.

Weil wrote her only book-length work, *The Need for Roots* (1943), while serving with the partisan Free French in London. The text presents a historical and theoretical analysis of French patriotism and a programmatic vision for 'refashioning the soul of a country'. In this final work she declared the 'earthly roots' of country to be one of the greatest needs of the human soul. She also advanced a powerful condemnation of nationalism as '*ersatz* greatness' and urged her fellow French to develop instead a compassion for their country that is 'the spiritualization of sufferings being undergone'. The new patriotism she proposed was an attempt to reconcile certain spiritual values – compassion, attention, righteousness and truth – with political belonging, and to offer a 'medicament' for the damage done not only to France but to all of post-war Europe.

See also

Camus.

Works

Waiting for God, trans. E. Craufurd, New York, Harper, 1951.
The Need for Roots, trans. A. Wills, Boston, Mass., Beacon Press, 1952.
The Iliad, or, The Poem of Force, Wallingford, Pa, Pendle Hill, 1954.
Oppression and Liberty, trans. A. Wills, Amherst, Mass., University of Massachusetts Press, 1973.

Other works

Simone Pétrement, *Simone Weil: a Life*, New York, Panthenon, 1976.
Robert Coles, *Simone Weil: a Modern Pilgrimage*, Reading, Mass., Addison Wesley, 1987.
Mary Dietz, *Between the Human and the Divine: the Polit-ical Thought of Simone Weil*, Totowa, N.J., Rowman & Littlefield, 1988.
L. Blum and Victor Seidler, *A Truer Liberty: Simone Weil and Marxism*, London, Routledge, 1989.
David McLellan, *Simone Weil: Utopian Pessimist*, London, Macmillan, 1989.
Peter Winch, *Simone Weil: 'the Just Balance'*, Cambridge, Cambridge University Press, 1989.

Raymond Williams
1921–1988

Raymond Williams is regarded by many as Britain's leading socialist intellectual of the past three decades. The range and diversity of his writing is extraordinary. It includes works of literary and cultural history, an original contribution to cultural theory, major work in literary theory, a wide range of literary criticism, studies of modern popular culture, more direct political analysis, several important novels – including a posthumously published novel about the history, people and landscape of Wales – a mass of scholarly and occasional articles, in addition to the seminal reference work on how key historical shifts are reflected in the changing meanings of concepts, and an extended conversation with the editors of *New Left Review* about his life, work and politics.

Williams was the son of a railway signalman. He was born in Gwent, in the Welsh border country (the title of his early novel), with roots in both the rural and the industrial Welsh working class. He retained a strong sense of identification with Wales, its people and communities. Though he spent most of his working life in England, he always described himself as 'a Welshman and a European'. He went to Cambridge as a 'scholarship boy' in 1939 but was called up (1941) and completed his studies only after the war. For many years he worked in adult education for the Oxford University extramural department. He was elected fellow of Jesus College, Cambridge, in 1961, and Professor of Drama in 1974.

His influence has been considerable, especially among critical intellectuals. Yet only a small portion of his enormous output is *directly* about politics in the conventional sense, and few leading Labour politicians would have more than a nodding acquaintance with his ideas. There are many reasons (apart from the general anti-intellectualism which afflicts parts of the British Labour movement). Williams was a lifelong democratic socialist, and participated in many left causes (for example, against the invasions of Suez and Hungary in the 1950s, in the Campaign for Nuclear Disarmament and the anti-Vietnam War movement in the 1960s, with the miners' strike in the 1980s). But he was an independent socialist intellectual, never a 'party' figure; he was never closely aligned with any political organization, though he was active in the early British New Left, edited the *May Day Manifesto* (1968) and remained a regular contributor to *New Left Review*.

The principal organizing concept of his work was culture. The many different forms of his writing all converged on what turned out to be a strategic, emerging terrain of modern politics; the intersection between culture and politics. Williams rejected abstract, idealist and elitist conceptions of culture in favour of more democratic, 'key' meanings: culture as 'a whole way of life', constituted through 'the giving and taking of meanings'. The other, related, 'key word' in his work was 'community' – the shared historical formation, experience and meanings within which culture is created. For him, these two ideas were interdependent. 'Since our way of seeing things is literally our way of living, the process of communication is in fact the process of community: the sharing of common meanings, and thence common activities and purposes; the offering, reception and comparison of new meanings, leading to the tensions and achievements of growth and change.' This passage from *The Long Revolution* well represents the 'organic' character of his thinking on these issues.

Culture, he believed, was always complex – the result of intricate historical processes of struggle, communication and negotiation, in

which the dominant and subordinate 'class cultures' of an epoch or society interacted – of course, in very uneven ways – and, together with other practices (production, consumption, politics, the family, work, etc.), created distinct 'structures of feeling'. These, he argued, played as crucial a role as the mode of production in both the maintenance of certain forms of social organization (e.g. industrial capitalism) and in the struggle to change them (e.g. socialism). Every major historical transition had to be understood in cultural terms. Literature, drama, language itself, made sense only in this context. It followed that no new form of society could arise without this also involving a struggle over the construction and transformation of our common meanings. Hence the study of the genesis, construction and transformation of all these practices (none of which was accorded explanatory priority) would produce a theory of 'cultural materialism', and Williams came to call this intellectual work 'cultural politics'. In *Marxism and Literature* (a wider-ranging theoretical enterprise than its title suggests) he re-read Gramsci's 'hegemony' in terms of the tension between dominant, emergent and residual elements in cultural systems.

Williams was thus not only the formative figure in what is now called 'cultural studies' but also one of the first to offer a substantive and original theorization of the new concern with 'cultural politics' which has become such a feature of our time.

Marxism was a formative influence, but not of a doctrinal kind. Indeed, much of his writing represents a critical engagement with it, including what he saw as some of its deficiencies (for example, his critique of the base/superstructure metaphor, Marxism's tendency to economic reductionism, and its dismissive neglect of culture and cultural practices as merely 'superstructural'). His work thus had wide-ranging political implications, though his major writing is not about immediate political issues. What is more, he had a much expanded conception of 'politics', so that the interest of this aspect of his work lies in the breadth of his treatment of political themes and the way he reconstructed the traditional boundaries and concerns of academic scholarship.

Williams was strongly committed to democratic and egalitarian values. Yet much of his work was directed to rethinking and reworking the 'project of the left', in what he saw as new historical conditions. One thinks, for example, of his critique of the rather narrow conception of 'democracy' in the Labourist tradition; his questioning of the 'productivist' emphasis in the British left and its neglect of issues like consumption and the environment; or his rethinking of questions of 'class' in the light of the rapidly changing character of modern work.

In short, he rarely settled for the existing formulations – the conventional wisdom – of the left, which make for easy acceptance. His writing, which some find rather abstract and difficult is characteristically 'knotty' – reproducing in its cadences and structure the efforts of intelligence required to produce a description which matched, in complexity, the problems he was wrestling with. *Towards 2000*, for example, is an ambitious attempt to rethink some fundamental socialist questions through a deep and challenging analysis of changes in British life and culture since the 1960s. These, he argued, are significant, 'but it is not possible to think about them, politically, if we retain the false assumption of the "socialism of the classical proletariat or old working class" or if . . . we treat "the Labour vote" or "trade-union vote" as if they were simple and uniform properties' (p. 157). He retained a stubborn faith in the capacity of ordinary working people to bring about change and create a distinctive culture of their own – 'culture', he insisted, 'is ordinary'. But he recognized that historical change is complex and difficult. The 'long revolution' is the (rather unexpected) phrase he used to describe the efforts of working people to reshape industrial capitalist culture in more democratic forms.

Williams exercised a formative influence on several generations of the left. He brought a stubborn and penetrating critical intelligence to bear, from the left, on the difficult issues of his time. He combined a strong sense of 'rootedness' in the values of the working-class community, and the way these had been transmuted and generalized within the wider culture of socialism, with a sustained exercise of independent critical intelligence. He was probably the most distinctive intellectual voice on the British left during his lifetime.

See also

Gramsci.

Works

Culture and Society, 1780–1950, London, Chatto & Windus, 1958.
The Long Revolution, Chatto & Windus, 1961.
Modern Tragedy, London, Chatto & Windus, 1966.
May Day Manifesto to 1968, Harmondsworth, Penguin, 1968.
The English Novel from Dickens to Lawrence, London, Chatto & Windus, 1970.
The Country and the City, London, Chatto & Windus, 1973.
Television: Technology and Cultural Form, London, Fontana, 1974.
Keywords, London, Fontana, 1976.
Marxism and Literature, London, Oxford University Press, 1977.
Politics and Letters: Interviews with New Left Review, London, New Left Books, 1979.
Problems in Materialism and Culture, London, Verso and New Left Books, 1980.
Towards 2000, London, Chatto & Windus, 1983.
People of the Black Mountains 1, *The Beginning*, London, Chatto & Windus, 1989.
People of the Black Mountains 2, *The Eggs of the Eagle*, London, Chatto & Windus, 1990.

Other works

J. Gorak, *The Alien Mind of Raymond Williams*, Columbia, Mo., University of Missouri Press, 1988.
N. Belton, F. Mulhern and J. Taylor, *Raymond Williams – What I Came to Say*, London, Hutchinson, 1989.
T. Eagleton (ed.), *Critical Perspectives*, Cambridge, Polity Press, 1989.

Monique Wittig   1935–

Feminist, theorist of lesbian separatism and novelist, Wittig was active in the early 1970s in the French women's movement, acting as a spokeswoman for the group Féministes Révolutionnaires and working on the editorial collective of the journal *Questions Féministes*, for which she wrote a series of articles analysing heterosexuality as a mode of political, epistemological and psychic domination. Her central argument is that sexual difference as a category establishes men as the normative term and makes a focus on women as women impossible ('The straight mind'). Her statement 'A lesbian is not a woman' ('One is not born a woman') points to the subordinate status of heterosexual women, defined only in relation to men, and to the conceptual and social freedom available by contrast to women who step outside the heterosexual contract. In her literary texts Wittig transforms canonical genres developed by men by using them to explore relations among women: the schoolgirls of *The Opoponax*, the female tribes at war with men in *Les Guérillères* (a classic of radical feminism in the United States), the amorous couple of *Le Corps lesbien*, the past and future amazons of *Material for a Lesbian People's Dictionary*, the explorers and inhabitants of hell in *Across the Acheron*, the female Quixote and Panza of the drama *The Constant Journey*. Wittig's incisive critique of heterosexual culture and the mixture of violent satire and utopian fantasy in her novels have made her work important to feminists in the United States and Britain as well as in Europe.

See also

Clément, Delphy, Kristeva.

Works

Les Guérillères, 1969, trans. David Le Vay, London, Owen; New York, Viking, 1971.
'La Pensée straight', *Questions Féministes* 7 (February 1980), trans. as 'The straight mind', *Feminist Issues* 1 (1980).
'One is not born a woman', *Feminist Issues* 1 (1981).
'The category of sex', *Feminist Issues* 2 (1982).
'The mark of gender', *Feminist Issues* 5 (1985), revised in

The Poetics of Gender, ed. Nancy K. Miller, New York, Columbia University Press, 1986.
'On the social contract', *Feminist Issues* 9 (1989).

Other works

Hélène Wenzel, 'The text as body politics: an appreciation of Monique Wittig's writings in context', *Feminist Studies* 7 (1981), pp. 264–87.
Diane Griffin Crowder, 'Mothers of amazons? Monique Wittig, Hélène Cixous and theories of women's writing', *Contemporary Literature* 24 (1983), pp. 117–44.

Virginia Woolf   1882–1941

Virginia Woolf is better known for her beautiful prose and innovative fiction than for her political analyses. Although she was a lifelong pacifist who moved among political figures – her husband, Leonard Woolf, was a prominent socialist, her circle of friends included, eclectically, John Maynard Keynes, Harold Nicolson and Dame Ethel Smyth – her imagination is clearly not the product of any specific political affiliation. Yet her novels are infused with political awareness, and several of her essays, most notably *A Room of One's Own* and *Three Guineas*, are skilled political polemics. Decades before Kate Millett coined the term 'sexual politics', Woolf anatomized the reciprocal relationship between the restrictions of domestic life and the structures of the public realm. Taken as a whole, Woolf's *oeuvre* plots the co-ordinates of gender on the map of social power.

Four of her novels, in particular, explore the contingent relationship between metaphysical speculation and mundane shifts in political and cultural phenomena. *Jacob's Room* shows how the education that acculturates its hero, Jacob Flanders, as a male member of the English bourgeoisie orchestrates the First World War as well, and turns Jacob into cannon fodder. *Mrs Dalloway* makes even more explicit the connection Woolf draws among patriotism, militarism and patriarchal values. Examining the post-war life and death of Septimus Smith, a shell-shocked soldier who kills himself rather than become conventionally manly and emotionally anaesthetized, the novel contrasts the imperatives that destroy Septimus with Clarissa Dalloway's parties, life-affirming gestures offered as an alternative to a political ethos that requires slaughter, suffering and suicide. *To the Lighthouse* exposes the complicity between the highly formalized gender structures of late Victorian society and the cataclysmic war and domestic dissolution that were their logical outcome and their nemesis. *Between the Acts* makes a local pageant and the private lives and transgressions of its author, audience and actors the occasion for a meditation on history, historiography and the fate of England facing the onslaught of the Second World War.

Woolf's two major essays extend her fiction's themes. *A Room of One's Own* argues that we know little of the history and lives of women because, financially dependent and hampered by cultural assumptions about female intellectual inferiority and moral weakness, women have, for the most part, left no written record, dissembled in order to produce socially acceptable accounts, or marred their writings out of overwhelming rage. Remedying this situation requires changes in the material relationship between women and society. An independent intellect is the product of an independent income; women's writing, therefore, must rest on an economic base – £500 a year and a room of one's own. *Three Guineas* is Woolf's most explicitly and well researched account analogizing the systems of fascism, militarism and patriarchy as hierarchies resting on institutionalized violence legitimized by public rituals, reverencing rage represented as a hypertrophied masculinity, subordinating what is seen as feminine to masculine authority, and effacing the individual in a group identity. Those who make war, Woolf observes, have historically not been women. The maintenance of peace, she thus contends, mandates a new polity, one that might be generated if women – educated, self-supporting and active in the world's affairs – none the less preserve the ethos of

selflessness and nurturance traditionally associated with femininity. Conjuring up what she calls a Society of Outsiders, open not just to women but to men as well, Woolf envisages an Archimedean point where those who refuse to sell themselves for money or for status, who refuse both guns and anger and reject official honours and the state's authority as unreal abstractions, could move a lever that might change the world.

See also

Keynes.

Works

Jacob's Room, 1923, London, Hogarth Press; New York, Harcourt Brace.
Mrs Dalloway, 1925, London, Hogarth Press; New York, Harcourt Brace.
To the Lighthouse, 1927, London, Hogarth Press; New York, Harcourt Brace.
A Room of One's Own, 1929, London, Hogarth Press; New York, Harcourt Brace.
Three Guineas, 1938, London, Hogarth Press; New York, Harcourt Brace.
Between the Acts, 1941, London, Hogarth Press; New York, Harcourt Brace.

Other works

Lee R. Edwards, 'War and roses: the politics of *Mrs Dalloway*', in Arlyn Diamond and Lee R. Edwards (eds.), *The Authority of Experience*, Amherst, Mass., University of Massachusetts Press, 1977.
Phyllis Rose, *Woman of Letters: a Life of Virginia Woolf*, New York, Oxford University Press, 1978.
Susan Squier, *Virginia Woolf and London: the Sexual Politics of the City*, Chapel Hill, N.C., and London, University of North Carolina Press, 1983.
Alex Zwerdling, *Virginia Woolf and the Real World*, Berkeley, Cal., University of California Press, 1986.

Yoshino Sakuzō   1878–1933

Political scientist and theoretical leader of Japan's movement for Taishō democracy, Yoshino Sakuzō was born into a middle-class merchant family in Miyagi prefecture. Yoshino was converted to Christianity while a high-school student in Sendai, in northern Japan and as a law student in Tokyo Imperial

University joined the Hongō Church, where he became acquainted with the Christian socialists Abe Isoo and Kinoshita Naoe. After graduating in 1906, Yoshino accepted an invitation from the Chinese political and military leader Yuan Shih-k'ai to reach law and politics in a Tianjin school. When he returned to Japan in 1909 he was appointed assistant professor at Tokyo Imperial University. After studying abroad in Europe from 1910 to 1913, where he came into contact with European social movements, Yoshino became a full professor at Tokyo Imperial University in 1914.

At about the same time, breaking with the traditional academicism of the imperial universities, Yoshino began to publish articles dealing with politics in the monthly *Chūō Kōron* (Monthly Review). Articles that appeared in 1916 concerning the establishment of constitutional government that called on Japan's political leaders to consider popular opinion in formulating policies came to have a particularly strong impact on the liberal and social movement in Japan. Late in 1918 Yoshino joined other Tokyo Imperial University professors in founding the Reimeikai (Enlightenment Society), which worked to disseminate democratic thought in Japan. Beginning the following year, Yoshino held lecture meetings with another leader of the democratic movement, Ōyama Ikuo. He remained active in journalistic writing, calling for the reduction of the powers of the elite upper House of the Diet and the Privy Council and for universal suffrage, and criticizing Japanese militarist leaders.

During these years Yoshino's liberalism was challenged by the growing influence of currents of thought further to the left in the aftermath of the Bolshevik revolution. In 1924 Yoshino resigned his position at Tokyo Imperial University and took a position as leader writer on the *Asahi Shinbun*. His continued activity writing editorials on politics brought government censorship, and he was forced to resign from the paper. The same year he founded the Meiji Bunka Kenkyūkai (Meiji Culture Research Association).

Together with associates of this group, Yoshino edited and published a twenty-four-volume work entitled *Meiji bunka zenshū* (1927–30). The collection included major sources for the study of Japanese culture in the Meiji era (1868–1912). Yoshino's political activism did not abate on his return to the academic world, however. During the 1920s he joined the efforts of non-Communist Party leftists to create a single united-front proletarian political party and criticized harshly those former supporters of the social movement who turned to support the Japanese invasion of the mainland in the early 1930s.

Yoshino was an activist liberal in a polity which had borrowed the accoutrements of bourgeois democracy from Western Europe but maintained a concentration of power in the imperial institution and its supporting institutional structures. His brand of liberalism, however, differed in several respects from that of John Stuart Mill, Jeremy Bentham and other theorists of nineteenth-century England. Certainly Yoshino was critical of the limitations on democracy in Taishō Japan (1911–26), and the thrust of his reform campaign was to demand constitutional reform so that political arrangements would take more account of the wishes of the citizens who lived under them. In putting this argument forward, however, Yoshino redefined democracy. He rejected the concept of natural rights as the basis of democracy in Japan: unlike the British and the French, the Japanese had not fought for that right. Nevertheless, he argued that the ultimate end of any state was the well-being of its people. Thus in his view there were two conceptions of democracy: in the first, *minshu-shugi* sovereignty itself was vested in the people; the second, which Yoshino termed *minpon-shugi* (the view that the people are the basis or end of government), was more appropriate for Japan. This reasoning enabled him to argue that it was not necessary for the Japanese to accept popular sovereignty as the philosophical basis of their democracy; it was enough to borrow the institutions the functioning of which would assure that the popular welfare would be the basis of public policy. This was a functional approach to democracy that did not rely on a conception of individual rights. Within the context of the operation of state structures inherited from the Meiji era, however, Yoshino's was a radical prescription for Japan's political development.

Works

'Iwayuru tennō shinsetsu sonota o hyōsu' (A critique of 'imperial rule' and other theories), *Chūō kōron*, April 1916, pp. 100–43.
'Kanryō seiji o haisu' (Rejecting bureaucratic government), *Ōsaka asahi shinbun*, 26 September, 1917, p. 7.
'Kensei no hongi o toite sono yūshu no bi o sumasu no michi o ronzu' (A discussion of the means of perfecting constitutional government), *Chūō kōron*, January 1916, pp. 17–114.
Minshu-shugi ronshū (Collected Writings on Democracy), eight volumes, Tokyo, 1947.

Other works

Matsumoto Sannosuke, '"Minpon-shugi" no rekishi-teki keisei' (The historical development of 'minponshugi'), *Nenpō seijigaku* (The Political Science Annual), Tokyo, 1957.
Tanaka Sōgorō, *Yoshino Sakuzō*, Tokyo, 1958.
Bernard Silberman, 'The political theory and program of Yoshino Sakuzō', *Journal of Modern History* 31, 4 (December 1959), pp. 310–24.

Clara Zetkin   1857–1933

Born Clara Eissner, Zetkin was drawn into the liberal (or 'bourgeois') feminist movement by her mother, Josephine Vitale Eissner, and her teacher, Auguste Schmidt. She broke away from her family and respectable middle-class existence after meeting Osip Zetkin, becoming involved with his group of exiled Russian socialists, and joining the German Social Democratic Party (SPD). When Osip Zetkin was forced into exile again, Clara joined him in Zurich, and they later moved to Paris, where they lived together until his death in 1889. Although she had two children by him, and used his name, she never legally married Zetkin, as that would have meant losing her German citizenship. She made her first major political appearance in 1889 in Paris, at the founding congress of the Second Socialist International.

Equally committed to Marxism and women's rights, Clara Zetkin rejected the possibility of any alliance with the bourgeois feminists who comprised the woman suffrage movement of the time, and, beginning with an influential speech delivered at the SPD's congress in 1896, organized the first mass working-class women's emancipation movement in the world. Its policies were expounded and communicated at biennial conferences, and in the pages of *Die Gleichheit* (Equality), the radical magazine she edited from 1892–1916.

She was the leading activist and, after Friedrich Engels and August Bebel, the principal theoretician of the 'woman question' in the international socialist movement before the First World War. Her ideas had a profound influence on Alexandra Kollantai, among others. Although Zetkin's contemporaries, even her good friend Rosa Luxemburg, were irritated by her insistence on the need for women's full and equal participation in the running of society, since her death she has tended to be portrayed – and often dismissed by feminists – as an orthodox Marxist–Leninist. This may be in part because of her friendship with Lenin (her reminiscences of him were published in 1929) and because, despite writing many influential speeches and articles, she never wrote a book-length exposition of her theories.

In 1907 Zetkin created the Socialist Women's International. Although she may never have realized it, she was far too radical for the increasingly reformist SPD. In 1908 a new law gave women the right to organize politically with men, and gave the SPD an excuse for putting an end to separate women's organizations. Henceforth a woman would represent women's interests as a (non-voting) member of the party executive. Instead of Zetkin – the obvious choice – the lesser-known Luise Zietz was appointed. Continuing to promote womens rights internationally, and responsible, in 1910 at the second Conference of Socialist

Women in Copenhagen, for the establishment of an International Women's Day on 8 March (still celebrated), Zetkin also continued to edit *Die Gleichheit*, although she was allowed less editorial freedom, until, because of her outspoken opposition to the war (she helped organize the 1915 Berne peace conference), she was expelled from the SPD. In 1918 she became one of the founders of the German Communist Party, and in 1921 headed the Communist International Women's Secretariat. Maintaining strong connections with Germany, she spent most of the rest of her life in the Soviet Union.

See also

Kollontai, Lenin, Luxemburg.

Other works

Richard J. Evans, *The Feminists*, London, Croom Helm, 1977.

K. Honeycut, 'Clara Zetkin: a socialist approach to the problem of women's oppression', in J. Slaughter and R. Kern (eds.), *European Women on the Left*, Westport, Conn., Greenwood Press, 1981.

Richard J. Evans, *Comrades and Sisters: Feminism, Socialism and Pacifism in Europe, 1870–1945*, Brighton, Wheatsheaf, 1987.

Index